D0721933

From Monuments to Traces

Weimar and Now: German Cultural Criticism

Edward Dimendberg, Martin Jay, and Anton Kaes, General Editors

1. *Heritage of Our Times*, by Ernst Bloch
2. *The Nietzsche Legacy in Germany, 1890–1990*, by Steven E. Aschheim
3. *The Weimar Republic Sourcebook*, edited by Anton Kaes, Martin Jay, and Edward Dimendberg
4. *Batteries of Life: On the History of Things and Their Perception in Modernity*, by Christoph Asendorf
5. *Profane Illumination: Walter Benjamin and the Paris of Surrealist Revolution*, by Margaret Cohen
6. *Hollywood in Berlin: American Cinema and Weimar Germany*, by Thomas J. Saunders
7. *Walter Benjamin: An Aesthetic of Redemption*, by Richard Wolin
8. *The New Typography*, by Jan Tschichold, translated by Ruari McLean
9. *The Rule of Law under Siege: Selected Essays of Franz L. Neumann and Otto Kirchheimer*, edited by William E. Scheuerman
10. *The Dialectical Imagination: A History of the Frankfurt School and the Institute of Social Research, 1923–1950*, by Martin Jay
11. *Women in the Metropolis: Gender and Modernity in Weimar Culture*, edited by Katharina von Ankum
12. *Letters of Heinrich and Thomas Mann, 1900–1949*, edited by Hans Wysling, translated by Don Reneau
13. *Empire of Ecstasy: Nudity and Movement in German Body Culture, 1910–1935*, by Karl Toepfer
14. *In the Shadow of Catastrophe: German Intellectuals between Apocalypse and Enlightenment*, by Anson Rabinbach
15. *Walter Benjamin's Other History: Of Stones, Animals, Human Beings, and Angels*, by Beatrice Hanssen
16. *Exiled in Paradise: German Refugee Artists and Intellectuals in America from the 1930s to the Present*, by Anthony Heilbut

17. *Cool Conduct, The Culture of Distance in Weimar Germany,* by Helmut Lethen, translated by Don Reneau
18. *In a Cold Crater: Cultural and Intellectual Life in Berlin, 1945–1948,* by Wolfgang Schivelbusch, translated by Kelly Barry
19. *A Dubious Past: Ernst Jünger and the Politics of Literature after Nazism,* by Elliot Y. Neaman
20. *Beyond the Conceivable: On Germany, Nazism, and the Holocaust,* by Dan Diner
21. *Prague Territories: National Conflict and Cultural Innovation in Kafka's Fin de Siècle,* by Scott Spector
22. *Munich and Memory: Architecture, Monuments, and the Legacy of the Third Reich,* by Gavriel D. Rosenfeld
23. *The UFA Story: A History of Germany's Greatest Film Company, 1918–1945,* by Klaus Kreimeier, translated by Robert and Rita Kimber
24. *From Monuments to Traces: Artifacts of German Memory, 1870–1990,* by Rudy Koshar
25. *We Weren't Modern Enough: Women Artists and the Limits of German Modernism,* by Marsha Maskimmon

From Monuments to Traces

Artifacts of German Memory, 1870–1990

Rudy Koshar

UNIVERSITY OF CALIFORNIA PRESS
Berkeley · Los Angeles · London

University of California Press
Berkeley and Los Angeles, California

University of California Press, Ltd.
London, England

Library of Congress Cataloging-in-Publication Data

Koshar, Rudy.
From monuments to traces : artifacts of German memory, 1870–1990 / Rudy Koshar.

p. cm.—(Weimar and now; 24)
Includes bibliographical references and index.
ISBN 0-520-21768-3 (alk. paper)
1. German—History—1871–1918—Historiography. 2. War memorials—Germany. 3. National monuments—Germany. 4. Symbolism in politics—Germany. 5. Germany—History—20th century—Historiography. 6. War and civilization. 7. Political culture—Germany. 8. National socialism—Moral and ethical aspects. I. Title. II. Series.
DD222.K67 2000
943.08—dc21 99-088549
CIP

Manufactured in the United States of America

09 08 07 06 05 04 03 02 01 00
10 9 8 7 6 5 4 3 2 1

The paper used in this publication meets the minimum requirements of ANSI/NIZO Z39.48-1992 (R 1997) (*Permanence of Paper*).

For Judy, Drew, and Annie

Contents

Figures

readers for the press, whose careful comments and suggestions on an earlier draft of the manuscript were invaluable. Finally, for the third time since I started publishing books, I want to acknowledge the tremendous emotional support given by my family, Judy, Drew, and Annie, whose daily lives framed the steady progress of this project.

Introduction

In the tumultuous last days of the former German Democratic Republic (GDR), demonstrators in Berlin carried a sign reading, "Forward, but forgetting nothing." The lines came from the revolutionary playwright Bertolt Brecht's 1931 "Song of Solidarity," written for the film *Kuhle Wampe*.[1] One of many well-known socialist slogans usurped by the demonstrators of autumn 1989,[2] the phrase expressed support for the political transformation then underway, but it cautioned that a reunified Germany could not leave history behind. This was a controversial and disturbing position to take. For East Germans, "forgetting nothing" could be extremely painful because many, especially those in positions of authority, collaborated with the State Security Police, or *Stasi*. This organization raised secrecy to a central political principle as it created a perverse empire of documents recording every aspect of East Germans' co-optation by the state. Stasi files turned the idea of forgetting nothing into a threat. What would be uncovered if these documents reached the wider public? What misdeeds of spying and denunciation would be revealed about one's friends or neighbors, or indeed about oneself?

West Germans did not have it much easier, because to forget nothing was to be reminded of the reasons for German disunity in the first place. Many West Germans satisfied themselves that the most important goal was to get East Germans to take a critical perspective on their own history. Yet for thoughtful observers it was hard to overlook that both former Westerners and Easterners shared a common origin in the disasters of Adolf Hitler's politics. Germans had lived under two dictatorships in the twentieth century, and not even citizens of the Federal Republic, well-to-do and democratic, could escape this historical reality even though many tried. To exhort people to forget nothing was a harsh abrasion on the historical scar that many felt had been healed with the evolving unification of the two Germanys.

Germans forgot much after unification, but they also remembered a great deal—enough to remind observers that the slogan carried by the Berlin demonstrators had a palpable effect. Despite their firm goal of creating the future in the form of a country more prosperous, more democratic, and more "European" than any previous incarnation of a single German nation-state, elites as well as ordinary citizens in the Federal Republic began debating German history with an intensity that surprised many observers. Despite the desire of most GDR citizens to leave the former Communist state in the landfill of the past, many East German intellectuals also participated in such debates, partly to remind the West that "real existing socialism" had had some positive and humane features. Daniela Dahn, a perceptive writer from the former East Berlin, gave voice to this impulse in *Westwärts und nicht vergessen [Westwards and Do Not Forget]*, a powerfully argued book that accepted reunification but also identified—and not without some rancor—socialist and democratic elements of the East German system that political unity eviscerated.[3]

The physical environment was at the center of such discussions, as it should have been. The symbol of divided Germany had been an architectural "landmark," the Berlin Wall, built hastily in 1961 by an East German regime trying to prevent its medical doctors, engineers, and technicians from escaping to the more prosperous West. The Berlin Wall was more than just a wall. It was made up of concrete slabs and fortifications, metal fencing, inner and outer walls, barbed wire (as much as ten thousand kilometers of it when first built), antitank installations, boarded-up buildings, death strips, automatic firing devices, trip wires and flares, the banks of canals and rivers, electrified screens in underground sewers, border checkpoints, and more than two hundred dog runs and watchtowers. The "border security system for the national frontier west," as GDR officials called it, went through several generations as an "antifascist protection wall" designed to keep the West out as much as it kept GDR citizens in. The Wall was quickly dismantled in a process so breathtaking that preservationists had to scramble to save a few shards of this artifact of Cold War disunity. But the Wall did not drop out of memory. Graffiti-daubed chunks of it were scattered throughout Germany and abroad, reappearing in museums, stores, corporate offices, city halls, souvenir stands, schools, and not a few living rooms. Tourists and entrepreneurs (some adding their own graffiti to Wall fragments for authenticity's sake) turned the marketing of the Wall into an unofficial heritage industry; everyone got a piece of the past. Perhaps only the fate of the Bastille in Paris was comparable. François Palloy demolished this hated symbol of the French monarchy soon after it had been stormed by a revolutionary crowd in 1789. He produced innumerable souvenirs, medals, and even pieces of jewelry from its remains. Just four years after unification, less was left of the Berlin Wall in its original place than of the Emperor Hadrian's Wall, designed more than eighteen hundred years previously to protect Rome's frontiers not from Western imperialists but barbarian tribes.[4] In the rapid dismantling of the Wall, the world found a fitting symbol for the rapid dissolution not only of East Germany but of Communist East Europe as a whole.

If the Berlin Wall met a sudden and undignified end, the fate of other objects was debated with a riveting thoroughness. Should former Nazi concentration camp sites in the East now be reorganized also to commemorate the incarceration and death of Stalinism's enemies after World War II? Should Berlin, the future capital of a reunified Germany, be the site of a massive national Holocaust memorial? Should streets and public squares in the former GDR be renamed to obliterate memory of their once commanding "antifascist" symbolism? Should grand historical landmarks on GDR territory such as the former imperial palace of Berlin or the Church of our Lady *(Frauenkirche)* in Dresden be reconstructed? Should the political monuments of the GDR be destroyed, or should they be used in new, perhaps more playful, symbolic gestures, such as artist Stefan Moses' evocative cloaking of the Marx-Engels Monument in Berlin in 1990? Should there be a "sculpture park," like that constructed by the Hungarians outside Budapest in 1993, where tourists could see Communist-era statues of Lenin and Marx displayed in a state of commemorative irony, and where recordings of old revolutionary songs and toy Trabants, the flawed East German answer to the Volkswagen, could be purchased at a souvenir stand? Reunification was not only a process of economic and political synchronization but also a struggle over symbols, a struggle no less revealing of the society in which

Figure 1. The Berlin Wall near the Reichstag, 19 February 1990. Bildarchiv Preussischer Kulturbesitz.

it took place than was the battle over Republican imagery in nineteenth-century France, compellingly discussed in historian Maurice Agulhon's classic *Marianne into Battle.*

Contemporaries explained the sudden onrush of memory by noting that the end of the Cold War had lifted the ideological blinkers, both capitalist and socialist, that had prevented Germans from "mastering the past," to use a phrase widespread in the postwar era. They noted that many of the survivors of the Holocaust were elderly and near death, creating a moral imperative to fix their story in the public mind. They pointed to the fact that the fiftieth anniversary of the end of World War II, a major event attended by heads of state and fully covered by the media, aroused new controversies about the history of resistance and collaboration in all European nations. Throughout such commentary, many journalists and scholars assumed that a typically German silence about the past had now given way to a preoccupation with history. "Forty-four years of distraction," to use journalist Jane Kramer's phrase, had given way to memory.[5]

But were such debates really so surprising or unusual in their European context? Germans after all were not the only ones to engage in intense and often emotional debates about recent history. The Italians and

Figure 2. The Marx-Engels Monument behind the Palace of the Republic, Berlin, August 1990. Photograph by Stefan Moses. Deutsches Historisches Museum.

the French also debated whether previously accepted stories about heroic resistance to fascist rule were as unproblematic as many assumed. Italian television and newspapers commented daily on the memory of World War II as the fiftieth anniversary of Italian liberation from Nazi occupation approached in 1994. One Italian observer writing in the leftist daily *L'unità* raised the question any number of Europeans could have asked (and still could ask): "Have we really come to terms with the legacy of fascism?"[6] Public controversies in Russia over historic artifacts from the former Soviet Union have been very contentious and at times unusually macabre, as when they revolved around the fate of Lenin's embalmed body in Red Square and the bones of Nicholas II, the last tsar of Russia, who was executed along with his family and servants by Bolshevik revolutionaries in 1918. The workings of historical memory had vicious consequences in the former Yugoslavia, where, during a murderous civil war in the 1990s, Croats and Serbs reminded each other of the atrocities the other side committed in World War II. In Croatia, the memory of World War II actually strengthened rather than chastened that country's neo-fascist movement. On top of such debates over political history, intellectuals in Europe and North America worried about

Benjamin's archaeological metaphor for comprehending the past. Benjamin wrote: "He who seeks to approach his own buried past must conduct himself like a man digging."[32] In this book I am also selectively digging for the varied levels and paradigmatic representations of the memory landscape that have accumulated over more than a century of German history. In doing so, I hope to offer an affirmative preliminary response to historian Etienne François's intriguing question whether it is possible, through collective scholarly effort, to write a history of German "realms of memory" analogous to that developed for France by Pierre Nora and now emulated in the Netherlands and Italy.[33]

It is only fitting that in this age of anxiety over connections to the past, scholarship on memory has achieved a landmark status no less compelling in its own right than the role enjoyed by the "heritage industry" in the wider society.[34] This is not the first book about the history of German memory, and it will certainly not be the last.[35] But it is the first to synthesize a growing body of English and German language scholarship on the production and consumption of many physical traces of German history over a period of great complexity. If it sums up and makes sense of a large amount of rather specialized information until now closed to many scholars, students, and interested lay readers of European history, then it will have fulfilled one of its central goals. As a synthesis, the study engages current scholarly debates only to the degree this is necessary to clarify terms or arguments, and it keeps notes and bibliography to a minimum. The German ethnie became increasingly identified with a political nation established in 1871 and then expanded, shrank, or divided in subsequent periods; the narrative focuses on that political core and necessarily goes into little detail on German-identified cultures in Austria-Hungary, Switzerland, the Balkans, and East Central Europe. These and other sins of omission and commission are necessary in writing such an overview. But useful synthesis does not mean eschewing interpretation, and it is hoped that this book also develops an original argument that redirects the reader's attention to the continuing emotional authority of the artifacts of German memory. In the journey from monuments to traces, I argue, the German nation has remembered itself not so much as an invention or product of the imagination, but as an enduring and tangible community capable of enormous societal success as well as fierce human trauma.

CHAPTER ONE

Monuments

Germans unified under a single territorial state for the first time in 1871, when, after wars with the Danes, the Austrians, and the French, the so-called Second Empire was formed. For many European and German observers, German unification was an anomaly, if not a perverse departure from tradition. Only three-quarters of a century earlier, the great poet and philosopher Friedrich von Schiller typified contemporary opinion by asking rhetorically: "Germany? But where is it? I cannot find any such country."[1] Nonetheless, Imperial Germany, or the *Kaiserreich*, was not as bereft of historical precedents as many assumed. The loosely organized Holy Roman Empire of the German Nation, originating in the eighth century, had persisted until 1806, though in a much-altered and weakened form. The Second Empire claimed it as its noble predecessor and could in fact point to documents from the tenth century speaking of an accomplished *regnum teutonicorum*, which suggested a broader sense of national self-consciousness and German hegemony over the rest of Europe.[2] Since the sixteenth century, German scholars and teachers, drawn first from the aristocracy and the articulate middle strata, or *Bürgertum*, promoted standardization of the German language and "humanistic nationalism." The idea of a common cultural identity became even stronger for larger parts of the Bürgertum by the late eighteenth and early nineteenth centuries, and decades before the Franco-Prussian War a large and increasingly organized national movement developed. Many nationalists envisioned a larger German state than the one formed in 1871, but when the moment of unification came, they were more than ready to jettison Austria in return for a smaller German entity. This movement was shaped above all by liberals who did not see eye to eye on many social, territorial, and economic issues, but who were united in their desire to establish a national state grounded on constitutional monarchy, an end to feudal privileges, the rule of law, representative parliamentary bodies, and freedom of the press, assembly, and association. Although one could find support for a nationally oriented liberalism among state officials as well as parts of the aristocracy, it "was generally strongest among the still amorphous middle strata of German society, especially among the educated and the professionals, stretching down to notaries, schoolteachers, journalists and other members of the academic proletariat."[3] Manufacturing networks and a broader commercial culture had already laid part of the foundation of economic nationalism and political unity. A North German confederation was formed after the Austro-Prussian War in 1866, and when Bavaria and other southern German states joined the Second Empire in 1871, many of the confederation's laws, commercial codes, and practices were carried over into the new entity.

These precedents were by themselves insufficient to create the necessary emotional context for national unification. The new German empire was more than a top-down dynastic creation. Although it was the product of Prussian military victory, and although legally it was constituted by the unity of the German princes, it had a significant emotional valence for the larger populace. The events leading up to national unity —a diplomatic crisis with France over the seemingly innocuous issue of succession to the Spanish throne, a bitter and bloody war with France starting in 1870, and decisive military victory for German forces—formed a constitutive experience, or what historian Michael Jeismann has described as a "short emphatic moment in which regional, confessional, and political differences faded into the background and it was possible to experience or imagine that one's primary identity was German."[4] Those who witnessed Germans dancing atop the Berlin Wall in 1989 will have little trouble understanding this statement. Nor would they have had trouble envisioning the scene on 16 June 1871, when returning German troops paraded through the streets of Berlin in a great victory celebration. They proceeded from the Tempelhofer Field along the wide boulevard called Unter den Linden and then on to the imperial palace. Built in 1788–1791 and capped by a quadriga, a chariot with four horses symbolizing peace crafted by the masterful sculptor Johann

Figure 3. The Brandenburg Gate, 1887. Bildarchiv Preussischer Kulturbesitz.

Gottfried Schadow, the Brandenburg Gate was the central symbol in this triumphal march. Twenty-six meters high at the top of the quadriga, the gate was made of sandstone and consisted of five separate passages defined by Doric columns. The quadriga itself had an important history. Its formal precedents were ancient since Roman tradition determined that no triumphal arch was complete without such a sculpted group.[5] The Berlin quadriga had been captured by Napoleon in 1806, then retaken by the Prussians after 1813 and returned to Berlin in a mass celebration. The gate and its impressive sculpture were now transformed into symbols of German military victory.

The forceful experience of unification, the sheer emotion of the moment, could not last, especially in the light of Chancellor Otto von Bismarck's reluctance to beat the nationalist drum. But many Germans, and not just state officials and elites, believed that national loyalty could be reinforced and institutionalized. Charles de Montalembert, a nineteenth-century, liberal French Catholic who had advocated saving historic cathedrals and castles as national monuments, had once said that "long memories make great peoples." Many German historians, schoolteachers, state officials, monument builders, historic preservationists, architects, and local patriots agreed. They felt that a cultural substratum of history and memory could be called up and manipulated—that a

A lack of serious debate nonetheless did not preclude the voicing of criticisms of and reservations about Berlin—as symbol of Prussian-national military and political might, as a motor of materialism, or as a center of "decadent" cultural modernism—in later decades of the imperial era.

As the Prussian claim on German history suggested, moreover, the new Germany's problem was too much memory rather than too little. The cultural landscape was already suffused with rich and tangible historical associations, though they were neither automatically conducive to the historical legitimacy of the new nation state nor indicative of a special Prussian mission to resolve the contradictions of German history. Rather they were linked to a sense of German cultural identity that preceded loyalty to a specific state—in contrast to France, for example, which I discuss below—or they were oriented to regions and dynasties. They were, in short, linked to the idea of "Germany" as a cultural, ethnic, and historical *place* in Europe rather than as a unitary political structure.

The sociologist Anthony D. Smith uses the term "ethnie" to describe and analyze such formations, which in his view make up the cores of all modern nations.[11] A rough equivalent is the term "cultural nation," which Germans have used to define a community rooted in language, genealogy, and custom—all ultimately independent of specific national and territorial states. From this point of view, political and state systems were the expression rather than the determinant of characteristic cultural and historical entities. Whether we use "ethnie" or "cultural nation," it is important to indicate that the subject is not a racial or biological category—despite later attempts to define the nation in precisely this way—but an enduring *sense* of ancestry and shared history that is worked out and continuously elaborated over time. The German example reminds us, moreover, that ethnie may become identified with reduced political forms: the Kaiserreich emerged from a political split in Germanophone Europe between Austria and Prussia, the latter increasingly representing the German ethnie. The cultures and memories of German-identified groups outside the Kaiserreich henceforth became subsidiary or marginal to the German ethnic-political core.

The intellectual movement of Romanticism had done much to arouse interest in the memory landscape as a source of a broadly German cultural identity. Emphasizing feeling and emotion rather than the rational certainties of the Enlightenment, Romantics thought of the individual not as an isolated atom but as a being profoundly shaped by early childhood memories, folk culture, and the natural and physical landscape.

The key influence on Romantic thinkers was Johann Gottfried von Herder, who regarded the state as a "cold monster," but who saw the nation as a force of nurturance and the source of a distinctive "national spirit," or *Volksgeist*.[12] In the Rhineland, Romantic poets, painters, and travel writers armed with Herder's ideas connoted the workings of time and nature on the national spirit by depicting medieval castle ruins and natural settings as parts of a German cultural landscape independent of states or contemporary political boundaries. Rhenish Romanticism was in fact an international phenomenon elaborated first by English intellectuals and tourists, then taken up and adapted in Germany at the beginning of the nineteenth century. "Nothing can embellish or strengthen one's impression more than the traces of human audacity on the ruins of nature," wrote Friedrich Schlegel in 1805 after returning from a tour of the Rhineland, "daring castles on wild cliffs: monuments of a time of human heroism at one with the wonders of a golden age of nature. The source of this inspiration overflows before our eyes, and the old river of the Fatherland appears to us as a powerful stream of poetry prophesied by nature."[13] Anthony Smith has argued that "poetic spaces" have served nationalists worldwide "to integrate the homeland into a romantic drama of the progress of the nation."[14] The Rhineland was one such highly evocative poetic space.

Dynastic governments had done much to shape the memory landscape before unification as well. Prussia completed the process of national unification, but before the 1860s its cultural politics had aimed at developing loyalties to the monarchy within a larger German fatherland. The Prussian state bowed to Romantic and popular interest in the medieval age by starting the long process of finishing the Cologne cathedral in the 1820s. Although the huge torso of this medieval monument had reminded many Germans of the incompleteness of German national identity, the Prussian monarch Friedrich Wilhelm IV used the project to arouse popular expectations of national unity while seeking not to disturb the political status quo. Restoration of the Marienburg fortress, a symbol of Germany's knightly expansion to the East in the Middle Ages, accomplished similar goals, at least earlier in the century. Its restoration was also a response to popular pressure. Prussian monuments commemorating the fallen soldiers of the struggles against French armies in the War of Liberation of 1813 drew on religious traditions of Protestant pietism, which stressed a deeply personal religiosity but also transferred a sense of Christian sacrifice to the nation.[15] Such monuments had also contributed to a growing hatred of the French, whose differences with the Germans were increasingly seen not only as products of political conflict but of historically etched-in ethnic differences. It was this sense of difference from France—and the universal values of freedom and liberty that the country stood for in the French Revolution—that produced the notion of a German *Sonderweg,* or special path through history, which German historians would later refine and institutionalize. The use of poetic spaces to promulgate a Sonderweg narrative was also associated with the idea of Germany as a culturally identified community rather than as a unitary political entity.

Competing with Protestant Prussia, Catholic Bavaria restored castles, built monuments, and undertook other projects designed to stimulate loyalty to Germany but also enhance the prestige of the Bavarian dynasty. Drawing on the French model of the Pantheon, the former St. Geneviève church, transformed in 1791 into a hall of fame of the French nation, Bavaria's Ludwig I had the idea of creating a similar site for German heroes, the Walhalla, named after the palace of the mythical warrior Wotan, which was finished in 1842 near Regensburg. The inclusion of heroes was defined by membership in the family of Germanic languages, and thus not only Germans and Austrians but the Swiss and Dutch gained entry. In 1848 German political representatives would debate if the German state should be a "small-German" (*kleindeutsch*) state defined by Prussia or a "greater-German" (*großdeutsch*) entity in which Austria and Prussia shared influence. The Walhalla drew on the latter tradition. In such cases long-standing historical and cultural differences between southern and northern Germany, Catholics and Protestants, and *großdeutsch* and *kleindeutsch* visions, continued to shape a memory landscape that was now inherited and recast by the new German Reich.

If the memory landscape held such rich traditions and memories, how could it be transformed into something that connoted the long-term historical legitimacy of the Prusso-German Reich? How could the surfeit of memory, the sheer excess of "Germanness" in Europe, be controlled and contained so as to benefit the Prussian "mission"? How could the stifling particularism of the individual German states, the *Kleinstaaterei* against which liberals railed, be neutralized? How could the new German Reich carry out what was in essence an act of destruction in the memory landscape, an act of forgetting much of the past and recasting or quite literally "re-remembering" other parts of it? In short, how, and by what means, would a framing strategy be devised that made Prusso-German authority hegemonic within the Kaiserreich?

The German Chancellor Bismarck's solution until his departure from office in 1890 was to emphasize preexisting attachments to the princely dynasties. "German patriotism needs the mediation of dynastic loyalties if it is to become active and effective," he wrote.[16] This approach in effect allowed the weight of the past to exert pressure on the present. It severely delimited the production of new historical associations linked to the Reich and shrank from challenging too greatly the right of the federal states to conduct their own policies of national unity. It took the legal foundation of the Reich as a unity of the princes as the premise of all efforts to encourage emotional ties to the German nation. It catered to those parts of the German educated strata who, even if they attacked provincialism, regarded a degree of political decentralization to be a good thing, and who thought that the key to German unity was not a concentrated state on the French model but a more uniform policy exercised by dynasts who retained a degree of maneuverability. It was reflected quite materially in Bismarck's reluctance to promote building projects that symbolized Berlin's status as the national rather than the Prussian capital. The Iron Chancellor was satisfied that the Reichstag, the national parliament, met in a former Prussian porcelain factory, which served as the "provisional" home for the delegates for twenty-three years. Not incidentally, the Reichstag gained a substantial popular legitimacy in the 1870s, challenging Bismarck's authority and reinforcing the Iron Chancellor's will to do what he could to reduce the substantive and symbolic power of this national institution.

If Bismarck's policy downplayed expressions of loyalty to the new Reich unless they were directly mediated through the federal states, many social groups were dissatisfied with the sporadic and partial quality of German national identity. This was one of the causes of the harsher and more organized movements of nationalism and racism that appeared in Germany in the 1880s and developed in the following decades.[17] In one respect, the radical nationalists were departing from the German tradition of political decentralization by advocating a more integral state. But this departure could also be seen as consistent both with the liberal desire to overcome particularism and with the well-established assumption that an ethnic core or, increasingly, a "race," underlay the drive for national unity. These movements gained support from government elites, the right-wing liberal (National Liberal) and conservative political parties, and many other popular groups. But it was once again the broad middle strata, this time with a substantial opening to the lower middle classes and peasants, that gave the new nationalism its dynamism and legitimacy. They directed their hostility against domestic minorities, especially the Poles, as well as against Germans whose national loyalties were thought to be somehow tainted or incomplete: socialists, Catholics, and Jews. Hypernationalism spawned an array of new associations and national monuments including the Kyffhäuser Monument and the Leipzig Monument to the Battle of the Nations.

The more virulent nationalism of the age gained momentum from (but was definitely not controlled by) Kaiser Wilhelm II, who came to power in 1888 and chose a more activist political-cultural strategy after Bismarck left office two years later. The kaiser faced much the same dilemma, if not on the same scale, that the makers of liberal Italy did: a tradition of loyalty to the new nation had been established, but it was fragile, discontinuous, and antagonistic.[18] An imperialist and anti-Semite, Wilhelm II wanted to create more powerful emotional ties to the Reich, and he felt the memory landscape was a key resource in this project. He thus devoted much time and energy to the restoration of castles and churches as national monuments. He supported continued restoration of the Marienburg in the East and devoted funds to the costly restoration of the Hohkönigsburg, a completely deteriorated Alsatian fortress that was to be the Western counterpart to the Marienburg. The neo-Romanesque style appealed to him because it associated his rule with a centuries-old dynastic tradition. In contrast to Bismarck, he wanted to promote Berlin as the Reich capital and turn it into "the most beautiful city in the world," in his own overheated words. Many buildings planned under Bismarck were now completed, including the new Reichstag and several museums, and many new projects were started and finished, such as the Kaiser Wilhelm Memorial Church. Wilhelm II's most grandiose architectural project was the so-called Avenue of Victory, or *Siegesallee,* in Berlin, dedicated in 1901. This long, tasteless avenue of marble statues of Hohenzollern monarchs attempted to place the new Reich in the succession of kingly power. It also symbolized the monarchy's embrace of classical Greek and Roman motifs, an embrace that was in turn fed by the long history of German Graecophilia.[19] At the dedication ceremony, Wilhelm II proclaimed that the Siegesallee gave the German people, and workers in particular, a historical model of "beauty and harmony" to which they could aspire in their daily lives. The press and modernist architects of the capital shuddered, all the more so because in the same year the kaiser attacked modern art as ugly "factory work."[20] The German kaiser became a highly visible proponent of well-established ideas of classical beauty and proportion in German public life. These ideas would continue to inform cultural debates in the country for decades to come.

The kaiser also became Germany's most visible tourist. Nicknamed the *Reisekaiser,* or traveling kaiser, Wilhelm II made hundreds of highly publicized and showy visits to historic sites and repeatedly stayed and held lavish ceremonies or costume balls in historical fortresses such as the Marienburg. In Berlin by the last half-decade before the war, the kaiser's motorcade, departing or returning, had become a tourist attraction, and the "melodic trumpet signal" of the royal automobiles was identified as a distinctive feature of Berlin life.[21] Of course, this activity had important historical precedent in the long tradition by which "kings take symbolic possession of their realm." "When kings journey around the countryside, making appearances, attending fêtes, conferring honors, exchanging gifts, or defying rivals," wrote anthropologist Clifford Geertz, "they mark it, like some wolf or tiger spreading his scent through the territory, as almost physically part of them."[22] Yet aside from the fact that Wilhelm II traveled about much more frequently than his predecessors did, there was something more specific and original about his peripatetic behavior. Given the new popularity of tourism in Europe in this age of rising material wealth, the kaiser's travels illustrated that national identity was now also increasingly a product of consumption. The "buying" and "selling" of historical sites to the public, indeed the buying and selling of many images of those sites in the form of photographs, mugs, and playing cards, potentially united Germans from different backgrounds with their kaiser and with each other. In the process, the kaiser created himself as Germany's leading consumer of touristic spectacles just as he became a spectacle to other consumers.

I have noted that etched-in genealogies were central to the nineteenth-century theory of the modern nation. But this was more than theory, particularly at the end of the century. Michael Kammen has argued that the drive to give the nation a long history was an international development that shaped state policy, public life, and commercial practices in the last decades of the century in the United States, England, France, Italy, Scandinavia, and even Japan. Although patterns varied from country to country, there was a worldwide tendency "to appreciate cultural identity in historical terms" and to use cultural identity to build loyalty to a national community or national state. Both popular and elite culture joined in the game. In England, the popular novels of Sir Walter Scott directed readers to what were perceived as the medieval origins of

Figure 4. Wilhelm II (bottom left) at dedication ceremony of Monument to the Battle of the Nations, Leipzig, 1913. Bildarchiv Preussischer Kulturbesitz.

the English people, while in both England (Carlyle) and France (Michelet), historians acted as prophets, linking the national destiny with past glory. English Whig historians, convinced that British constitutional history was a story of inevitable progress toward humanity and liberty, were even more teleological in their treatment of the past's relationship to the future than were German historians like Heinrich von Sybel or Heinrich von Treitschke, who saw Prussia's leadership as a logical outcome in a centuries-old history of the German states.[23]

Such examples make it clear that in each national community a politically expedient way of adjudicating between history and anticipation had to be found. In the United States a strong tendency developed to depoliticize regional and ethnic traditions in an attempt to lessen the pull they exerted on a democratic politics based on a painfully learned tradition of reconciliation and balance. Germany's response to having too much memory from the preunification period was to create a new layer for the memory landscape, the goal of which was to channel and transform earlier pasts while retaining some of them and destroying many others. It was a piecemeal and partial approach that suited the complex balancing of national, regional, religious, and class loyalties in the German state. It corresponded to a general German tendency to force modernization in the economy and society while also retaining and reinforcing certain cultural and political traditions. Students of modern architectural theory often distinguish between the methods of the *bricoleur* and the engineer, the former adapting his tools and methods to the work at hand without subjugating his labors to a grand theory, the latter motivated by a single and often highly authoritarian central vision.[24] In approaching the problem of national memory, the German Empire was more like a bricoleur than an engineer.

A comparison with France, the engineer-state *par excellence,* illustrates the German path and its complexity even more clearly. Historian Maurice Agulhon wrote that not only for France but for much of nineteenth-century Europe, "changing the state and the principles upon which it rested meant abolishing its symbols and therefore being obliged to invent new ones." Because the new German Empire basically changed neither the state nor the principles it rested on, it was not compelled to make a clean sweep of all preexisting political symbols.[25] Indeed, the German Empire rested to a considerable degree on Bismarck's and the kaiser's usurpation of national symbols and the national movement to legitimate Prussian hegemony. If we focus more specifically on the French Third Republic in relation to the new German Empire, we have another significant comparison. "Since the Revolution had established the fact, the nature and the boundaries of the French nation and its patriotism," wrote Hobsbawm, "the Republic could confine itself to recalling these to its citizens by means of a few obvious symbols—Marianne, the tricolor, the 'Marseillaise,' and so on—supplementing them with a little ideological exegesis elaborating on the (to its poorer citizens) obvious if sometimes theoretical benefits of Liberty, Equality and Fraternity."[26] Conversely, in Germany allegiances to the new empire were less definite, the nation's boundaries less established, and the historical referents of nationhood more confused. Hence under Wilhelm II in particular, the German Empire resorted to more numerous and complex historical references.

Still, it would be inaccurate to take this contrast too far. The memory of 1789 aroused much partisan conflict in France in the succeeding century, much more than the American Revolution, whose commemorative status was uncontroversial.[27] Hobsbawm overstates the degree to which the Revolution held an unassailable authority in French memory, especially until the Third Republic was established on fairly stable political and symbolic ground by 1880, and he overlooks the way varying depictions of statues of Marianne, the preeminent symbol of the Republic, reflected competing group understandings of Republican values. By focusing only on intended monuments, moreover, Hobsbawm underestimates the number of architectural landmarks (such as Notre Dame) used to symbolize French national heritage. A brief look at the French Monument Act of 1887 would have provided a more balanced view. His statement does not do justice to what historian Maurice Agulhon called a "statuomania" that gripped France and other European states in this period. He does not consider that French political iconography went much further beyond the Revolution for its inspiration, relying for instance on the story of Joan of Arc, who, although she became a symbol of French nationalism and an increasingly powerful weapon among French anti-Semites before World War I, also was used as a symbol of Republican patriotism by those on the Left. Nor does he recognize that the Germans agreed a good deal more about the status and significance of national foundation myths than the French did.[28]

Historians often contrast France's civic basis of identity—the idea of the nation as a social contract—with German notions of the nation as a product of objective ethnic-cultural characteristics. Scholars base this contrast on a larger conceptual distinction between two types of nations: those formed on the basis of coherent territorial boundaries in which civic and political traditions developed, and those that emphasized ethnically defined characteristics. England, France, and Spain represent Western "territorialism" in the former case, while Germany, Italy, and much of Eastern Europe stand for "ethnicism." I have already remarked on the centrality of the idea of the cultural nation to German identity. But Germany is also recognized as a country in which territorial and ethnic models clashed. Prussia's leadership, the Holy Roman Empire, a nationalist consciousness starting as early as the sixteenth century, and the princely dynasties all established a territorial precedent, but this precedent was weaker than that enjoyed by France well before the modern era. Ethnic ideas gained legitimacy in Germany, as they did in France, although in Germany they often functioned to provide the nation with a historical basis not provided indisputably by territorial boundaries.[29] Such points suggest that skepticism is in order regarding the utility of a strict version of the contrast between France and Germany, between the engineer and the bricoleur, or between territorial and ethnic models of nation formation.

Hobsbawm's comparison is therefore a useful one not because it highlights significant differences but because it leads one to consider how differing political contexts led to roughly similar outcomes in the appropriation of historical memories. The *relatively* powerful aura of the Revolution allowed the Republic to treat French political history as something natural; a *relatively* small number of political landmarks referred citizens to their unquestioned and hence dehistoricized heritage. In the German state, a panoply of historical symbols shrouded the political uncertainties of the new nation, linking German nationhood to something notionally "deeper" than political events even when it used the Franco-Prussian War as a stimulus for national feeling. In France, the political nation dislodged national memory from history, substituting the foundation myth of the Revolution in its place, although not abandoning pre-Revolutionary history. In the German Empire, the political nation tried to use the social heritage to subjugate history not to the aura of a founding political event but to that of cultural-ethnic myth. In neither case, moreover, was this resort to a mythic past unprecedented. Revolutionary France returned to Roman times for its inspiration, while Germany in the same period drew on the memory of freedom-loving Germanic tribes.[30]

THE MANY IN THE ONE

The dual movement of creating a new past for the Second Empire and at the same time controlling, directing, and dispersing the preunification past was reflected in the way the memory landscape was framed by both state and society after 1871. Commemorative monuments had been used throughout the nineteenth century, most often to honor monarchical and military power, but increasingly to envision a national community. This could be done by putting up statues of kings, princes, and generals, or, as in the case of the famous Goethe-Schiller monument made by Ernst Rietschel in Weimar in 1857, of important cultural figures. Later in the nineteenth and early twentieth centuries in cities such as Essen in the Ruhr, in the heart of a great coal-mining and manufacturing district, statues commemorated industrial magnates such as Alfred

Krupp, the armaments king. This reflected the way in which industrial prowess had become an important part of German memory and identity. Maurice Agulhon has argued that throughout Europe public statuary moved down the social scale, increasingly depicting less exalted personages as a result of the spread of liberal humanist ideologies. The nineteenth century was in any case the age of monuments, and the characteristic liberal and national movements of the day chose monuments as an effective form of representation. Nineteenth-century monuments were products of that "bourgeois public" that had gained power and influence, and even where governments and monarchs built monuments, as they often did in Germanophone Europe, they did so with reference to the ideas and values of architects, nationalist groups, literary societies, and other typical representatives of bourgeois society.

After the Franco-Prussian War, war memorials and commemorative tablets appeared all over Germany. But the intended monuments for which the Second Empire was best known were grandiose national monuments, whose size, iconography, or intent distinguished them from any preceding monuments. Defining a "national monument" is no easy task. Reinhard Alings has recently written that a national monument should not necessarily be seen as a "thing," but rather as a process, an "attempt to create a generally comprehensible and durable national symbol." But he cautions that the real measure of a national monument was whether it became widely regarded as such; a national monument did not exist but rather "became."[31]

The list of possible national monuments includes the Victory Column, erected in 1872 in Berlin to celebrate German triumph over the French and topped with the mythic female figure Germania, a symbol of the unity of Prussian dynastic and national liberal aspirations; the monument of Hermann the Cheruscan (in reference to a Germanic tribe) in the Teutoburg Forest near Detmold, finished in 1875; the Niederwald monument, built from 1877 to 1883, at Rüdesheim above the Rhine, and symbolizing national unification; the monument atop the Kyffhäuser mountain in central Germany, erected from 1890 to 1896; the monument on the so-called Deutsches Eck, the confluence of the Rhine and Moselle rivers in Koblenz, from which French claims to the left bank of the Rhine could be resisted, built from 1894 to 1897; and the centenary monument for the Battle of Nations in Leipzig, inaugurated in 1913. By the end of the decade, and well into the first decade of the twentieth century, Germans also erected more than three hundred Bismarck monuments in a veritable cult of commemoration for the Iron

Chancellor. By this time, moreover, more than three hundred statues and other types of monuments had been built to commemorate Wilhelm I, official German nationalism's founding father, including the gargantuan Porta Westfalica Monument, dedicated in 1896. Keeping in mind the difficulties of categorization and comprehensiveness, scholars estimate that the total number of national monuments in Imperial Germany exceeded one thousand.[32]

The appearance of national monuments in the German landscape is significant for a number of reasons. The origins of the idea may be traced back to the English garden of the eighteenth century—or more precisely to the idea of a natural "park" containing numerous statues and markers of historical personalities or even a "Temple of British Worthies," to use the contemporary phrase. While the English landscape garden was to have a universal symbolic appeal based on all-encompassing ideas of history and beauty, European and German architects adapted it to their own more narrowly focused national needs after the French Revolution and the Napoleonic wars. Writing early in the nineteenth century, Hegel argued that only a people derived from nature—and ultimately based on the family as the cell of the collectivity—could qualify as a nation. Thus the earliest ideology of the national monument developed closely with evolving definitions and representations of the natural world.[33]

Germany was by no means the only country to have many national monuments or to highlight monumentality as a key feature of national symbolism. Architectural traditions of noble monumentalism were well established in France, where, since the late eighteenth century, architects had tried to overcome the frivolities of baroque design with alternatives of simple grandeur. The Ecole des Beaux-Art's devotion to buildings of the ancient world encouraged designs of colossi and other monumental structures, and it was assumed throughout the nineteenth century that Republican art in the form of paintings, statues, or triumphal arches should be on "a gigantic scale."[34] Monumentalism of a truly overpowering kind could be found in newly unified Italy, where the attempt to create a civic religion of the nation resulted in the grandiose Monument to Victor Emmanuel II on the Capitol Hill in Rome. Begun in 1885 but finished only with great delay and debate just before World War I, this giant edifice of marble and bronze honored the monarch who had died in 1878 after leading the struggle for national unification. The monument jumbled together a copious supply of allegorical statutes, an altar to the motherland, a tomb to the unknown soldier of the wars of unification, massive marble stairways flanking the giant bronze equestrian statue of Victor Emmanuel II, representations of the most celebrated towns of Italian history, and at the summit a portico of sixteen columns offering a commanding view of Rome. This eclectic collection exemplified the Italian attempt to stimulate loyalty to the nation and monarchy while also incorporating the diversity of Italian history and culture in a central point of the memory landscape.

Nonetheless, in Germany the sheer number of national monuments does suggest a more substantial collective need for them and—not to forget the importance of Germany's industrial might to the evolution of the memory landscape—greater financial resources to initiate and erect them. Writing about the increasing disinterest in large static monuments in modern urban environments, Mumford stated "the more shaky the institution, the more solid the monument."[35] He referred to the fact that the desire by governments or other historical actors to symbolize permanence and grandeur in physical objects often belied weakness or even imminent decline. But in the case of the Kaiserreich's national monuments, this desire also reflected an uncertain relationship to a past and future that was now to be interpreted in terms of a coherent national history. National monuments had a presumed controlling and crystallizing function. They could serve as nodal points in the memory landscape that drew together the multifaceted history of the German states into a single, coherent sequence at the end of which was the Second Empire. They could serve the same function in their time as the electronic media do for advanced nations in the late twentieth century: the "staging" of the past in spectacular cultural productions.[36]

The great monuments of the Empire would thus be symbolic command posts of a nationalized memory. But they would make this attempt in a way that continued and legitimated the multicentered nature of German nationhood. Not clustered in the capital but spread out over the cultural landscape, the monuments strengthened an important continuity of national tradition by retaining the "many" in the "one." In Italy, Rome was the inevitable choice as capital, and the natural site for the grandest national monument; in Germany, although Berlin's stature as the national capital increased in the last decades of the empire, national monuments were still scattered throughout the memory landscape, albeit with a clear bias for Prussian territory. Given this pattern, it is unsurprising to find that among the strongest supporters of national monuments was the liberal press. While conservative newspapers often stressed Prussian themes when commenting on the Victory Column or the Niederwaldenkmal, the liberal *National-Zeitung* of Berlin, the *Vos-*

sische Zeitung, and the *Münchener Neuesten Nachrichten* emphasized national symbolism. The Victory Column was not a commemoration of the Prussian monarchy's military victory, according to the *Vossische Zeitung,* but a symbol of the "Volk in arms."[37] Even so, liberal nationalism had been based on a strong sense of regionality, and the idea of the German nation as an entity uniting the many in the one was therefore perfectly compatible with liberals' interpretations of national monuments. German nationality had overcome the poverty of provincialism, but national monuments reminded Germans that unity did not dissolve the rich panoply of local identities. National monuments would be scattered throughout the political landscape to emphasize not only national unity but also the diversity of the provinces' participation in the larger collectivity.

A comparison with Hungary illustrates this point even more succinctly. Hungary had established a position of incomplete national autonomy within the Hapsburg Empire in the Austro-Hungarian Compromise of 1867. Seeking to consolidate Hungarian national feeling and at the same time establish Budapest as the national capital, the Hungarian parliament voted to build a massive monument commemorating the millennium of the conquest and settlement of Hungary as part of a larger millenial celebration. The monument would legitimate Hungary's borders within the Hapsburg Empire and treat the current state of the Hungarian nation as an inevitable outcome of a thousand-year-long past. With construction beginning in 1896 and continuing until 1929, the Millennial Monument was designed by sculptor György Zala and architect Albert Schickedanz to condense all of Hungarian history in a single powerful symbol. An eighty-five-meter-wide colonnade formed a double semicircle anchored by a thirty-six-meter-high column with the statue of the archangel Gabriel. Designed to give the impression of an open triumphal arch facing the city, the colonnade featured a central group of equestrian statues depicting Árpád, chieftain of the Magyar tribes that conquered Hungary, and his six tribal leaders. In between the columns were statues of leading figures from Hungarian history; below each statue was a relief representing a relevant moment in Hungary's past.[38] This giant structure was thus designed to sum up Hungarian history and represent it in a single sacred space of national authority. The site would be renamed Heroes' Square in 1932, and later regimes would add or subtract important historical figures to the colonnade as they saw fit. But the original intention of the monument persisted. No comparable effort at condensation of the national history could have been made in the German context even though monument builders and political powerholders tried.

Like the Millennial Monument, German national monuments were massive edifices. The size of the monuments suggested the need to use the past not to inform but to overwhelm or intimidate. Reaching a height of ninety-one meters, the Leipzig monument was the biggest structure of this genre and taller than the Statue of Liberty in New York City.[39] The Kyffhäuser Monument was sixty-five meters high, the Kaiser Wilhelm I monument at Porta Westfalica nearly sixty-two meters. Popular culture did much to reinforce the theme of bigness. A prewar postcard depicted the Leipzig monument along with six other German national monuments, reminding its buyers that sixteen Kyffhäusers could fit in the area of the Leipzig colossus. The Leipzig monument weighed 500,000 tons and cost six million marks, according to the postcard.

But who specifically was to be impressed or even intimidated by such size and numbers? The siting of the great monuments reflected a certain ambiguity about how they were to engage audiences. Many such monuments (Leipzig's excepted) were built atop mountains or in forest clearings, making them richly symbolic or scenic but also relatively inaccessible to those without money, time, and transport. Moreover, if one compares the great public spaces anchored by monuments in East Berlin or any other Soviet Bloc city after World War II, the allowance made for truly mass audiences around the monuments of the Kaiserreich (with the exception again of the Leipzig monument) was modest. The Walhalla with its hall of fame of German heroes provided no meeting place for the assembled masses. This reflected a presumption that a relatively small public was capable of shaping national memory, a presumption consistent with the impulse of the liberal movement in Germany to speak for the *Volk* as a whole but in fact to cater to the outlook and values of the educated middle strata. Moreover, most national monuments were sited in the north—it is estimated there were five Prussian national monuments in the broadest sense to every non-Prussian monument in Imperial Germany[40]—reflecting once again Prussia's claim to have realized a long-standing national mission and the Catholic south's ambivalence toward the new Reich.

Such potential limitations on the intended audiences derived in part from the composition of the committees that selected sites for the monuments, awarded commissions to architects and sculptors, organized finances, saw projects through to completion, orchestrated publicity and unveiling ceremonies, and maintained monuments after they were built.

State agencies or private groups such as student associations (in the case of Bismarck monuments) or veterans' societies (for the Kyffhäuser) sponsored individual monuments. But the committee members invariably came from the ranks of upper-level bureaucrats, especially mayors and county and provincial officials, nobles and estate owners, university professors, military officers, and industrialists. The composition of various monument committees reflected local circumstances, but generally it was the upper Bürgertum (along with select groups of nobles) that carried the day. Workers and peasants were virtually shut out from leadership positions (although they would sometimes give donations), while artisans and individuals from the free professions were underrepresented. Significantly, party-political differences within the Bürgertum seemed to have weighed less than might be assumed in the formation of local and regional commissions. Center party representatives got along with National Liberals, just as conservatives or individuals from radical nationalist groups worked with members from the left-liberal parties. Only the Social Democrats were consistently excluded from such groups. It appeared that local and regional loyalties and the representation of local hierarchies—which may or may not have reinforced party-political conflicts within the upper middle strata and elites—were more important in shaping the makeup of local sponsors of national monuments than were other factors.[41] In this sense, many of the sponsors of national monuments, though speaking to the nation as a whole, were in fact carrying on a conversation within a relatively constricted circle of elites.

National monuments were shaped by certain iconographical traditions, including myths of origins in time and space, myths of liberation depicting how a national community freed itself from bondage or attack, and myths of a golden age in which the best features of the national community were defined and elaborated. Constructed from 1841 to 1875, the Hermann Monument, or *Hermannsdenkmal,* represents a link between mid-nineteenth-century German nationalism, indeed the developing national consciousness of the second half of the eighteenth century, and the monument building of the Second Empire. At the same time, it is a good example of some of the principle ideological characteristics of the national monuments.[42]

The obsession of a single man, Ernst von Bandel, the Hermann monument could be constructed only after repeated attempts by Bandel and voluntary groups to raise money. At one point, the fundraising effort, which was based on two major campaigns in 1838–1843 and 1862–1871, included getting the best pupil of each German high school class

Figure 5. Hermannsdenkmal. Bildarchiv Preussischer Kulturbesitz.

to raise money for the project. Although shaped by regional deviations, donations came in from all over Germany, including Switzerland and Austria, and in the earlier fundraising drive in particular a not insignificant share of the donors came from nonbourgeois groups such as artisans and peasants who joined the more prevalent Bürgertum in contributing to the cause.[43] Bandel's singlemindedness would later earn him a sizable pension and a grant from the Prussian monarch and the Prussian Diet. Official support came rather late in the game, however, and the Hermann Monument was not mainly a product of state policy or monarchical generosity but of a national movement.

Hermann was the legendary Germanic chieftain who successfully repulsed attacking Roman legions and massacred them in the first century A.D. The battlefield was said to have been in the Teutoburger Forest near Detmold, where the monument was built. Although studied by German-speaking scholars since the fifteenth century, Hermann had become a well-known figure in the late eighteenth century among the educated strata who promoted the idea of German cultural identity, and plans for a Hermann monument had been drawn up as early as 1768. Between 1750 and 1850 approximately two hundred poems and operas used the Hermann theme. The patriotic movement of 1813, spurred by Prussia's role in an alliance against Napoleonic armies, enhanced Hermann's symbolic capital even more for educated German speakers. Even left-leaning German nationalists used the Hermann legend in their poems and songs, as exemplified in the work of the democratic member of the student fraternity (*Burschenschaft*) movement, Karl Follen, in 1818 and of the leading radical writer Ferdinand Freiligrath before the 1848 revolutions. Thomas Nipperdey gave one reason for Hermann's popularity as a symbol of the German national movement: at a time when historical churches, "temples of honor" (like Walhalla), or grandiose architectural monuments seemed to speak to rather abstract or distant themes and symbols, the direct, personalized representation of a single individual, a single German hero, was both more specific and more functional to a national movement seeking a counterweight to German territorial, cultural, and political fragmentation. This impulse was even more relevant to the members of the Bürgertum who interpreted Hermann as a symbol of German nationhood *and* a liberal, cosmopolitan figure whose first-century battle struck a blow for "Germanic" individuality against "Roman" centralization, for the multiplicity and "diversity" of all national groups against the universalizing tendencies of a "Latin" imperium. This form of "Germanism" had adherents in the late eighteenth century in many other European countries as well as in North America, where Thomas Jefferson proposed that the seal of the United States feature not only the children of Israel being led out of the wilderness but the "Saxon chiefs" Hengist and Horsa, who were seen as political ancestors of the American revolutionaries.[44]

Hermann's liberal-national "internationalism" flagged as time went by just as the national movement's aims became narrower and more selfish. The Germanic chieftain's heroism came to stand increasingly for German culture's defense not primarily against centralizing, universalizing, and imperial "Roman" influences but against the hostile designs of a single national enemy, the French. The historical complexity of French relations with the German states was thereby reduced to a predestined ethnic-national antagonism, an "organic" conflict. Such ideas gained contemporary resonance when the Hermannsdenkmal was dedicated in August 1875, shortly after the previous spring's worsening relations between France and Germany precipitated a war scare. Hermann was designed as a warrior holding a massive sword directed toward Germany's western frontier. The massive pedestal symbolized the strength and resolve of the barbaric defender of German culture. That it was a defensive posture should not lead one to overlook that a more martial nationalism could give the raised sword a pronounced militant and aggressive meaning. Hermann's status as leader of his tribe came to symbolize the German people's unity with their princes. The liberal movement's stress not on revolution but on cooperation and compromise with the German states fit well with the Hermann Monument's evocation of solidarity between the *Volk* and their leaders. This unity was also to be defended against internal enemies. The dedication of the Hermannsdenkmal in 1875 fell in the midst of the *Kulturkampf*, a "cultural war" carried out by Bismarck with liberal support against the influence of the Catholic church. The struggle against France could be easily linked with the internal Catholic "enemy." Bundled together with themes of solidarity and defense against internal and external enemies was a broader dynamic whereby cultural nationalism had given way to state nationalism. Having begun life as a symbol of Germanic, cultural-national, and even international identities, Hermann was now embedded in the political iconology of a specific national state and lauded by both state officials and middle-class nationalists as a symbol of the German Empire.

It is intriguing to compare Hermann with his functional equivalent across the Rhine, the Gallic warrior Vercingetorix, symbolized in several national monuments for which the Hermann Monument may have served as direct inspiration.[45] Unlike Hermann, Vercingetorix was martyred in his battle against the Roman Legions. But his martyrdom came to stand for the vigorous and positive interaction between Gallic and Roman peoples, and thus Vercingetorix became a symbol not of closure against outside influence but of a civilizing process led by Rome but supported in Gallic culture. From the French point of view, Hermann's barbarism was a symbol of Germany's lack of civilization; from the German point of view, Vercingetorix was a sign of France's succumbing to decadent foreign influences. From the French point of view, Vercingetorix was a symbol of a Gallic-Roman symbiosis the outcome of which was a sovereign and civilized nation; from the German point of view, Hermann was a sign of cultural purity the outcome of which was an organic identity between a barbaric people and its princes. National symbols developed as mirror images of other national traditions. These national traditions in turn became products of a continuous, centuries-long history, whether that of a civilizing process or an organic unfolding.

The theme of violent resistance to outsiders who had victimized Germans and stood in the way of the organic development of their own history would appear again and again in many new guises and permutations throughout the following century and even after World War II. Monuments were there to inspire national comrades but also to deter and admonish outsiders. This tendency was shared by other national groups in East Central Europe and the Balkans, such as Poland, Hungary, and Serbia, that had experienced foreign occupation and depended on myths of victimization, admonition, and unprecedented resistance to outsiders. Polish national identity was virtually synonymous with the idea of resistance as developed by the Court, the nobility, and the clergy. In Hungary, there was a well-established tradition of portraying the nation as the last bulwark of European civilization in the struggle against the Ottoman Empire, the Turkish infidel. Hungarian history was seen as a story of one nation's selfless contribution to European resistance against un-Christian and uncivilized forces.[46] In both cases, myths of resistance and warning to outsiders solidified claims of national independence or autonomy to the outside world but also legitimated elite rule over a culturally mixed peasantry and artisanate within each national community.

A central difference between these other nations and Germany was that the theme of bloody resistance to foreign domination was taken up in the latter case by a country whose material and military might was unparalleled on the Continent. The destructiveness of the resistance theme derived less from its cultural peculiarity than from the organizational and material resources Germany had to back it up. Even then, one cannot ignore a central difference in the content of some of the myths: unlike the Cheruscans, for example, the Serbians lost an epic battle on Kosovo Polje, the Field of Blackbirds, against the Ottoman Empire on June 28, 1389. This battle became the stuff of nationalist epic poetry, art, and literature and a recurrent theme of Serbian nationalist politics, so much so that it is doubtful any European nation could point to a single myth so incomparably instrumental to its sense of history and identity. Despite the fact that initial reports of the battle led Europeans to celebrate a triumph over the Turks, the Kosovo myth came to symbolize the "normal fate of Serbs": to fight valiantly but to be denied a well-deserved victory against foreign threats and oppressors.[47] In contrast, the German theme of resistance was based on a memory of bloody triumph and ultimate deliverance and was therefore much more confident and self-assured than its Serbian counterpart. The Kosovo legend was at times transformed into a promise of national salvation, but it *began* with defeat, and it included the idea that Serbia's leader, Prince Lazar, when given the choice between an empire on earth or in heaven, chose the latter. The legend tells that he was beheaded in the Kosovo battle. Such differences in national myths are significant given that scholars have so often focused on the pessimistic or resentful qualities of German national identity.

The Kyffhäuser monument to Wilhelm I exemplified another aspect of the national mythology, namely the myth of decline and rebirth. The Kosovo myth contained this element as well, since the martyrdom of the Serbs was to be made good in the revival of their medieval kingdom in the modern period. Thought to be the geographical center of Germanophone Europe, the Kyffhäuser mountain in Thuringia was already deeply etched in German memory and folklore before the monument was built between 1890 and 1896. The medieval king Friedrich Barbarossa was said to be sleeping below the mountain as he awaited the renewal of German glory after the nation's fall from grace in the late Middle Ages and early modern periods. His magical slumber symbolized not only the fall from medieval glory and anticipated renewal; for many Germans it also represented Catholic treason because the Catholic church was held responsible for the degradation of the dynasty represented by Friedrich. Barbarossa's slumber would be ended only when Germany was freed of "Roman ways," as an 1849 nationalist pamphlet put it. When the end of the Franco-Prussian War was celebrated at the site, one speaker proclaimed that "the black ravens that circle the site are Catholic priests and Jesuits who actually belong in the camp of the Gauls, that is in France."[48]

Such sentiments linked medieval imagery, nationalist anticipation, and Prussian and Protestant antipathy to Catholic Germany in a web of historical associations. They reinforced the idea that, as suggested in the association of the Hermann Monument with the Kulturkampf, a significant part of German national unity consisted of fighting internal enemies. The Kyffhäuser's association with the struggle against "priests and Jesuits" was an even more powerful sign of the nation's drive to suppress internal opponents than that provided by Hermann's menacing sword.

Figure 6. Kyffhäuser Monument, 1897. Archiv für Kunst und Geschichte, Berlin.

Even so, when the Kyffhäuser Monument was completed, the anti-Catholic struggle had resided, and the most significant internal enemy for nationalists was red rather than black, socialist rather than Catholic. One finds themes of internal repression of supposedly treasonous elements in other national legends as well, particularly in those used by nations where ethno-cultural factors played a major role in forging unity. In the Kosovo legend, the battle was lost in part because of the treachery of one of the Serbian chieftains, Vuk Branković. Based on dubious historical sources, this narrative of treachery became a stock item in Serbian epic poetry. Translated into political action, it served those Serbian leaders who would brook no internal opposition to their drive to reestablish the medieval Serbian empire in the modern era—and who would take no personal responsibility for defeat because of the alleged scheming of others.[49] The potential for radical militancy and violence inherent in such internally directed nationalism and the pinpointing of domestic perfidy would have significant and tragic consequences for both Germany and Serbia, though at different times and under different conditions, in later decades. That this was the direction of nationalism in the modern world—toward a more aggressive and even violent attack on internal groups that allegedly stood in the way of an "integrated" and militant identity—suggests the Kyffhäuser's relevance as something more than only the product of a hyperventilated German nationalism.

Shortly after Wilhelm I's death, the board of directors of the influential German Veterans' Association initiated a drive to have a monument to the deceased kaiser built atop the Kyffhäuser. The iconography reflected Prussia's insinuation into prior myth and legend. Viewers could ascend a flight of stairs to a massive platform on which a fortress-like wall surrounded the monument. They would look through one of three stone arches at a massive stone sculpture of the aged Friedrich Barbarossa sleeping as he awaited the restoration of his medieval power. His figure arose from a gigantic stone mass that seemingly placed German history in the context of geological time. Above him emerging from a high stone pillar was the equestrian statue of Wilhelm I, who would realize Barbarossa's dream, and who in popular parlance was often referred to as Barbablanca to signal even more directly his association with the medieval emperor. From below, the colossal, heavily veined horse on which the Prussian monarch rode appeared literally to overrun the viewer. From the platform on which the monument stood, one gained commanding views of the landscape in all directions, an evocation of the intended goal of the monument to dominate and centralize the German past and future.

It should be noted that although this imagery praised the national state, monuments such as the Kyffhäuser relied heavily on popular action, and they thereby upheld the relationship between the modern monument and the liberal-bourgeois public sphere. Since the early nineteenth century, various groups had pushed state governments to complete the Cologne cathedral and restore the Marienburg fortress. They now agitated to build national monuments. Bandel's campaign relied on many donations. The Kyffhäuser had been started through the initiative of German veterans. Reich or federal state financing of national monuments was uneven, as public monies were used for building monuments to Wilhelm I in various major cities but generally not for Bismarck or other kinds of national monuments, which relied more on private donations. This made broad popular support all the more necessary. Radical nationalist groups were thus active in drumming up enthusiasm for the great Leipzig monument of 1913. The national monuments had the potential to function like the constitution of the French Third Republic insofar as they established a popular legitimacy and activism for the nation.[50] Germany's "social contract" relied heavily on the symbolism of such monuments to give the national community a tangible purchase on the public imagination even when the nature of liberalism and nationalism changed.

Some national monuments were much more traditional than the Kyffhäuser Monument, which combined elements of the baroque and Germanic myth. Reinhold Begas's Kaiser Wilhelm Monument in Berlin, built from 1893 to 1897 and financed entirely by the Reich government after rancorous debate in the Reichstag, was an elaborate, nine-meter-high equestrian statue situated on the west side of the city's famous imperial palace. The monarch's powerfully depicted steed was accompanied by the Goddess of Victory. The monument had 157 animals and 53 partly clothed figures, all elaborately sculpted and designed to represent movement in the baroque fashion. Although it became a central tourist attraction, its busy imagery was heavily criticized in the press and in architectural circles. This was only one of many instances in which popular reception differed greatly from expert opinion on monuments. A leading architectural journal attacked its numerous figures in an 1899 article entitled "On the Zoology of our Monuments." Well known for their satirical slant, Berliners commonly referred to the monument as "Wilhelm in the Lion's Den," a reference to the biblical Daniel and the four lions flanking the equestrian statue of the Prussian monarch.[51] For many critics, Begas's monument was decadent and inappropriate to the simplicity and modesty that were said to characterize German identity. This argument of course filtered the idea of German identity through the lens of a tradition of Prussian austerity. The monument nonetheless acted as a spur to those who advocated new formal criteria for national monuments.

The Leipzig Monument to the Battle of the Nations was a rallying point in this search for new forms—and in the search for more lasting and emotionally resonant ways of relating to the German nation. Built between 1894 and 1913, the Leipzig monument derived from plans published a hundred years earlier by the masterful architect of southern German classicism, Friedrich Weinbrenner, who wanted to memorialize and distinguish Prussia's role in the multinational military victory over Napoleon in 1813.[52] But it departed from all previous national monuments in a number of important respects. It was designed by Bruno Schmitz, also the creator of the Kyffhäuser. Like the latter monument it had a pyramidal structure that commanded its surroundings and overawed the viewer. But its monumentality was even greater than any previous model, and it was quickly recognized as the largest national monument in Europe before World War I. It influenced monument design in other countries also. The accomplished architect Ivan Meštrović, a Croat who held pro-Serb views before World War I, based his St. Vitus Day Temple honoring the dead of Kosovo on the still unfinished Leipzig monument. Although the project was never carried out, Meštrović's model for the temple was one of the main attractions of the Serbian pavilion at the Rome Exhibition of International Art in 1911.[53] A symbol of more intense German nationalism, the Leipzig monument nonetheless occupied a central role in a broader European design discourse.

The Leipzig monument did not try to represent the monarchy or embody the nation in a human figure, as with Hermann, but had a more abstract and "architectonic" approach, concentrating on massive, fortress-like forms rather than elaborate statuary. Its goal was to reduce the number of historical associations surrounding national monuments and to centralize historical memory through simplified architectural forms. More than previous monuments, it revived völkish and Germanic themes that appeared early in the nineteenth century but were then understated as classical motifs gained ground. Unlike the Kyffhäuser Monument, which explicitly linked Wilhelm I, the newly founded Reich, and German identity, the Leipzig monument took 1813 as the founding moment of the national community. This reading of German history was typified in the statement of nationalist J. E. Freiherr von Grotthuss, who wrote in 1913 that "in a specific sense, the Wars of Liberation will be to Germany what the War of Independence is to the Americans and the great Revolution to the French: the beginning of modern, nationally conscious political life." The Leipzig monument symbolized this perspective, focusing on the political maturation of the ethnie rather than on the accomplishments of the monarchy and national state. In its central hall four massive sculpture groups, each more than nine meters high, represented the "original" Germanic qualities of bravery, willingness to sacrifice, strength of belief, and fertility. These were done up not according to classical motifs but (like parts of the Kyffhäuser) as Egyptian or Assyrian figures connoting the centuries-old

Figure 7. Monument to the Battle of the Nations, Leipzig. Bildarchiv Preussischer Kulturbesitz.

achievements of great empires. In the land surrounding the monument were to be planted German oaks, favorite symbols of prehistorical Germanic traditions. The oak also represented masculine strength and endurance, again linking the nation with primeval times. By contrast, evergreens, though also found in nationalist symbolism, represented the feminine virtue of fecundity and occupied a subordinate position in relation to the male oak.[54]

While Gothic imagery could represent a hierarchical and Christian society untainted by modern social and political development, ancient and völkisch imagery could be used to revive memories of a purported Germanic egalitarianism. This idea stemmed in part from the neo-Romantic revival of the last decade of the nineteenth century. Julius Langbehn, author of the wildly popular *Rembrandt as Educator,* published in 1890, argued that Germany needed to find its own artistic styles based on the "fine barbarism" of Germanic tradition.[55] Fine barbarism would situate the Second Empire in a long historical tradition that Gothic, Renaissance, and classical perspectives only weakened. To eradicate these other traditions was to perform an act of patriotism, a symbolic cleansing. To reduce the chaos of historical associations in nationalist imagery was to carry out an act of creative destruction. In Langbehn's view the Germans were barbarians—irrational, wild, individualistic, and spontaneous—who had been separated from their distinctive social heritage and their ethnic memory by foreign influences. That such creative destruction had a "democratic" tinge should not be overlooked. Stripping national monuments to their bare symbolic essentials was in line with the contemporary European practice of streamlining or reducing iconography on statues and monuments so as to connote "simple democratic goals," as in the French Third Republic.[56]

This view was taken up by a larger public, now mobilized by a more radical nationalism than that represented by the kaiser or the conservative and liberal parties and organized in associations such as the Pan-German League, or *Alldeutscher Verband.* More than previous nationalist groups, these organizations stressed popular mobilization, imperialism, and in some cases racism. But radical nationalism was also widespread in more moderate nationalist groups, among which the German Patriotic League, the sponsor of the Leipzig monument, could be counted. The Leipzig monument thus had a more critical perspective on Wilhelmine public culture. More than other national monuments, the Leipzig monument stood more explicitly against Wilhelm II's embrace of classicism just as it stood for the radicalized ethnie instead of the

Reich government as such. Although its supporters hated the politics of the modernist critics of Wilhelm II's "court art," they shared with the modernists a desire to leave traditional artistic styles behind in an effort to more effectively symbolize the German *Volk*.[57] Positioned within this context of crosscutting anxieties about Wilhelmine national identity, the Leipzig monument stood at the end of the sequence of national monuments that had begun earlier in the century—but also at the beginning of a new genre of radical national monuments of which only one would exist due to the interruption of World War I.

The reception to the Leipzig monument was mixed. Architectural critics wrote that the structure maintained a sense of bigness from all angles because of its simplified form, but there were still problems of siting and design. The kaiser attended the dedication ceremonies in October 1913, but he did not give a speech. Nor did he give the architect Schmitz or the sculptor Franz Metzner the normal honors for their work. The monarch's reserve aroused the anti-Berlin sentiments of Leipzig citizens who favored the monument. For its part, the Leipzig Social Democratic party called the monument an awkward "pile of stones" and played up the differences between Wilhelm II and the radical nationalists.[58] Tourists, however, had no compunctions about gawking at the monument or reveling in its size. They were willing to follow the lead of tourists' guidebooks, which described the bulk and commanding presence of the structure, its sixty-meter-wide relief featuring a central image of the archangel Michael, and its sixty-meter-high inner hall and crypt.[59]

Germanic motifs were found in Bismarck monuments as well. When sponsored by the national organization of German university students, the Bismarck monuments were often simple towers that stylistically linked them to ancient Saxon and Norman forms as well as to classical symbolism of the eighteenth century based on the pillar. Rejecting direct representation, these abstract shapes seemed to place the Iron Chancellor above everyday political history, even above history itself. The pillar had also come to represent Germanic manliness, and thus Bismarck stood for the masculine power of the new German nation. But if they were stylistically linked to classicism and Germanic ideology, they were by no means incompatible with modernist impulses because in such simple structures pure form dominated rather than realistic representation. Bismarck monuments could also take other forms, however, as in the case of the Hamburg monument, built from 1901 to 1906. This twenty-three-meter-high monument portrayed Bismarck as the medieval knight Roland, a symbol of German civic power. Armed and ready for battle, Bismarck stood overlooking the Hamburg harbor at a spot where, from the perspective of incoming ships, he surveyed Germany from the heavens.[60]

The size and monumentality of the structures belie their often limited effect in the built environment, as many critics of nineteenth-century monuments would argue in World War I and thereafter. Nationalist festivals held at some of the monuments were highly formalized, and their long-term impact for participants may have been limited. Neither the Kyffhäuser memorial nor the Niederwaldenkmal became commanding centers of nationalist demonstrations or festivals. Estimates indicate that the Hermann Monument attracted between fifteen hundred and two thousand visitors annually between 1875 and 1890, and after Detmold got a rail station, these numbers climbed higher than forty thousand just before World War I.[61] Still, such numbers were small when compared to the potential mass audience, and it is of course notoriously difficult to determine what tourists in the past got out of their travels in terms of political education. Later political uses of the monuments varied. The Nazis for example disliked and ignored the Hermann Monument, perhaps because its Gothic form represented an anachronistic version of German identity to them.[62] In general, the monuments had their greatest public impact at their unveiling or during important national commemorations. Outside of these high points of public mobilization, they settled into their respective landscapes, becoming a part of everyday community identity.

On the other hand, the reproduction and consumption of monuments in schoolbooks or commercial products suggests that such images reached many Germans. This alone indicates that not only the monuments but other forms of communication—books, popular illustrated magazines, postcards, playing cards, food tins, cheap plaster reproductions and busts—also carried the burden of representation into the twentieth century. Scholars of art history note that it was in the nineteenth century that miniature busts of Napoleon, Bismarck, or the Polish patriot Tadeusz Kościuszko began to appear on the bookshelves and pianos of the European middle and upper classes. Small plaster statues or busts of Marianne, the symbol of the French Republic, appeared in homes and small patriotic altars all over France on important commemorative holidays such as 14 July, Bastille Day. Scholars of German culture have demonstrated how popular family magazines such as *Die Gartenlaube,* with an estimated circulation of around two million, carried pictures of German landscapes and national monuments to their readers. *Die Gartenlaube* was particularly enthusiastic about the Niederwaldenkmal, whose sponsors often wrote articles in the magazine to drum up popular enthusiasm. Even satirical treatments of national monuments, from the journal *Kladderadatsch*'s attacks on the Kyffhäuser to Berliners' description of the Victory Column (*Siegessäule*) as the "asparagus column" (*Spargelsäule*), kept the structures before the public eye.[63] From this perspective, Mumford's notion of the death of monuments is inadequate because it overlooks the ways in which such objects resonated as "virtual" monuments. Because books, illustrated periodicals, postcards, and miniatures circulated as commodities, moreover, the national monuments became "naturalized" as images fully integrated into daily life and exchange.

Still, it is a matter for debate if even such virtual monuments "nationalized" the masses, at least in any really active way. To enter the everyday realm of circulation and commercial exchange was also to risk reducing the impact and originality of such representations. As a way of disseminating mental pictures of the nation, the national monuments and their numerous representations were the most unusual and dynamic elements in the memory landscape of the Second Empire. But when one considers these structures cumulatively and in relation to the landscape as a whole, they could have appeared not as dominant elements or nodal points but as gestures of unintended compromise or indecision. In this sense, they also reflected the peculiar political realities of the Prusso-German Reich, a system built up on the difficult and anxious emotional foundations of compromise and deferral. Despite the heated building activity of the imperial period, Albert Hoffmann, writing in an architectural journal in 1917, felt compelled to plead for the construction of a single, definitive German-Austrian national monument, as if World War I offered one last chance to create the widely recognizable and unanimously accepted national symbol so many other monuments had tried to create. Hoffmann's plea for a German-Austrian monument demonstrated that the memory of a broader German ethnie was still influential, especially at moments of political crisis.[64]

If their impact was possibly less than their creators intended, the national monuments nonetheless reinforced an ancient practice through their consumption and circulation. It has been noted that in the nineteenth century the national monument functioned in much the same way that the sacrament did in the Christian religion.[65] Based on twelfth-century theology, the idea was that the individual body of Christ, the *corpus Christi,* was the sacrament of the collective and mystical body or soul of the Church, the *corpus mysticum.* In the nineteenth century, the monument became the sacrament of the nation, which, like the Church, was thought to have its own "soul" by many contemporary thinkers. The substance of the sacrament was provided by acts of heroism, either of mythic figures or of historical personalities (Napoleon, Wilhelm I, great military officers). These personages and their heroic acts constantly returned in the monuments that commemorated them. By its nature as the sacrament of the nation, the monument had to circulate and be available to the people, who by participating in the ritual of the sacrament also participated in and demonstrated their loyalty to the nation. In this sense, the monument, though made of brick, bronze, and stone, was constantly in movement. Just as the Church in the twelfth century had instituted the procession of Corpus Christi in which the host was paraded through the streets, the monument as sacrament circulated in daily life as both image and body of the nation.

Although grandiose national monuments commanded the greatest public attention, many other kinds of intended monuments were built in the Second Empire. Given the importance of the Franco-Prussian War to the new Reich's existence, war monuments commemorating that event were important indicators of historical memory. Already in 1871 sporadic efforts to commemorate peace occurred as Germans planted "peace trees" and conducted similar symbolic actions. But much more dominant were obelisks, granite blocks, soldier figures, and sculptures of lions and eagles that began to appear throughout the cities and towns of the new Reich. The wave of monument building directly related to the aftermath of the Franco-Prussian War lasted into the mid-1880s. The iconography and inscription of these monuments expressed loyalty to "Kaiser and Empire" or to "King and Fatherland," thus combining increasingly powerful national identity and dynastic loyalty. But the pull of the preunification past could not be denied. Earlier war monuments had treated the ordinary soldier as part of an anonymous mass, reserving individual recognition only for the aristocracy and military leaders. Although this tendency was breaking down after 1871, the predemocratic forms of memory prevailed until after World War I, and monuments to the Franco-Prussian War generally left the common soldier unmentioned. This lessened the impact of such monuments for the larger populace.

The weight of the past was also strong in Catholic states such as Bavaria, where, especially after the Kulturkampf, war monuments reflected an ambiguous relationship between the national state and religious identity. Commemoration of the war dead took place more often in the form of plaques or other objects inside Catholic churches, and larger and more visible war monuments in open spaces were less ubiquitous than in northern Protestant regions. In these places the Church rather than the nation still seemed to have the upper hand. In general, Bavaria was well behind Prussia, and non-Prussian states such as Württemberg, in erecting national monuments, as we might well expect considering the continuation of regionalist loyalties in the southern state. Another variation was that in states such as Württemberg, proximity to France and the fact that the Württemberg army had participated only in the conflict of 1870–1871 rather than all three wars of unification produced veterans' monuments that were much more exclusive in their emphasis on the Franco-Prussian War. In Hannover, meanwhile, a large provincial war monument created a potential split between regional and national identity. A group of local notables headed by the influential liberal Rudolf von Bennigsen had sponsored the monument, which was unveiled in 1884. Atop the imposing structure appeared a heroic Germania, eyes focused in the distance as she was crowned by two victory goddesses and flanked by Prussian eagles, while below her was the mythical figure Hannovera, eyes downcast as she mourned local sons who died in the Franco-Prussian War. An unsigned letter to the editor of a local daily suggested that the monument placed the two symbols in contradiction with one another, thereby casting doubt on Hannover's full integration with Prussia and Germany.[66] The war monuments thus came to stand not for a unified national experience but for specific regional relationships to the process of unification. Whether war monuments referred more to religious or regional identity in such instances, they limited and dispersed the growing presence of the national state in the memory landscape.

Dynastic governments had been involved in promoting a sense of German cultural identity throughout the nineteenth century. Whereas this tendency continued after 1871, Bavaria, Württemberg, and other states now also revived efforts to promote identity with the federal state, the existence of which was threatened by Prussia's claim on the German past and national unity. Even when such efforts were undertaken in competition with Prussia, the non-Prussian dynasties shared with Prussia a tradition of regarding the German nation as a unity between the German princes and their peoples. Thus in Württemberg, inclusion in the new Reich provoked a cult of dynastic memory symbolized in equestrian statues and other kinds of monuments. The dynasty was declining politically within the new Reich and losing legitimacy with its own subjects. To stop the bleeding, it set off a flurry of memory work to reinforce the monarchy's historical links with the people and the coherence of Württemberg as a distinct regional entity.[67] The resort to dynastic monuments was even more elaborate in Bavaria.

AGE VALUE

National, war, and dynastic monuments were not the only parts of the memory landscape that became important to the symbolic capital of the new German nation. Riegl argued that the "cult of monuments" of the turn of the century depended most heavily on "age value."[68] By this he meant that many objects, most notably historical buildings, had become monuments not because of the intention of their builders, or because they had a specific historical or aesthetic value, but simply because they were old. In contrast to intended monuments such as national monuments, Riegl referred to unintended monuments whose primary attraction was their patina of age.

The movement to preserve historical buildings was European and international in scope.[69] It was rooted in the early nineteenth century (although Riegl and others saw its intellectual roots in the Renaissance), especially in the age of Restoration in which states and social groups throughout Europe reacted to the French Revolution's destruction of monuments by stressing the need to restore and preserve artifacts that linked the nineteenth century with its eighteenth-century and pre-Revolutionary roots. Although the French and the Greek states led Europe in terms of enacting legislation to save historical buildings (and states such as Serbia and Romania had the most draconian preservationist statutes), it was the German federal states that, by the last decade of the nineteenth century, were in the forefront of preservationist activity. Eschewing national preservation legislation, Germany relied on a dense network of provincial laws and regional preservation organizations. Historic preservation policy was not seen by contemporaries as a sign of reaction or antimodern feeling, but as a reflection of Germany's impressively modern state and municipal governments and as a commitment to civilized stewardship of the national heritage. This view was endorsed by German as well as non-German observers. In contrast, commentators within and outside Great Britain considered that country's preservation efforts to have been relatively haphazard and unduly influenced by the power of private property.[70]

Buildings dating from the medieval period were especially favored by German preservationists throughout much of the nineteenth century, and this tendency was inherited in the Empire. Germans were fond of saying that preservation was a child of Romanticism, whose love of the medieval age found direct expression in the activity of maintaining or restoring monuments. But the more exclusive focus on the medieval age highlighted the fact that preservation also meant the destruction of monuments from other historical periods. If the medieval age connoted the glory of imperial power for German monarchs, it also recalled an age of bourgeois abundance and influence in numerous urban centers. One key geographical center of medievalism was the Prussian Rhineland, where government-appointed conservators, including Bonn art historian Paul Clemen and his successors, had more medieval monuments under their jurisdiction than any other conservators in Europe. The Rhineland's stature stemmed from its abundance of castles and Romanesque and Gothic churches in Cologne, Aachen, and other cities. Here Catholics could see churches and other urban monuments as symbols of their cultural persistence in the face of Prussia's absorption of the Rhineland, just as Prussian officials could use preservation to represent their benevolent rule over Catholics. Despite their love for the medieval, Germans had begun to widen their view of monuments to later periods, and Clemen himself was one of the leaders in this effort. He had studied with the prolific historian Karl Lamprecht, whose conception of cultural history was extremely eclectic and interdisciplinary.[71]

As monuments were defined more broadly, the memory landscape came to include a greater variety of historical buildings, including not only major cathedrals and castles but also vernacular buildings such as peasant architecture, windmills, and workshops. Just as the trend toward building national monuments was in part a response to the mobilization of an increasingly complex society in need of new forms of collective identity, the elaboration of the field of historical buildings reflected twin processes of fragmentation and consolidation. More and more groups needed historical artifacts that situated them in meaningful historical sequences explaining the relationship between the past and an ever more complicated present. At the same time, those groups required a point of reference whereby the variety of symbols and objects being preserved could be reduced to a common denominator of identity.

Even so, "star" monuments continued to receive the most attention and the most funding. Historic churches were particularly important parts of the memory landscape. "Religion as well as the churches are not embedded in the nineteenth century like some relic of tradition," Thomas Nipperdey wrote, "rather they are simultaneously products of and constitutive factors of this century."[72] Part of the churches' continued status derived from their close association with German national identity. In countries such as France or Italy, national identity evolved with a strong anticlerical quality. Pre–World War I Italian nationalists influenced by modernism argued that they yearned for a national loyalty that amounted to a "religion of the irreligious."[73] It was not that churches, either as historical buildings or new edifices, were unimportant to national iconography in either country. In France a major campaign extending from the 1870s to 1919 was mounted by Catholic conservatives to erect a monumental church in Paris, the Basilica of Sacré-Coeur, as a symbol of national solidarity based on a revival of religious piety. Renewing the nation's Christian foundations was thought to be a necessary antidote to the violence caused by the revolutionaries of the Paris Commune of 1870–1871. Republican opponents lost the battle over Sacré-Coeur but not after they used explicitly anticlerical arguments that demonized the Church and reaffirmed attacks on the clergy as a staple of national allegiance.[74]

In Germany, both the Catholic and Protestant churches remained at the center of national thinking, even when, in the course of the late nineteenth century, a nationalism less directly tied to Christian imagery began to take hold, and even when Catholics and Protestants disagreed over national questions. In the aftermath of the Wars of Liberation, German architects such as Schinkel and Klenze called for the building of monumental churches that would symbolize German unity and the coming of peace. The popular demand to complete the Cologne cathedral emerged from such desires as well.

The Cologne cathedral was without doubt the most important historical church in the German memory landscape.[75] Begun in the thirteenth century, construction of the church stopped in 1560, and the crane at the south end of the massive cathedral's torso had itself become a symbol of Cologne over the centuries. Spurred partly by Romanticism, partly by the desire to have a national monument that would remind Germans of their victory over the French in 1813, the movement to complete the cathedral enjoyed tremendous popular resonance throughout German-speaking Europe in the nineteenth century. In the age before the railway network began to knit together the German nation, the cathedral served as a well-known "dominant" in the memory landscape. The church appealed to those with conservative-federalist leanings because it symbolized an age of hierarchy, religiosity, and monarchical power. Yet it also appealed to the proponents of a liberal nationalism because its buttresses and arches suggested an age of bürgerlich power, urbanity, and national coherence unsullied by contemporary social and political conflicts. Particularly up to the middle of the century, the church's Gothic style represented democratic principles as much as it did conservative ones. Beyond political tendencies, it appealed to those who saw art, and particularly Gothic art with its rich religious associations, as a specifically German phenomenon. For Rhenish Catholic political leaders such as the influential August Reichensperger, the church was a product of Catholicism's centrality to German identity. For Protestants, Gothic design was a precursor of the Reformation's stress on freedom and inwardness.

By the time of national unification, the cathedral did more to symbolize the country's confessional splits than to offer a unifying mystique. Bismarck's Kulturkampf, begun in 1871, exacerbated such conflicts. In coalition with liberals and his cultural minister, the chancellor undertook a repressive campaign, the goal of which was to eliminate Catholic influence from public life. The bitterness of the Catholic clergy and their followers was dramatic, and Catholic leaders took a position of "respectful caution" toward the ceremonies that were to dedicate the cathedral on its completion in October 1880. Attended by the royal couple, the festivities included a massive historical parade and the first electrical illumination of the cathedral. The representative of the Catholic church received Wilhelm I at the cathedral door. Approved by the government censor, the message he delivered to the monarch nonetheless included the words "may the day we have longed for soon come, which returns peace to the Church and gives the completed cathedral back to its shepherds."[76] No Catholic church service was planned for the official ceremony, and when the final stone was raised up, celebrants sang a Lutheran hymn. Although Cologne was filled with visitors, and although many Catholics participated in the festival, it was largely a conservative Protestant affair for which most Protestant liberals had lost enthusiasm.

Beyond the specific tensions surrounding the Cologne cathedral, it is clear that historical churches' status as architectural landmarks meant they could have subtler and more varied meanings within the memory landscape than those given to them by nationalist thinkers. Romanesque churches in cities such as Cologne were important to the identity of Rhenish Catholics suspicious of Prussian designs, for example. Churches in small towns and villages were important parts of local identity because of their centrality to everyday social life. For clergy, the churches as physical structures were the fundaments of a religious practice rooted in centuries-old traditions. This function often clashed with the goals of preservationists, who regarded Germany's old churches as important art-historical documents the daily use of which needed to be controlled and managed. The local priest or the chair of a local church board might take offense when a government conservator tried to "educate" them about the proper care of historical churches.[77]

The nineteenth century's desire for historical accuracy had led many churches to undertake damaging restorations in which facades, historical altars, and organs from the Renaissance and baroque periods were altered or even removed. These artifacts made way for "Gothic" style, which was presumed to be more authentic and more national. In one respect such restorations had the positive effect of reducing the number of historical associations found at a given site. The church's symbolic import could thus be more clearly illustrated to congregants and tourists. The completion of the Cologne cathedral as a specifically Gothic monument derived from this restorationist logic. So did the abstraction and simplification of historical forms on national monuments. Based on a redefinition of the ethnie, such efforts dispersed some parts of the memory landscape while crystallizing or concentrating others. The resulting architectural forms were not inventions but rather recastings or reframings of preexisting material culture.

Some preservationists conducted a running battle against the churches over such matters well into the twentieth century.[78] They assumed that the meaning of the historical building lay in its accretion of various styles over the ages. In making this argument they adopted Riegl's concept of age value. This approach was also associated with the idea that buildings would eventually "die" just as human beings did. The goal was to allow landmarks to develop, historical accretions and all, but not to preserve them beyond their natural life, however that was defined. The proponents of this approach often hesitated when it came time to accept the consequences of the theory, which meant accepting the loss of many historical buildings to natural decay. Whether restored or allowed to evolve with their historical accretions, churches as monuments remained at the center of German national identity throughout the twentieth century.

Of particular interest to the Bürgertum in Imperial Germany was historical urban architecture. Bürgerlich liberals saw the medieval city as a fundament of popular national identity. The city's town hall, patrician houses, and fortified walls and towers were reminders of the material wealth, civic prestige, self-government, and political power of the Bürgertum in the Middle Ages. Urban development and industrial growth threatened many such buildings in the late Empire. The most richly symbolic monuments of the medieval city were the numerous fortifications that ringed communities and added medieval ambiance with their towers and walkways.[79] Proponents of growth saw the walls and towers as obstacles to expansion and increased traffic, which indeed they often were. Defenders of such urban monuments put up a vigorous struggle, first in the early part of the nineteenth century in the bigger cities, then by the end of the century in smaller communities where commercialization and urbanization began to break up centuries-old urban morphologies. The results were mixed, as some communities did away with more or less all their fortifications while others saved a few reminders in the form of gates or well-preserved towers. Solutions that balanced the need for memory with the functional requirements of the modern city were most successful. That such balance was achieved in many instances reflects the Second Empire's willingness to compromise and to defer definitive solutions. This willingness would contrast sharply with the dominant tendency of the interwar period, which was to offer sweeping and "total" decisions.

Germans also showed an interest in salvaging industrial or farm artifacts from the past. One of the leading figures in this drive was Oskar von Miller, creator of the German Museum of Technology in Munich before World War I. Miller's idea for a technical museum reflected the growing status of engineers and technicians in Wilhelmine culture and the growing claim these groups had on public memory. The memory landscape consisted not only of the grand creations of the medieval Bürgertum or the aristocracy but also of artifacts of the technical intelligentsia and, even more broadly, of artisans and peasants. Miller was inspired by his visit to the first open-air museum in the world, organized by Artur Hazelius in 1891 in Skansen near Stockholm and featuring complete reconstructions of artisanal and peasant work settings. Miller's plan was to construct an open-air museum in the garden of the Museum of Technology, but World War I delayed plans. It would not be until the interwar era that the organized preservation of technical artifacts gained more momentum.[80] But the idea that the memory landscape must also reflect the history of ordinary work practices, industry, and technology was established in the imperial era. Such efforts had little to do with contemporary workers' and peasants' historical memories and even less to do with the political representatives of workers such as the Social Democrats. Instead, adoration of the artifacts of ordinary people usually derived from middle-class intellectuals' idealization of simple village life or craft customs.

THE ARCHITECTURE OF MEMORY

New architecture also played a significant role in the memory landscape of the Kaiserreich. As with monument building and preservation, architectural design felt the irresistible pull of historicism throughout most of the nineteenth century. In an age of economic and political revolutions, historicism reflected Europeans' heightened sense of discontinuity and of living in historical time. This greater awareness of time affected scholarship, philosophy, art, politics, and of course architecture. Drawing on a rich symbolic language, architects used specific historical styles for buildings with specific purposes. Just as historians of the nineteenth century depicted the past "as it really was," to use the German historian Leopold von Ranke's famous formulation, historicist architects constructed buildings that would accurately reflect what they thought to be the distinctive style of a bygone epoch. The point was not to give the architect room for individual creation or genius, but to work within an accepted historical genre, and thereby to express an ideology that had a broader social purpose. This meant that the actual edifice would not necessarily be like any building that existed in the medieval or baroque age, but rather would exemplify, in "pure" form, the perceived style of that age. Historicist architecture celebrated the weight of the past, accepted it fully, and derived meaning from history's continued elaboration in the present.

Intellectuals were vigorous proponents of particular styles, and in the case of the Rhenish Catholic writer and parliamentarian August Reichensperger, neo-Gothic found an especially powerful supporter who participated in an international Gothic movement led by Pugin in England and Hugo, Viollet-le-Duc, and Montalembert in France. In contrast to the situation in England or France, in Germany the neo-Gothic movement was highly politicized because it was marked by the religious and political struggles of German unification. For Reichensperger and many others, artistic style was much more than a matter of aesthetics. Disorganized or ambivalent artistic or architectural images represented a disorganized sense of national mission or even the dissolution of racial purity, as in the case of the musician Richard Wagner's thinking. Stylistic unity represented national unity and a clear sense of the present's relationship with the past. Although the racial issue played a marginal role in Reichensperger's thought, he nonetheless felt that Gothic was the architecture that most effectively linked contemporaries with the Middle Ages and that suited a decentralized state shaped by "contending but interlocking institutions," as Michael Lewis writes. Reichensperger "proposed a Gothic image for a modern Germany, and a Gothic model for German nationhood."[81]

Even when most Germans realized after midcentury that Gothic was originally French rather than German, church builders continued to use Gothic because it represented religiosity and religious unity. Architects for new town halls in Vienna and Munich also used massive Gothic designs because they connoted the civic culture of the medieval urban Bürgertum. In Vienna in particular, liberal culture represented the tradition of bürgerlich municipal autonomy in a massive Gothic Rathaus that was one of the most important buildings on the newly designed Ringstraße.[82] German industrialists and manufacturers often favored Romanesque and neo-Gothic styles for factories and other industrial sites, but they also turned to a more eclectic mix of historical forms before the turn of the century. Red brick neo-Gothic was particularly appealing because of its emphasis on structural "truth." By the 1890s most German industrialists, with the exception of the magnates of the iron and steel industries in the Ruhr valley, turned away from explicitly historicist styles in favor of *Jugendstil*, the German interpretation of Art Nouveau.[83] Libraries and universities were often built in the Italian Renaissance style to reflect humanistic aims and traditions. The late nineteenth-century German bourgeoisie favored Renaissance architecture for their homes. They could think of no better compliment than that which an Italian visitor gave to the wealthy German owner of a Renaissance residence designed by the architect Gottfried Semper: "E una villa di Toscana!"[84]

A veteran of the 1848 revolution in which Germans fought unsuccessfully for national unity and a liberal constitutional system, Semper had been instrumental in promoting Renaissance style in Dresden.

Many other architects and intellectuals took up the cause of Renaissance style, and in the first two decades after national unification, it became the symbol of Protestant liberal nationalism. Proponents of this tendency respected and admired Gothic architecture but also felt it had become too closely tied to conservative and clerical political causes in Germany. For these individuals, Renaissance architecture was linked to the time of Luther, who became a symbol of the (mainly Protestant) origins of modern German nationality. This of course did not prevent the Catholic Church from building neo-Renaissance churches that symbolized German Catholics' allegiance to Rome. Semper himself had championed architecture adapted to modern conditions, and for him and many others Renaissance was therefore also equated with modernity, while Gothic represented the outmoded past. Racial thinking could again be found on the margins of those holding such historical viewpoints. A few thinkers tried to demonstrate that the Italian Renaissance actually stemmed from Nordic and German influences. Like the proponents of neo-Gothic architecture, the advocates of the Renaissance in Germany wanted to combat "the formless Moloch of tastelessness and lack of style," in the words of the Munich publisher Georg Hirth in 1880, that befell the country. If the neo-Renaissance could be associated with liberal nationalism, it could nonetheless also be taken up by conservative monarchists, as it indeed was once the prospects of liberalism were in full decline later in the Second Empire.[85]

If the supporters of the neo-Renaissance hoped for a new unitary national style, then the Berlin Reichstag was one of their most powerful symbols. It was built on the Königsplatz, or Royal Square, by the Frankfurt architect Paul Wallot from 1884 to 1894 after a protracted and contentious struggle. A competition for the design had been held as early as 1872, but after considering more than sixty sites, the Reich initially failed in its attempt to buy land for the project. When the central government finally secured land and hit upon a design, no one was satisfied because the plan called for a compromise between the then regnant neo-Gothic style and Berlin neo-classicism, which had very strong proponents. Wallot was all too aware of the difficulties of the enterprise, stating that "we are building a national edifice without having a national style."[86] In Vienna, the Ringstraße development reflected a multiplicity of memories and design vocabularies dispersed over a larger urban fabric including public buildings, churches, and residences. In the Berlin Reichstag, Wallot concentrated this multiplicity in a single entity. He tried to accommodate the spirits of the time, placing a massive and

Figure 8. West facade of the Reichstag, Berlin, 1896. Bildarchiv Preussischer Kulturbesitz.

very modern-looking cupola of iron and glass above the huge central entrance to the building and larding the rest with statuary, towers, and columns done up in an ornate Renaissance style. Critics rightly criticized the structure for what appeared to be its indecisiveness, and modifications undertaken after World War II did away with some of the building's elaborate facade and statuary. In the 1990s, the British architect Norman Foster returned a modernized version of the glass dome to the edifice, which now houses the national parliament of reunified Germany.

Rumors circulated in the 1890s that the kaiser had scotched plans to build the glass dome even higher because it would overshadow the cupola of the imperial palace. Wilhelm II's intervention on this score is unsubstantiated, but he did successfully prevent Wallot from having the words "To the German People" placed on the Reichstag's massive gable. This phrase smacked of popular sovereignty, all the more so since the leader of the socialist movement, August Bebel, had praised the Reichstag precisely because it took the architecture of privilege and transformed it into a symbol of parliamentary government. Wilhelm II had become disillusioned with a Reichstag to which Social Democrats were increasingly elected and with a capital city in which liberal political and avant-garde cultural ideas had gained much influence. The monarch's sensitivity on such issues was of course heightened on the very first day the new Reichstag was in full operation, 6 December 1894, when several Social Democrats ostentatiously remained seated while the other representatives stood to hail Wilhelm II in the traditional manner. The kaiser once referred to the Reichstag as the "imperial monkey house." Only in 1916, when the war made the kaiser's opposition to Wallot's inscription almost unpatriotic, were the now-famous words etched in stone on the parliament building. The incident was a fitting symbol of the struggle for democracy in the imperial period.[87]

Historicism reflected divergent memories and a multiplicity of historical styles. From one point of view the multiplicity of styles could represent the harmonization of interests in a liberal national culture. But this hardly satisfied those who equated the lack of a unitary artistic style with the weakness or downfall of the culture or the racial community. For them, Julius Langbehn's call for a unified German style in all architectural and artistic matters was much more to the point. The kaiser's adoption of neo-Romanesque reflected similar concerns, although his artistic tastes were still too favorable to foreign influences in the eyes of nationalists. Despite the seriousness with which architects and publicists pursued such issues, it is true that historicism was reduced to a kind of cafeteria of styles by the end of the century. The proliferation of architectural firms and the general growth and diversification of the economy led to a situation in which historical forms became superficial fashions rather than attributes of a "world-view architecture" (*Weltanschauungsarchitektur*). In the eyes of many, the philosophy of historicism had been commercialized and trivialized.

Scholars have often seen historicist architecture as evidence of the Bürgertum's anxiety about the appearance of a modern industrial society. They argue that ornamentation and multiple historical references revealed a wish to live in the past rather than the present. That such anxiety existed could hardly be denied. One could find much evidence for it in Germany, England, France, and the Scandinavian countries. But the evidence could just as easily be used to argue that historicist architecture did not represent a flight from the industrial and urban society that was being built, but an attempt to adapt to that society and create an architecture appropriate to it. The pluralism of historicist architecture after all matched the multiplicity and plurality of a changing society increasingly divided into classes and strata. Historicist architecture was a product of the kind of detailed scholarship and highly technical research that characterized the more elaborate organization of the historical and natural sciences in the nineteenth century. Historicist architecture matched the desire for social and cultural reform that captured the imagination of many Europeans at this time. And of course historicist architecture emerged from attempts to capture and represent specific national traditions in a way demanded by the modern national state itself. Protagonists of Gothic, Romanesque, or Renaissance architecture argued that their style was most appropriate to express national identity. If they excluded other styles, they nonetheless shared an impulse to find a single form of artistic representation that could embody the moment of historical time in which they lived.

Modernist architecture drank from the same well. Like historicists, modernist architects tried to control the surfeit of historical models in an attempt to create forms appropriate to the age. They too were involved in an attempt to channel or even destroy the past in order to recreate it. We associate modernist architecture with the functionalist architecture that appeared most forcefully in interwar Europe in the work of the Bauhaus school and Walter Gropius, Le Corbusier in France, and El Lissitzky in Germany and the Soviet Union. Yet at the turn of the century, modernist architecture was more varied and less hostile to historical influences than its interwar successor would be. Men such as Peter Behrens, Alfred Messel, Paul Bonatz, and Bruno Taut tried to limit the historical static of historicism and create a new, cleaner architectural style that could also represent Germany's status as a global economic power. Despite its indisputable links with the interwar internationalism of the architecture of "constructivism," modernism in its earlier stages also had a strong nationalizing impulse. In Germany, this impulse corroborated and strengthened other efforts to gain a more useful past for the Second Reich. No less than their historicist brethren, modernists were interested in using architecture to bring about a national renewal based on a healthier and more consistent relationship between the past and future.

Modernist architecture therefore belongs in a discussion of the memory landscape just as much as national monuments and historic sites do, and not only because modernist architects challenged the historicists and preservationists. Barbara Miller Lane referred to the modernist architecture of the late imperial period as an abstracted historicism. Modernists stripped away what they regarded as the chaotic facades of historicist architecture and either added their own simplified designs or did away with ornamentation altogether. In doing so, they did not reject his-

Figure 9. Wertheim's Department Store, Berlin, 1905. Bildarchiv Preussischer Kulturbesitz.

torical styles as much as they recodified and reduced them. Alfred Messel's Wertheim store, built from 1897 to 1904, was one of the first great department stores in Berlin. Messel created a dramatically new interpretation of the verticality of Gothic facades by transforming granite mullions, uprights dividing windows into two or more sections, into a regular pattern that was more orderly and dynamic than the heavily decorated facades of the seventies and eighties. This department store became a popular tourist attraction not only because of its high-quality goods but because of the building itself. Paul Bonatz was more radical in his Stuttgart railway station, begun in 1913. This influential and much-praised building used the baroque pattern of elongated vertical windows separated by ornamented panels. A classical colonnade stood astride the central block of the building. But such historical associations were integrated into a radically new design in which the base of the building was eliminated and the cornice only suggested. Asymmetrical and massive, the creation resembled an arrangement of simplified cubic forms in which the echo of historical tradition was faint to say the least.[88]

Bonatz's building was one of a number of late imperial creations that hovered on the border between abstracted historicism and interwar functionalist architecture. Yet even when architects explicitly attacked historical styles, as they were to do vociferously after World War I, they never cut the thread linking them to the past. Moreover, even when they assumed a more pointed and critical stance toward German architectural tradition, they continued to produce buildings that would be conducive to the creation of a strong national cultural life. In short, they continued to build national monuments, just as their historicist colleagues did, even if these monuments depicted a very different nation.

EXPANDING THE LANDSCAPE

All the examples used so far have considered isolated parts of the memory landscape rather than larger ensembles and groupings. My last two examples, urban planning and the *Heimat* movement, dealt with discourses that had a broader view of the built environment and a correspondingly more expansive view of the memory landscape. Even though urban planning designed or remapped cities to accommodate the future, its decisions affected how or whether buildings and monuments from the past would survive. For urban planners the memory landscape potentially consisted not just of individual monuments and buildings but of whole cities as national monuments. Their work in the Imperial period could thus anticipate that of late-twentieth-century thinkers who thought of the memory landscape in terms of whole topographies.

Urban planning had a marginal role in the early modern period, but it emerged as a coherent and influential discipline in the nineteenth century when the technical and hygienic problems of rapidly growing cities demanded solutions. The commanding figure of midcentury urban planning was the Alsatian civil servant and prefect of the Department of the Seine in Paris, Georges-Eugène Haussmann. Carrying out Emperor Napoleon III's wish to remake Paris as an imperial capital in the 1850s and 1860s, Haussmann transformed the city relying on classical traditions of regularity and monumentality as well as on rather shifty financial policies.[89] Besides building sewers and creating wide new traffic arteries, Haussmann also restored historical buildings and monuments. His vision of historical landmarks was characteristic of mid-nineteenth-century culture, for he saw the memory landscape as consisting of a limited canon of national monuments, the qualities of which could be appreciated only under highly controlled conditions. From this perspective, one viewed a grand cathedral or important monument as one would an artistic masterpiece in a museum. A static (and usually male) viewer observed the painting isolated from its historical context but would nonetheless gain a sense of the work's historical meaning by virtue of his education and general cultural learning. In practical terms, this meant that Haussmann resorted to the widely accepted procedure of restoring many monuments to accentuate the "purity" of their particular historical style. It also meant that large parts of medieval and working-class Paris—a palimpsest of ancient alleys, narrow streets, and jumbles of old buildings—were torn down so as to "disencumber" monuments from their accretions and create wide streets conducive to the traffic of an imperial city.

Germany had no experience to compare with Haussmann's remaking of Paris. But in 1862 the engineer James Hobrecht developed a comprehensive plan to manage the extraordinary expansion of Berlin by creating a grid pattern of large blocks of land adapted to the roads and property lines that already formed the Berlin suburbs. Although Hobrecht spoke to the problem of new urban expansion whereas Haussmann dealt with a historical urban core, both regarded regularity of design, traffic flow, and hygienic and sanitary improvements as key elements of town planning. In practice, Hobrecht's approach encouraged other planners to apply the standards of uniformity and sanitary improvement to older cities in efforts to reorganize what was seen as the chaotic and disorganized architecture and street layouts of the past. In the eyes of one planner, Carl-Friedrich Reichardt, German urban planning would necessarily be directed against "the uneven, unregulated streets and the disorderly arbitrariness and lack of refinement of the much-praised Middle Ages."[90] Based on an optimism about the future, such ideas were cut from the same cloth as those employed by the builders of national monuments, the restorers of historical buildings, and historicist architects. All wanted to reduce and reorganize the memory landscape in order to recenter it around a unitary national vision.

Planners such as Reichardt, Reinhard Baumeister, and Josef Stübben did praise the aesthetic qualities of medieval cities and old townscapes, but they considered such qualities to be marginal to the larger tasks of urban reorganization demanded by the new age. While they were willing to allow some medieval fortifications or ensembles of medieval buildings to stand, they considered such parts of the built environment to be isolated elements rather than integral resources. Some architects had already criticized this imbalance in the 1870s, though with relatively little effect, and Stübben would gradually rethink the role of historical buildings in urban planning by the turn of the century.

The design culture of the German ethnie still had strong Central European connections, and it is unsurprising to find that one of the most enduring impulses in town planning came not from Berlin or Cologne but from Vienna. The most influential alternative to the city of geometry and the grid was offered by the Viennese planner Camillo Sitte, whose 1889 book *Town Planning According to Artistic Principles*, envisioned monuments and squares in a broader relationship with their surroundings. Sitte was concerned mainly with the construction of picturesque urban squares that would relieve the monotony of geometrically planned cities and revive memories of the civic pride and local identities of the premodern city. He stated his premise succinctly: "We have lost the thread of artistic tradition in city planning, although it is not clear why."[91] This artistic tradition meant what amounted to ad hoc planning principles rather than submission to the dictatorship of the slide rule and straight line; it was, to use a vocabulary introduced earlier in the chapter, closer to bricolage than to "science." The Sittian principle translated into an aesthetic vision in which irregularity was incorporated into urban vistas, as when a monument was placed at the side rather than in the center of the square. Such ambiance would provide the proper setting for traditional folk customs and festivals, indeed for the fuller development of what Sitte called "national life," or *Volksleben*, which in the architect's eyes had disappeared from the monotonous and congested traffic arteries of the modern city. Squares, monuments, streets, and social life added up to a cumulative vision of urban exchange based on a memory landscape that was fuller and more evocative of national tradition than anything offered by the urban geometricians. Historically resonant urban squares and the interactions that went on around them thus became national monuments for Sitte and his followers.

Sitte's vision would have great impact in Germany at the turn of the century, although the planning principles outlined by Baumeister and others would still hold sway. Sitte offered a vision of the city that saw the memory landscape as a true environment or living ensemble of objects, actions, and memories. This vision would be taken up again in later periods of German urban history, as I will show. Sitte had also introduced a narrative of urban decline and possible renewal that fit the desires of those who envisioned a new Germany. Like the slumbering Barbarossa at the Kyffhäuser mountain, the German city, both symbol and motor of the ethnie, would arise again after a period of decline and alienation from its historical roots. But if Sitte offered an urbanistic myth of national revival, his treatment of the city reduced and contained historical memories just as much as the geometricians' approach to the city did. Carl Schorske has noted that Sitte was willing to concede large stretches of the modern city to the forces of commercial exploitation, traffic, and utilitarian principles.[92] Only a few resonant squares and ensembles were left over to realize Sitte's vision of renewal. Reflecting the influence of dominant urban planning themes, Sitte also accepted the argument for urban hygiene, and he referred to the urban park and green space as the "lungs" of the city.[93] The limitations of Sitte's perspectives were often overlooked by later urban planners, who, inspired by postmodern viewpoints, saw his principle of artistic planning as a radical signal to transform whole cities into museums. In his time, Sitte's vision thus also shared the collective desire to limit and control the past, to reframe it selectively for specific national purposes. No less than the builders of national monuments, Sitte was an architect of destruction as much as he was a prophet of memory.

An even more expansive definition of national monuments could be found in a group of organizations with the goal of protecting the German "homeland," or Heimat. The Heimat movement was not a unitary phenomenon but a varied group that tried to unite the preservationist, historical, cultural, and environmentalist groups that had emerged in Germany by the turn of the century.[94] Heimat advocates revived Romanticism's emphasis on the natural and built environments' deep impact on individual and collective identity. Picturesque landscapes or medieval townscapes were total environments that were at the same time national monuments worthy of preserving. This perspective led Heimat devotees such as the Berlin music professor Ernst Rudorff and architect Paul Schultze-Naumburg to criticize the effects of railway building, urbanization, suburbanization, and commercialization. Disruptive industrial building, colorful commercial advertising, and shoddy residential housing defaced such total environments and cut the historical traditions uniting modern landscapes with their predecessors. Given the close interaction between the environment and the national identity, to deface the environment was also to diminish the vitality of the people. The Heimat movement's most prolific and visible representative was Schultze-Naumburg, whose writings were often obligatory reading for building officials and other civil servants in municipal and state governments.

The Heimat movement's "totalistic" vision and strident criticism of industrial society suggested radicalism, but its approach to planning and preservation was in practice rather moderate. The defenders of Heimat wanted to shield the countryside from industrial development, but they were willing to countenance more efficient land uses and rational railway building. They adored what were interpreted as traditional peasant costumes or folk architecture, but they also engaged in highly technical discussions about agriculture, land and village planning, and transportation needs. They loved the countryside, but they were based in cities such as Dresden, Berlin, and Cologne. They developed the most expansive definition of memory landscape in the imperial period, but they were explicit in their willingness to accommodate the past to future national needs. If their often breathless nationalism had traces of racist thought in the imperial period, their political practice engendered compromise and negotiation. In World War I and in the Weimar Republic, the racial and radical nationalist elements of their thought would come through more clearly. In the imperial era, in contrast, radicalism would be tempered by pragmatism.

The Heimat movement's perspective rested on the idea that the landscape revealed the unique memory and culture of the people. This linked it with the radical nationalists and neo-Romantics of the age, who wanted to dislodge foreign influences from German culture and rediscover the "real" social heritage. It is important nonetheless to remember that such ideas had a broad international resonance in this age of spreading industrialization and urbanization. The Heimat movement took a part of its intellectual stimulus from the work of John Ruskin and William Morris, who criticized the culture of English capitalism, and it had similarities to the ethnic revival movements of the various British nationalities in the third quarter of the nineteenth century.[95] The national Heimat organization patterned itself after the French "Société pour la protection des paysages de France." In France at the end of the nineteenth century, it had become common to hear conservative intellectuals such as Maurice Barrès and Charles Maurras use a distinction dating back decades, namely that between *le pays légal,* the country as represented by the political system, and *le pays réel,* the country as represented by the peasantry, the rural family, and devout Catholicism. Political systems would change, but authentic France, the country of village and field, endured. Conservatives argued that every Frenchmen simultaneously belonged to a *petite patrie* bounded by the local region and the *grande patrie,* the whole of France.[96] The latter could only be true to French national character if it were based on the values of the former. Despite state centralization, the idea of the nation as rooted in the local community became widespread in French political culture.

All such ideas were analogous to the German Heimat movement's idealization of rural life and architecture; all such ideas posited a "true" national existence whose foundation lay in a memory landscape that would reveal its mysteries only to those who were willing to preserve the artifacts of a culture threatened by big cities, modern transportation networks, and mass politics. Considered in an international perspective, then, the argument of national uniqueness was part of a series of parallel gestures. Nationalist thinkers revealed their broadly European heritage by stressing the unique and irreducible qualities of the history of their home culture. This too would be an enduring and constitutive element in the memory landscape for the whole period covered by this study.

OUTSIDERS

It may be useful to mention some other parts of the memory landscape that were either not elaborated or were suppressed through the mobilization of framing strategies during the Kaiserreich. Throughout the nineteenth century, "the subject of history and its agent was the male citizen."[97] The nation was seen as a fellowship of men, or rather of male-dominated households in which women participated in the nation only as wives and mothers. This predominant view also shaped perceptions of the memory landscape, which was built out of monuments, buildings, and sites that had a strong public visibility. To the considerable degree that a "separate spheres" ideology segregated men and women, the public and the private, and work and home, the memory landscape of the era from the French Revolution to World War I was very much a male invention. Because monuments were products of the bourgeois public sphere and the state, and because these realms were constituted primarily by dominant male subjects, monuments both reflected and ensured the subordination of women.

It was not that the memory landscape was without representations of females.[98] European urban architecture was full of elaborate female forms, including sylphs, the Muses, goddesses, dryads, caryatids, nymphs, and angels. Such figures were part of a broader allegorical tradition in classical and Christian civilization in which symbolic representations of females expressed widely held "desiderata and virtues." But the strength and pervasiveness of this allegorical tradition often depended "on the unlikelihood of women practicing the concepts they represent." The fact that French Republicanism was associated with the feminine figure of Marianne does not challenge this assessment. For many French citizens, Marianne was not a symbol of political fortitude, least of all for women, but a substitute for the traditional emotive force of the Virgin Mary. And for the defenders of the Republic, Marianne caused as many problems as she solved because conservatives saw her as a sign of the weakness of the French nation or, in more extreme critiques, as a prostitute. The French Right offered Joan of Arc, "the anti-Marianne par excellence," as the appropriate feminine symbol of virginal innocence, peasant authenticity, religious faith, and national tradition in opposition to the Revolution. Even for the French then, it was, as Agulhon remarked, a "phallocratic" age, and Marianne's ubiquitous presence only reflected and strengthened male actors' instrumentalization of female forms.[99]

The iconography of German national monuments reinforced a male-oriented view as well, as Wilhelm I or Bismarck were represented as strong masculine figures engaged in political and military struggle. Hermann's raised sword had obvious phallic overtones for both the sculptor Bandel and contemporary observers, who spoke of the power elicited by the warrior's "masculine beauty." Radical nationalists emphasized and elaborated such perspectives for other monuments and political activities.[100] To the extent that women were portrayed in nationalist symbolism, they assumed traditional roles, in this period usually as mythical figures such as Germania—found on the south gable of the Walhalla, the Victory Column, the Niederwalddenkmal, and the Reichstag—who ratified and mythologized men's heroism. Germania could stand for many things, and she was at times, as in 1848, linked with the liberal and democratic values that Marianne had for many French citizens. In the Niederwalddenkmal in particular, where she symbolized German unification, she assumed the same aggressive stance toward enemies of the nation that Hermann did in the Teutoburger Forest, or that Joan of Arc did, in numerous monuments and other representations, initially *vis-à-vis* the English but then all foreign invaders on French soil. But the German symbol also had a more inward-directed meaning. "Germania is the victor," said Johannes Schilling, the creator of the monument, who depicted Germania gazing inward toward the nation rather than toward the French, who belonged to the past because they had been beaten. Later, Germania would take up arms in World War I–era pictorial representations, she would appear on bank notes and as a symbol for business corporations, and she would experience her most embarrassing degradation at the hands of Hitler, who wanted to rename his capital after her. Despite the variations of meaning and expression, Germania remained an instrument of masculine renderings of the nation right up to the time when she disappeared from German national discourse after the war.[101]

From another angle, tourists and preservationists who valued scenic villages or historic urban centers reinforced dominant interpretations of "picturesque" settings, to which both male and female viewers often ascribed "feminine" characteristics of beauty and naturalness but also incompleteness and lack of organization. Those who preserved or reorganized such settings assumed a masculine position as they cared for and completed a feminized landscape. The builders of the memory landscape, finally, were predominantly male, since few women entered the ranks of professional architects, engineers, sculptors, art historians, building officials, city planners, and preservationists. With few exceptions, the organizing committees for the national monuments were made up of men.[102]

Even so, a completely black-and-white picture will not do for Germany.[103] The memory landscape was available for "private" memories created and reinforced by women in families, churches, and schools. But even more importantly, the symbiosis in Germany between religion and politics (as in the Catholic movement) created a situation in which women could play a greater public role. The "spiritualization" of the national movement, its reliance on religious motifs and symbols, also meant that the confinement of religion to the private sphere, and hence the reduction of women to private roles, did not proceed quite as far as it did in France, where religion and politics were more radically separated. Women played subordinate roles within the nationalist movement, but when they gathered donations for the building of the Hermannsdenkmal or other national monuments, or when they participated in nationalist festivals at the base of such monuments, their activity became more public. The male geometricians of German national memory celebrated women as symbols, but dominated them as human beings. Women for the most part accepted their roles, but their activity often unintentionally blurred the lines between public and private memory, between politics and religion, and between the nation and the household.

In contrast, the German Social Democratic workers' movement, itself the representative of mainly Protestant male workers, actively promoted a view of the German past and future that opposed the Reich, the states, and the Bürgertum. Having adopted Marxist ideology as the official

Figure 10. Woodcut of Germania on Niederwalddenkmal, 1879. Bildarchiv Preussischer Kulturbesitz.

viewpoint of the Social Democratic party by the last decade of the century, socialist workers framed the past as an age of exploitation of the working man and the future as the site of new and more humane conditions.[104] The Social Democrats were the only political party in the Reichstag not to vote for a 4-million-mark Reich donation to Begas's Kaiser Wilhelm Memorial in Berlin. Against the campaign to collect money for the building of the Leipzig Monument to the Battle of the Nations, socialists warned "eyes open, pockets closed."[105] Social Democrats not only had a strong sense of separateness from efforts to build up the memory landscape of Imperial Germany; they were also branded as the "fellows without a fatherland" by the kaiser and others. This epithet stemmed directly from the tendency of German nationalism to undertake a militant struggle against internal opponents.

Still, the Social Democrats shared many assumptions with the official and bourgeois proponents of national identity. At the moment of national unification, they identified strongly with the bourgeois press's attacks on Napoleon III and praised the "animation" of the national spirit in all German states. Social Democrats emphasized class loyalty, but their political rituals and symbolism indicated they accepted the new German nation as the basis of their political action. They too participated in a cult of adoration for the authors of classical German literature such as Goethe and Friedrich Schiller. They too retained religious elements and symbols in their festivals and speeches even as class antagonisms mounted in the last two decades of the empire. Sponsored directly by the Social Democratic party, "March Festivals" honoring the martyrs of the 1848 revolutions, the *Märzgefallenen,* and later also of the Paris Commune of 1871, added to the richness of the German memory culture. Heavily controlled by police authorities, such festivals featured the laying of wreaths at the gravestones of revolutionaries, speeches, processions, and sociability. By the last decade of the century, May Day demonstrations and festivals were the most important of the explicitly political celebrations of the socialist movement.[106] In working-class nature and hiking associations, workers shared bourgeois assumptions that natural environments represented not only a respite from the city but a quasi-religious path back to an authentic source of German national being. In doing so, they participated in a broader European movement whereby nature assumed a new centrality to national identities built less on martial glories than on authenticity and simplicity.[107] Nature too could be used to limit the multiple messages of the German past and centralize national feeling; nature too could be a monument.

Figure 11. Police controlling commemoration of 1848 martyrs, Berlin, 1912. Deutsches Historisches Museum.

The Social Democrats were not as concerned with the optical characteristics of the nation as their bourgeois opponents were; the political struggle and the everyday world were much more important. Even so, historically, workers had not been absent from local efforts to erect monuments, as when earlier in the century they participated in veterans' associations that sponsored the building of memorials to honor their fallen comrades.[108] When in the late empire workers added their own national monuments to the memory landscape, their creations drew heavily on the practices and forms of the national culture. Workers used Schiller busts at party festivals and incorporated the Nibelungen myth in a *tableau vivant* at the 1900 party congress. More substantially, they began to build their own form of monumental architecture. After 1905 there was a building boom of trade union halls, nicknamed "red city halls" or in some cities simply "people's houses *[Volkshäuser]*."[109] The Social Democratic leader August Bebel called the Hamburg trade union hall "the armorer of the proletariat," while critics referred to the structures as working-class "castles." At the turn of the century there were fifteen such buildings, at the start of World War I, eighty. About 10 percent of all local trade union cartels had halls by 1914, up from 5 percent at the turn of the century. Although the cost of trade union halls was very high and all of them except the Frankfurt am Main hall proved to be financially unprofitable before the war, there was much popular support for such ventures, although because of anticipated costs this support was never unanimous.

Supporters thought that the red city halls would serve as symbolic rallying points and communication centers for an increasingly diverse and internally contentious working class. The goal was not only to create an outward demonstration of working-class strength but to draw together the working-class movement from within just as national monuments were thought to bring together the disparate elements of the nation. The local milieu was the most immediate context in which such solidarity could be demonstrated. The red city halls were also planned as local business enterprises, and thus they participated in the growing commercialization of city centers and historic districts. In Hamburg, a huge trade union hall was dedicated in 1906, the same year in which that city erected its Bismarck monument at the city harbor. The Hamburg hall was a kind of counter-monument to local bourgeois architecture. Its colossal size and imposing facade, which resembled the Hamburg city hall built in 1897, was seen by some sympathetic commentators as proof that it was not only the Hamburg bourgeoisie that had a taste for monumental buildings. Workers too could erect grand edifices that gave them historical legitimacy and a place of honor in the national genealogy.

Although many German Jews joined the Social Democratic party, the majority of Jews were members of the Bürgertum who supported liberal political parties and considered themselves good German patriots. German national monuments were therefore also their monuments. Jewish culture contributed vitally to the monumental style in German architecture in this period. The massive Oranienburger Straße synagogue, based on designs by the noted German architect Knoblauch, completed in Berlin in 1866 and constructed in an imposing Oriental style featuring a gilded dome and an impressive brick facade with granite and sandstone details, was one such example. In 1889 the Baedeker guide to the German capital referred to the grand edifice as "one of the most important and original products of modern architectural activity in Berlin."[110] Like their Protestant and Catholic counterparts, Jewish preservation societies were also active. A society organized to research Jewish monuments was formed in Frankfurt am Main in 1897. Besides wanting to study and preserve Jewish artifacts, it aimed to create a topography of Jewish art and material culture in the city. State authorities also financed

Figure 12. The Oranienburger Straße synagogue, Berlin, 1892. Bildarchiv Preussischer Kulturbesitz.

and organized research on Jewish architecture and remains such as the medieval baths of Jewish ghettoes. These activities should be seen in the context of the wider formation of a secular German Jewish culture that took shape earlier in the nineteenth century, consolidated itself in the last quarter-century before World War I, and culminated in the Weimar Republic.[111]

Such objects and activities highlighted the double bind of German Jewish existence. Jews strongly identified with national monuments and contributed to the modern project of situating the nation in historical time. For them the memory landscape could symbolize their assimilation to German national culture, which could also mean their adoption of the Christian religion. At the same time, their separateness was symbolized in the ruins and other objects of Jewish culture that could be used to recall a history of persecution and segregation or to remind contemporaries of the presence of a populist anti-Semitism in the Second Empire. The German nation was a Christian nation oriented in part to the ruthless struggle against internal "enemies." Historian Omer Bartov has recently argued that "the Jews can be seen as the paradigmatic example of the preoccupation with identity and solidarity, exclusion and victimization that numerous states or at least some of their agencies have manifested in the modern era."[112] In this context Jews were always vulnerable to persecution and even violence when nationalist ideology assumed more militant forms.

Finally, by the end of the nineteenth century, many European thinkers criticized the dominance of history and the idea of a collective past as such. For them, the memory landscape, whether German, French, or Serbian, was not exclusively a symbol of national history. Rather, it could also symbolize personal experiences and a private memory that was never identical to the past created by nationalists and their followers. New scientific analyses of memory and forgetting, philosophy, psychoanalysis, developmental psychology, painting, and the theater contributed to the trend, as did more popular pursuits such as mysticism, nudism, nature reform, and vegetarianism. It was not that adherents of such practices disavowed national history, but rather that they insisted that to ignore or leave unexplored the impact of personal memories and feelings was to risk living an inauthentic life. This perspective would have its own history, its own deep continuity, and would be powerfully expressed in the period after 1970, when for many Germans the landscape became a topography of historical traces resonating with both national and personal memories.

Nietzsche's emphasis on forgetting, as well as his criticism of the overpowering weight of the past in German culture, inspired such trends even if many advocates of the new personal culture had gained access to the tortured philosopher's thought only by the most indirect and misleading routes. "This shift in attention from the historical past to the personal past was part of a broad effort to shake off the burden of history," writes historian Stephen Kern. Germans contributed significantly to the shift. But as with other Europeans, Germans who embraced a more developed sense of personal memory did so partly out of the fear that "germ cells and muscle tissues, dreams and neuroses, retentions and involuntary memories, [and] guilt and ghosts" overpowered the individual.[113] Was the personal and familial past a prison house of the soul just as much as the collective and national past was? Few Europeans could deal seriously with this possibility before 1914, and many of those who did, in Germany or elsewhere, soon succumbed to the ever louder drumbeat of nationalism in World War I. For most, the theme of personal memory would have to operate "between the monuments," as it were, before it would become elaborated more fully—and then ritualized—on the stage of public life later in the century.

Earlier in the nineteenth century the famous historian Jacob Burckhardt argued that culture was the product of the mastering and sublimation of basic human drives and emotions. Burckhardt's definition of culture was extremely broad, encompassing the state and religion as well as art, architecture, literature, and music.[114] The process of national memory work in Germany was analogous to Burckhardt's model of cultural production. From the Kyffhäuser and Leipzig monuments to medieval churches, from industrial artifacts to Jewish sites of memory, Germany built and maintained national monuments in an effort to sublimate and transform the effects of a rich but ultimately chaotic preunification past. In this process the cultural nation was reframed and reconstructed to serve the political exigencies of the new national state, which in the eyes of Wilhelm II was quite literally a work of art. The emergent German nation participated in a broader European trend whereby "long memories" were channeled and selectively reoriented to symbolize the accomplishments of "great peoples." But if grandeur, longevity, and monumentality characterized national cultures in this age, then so too did aggressiveness and militarism. The prewar battle of monuments prefigured the bloody, elemental war of real people in 1914–1918. Burckhardt's narrative of the development of culture could apparently work in reverse as well, as base human aggression was desublimated in a war of supposedly civilized nations. As that war unfolded, a disturbing new artifactual form emerged to reconfigure the memory landscape and the nation it represented.

CHAPTER TWO

Ruins

The Bonn art historian Paul Clemen was a leading preservationist appointed by the German government to oversee the protection of monuments and artistic treasures wherever the German military operated in World War I. Pessimistic about the chances for comprehensive wartime preservation in the future, Clemen, writing in 1919, envisioned a new war in which not France or Belgium but Germany was the victim. "What would all the theoretical considerations signify," asked Clemen, "if today from the French and Belgian, the Czechoslovakian and Polish borders, an army of airplanes took off that in twenty-four hours could transform all German big cities into a sea of ruins?"[1] A conservative nationalist whose heart remained in Imperial Germany, Clemen nonetheless gave moderate support to Germany's first democratic republic in 1918. But he was convinced that the Versailles peace treaty, signed with great reluctance in 1919 by the Weimar Republic's representatives, made it impossible for Germany to defend itself against attacks that would transform the World War I ruins of Louvain, Reims, and Amiens into the ruins of Cologne, Berlin, and Dresden in a future conflagration. Clemen had the dubious opportunity of seeing his nightmare vision become reality before his death in 1947, and although he was not the only leading intellectual to imagine such imminent disasters, his proximity to the world of art made the dream of unprecedented cultural destruction particularly unbearable for him.

Figure 13. Ruins of city hall and church in Belgian town Dixmuiden, World War I. Bildarchiv Preussischer Kulturbesitz.

Paul Clemen's nightmare suggested that the most imposing and "creative" feature of Germany's memory landscape in this period was the ruin. "Ruins are ideal: the perceiver's attitudes count so heavily that one is tempted to say ruins are a way of seeing," writes the architectural historian Robert Harbison. Ruins are physical artifacts, to be sure, but since the eighteenth century at least, they were much more. "Practically any human thing slipping into dereliction, the forecast of ruin," continues Harbison, "engages our feelings about where we see ourselves in history, early or late, and (in poignant cases) our feelings about how the world will end."[2]

The ruin had a long and noble standing in Western culture but it now not only took on new meanings but allowed Europeans to reframe the significance of other parts of the memory landscape as well. Romantics of the late eighteenth and early nineteenth centuries had taken delight in ruins, regarding them as symbols of the irrevocable workings of nature and time against artifice. For some the ruin was a negative symbol, as in the paintings of Caspar David Friedrich, who lamented the decline of religion and saw the landscape as a vast repository for the broken remains of spiritual certainty. In 1907 the German sociologist Georg Simmel wrote that the architectural ruin created a sense of peace for the viewer. The ruin was a specific artistic form that derived its unity and resonance from the fact that it embodied and momentarily preserved an eternal "tension" between "utility and decay, nature and spirit, past and present."[3] All human history could be read from observing ruins, Simmel wrote. Like other admirers of ruins before him, Simmel implied that the ruin, even when it was under attack by those who wanted to restore crumbled castles and churches, could still impart a sense of immortality. The struggle between past and present, nature and spirit, could remind the individual that in spite of her or his own death, human life wages its struggle for existence.

The nineteenth century had become uncomfortable with ruins. But in the interwar era, ruins came to signify something much more than the drag of the past on a society oriented to material progress and civilization. In the Middle Ages, many thinkers thought of the City of Earth as an organic cosmos that would eventually die just as human beings did. In the interwar period, this organic metaphor was applied to civilization, and ruins now signified a deep and virtually unavoidable process of decline in the Occident. The German philosopher Oswald Spengler finished his three-volume *Decline of the West* before World War I broke out, but the war delayed its publication and allowed the philosopher to make further revisions in the manuscript. When it appeared from 1918 to 1923 it created a world-historical counterpart to Clemen's vision of a Germany in ruins.

Spengler wrote that his was a "philosophy of the future, so far as the metaphysically exhausted soil of the West can bear such." He argued that all great civilizations had gone through comparable patterns of rise and decline. Great cities reflected and embodied such patterns as they grew from primitive barter centers, into what Spengler called the "culture city," and finally into "world cities." The fate of world cities was predictable from history. "In a long series of Classical writers . . ." he argued, "we read of old, renowned cities in which the streets have become lines of empty, crumbling shells, where the cattle browse in forum and gymnasium, and the amphitheatre is a sown field, dotted with emergent statues and hermae." This vision resonated for contemporary society. For Spengler, "the stone of Gothic buildings" had become not the symbol of a resurgent national identity, as it had been for so many nineteenth-century patriots, but "the soulless material" of a "demonic stone desert" that arose from a process of ineluctable decay. Spengler hated the big

European cities, decrying their commercialism and soullessness in terms one would find in Nazi thinkers' writings also. But he did manage to leave room for an austere and rather frightening hope in the future, at least in the short run. Basing his analysis on the murky idea of race as "Ethos" rather than biology, Spengler argued that life "lets choose *only* between victory and ruin, not between war and peace, and to the victory belong the sacrifices of victory." Only the race that was "in condition" and willing to struggle to the death could avoid, for a time, the inevitable.[4] The images of future slaughter this perspective raised would have to be met with a shrug of the shoulders, for life and race, like time and destiny, were without conscience. In part because he was assailed as a pessimist, Spengler wrote pamphlets and gave speeches that developed the idea that an authoritarian socialism rooted in Prussian tradition—and based on the image of the eighteenth-century Prussian king Friedrich Wilhelm I as the first true socialist—would gain the future.

Such apocalyptic visions could hardly fail to have an impact when sober conservatives like Clemen were imagining German cities as "crumbling shells" not as a result of historical inevitability but as a result of Allied bombs. Many Germans would try to avoid the alarming meanings the ruin now held, reverting to earlier ideas of ruins as symbols of the constant renewal of life in the face of death. Some, like the Nazis, would take heart from Nietzsche's perplexing idea of eternal return. This made it possible to think of the decline and fall of civilizations as a constant process that would elevate the "Aryan" race to a privileged place in world history after its fall from a prehistoric Golden Age. Others would militantly suppress the more disturbing implications of the ruin metaphor. They created buildings that resisted the workings of time so effectively that even as ruins the buildings would be imposing. Finally, they would celebrate the ruins of devastated German cities in the last stages of World War II. They took heart from Spengler's idea of racial struggle and authoritarian socialism, even though they would suppress his work because of the criticisms he made of the regime's idea of a thousand-year Reich and, no doubt, because of the philosopher's obvious pessimism. But none could overlook the ruin as the central organizing metaphor of the terrains of national memory. Neither an anachronism nor the site of leisured musings about the transience of human life, the ruin was a disturbing and unavoidable leitmotif, a dominating framing strategy, that insinuated itself into cultural memory as it reconfigured the memory landscape.

A SEAMLESS WEB OF ANNIHILATION

The Kaiserreich had been built on a system of tense compromises between capital and labor, the Reich and the federal states, democracy and authoritarianism, the aristocracy and the Bürgertum, constitutionalism and monarchical arbitrariness, Catholics and Protestants, the avant-garde and cultural tradition. No less than the political culture as a whole, the memory landscape was shaped by a series of compromises that unsteadily balanced the national and the particular, the one and the many. German elites entered World War I not only for geopolitical reasons but also to break through such compromises at home. This attempt drew on the dominant political logic of the modern age, which envisioned the organized, coherent national community as the privileged referent of all identities. Breaking through the messy compromises of Imperial Germany thus meant "nationalizing" the populace more completely than ever before. Imperial Germany's attempts to nationalize the country more fully were finally inept and haphazard, but similar attempts by its successors, the Weimar Republic and Nazi Germany, were better organized, though in radically different ways. Still, even in the case of the Republic and, in more complex ways, of Nazism, the compromises and dualities established in Imperial Germany persisted. The ruins that marked the memory landscape in this period were the unintentional products of German leaders' inability to untangle and reorganize such complexities.

The memory landscape was transformed in the first days of World War I by the concept of the *Burgfrieden.* Resting on the kaiser's idea that parties and classes no longer existed but only German "brothers," the Burgfrieden connoted a medieval truce in which the inhabitants of the fortress buried their differences in a common attempt to defend themselves against outside threats. As such it recalled an age in which "Germany" was presumed to have been not only externally powerful but internally harmonious. But it achieved this internal coherence not by threatening violence against enemies within, but, theoretically at least, by settling differences. The Burgfrieden thus followed the tradition of the moment of national unification in 1871, or of 1813, more than it did the tradition represented by the Kyffhäuser or other monuments, which were marked by their aggressive posture toward domestic opponents. As in the past, war and the memories of past wars, provided the occasion on which Germans felt a moment of common identity and national compassion, a constitutive sense of euphoria based on true internal harmony.

The concept of the Burgfrieden connected with a larger and more European impulse, however. At the start of the war it was common in England, France, and many other countries to envision both soldiers and officers as successors to a long tradition of martial virtue extending from the medieval age into the present.[5] Chivalric images of the warrior were more appealing than accurate portrayals of the warfare that was to come. It could be argued that the wild celebrations accompanying the departure of soldiers to the front in all the major European cities derived in part from this traditional—and, as the war would show, increasingly unrealistic—social imagery of the soldier. One should thus discuss the concept of the Burgfrieden in the context of this popular and elite trend toward "medievalism" in European culture at the start of World War I. While it may have represented an important moment of civic activism in German history, the Burgfrieden cannot be understood without reference to the cultural authority that memories of war and medieval imagery had in this highly modern setting.[6]

The correlate of the Burgfrieden's internal harmony was violent struggle against the external enemy. Ruined monuments in the Western war zones were now symbols of German military might and national resistance. Adopting the policy of bleeding the enemy to death through a war of attrition, the German army conducted a "total war." This entailed blurring the distinction between soldier and civilian. If Germans were involved in the totality of a patriotic effort translated into warfare, then the enemy—soldier as well as civilian—would not be spared the full force of German military power. The German army adopted a policy of "frightfulness," or *Schrecklichkeit,* in the occupied areas, first in Belgium, and then in France and Russia. Whereas this did not result in the wholesale torture and slaughter of innocent civilians that Western propaganda claimed, it did result in the execution of a significant number of hostages, including women, children, and the elderly. It also resulted in extending battlefield operations more generally into civilian areas where many valuable monuments lay. "Better that a thousand church towers fall than that one German soldier should fall as a result of these towers," wrote one German historian in 1915. Such statements underscored a bizarre social arithmetic, as the sum of ruins on enemy territory equaled Germans' love for their countrymen.[7]

Accordingly, the *furor teutonicus* left many destroyed monuments in its wake—the library of Louvain, the thirteenth-century Rheims cathedral, the Cloth Hall of Ypres, and the cathedral at Albert. In October 1914 the Germans dropped twenty-two bombs on Paris, killing three citizens and scratching the Notre Dame cathedral in the process. In late 1914 they bombed British seaside resorts, and in 1915 and 1916 they conducted Zeppelin raids against London, Paris, and even the northern British industrial center of Lancashire. The military argued that such operations were necessary due to the enemy's use of church towers and other structures as observation points. To the outside world, however, especially to the propaganda specialists of England, France, and the United States, such actions were signs of German barbarism. But one cannot credit the propagandists entirely; in France, where the "sacred union" was declared as a crusade against the enemy, and where organized religion benefited from ordinary people's intensely felt spirituality in the trenches or in places of worship at home, the destruction of churches by German artillery gave World War I the quality of an apocalyptic religious struggle.[8] Had the Last Judgment finally come?

Germans inverted the terms of the argument. As international criticism of their nation's destruction of monuments, churches, and libraries on the Western front grew, Germans remembered the ruins left behind by foreign armies' military campaigns on German territory. Were not the actions of the French military toward German towns and cities in centuries past even more barbarous than those being carried out by the German army on French or Belgian soil in World War I? Were not these attacks rooted in the desire for plunder rather than the need to defend the nation? German intellectuals published articles in art history and preservation journals detailing French destruction of castles and other buildings in the sixteenth century or in the French Revolution. The ruined castles of Heidelberg and the Pfalz were now no longer picturesque tourist attractions but, as the architect and close friend of the kaiser Bodo Ebhardt remarked, sources of Germany's need for "hatred, revenge, and . . . battle to the bitter end."[9] This argument was extended to the Eastern zone when Clemen and others attacked the Bolshevists for their policies toward monuments in Riga and other Baltic cities. More broadly, as the Bolshevik revolution took shape in 1917, revolutionary historicide appeared as an extension of wartime cultural destruction. In the face of the revolutionary storm against monuments, German military policy appeared mild and limited only to military exigencies.

In keeping with this perspective, World War I ruins were used to signify German cultural superiority. The Germans fought the war not only for economic and military gain, it was argued, but for cultural dominance. Well established before the war, the distinction between German

Kultur and Western civilization now became general. In a war polemic noted for its attempt to identify the specific qualities of German culture, the great novelist Thomas Mann argued that civilization represented material progress, which many countries now shared, but that Kultur represented spiritual values, which Germany alone possessed.[10] Material progress was not to be gainsaid, wrote Mann, but it had also contributed to philistinism and narrow individualism. In contrast, Kultur accepted a degree of individualism but ranked holism, the nation, and community above it. The civilized man sought individual liberation, whereas the German prized attachment to the collectivity. Germans were national beings first; the nation had a moral obligation to seek life and, because the German nation was a "world people," expansion and global authority, even if these were attained through violence. The superior Kultur of the German nation was engaged in a deadly battle against the forces of Western civilization. Despite German *Schrecklichkeit,* German Kultur constrained German armies to destroy only those monuments that were militarily significant and to protect the unfortunate ruins left behind.

Germany's wartime cultural protection policy (*Kunstschutz*) was shaped by such reasoning, at least for its leading figures. Clemen was put in charge of protecting monuments in occupied Belgium in October 1914 and then in France, the Eastern front, and finally all areas occupied by the German military. Working as a Reich commissar, Clemen and his staff reported what had been destroyed, oversaw preservation measures, and encouraged military leaders to be aware of the cultural treasures at risk in the battle zones. Most importantly, this policy transformed battlefield ruins into symbols of two important ideas. First, it was the Germans who were the real defenders of European civilization. They alone understood the need to defend the values of organic collectivity against the insidious slide toward materialism and selfishness. Second, even if the military war was lost, the cultural war would be won. The war within the war would emerge as the most significant element of the great conflict, the true meaning of the unprecedented bloodletting. The world's failure to recognize the validity of this particular framing strategy caused much consternation and bitterness on the part of Germany's intellectuals and cultural leaders after the war. Clemen himself spent much time and energy in the Weimar Republic documenting his country's efforts at monument preservation in the battlefield for the international community.[11] Clemen's pessimism about the future emerged partly from this effort to set the record straight about Germany's obligation to fight a cultural struggle transcending narrow military, political, and economic interests.

The war also had the effect of transforming the meaning of the architectural ruin. The ruin had played an important role in the art of the Renaissance and in Romanticism, but the modern age's devotion to life had isolated the ruin and transformed its significance. In urban planning the ruin survived only as part of a larger complex devoted to change and movement, as in the Italian fascist dictator Benito Mussolini's Rome or the Roman ruins of the German city of Trier. This impulse made it imperative that the ruins of Belgian and French cities would be removed and that the buildings that had once been there would be rebuilt. "The old concept of the ruin and the shyness about disturbing it . . . must end. There are too many ruins," wrote Clemen, who offered advice to the Belgians and French as to how they should reconstruct their bombed-out cities.[12] Germans criticized their enemies' plans for rebuilding, and in Belgium in particular they faulted their adversaries for their allegedly low standards of taste and organization. The ruins of these cities were thus not only reminders of the German army's powerful artillery but of German planners' superior skills of reconstruction.

For Clemen, the problem was not only that the war had destroyed many monuments, but that destruction itself was part of the fabric of the age in which war, revolution, and cultural modernism operated in a seamless web of annihilation. When Chateaubriand returned to Paris in 1800 after having lived seven years in England, he shuddered at how the Revolution had caused the "crumbling and collapse of temples blackened by the centuries," and he complained that "no longer does the traveler see from afar those consecrated towers that rose up to the heavens like so many witnesses for posterity."[13] It was easy to hear the echo of the Frenchman's lament in Clemen's interwar commentary. "The Great Revolution destroyed French royal monuments, the Commune overturned the Vendome column, the November Revolution destroyed Hohenzollern statues in the Reich while in the East it was Polish hate that did the same, [and] the Russian revolution destroyed the monuments of the Romanovs," wrote Clemen in 1933. For the Bonn art historian, the long tradition of revolutionary destructiveness rested on a superficial understanding of the deep symbolic meaning of monuments for national communities. But it also hid a deeper and more radical strain in contemporary culture. "Can one not imagine," he speculated, "that there could be another completely different intellectual point of view, which, contemplating the source of all values, would consider the privileging of great age to be something that is a priori lifeless, a mere donnish construction, a museum system for corpses?"[14]

This danger was, after all, a central motif of Aldous Huxley's *Brave New World,* which Clemen called a "grotesque baroque utopia of mechanization" in which historical tradition was considered the enemy. It was the dominant motif in H. G. Wells's prewar novel *The World Set Free,* which in Clemen's opinion, revealed the author's "pleasant shudder" at the prospect of bombed-out cities made habitable for a new primitive civilization. It was the vision that was being realized in everyday life in the Soviet Union, Clemen insisted, where historical monuments were being "rooted out," and where churches, great works of architecture, and other outstanding structures were daily being turned into museums, schools, theaters, and clubhouses for the working classes —an ironically brutal radicalization of the very concept of adaptive reuse Clemen and many other European preservationists advocated. Such historicide was irrevocable. Clemen noted in January 1933 that only months earlier the Soviet Union had issued a decree to close the remaining Russian churches one by one and to turn them into Communist clubs and headquarters within five years. "That would then be the end," he stated.[15]

OBLIVIAN OR UTOPIA?

Clemen's science fiction–like vision rested on the idea of a seamless connection between battlefield ruins, the violence perpetrated against monuments in the Russian revolution, and cultural modernism. It is easy to see why Clemen would have regarded such phenomena as all of one piece. Bolshevik cultural policy did after all aim to transform the entire symbolic landscape. In Moscow, landmarks such as the All-Union Exhibition of the Achievements of the People's Economy, and Gorky Park, planned in the 1920s and built in the following decade, the Soviet Union tried to create utopian visions of the new society.[16] But such goals also meant that the landmarks of tsarist memory would be treated with unprecedented ruthlessness. Lenin proposed that the monuments of the Romanov monarchy be collected in a sculpture park ironically similar to that designed in Budapest in 1993 for defunct Communist-era monuments. Agitators cried "peace to the factories, war on the palaces." Revolutionary workers, soldiers, and peasants burned country homes, destroyed churches, or changed them into storage places and pulled down their bells. Communist artists and architects wanted the "grandiose destruction" of bourgeois forms and the "abstract deformation" of monuments and historical buildings through "cubo-futuristic" design. A sympathetic observer such as the German philosopher Walter Benjamin, traveling in the Soviet Union in 1926, could not avoid noting the "evisceration" of grand monuments such as St. Basel's in Moscow. It is true that some revolutionary agencies, such as the Petrograd Soviet, cautioned their comrades to be careful. "Do not touch a single stone," a proclamation read, "maintain the monuments, buildings, old objects and documents. All that is our history, our pride." Realizing that utopian plans to revolutionize the Russian cityscape were impossible, the regime in fact promoted the preservation of some historical monuments and sponsored museum collections of artifacts.[17] But such actions had to be legitimized with respect to the larger goal of revolutionary destruction, and the Bolsheviks treated the art collections and estates of the aristocracy as symbols of a distant historical epoch of slavery and degradation. The heritage of 1917 rested on a logic of deformation and strategic historicide.

Clemen envisioned similar threats for Germany, but they never materialized in the apocalyptic manner that, for example, prewar German novels predicted. Postwar political struggle and economic dislocation threatened Germany's architectural reminders of the national past, to be sure, but no major wave of revolutionary historicide washed over the memory landscape. No cloud of "abstract deformation" settled on German monuments. The exceptions proved the rule, as Rhenish separatists toppled the monuments of the hated Prussian monarchy in the immediate postwar years and French groups in Alsace-Lorraine celebrated the return of the "lost provinces" by pulling down Hohenzollern equestrian statues and other monuments from the Kaiserreich. In Metz, bronze souvenir medallions stamped from a destroyed statue of Wilhelm I could be had for a twenty-franc donation to the campaign to erect a monument of the French foot soldier, the *poilu,* where the German kaiser had once stood. Had Clemen and other alarmists taken a longer view of the history of the destruction of monuments on German soil, they might have expected a relatively nonviolent *demarche.* The last great wave of revolutionary enthusiasm that had swept German-speaking Europe in 1848 also saw no sustained major phase of historicide in the memory landscape.[18]

More serious was the incidental destruction of historic places due to the political dynamic of the moment. Large demonstrations and street fighting took place in Berlin in and around some of the city's most famous monuments including the Reichstag, the imperial palace, and the Reich chancellery. The Social Democrat Philip Scheidemann declared the founding of a republic from a Reichstag balcony and just hours earlier, Karl Liebknecht, speaking before a massive audience, called for a socialist republic from a portal of the imperial palace. The revolutionary Spartacists used the historic St. George's Church as their headquarters and were regularly attacked by government troops using tear gas. At first it was disconcerting for Berliners to hear bullets skipping by in some of the busiest and most historical districts of the city, but soon they adapted. One nationalist paramilitary fighter wrote a novel bemoaning the fact that bullet holes on the Reichstag, the imperial palace, and other Berlin landmarks were repaired so quickly that the country forgot the heroes of the struggle against Bolshevism—an exaggeration, but a revealing position nonetheless.[19] Material shortages had led some Germans to loot castles and other landmarks in the countryside. But finally preservationists were less concerned about these instances than about the fact that the country was spending more money going to the cinema than restoring German monuments.[20]

Throughout the 1920s, popular tourists' guidebooks continued to point out the places where serious street fighting had occurred. The Republic would later rename some streets to honor its heroes, as it did in 1925 when it named a Berlin avenue for the first president of the Republic, Friedrich Ebert, who died that year. But generally Weimar shied away from naming streets after important historical personages or revolutionary events, and thus traditional street names persisted after World War I. For the most part, this was the case in other centers of political turmoil as well, as in Munich, where the attempt to establish a Soviet-style Republic after the war led to bloody violence. Although the Left and the Right competed with one another to gain control over the public memory of the Munich violence, a relatively small number of plaques, monuments, and other types of memorials appeared during Weimar. Munich would have to await the Nazi dictatorship before a more radical commemorative politics occurred.[21] The streetscapes of Weimar-era cities would tell relatively little about the turbulent political disturbances that took place there or about the republic that emerged from them. Clemen's nightmare of historicide would find no immediate referent in the difficult first days of the new republic.

Figure 14. Crowds at the imperial palace, damaged by street fighting, Berlin, 1918. Bildarchiv Preussischer Kulturbesitz.

Of a more substantive and lasting nature for the memory landscape was the fact that the war radicalized some of the proponents of modernist architecture, creating a desire to break fundamentally with the past analogous to the Bolshevik avant-garde's desire to deform and destroy bourgeois art. "The war with its fury of hatred and destruction has proved that all things might be possible with a fury of love and labor," wrote Herman George Scheffauer, an observer of the new architecture in Germany. Praising Bruno Taut as the prime exemplar of a new "architecture of aspiration" rooted in Expressionism, Scheffauer unintentionally revealed the extraordinary violence that lay at the heart of the modernist impulse. "The first step in the liberation from the academic was the shattering of alien forms and outlived historical patterns," he wrote. The architecture of aspiration "seeks freedom through the obliteration, dismemberment and dissolution of the object." Experimental architecture might at first glance appear to be "an orchid-tangle reared upon the compost of wrecked and rotting art elements." But even though it was built on ruins and detritus, it expressed the "daemonic and prophetic in art" and the desire to "reshape the planet."[22]

In practical terms this astounding desire to "reshape the planet" led to a quite radical position toward not only other architectural styles (abstracted historicism included) but also toward preexisting architecture and monuments. Walter Gropius, Bruno Taut, and several others organized the Arbeitsrat für Kunst in late 1918. Besides calling for new utopian building projects and the creation of new, unified architectural schools, this revolutionary council demanded the destruction and "removal of all aesthetically worthless monuments and the demolition of all buildings whose artistic value is disproportionate to the value of their raw materials, which might be used elsewhere." In addition, the group wanted "the prevention of hastily planned war memorials, and the immediate cessation of work on the war museums planned for Berlin and elsewhere in Germany." In a 1918 article, Taut called for the melting down of public monuments and the demolishing of all triumphal arches and avenues. Taut had been inspired by the anarcho-socialism of Gustav Landauer, a perspective that led him to advocate garden cities, decentralization of the population, and the building of "people's houses" that would express the "pride of the social republic." "They cannot stand in the city," argued Taut of the people's houses, "for the city itself is rotten and will at some time disappear, just like the old institutions of power."[23] This critique of the big city was even more prevalent on the Right, and Taut's ideas suggest that numerous Germans across the political spectrum shared a deep distaste for major metropolitan centers. At the same time, they could not be said to be unambiguously antiurban, for they favored old city centers and small or medium-size medieval towns as examples of "organic" planning and architecture.

Such hyperbole was in any case typical of Taut, one of the most radical voices of modernist architects in the Republic. Yet many moderate architects built new buildings and housing projects that seemed indeed to herald the end of previous architectural forms and the end of an historical epoch. Using the memory of medieval building guilds as a model, the Bauhaus school, organized first in Weimar and then more influentially in Dessau, presented a radical vision of a functionalist architecture uniting art, crafts, and technology. In the summer of 1927, a

Figure 15. Ludwig Mies van der Rohe's memorial to Karl Liebknecht and Rosa Luxemburg, Berlin, 1926. Bildarchiv Preussischer Kulturbesitz.

new housing settlement on the Weissenhof hill overlooking Stuttgart featured the work of sixteen architects from Germany (including Gropius, Taut, and Behrens), Holland, Austria, Switzerland, and Belgium. Its modernist forms suggested an impressive unanimity of style among its practitioners, and the public success of the exhibition, which attracted five hundred thousand visitors in three and a half months, reflected the movement's broad impact. Modernist housing projects consisting of streamlined, low-priced apartment buildings in Berlin, Frankfurt, and other cities opened up a future of working-class control. In 1926 the modernist architect Ludwig Mies van der Rohe used an ensemble of large brick rectangles in a memorial to the Communist leaders Karl Liebknecht and Rosa Luxemburg, both murdered by Berlin police during the revolutionary upheavals of January 1919. This massing of planes used a hammer and sickle attached to a star to symbolize hope for Communist revolution. "By virtue of the consistency of their forms," wrote two architectural historians, "[the modernists] claimed to have established the international architecture of the twentieth century, relegating all other styles to secondary, provincial, or oppositional status."[24] All other styles had become ruins.

If ruins are a way of seeing, then artistic representations must also be discussed in this context. The modernist avant-garde contributed to the general preoccupation with ruins, particularly through the use of techniques such as montage.[25] The artist George Grosz constructed a heterotopy, a simultaneity of many different places, by juxtaposing and combining elements of the metropolis in his picture *Memory of New York,* completed in 1916. The skyscrapers, scraps of script, and disparate figures of American Indians and businessmen relate to one another as isolated ruins pulled together only by the artist's "memory" of a place he had not yet seen. This technique reminded one of the way in which early modern Italian architects had raided Roman ruins for motifs in churches and other public buildings. This approach was pursued in the photomontages of Paul Citroën and Hanna Höch in the 1920s, or even more famously and explicitly in A. Rönnebeck's *Wallstreet,* from 1928, in which the artist portrays New York City's Trinity Church overpowered by surrounding skyscrapers. Such images were not only about America, but about Germany's relationship to America and to its own future. A ruin of European culture, the tiny church symbolized America's drastic obliteration of history as well as its overwhelming power vis-à-vis Europe in the postwar world. In such pictures, German artists embraced America because it held out hope in a world ravaged by war and political chaos. But they also feared the American metropolis because it promised ruin and evisceration of tradition. Spengler's decadent world city on the brink of oblivion, or utopia? The artistic avant-garde could not decide what America stood for even when they used images of the big city in the United States to attack privilege and history at home.

DECENTERED MEMORIES

Partly because modernists advocated sweeping change and the destruction of tradition, nationalists fought back by defending their own iconography. Architectural monuments remained important as always, especially in border areas. Once a centerpiece of the drive to unify the German states, the Cologne cathedral now became a focal point of the Rhineland's resistance to French occupation. The resistance theme was prevalent in the thousand-year anniversary of the Rhineland in 1925 as well as in celebrations of the French army's departure from Rhenish cities one year later. Precisely because it was still a "sign of an harmonious holding together of all German tribes," as one newspaper article remarked in 1928, the great Gothic landmark also created much anxiety.

The national symbol was becoming a ruin, as a 1927 volume of essays entitled *The Cologne Cathedral in Danger* vividly demonstrated. Published by a Rhenish preservation group, this book described how the polluted urban environment of the Rhenish metropolis was rapidly causing the monument to deteriorate. Faulty preservation policies of the past added to the problem, and these policies became a significant source of contention at a national preservation congress in Cologne in 1930. That same year, the Rhenish city's populace celebrated the fiftieth anniversary of the completion of the cathedral. Speeches and festivities marked the occasion, but at least one newspaper commentator reminded Rhenish Catholics that bitterness about their treatment by Bismarck during the Kulturkampf had prompted many members of the Catholic leadership to stay away from the grand festival celebrating the completion of the church a half century ago.[26]

If monuments such as the Cologne cathedral could not obliterate the memory of past conflicts, then memory of the Great War appeared to be a good alternative for nationalists. Battlefield deaths were unprecedented, and Germany alone lost two million men in the war. But the reaction to this unprecedented slaughter was not enough to explain the waves of war commemoration that occurred throughout Europe in the 1920s.[27] Europeans mourned for their dead in deeply personal terms, it is true. The individual and familial aspects of bereavement have not received the attention they should from historians, as Jay Winter has pointed out. The tradition of personal bereavement produced one of the most moving sculptures of the century, the German artist Käthe Kollwitz's solitary granite figures of two mourning parents (one of which is shown in Figure 16) at the Roggevelde German war cemetery near Vladslo in Flemish Belgium. Designed to commemorate the death of her eighteen-year-old son Peter in October 1914 in the battle of Langemarck, this memorial was completed only in 1931, after Kollwitz had tried repeatedly—and finally successfully—to express the inexpressible, the sense of loss two parents felt at the death of a child who had sacrificed his life for a higher good.[28] Kollwitz's sense of loss was compounded by the fact that she had originally supported the war and her son's enthusiastic participation in it. Even so, the war also gained an important collective meaning that was only partly related to such profound feelings of personal loss, and it is this meaning that is of most consequence in discussing the significance of war commemoration for the longer-term evolution of the memory landscape.

Figure 16. Käthe Kollwitz's *The Mother,* from her 1931 memorial to her son, killed in World War I. Archiv für Kunst und Geschichte, Berlin.

Because the modern age would not countenance death as such but instead transformed it into an episode in the renewal of life, a larger meaning for the slaughter had to be found. Because the national state claimed the right and responsibility to create this larger meaning, it quickly framed (or tried to frame) the memory of the battlefield deaths to suit its own purposes. Because death had also become "democratized" since the French Revolution, the meaning of the war had to refer to the masses—or rather to the mass of individuals—who had lost their lives on the battlefield. This is why in France Armistice Day, which celebrated not abstract Reason or Marianne but "concrete citizens," and which derived much of its symbolic effect from the more than thirty-eight thousand war memorials put up on French soil, became the only really successful

Republican cult. Christian themes of sacrifice and resurrection remained central to all forms of national identity in the West, and the war would be seen as a massive but worthy sacrifice to the higher goal of national resurrection, a crusade or holy war against the devil, whether he had appeared in a German or French uniform.[29] Critics of the military and political leaders posed new memories of the war, and nationalists responded by fighting the war once again, this time on the terrain of culture and memory. Survivors also felt a sense of guilt in the absence of those who had died, a feeling made all the more powerful in Germany by the Right's argument that the home front had "stabbed" the military in the back. Käthe Kollwitz's memorial to her fallen son was moved in part by a sense that adults had sent innocent youth to a profoundly destructive slaughter. In this context of mourning, guilt, and political acrimony, towns and cities clamored to erect monuments and statues that would properly honor the fallen comrades.[30]

George Mosse has effectively described how a Myth of the War Experience drew on but transformed the reality of war during and after the bloodletting. The problem with Mosse's approach, however, is that it puts far too much emphasis on distortion and fabrication. The Myth of the War Experience did not divorce Germans from the reality of the war as much as it selectively remembered those aspects on which a positive sense of identity could be built—Christian sacrifice, youthful energy, manly honor, and of course spirited nationalism. That the political Right gained dominance over the Myth was therefore due not only to "the inability of the Left to forget the reality of the war and to enter into the Myth of the War Experience."[31] Instead, the Right was able effectively to emphasize and give shape to a particular reality of the war that the Left had never been able to endorse as its own because of its ambivalence about Christian and nationalist themes. The Left too often intellectualized memory as well, a tendency captured perfectly in Bruno Taut's proposal to create public reading rooms as war memorials. An outstanding idea from the point of view of creating a critical memory of the war, this suggestion nonetheless missed the populace's need for emotional responses to a transformative event. Books would not undo the grave sense of loss or the psychological and cultural trauma of war; history would not cleanse the wounds of memory.

War monuments and military cemeteries reflected a conservative and nationalist Myth. They served in effect as countermonuments to the pessimism inherent in Spenglerian visions of inevitable decline or to criticisms of the German military, which after all still enjoyed enormous respect as the school of the nation. But conservative nationalism had itself become more "democratic." Just as the American Civil War prompted authorities to create mass military cemeteries in which even ordinary soldiers were honored, World War I induced the belligerents to make similar efforts to honor the millions who lost their lives. The Treaty of Versailles made all countries responsible for military graves on their soil, essentially removing German control over the cemeteries of most of their fallen. But countries still had the right to design cemeteries for their own dead. Christian, nationalist, and pastoral symbols dominated the cemeteries of all countries, as did a uniformity that symbolized the comradeship of the trenches. Nonetheless, German designs differed in significant ways from those of the French and English.

More than those of the English, German cemeteries emphasized starkness and austerity. This corresponded in part with expert artistic opinion, which since before the war, even in its more conservative or nationalist forms, eschewed ornamentation of the kind that had predominated in the Victorian nineteenth century. It also suggested a relation with the war dead themselves, often represented as the simple yet genuine sons of the Volk. But austerity could serve even less obvious functions. It may be that even at the moment of commemorating death, even when transcendent meanings were yearned for to legitimize the suffering, the style and content of war memorials continued to reflect a German ambivalence about luxury, about overconsumption, even about the divisive or "degenerative" effects of Western-style commodification. Memorializing heroic death should not fall prey to the indulgences and inherently weakening effects of conspicuous display and overheated consumption; Kultur should continue its struggle against civilization even through memory of the fallen. Austere forms of commemoration also had an historical dimension, as they could be linked with memory of the War of Liberation a century before. One of the key architects of war monuments from that age was the great practitioner of a balanced neoclassicism, the architect Karl Friedrich Schinkel, whose war monument designs not incidentally were the subject of an important exhibition at the Schinkel Museum in Berlin in 1916. German cemeteries were also designed to adhere to the strictest rules. German architects argued that German soldiers' graves should not allow flowers but rather be built on lawns. Flowers and other plantings were expensive, it was argued, and they masked the tragic character of the war and German culture. True

Kultur accepted the tragic, as Spengler had argued, whereas mere civilization, weakened by rationalism as well as a propensity toward excess, could not.[32]

German austerity was based partly on the desire to distinguish German graves from those of their enemies. But it was also a product of German self-consciousness about the way other nations would regard Germany in the future. Among German intellectuals Clemen was a leading advocate of simple, tasteful, and masculine military cemeteries that reflected well on the always vulnerable German nation. The widespread resort to Christian motifs such as crosses and angels was also partly in deference to the populations who lived near the cemeteries of German war dead in areas occupied by the German army. Christian symbols were thought to be something all European nations could share. Similarly, patriotic inscriptions such as "Dulce et decorum est pro patria mori," which could be found on a cross at Origny St. Benoite, were thought to appeal to a sense of pride felt by all European nations.[33] Real and imagined attacks on German war graves by French or Belgian populations during and after the war reinforced such self-consciousness, as did reports of tourists' less than pious attitudes toward German war memorials.

Nature was a central motif in the military cemeteries of all nations, but it played a distinctive role in the German case. For example, soldiers would be honored with so-called *Heldenhaine,* or heroes' groves, where trees took the place of the graves. In such places oak trees symbolized German solidity and perdurability while large boulders stood for primeval nature. Both were meant to associate the nation's fallen with elemental forces and a form of being outside the vagaries of human history. The Romantic tradition had often transformed man-made buildings and ruins into nature by defining the landscape in the broadest possible terms. Heimat-movement representatives had revived this tradition in the Imperial period, and they played an important role in debates over war commemoration. The interpenetration between nature and monuments, either with regard to the setting of monuments and cemeteries or to the transformation of trees or other natural objects into monuments, was firmly within this tradition. But natural motifs also spoke directly to the memory of the soldiers. They had spent many months or even years in nature, whether in the trenches, where mud, rats, rain, wind, sunlight, and snow were their constant companions; or behind the lines, where they might have viewed ponds, rivers, plowed fields, and country lanes. Symbols of nature did not distort but rather elaborated a central thread of the experience and memory of war, even if that war had been the most industrialized in human history up to that time. Not incidentally, nature also played a major role in cutting short the life of battlefield sites as ruins. In 1920, tourists' guidebooks to battlefield sites could still point to the enormous destruction the war caused in the town of Ypres and the Salient that had girdled the town with graveyards. Only a decade later visitors to the same sites saw neatly plowed fields, flowers and trees, silhouettes of staid country towns, and a reconstructed Ypres that had lost much of its picturesque character.[34]

The symbolism of war commemoration was heavily gendered. All nations involved in the war stressed the youthful sacrifice of male warriors on monuments and other sites of memory. In Germany, the virility of the fallen was represented in statues of soldiers in modern uniforms or in nude or seminude figures of Greek warriors, imagery that associated memory of the fallen with timeless values of heroism. The classical male nude would reappear after 1945 in the commemoration of the military resistance to Hitler. Austere forms were also thought to represent manly virtues of simple comradeship. Whether the key symbol was the neoclassicist warrior or the realistic modern foot soldier, the gendering of war memorials had an important relation to the reality of World War I. The trenches had been a masculine world, and veterans' memory of the war revolved around feelings of lost comradeship—for those who had died as well as those who survived. The distance between the Myth of the War Experience and the palpable reality of the war was once again not as great as we might assume.

Female imagery was not absent from German war monuments and cemeteries. Indeed, the Pietà showing Christ dying in the lap of Mary was used at various memorial sites, and the Maximilian Church in Munich contained a plaque that called attention to the mourning of wives and mothers. The Pietà was widespread in war commemorations throughout Europe, but especially in Germany.[35] Mothers were also depicted passively mourning sons or husbands in German and Italian monuments, a reflection of the way in which mourning had become almost exclusively associated with women. In Serbian iconography linking the medieval Battle of Kosovo with Serbia's enormous human losses in World War I, the theme of the Maiden of Kosovo was continued in interwar paintings, reliefs, and sculptures. These depicted a young woman administering to the war wounded she encountered in her battlefield search for her betrothed.[36] In French war monuments one occasionally found realistic images of women, as in Germany, and in the highly unusual Péronne war

Figure 17. Mother mourning son. A detail from World War I memorial, Ehrenbreitstein near Koblenz. Bildarchiv Preussischer Kulturbesitz.

memorial in the Somme there was a figure of an enraged mother pointing an accusing finger at the German enemy. Nonetheless, throughout Europe, women in active, realistic forms were relegated to a marginal position or expressed in purely allegorical forms (winged Victory, for instance) in the statues and monuments commemorating the Great War. This continued a tradition of the memory landscape well established before 1914, but it also spoke to a contemporary need. In France as well as Germany, patriarchal gender norms were being questioned as males returned from the front and women took advantage of new commercial and employment opportunities or ran households in which returned veterans felt superfluous or emasculated. Gendered memory of the war thus functioned symbolically to reassert a lost stability, and war commemoration became a process involving "the unity of the nation in recognizing masculine sacrifice as its highest value."[37]

Clemen was one among many who criticized the pompousness and busy allegorical detail of the war memorials and graves from the Austro-Prussian and Franco-Prussian wars. Critics held up the neo-classicist monuments of the Wars of Liberation as a positive counterpoint to the lack of order and banality of the later veterans' monuments. Such arguments continued the debate begun in the Kaiserreich about the most appropriate forms of national memory. Discussions of the form and material of crosses used on graves and cemeteries constituted one such instance. During and after the war, some architects and officials argued that German soldiers' graves should be graced with the Iron Cross, a symbol of the German nation that had originated in the War of Liberation and had become the nation's highest military honor. The Iron Cross was also based on a design that went back to the Teutonic Knights. Germans recognized its noble asceticism not only in its design but in the cheap Upper Silesian iron used to make it.[38] Church spokesmen countered by supporting a Christian cross that stressed sacrifice and rebirth. Some advocated a combination of these or added a third variation: a cross that could also signify the occupation the soldier had in peace. Various spokesmen maintained that oak, steel, or even cement should be used for military crosses.

No less important was the debate over mass productions of monuments. The development and perfection of electroplating throughout Europe in the previous century had made it possible to mass produce from a single model headstones, crosses, angels, and many other items used in the cult of the war dead.[39] Local communities benefited from the wide availability of such objects because they were cheap and often helped officials avoid lengthy debates about style. They also enabled local communities to compete in the war of commemoration with their larger urban rivals, which could afford recognized sculptors and architects and could put on expensive national competitions for the design of war memorials. But mass-produced monuments were troublesome for many architects and preservationists, especially those in the Heimat movement. The problem was not so much that mass-produced monuments trivialized memory of the war dead or often descended into patriotic kitsch, though this was always a possibility. More significant to Heimat-movement representatives was the fact that mass-produced headstones or statues for monuments were maladapted to their surroundings. Soldiers' memorials, like all German architecture, should be integrated with nature or the city to stress the organic quality of the memory landscape. In this view the overall relation of the monument to its environment was a symbol of national identity as much as its form was.[40] Such tensions were by no means a German idiosyncrasy. One could find similarly strong misgivings among the prefectural review commissions set up by the French Interior Ministry after 1918 to advise locales on war commemoration. Commissioners often argued that the mass-produced monuments selected by small towns lacked originality or artistic merit and were unsuited to the historical ambiance of a village square or cemetery.[41]

Concerns about mass production remind us that memory of the war quickly became commercialized—indeed, that commemoration was a big business.[42] Mourners and veterans from all countries involved took guided tours of cemeteries, ossuaries (where unidentified remains from the battlefield were deposited), and battlefield sites. Such trips were often encouraged and organized by national tourist agencies. This occurred on both sides of the Channel; from 1919 to 1921 at least thirty guides to the battlefields were published in English alone.[43] Veterans' and civic groups in Germany and other nations organized festivals and Armistice Day ceremonies in front of monuments, in churches, and many other places. A thin line existed between these forms of commemoration and a more elaborate tourism based not on the idea of the pilgrimage but on curiosity or even lurid fascination. Even when pilgrims toured such sites of memory, they participated in the burgeoning business of mourning as they relied on guidebooks, hotels, and official tour guides, and as they bought souvenirs (at usually substantially inflated prices) or sent postcards.

It would of course be possible to see such commercial exploitation as another example of the distortions caused by the Myth of the War Experience.[44] Such commercialism did indeed trivialize the memory of the fallen. Yet it was also consistent with the nature of the Great War, which from the beginning had been a spectacle, sublime in its massive, inexplicable destruction and its ability to touch almost every individual or family in the belligerent nations. Battlefield tourism, war memoirs, novels, films, postcards, mass-produced monuments, children's war games—all reproduced the effect of a historical phenomenon both overwhelming and fascinating to the human imagination. Memory continued to register this theme of sublimity even after the battlefield sites had been plowed over and the war monuments reduced to symbols of an increasingly ritualized myth. In Germany, where additional effort was needed to transform defeat into something noble, the war had a special appeal as a phenomenon beyond human comprehensibility. The writer Ernst Jünger decried the commercialized memory of the war, but in his successful memoir *Storm of Steel,* he captured the idea of the war as spectacle, and later in the interwar period he wrote that the armored warrior-worker, possibly a prefiguration of the T 1000 cyborg from the film *Terminator II,* heralded an age of inevitable "catastrophic destruction."[45] It was to this impulse to represent spectacle and superhuman conflict beyond history that the seemingly trivial activities of the tour guides, monument makers, and hoteliers appealed as well.

It could be argued that commercialization of memory potentially lessened the national animosities that arose from the war. Prejudice would submit to the powerful logic of the commercial spectacle as tourists took in war memorials on the former battlefields or sites of wartime destruction. *Doux commerce* would soften nationalist enmities. But this argument is only partly convincing. Postwar German tourists were reminded of the war's bitter heritage of hatred when guidebooks of the early 1920s reminded them to observe "strict regulations" imposed by the French, English, and Belgian occupying forces in the Rhineland. When the Baedeker guide to Northern France represented the German execution of civilians in two Belgian towns near the French border as a response to sniper activity, inhabitants of the towns fought successfully in court to have the Belgian version of events—characterizing the German army's violence as an attack on innocent civilians—included in the guidebook.[46] Meanwhile, the Michelin illustrated guides to World War I battlefields, noted for their wider focus on German wartime atrocities, gave tourists vivid details of the German military's destruction of historical treasures such as the Rheims cathedral. Its history merged with that of the French monarchy, the cathedral at Rheims was the religious center of the nation where, until the Revolution, all but two French kings had been consecrated. One guidebook quoted a statement made in 1814 by the German patriot Josef Görres, who, reacting to Allied respect for the great cathedral during the War of Liberation, wrote "Destroy, reduce to ashes, this Rheims basilica . . . where was born that empire of the Franks, those turncoat brothers of the noble Germans." "In the course of the recent war the Germans followed the vindictive advice of Görres," the tour book continued, "although, less frank than he, they did not dare, in face of the indignation of Christendom and of the whole world, boast of their vandalism."[47] It is true that ex-servicemen's groups often stressed similarities between English, French, Belgian, and German pilgrims to battlefield sites,[48] but on either side of the Rhine, tourism nonetheless kept alive the memory of the war, hardening nationalist prejudices rather than assuaging them.

Collective memory has often been linked in history with the idea of vengeance, as Nietzsche reminded his readers.[49] When touristic memory fanned the flames of nationalist hatred, it thus reaffirmed a very old function of collective remembrance. The theme of vengeance was rarely found on war monuments, but it could be seen elsewhere. Examples of German feelings of commercialized and memory-driven vengeance abound, but as the example from the guidebook literature suggests, the French were as guilty as the Germans were on this count, if not more so. France's most important site for the cult of the fallen soldier was the memorial complex at Douaumont, near Verdun, where, at a cost of many thousands of lives, the French army, without the help of the British, won its greatest victory in World War I.[50] One of four major battlefield ossuaries, the Douaumont site was built by a private group with the supervision of the bishop of Verdun. More than any other nation, the French insisted on separating the remains of victors and vanquished at such sites. The Douaumont ossuary collected the disinterred skulls and bones of French soldiers and displayed them under glass while those of German soldiers were merely covered with earth. As George Mosse has observed, it must have been difficult identifying the national origins of soldiers on a battlefield where in 1916 one thousand men died for every square meter. Douaumont was a national monument, and the French government subventioned tours, pilgrimages, and memorial services in this sacred space. Before tourist and priest, before fatherless children and widows, continuing the "holy war" begun in 1914, France achieved revenge over the former German foe through the commerce of war commemoration.

In Germany, another debate ensued over the issue of a national memorial to the fallen, which had been planned for inauguration on the tenth anniversary of the war's end. Vigorous competition between regional interests prevented the monument from being built, and two other sites subsequently entered the picture.[51] First, in 1927 the Tannenberg monument in East Prussia near the village Hohenstein (today, Olsztynek) was dedicated before more than eighty thousand spectators. A fortress-like octagonal memorial heavily influenced by Expressionist designs and dominated by eight massive towers twenty meters in height, it contained the bodies of twenty unknown soldiers who had fought victoriously against the Russians on the Eastern Front in World War I under the command of the German general and later Reich president Paul von Hindenburg. The chief architects Walter and Johannes Krüger spoke of a modern Stonehenge. But their creation was a monument to Hindenburg's military victory more than a tribute to the primordial element of German culture or a generally recognized national monument. Even when public commemorations linked it to the Teutonic Knights' 1410 military victory at Tannenberg in East Prussia, and even when it became a popular setting for youth group outings and athletic events, the Tannenberg-Denkmal failed to be identified as the central memorial of German war dead. Hindenburg used the public dedication of the memorial in 1927 to rail against the so-called "war-guilt lies" against Germany. Seven years later he was buried there, as the Nazis transformed the place into a Hindenburg cult site. From a design standpoint, the Tannenberg monument suggested the shape of things to come even though no direct connection can be drawn between it and a more famous structure, the Nuremberg parade grounds designed by Albert Speer. In both cases, the architects inverted the traditional relationship between the monument and space by creating a vast open area within the monument rather than outside it. In World War II the remains of Hindenburg and his wife would be removed to the historic Church of St. Elizabeth in Marburg, and the Tannenberg memorial would be reduced to a ruin to prevent it from being captured by Russian troops.

The other potential national memorial was Schinkel's classicist Neue Wache, centrally located on the avenue Unter den Linden in Berlin. The noted architect Heinrich Tessenow was commissioned to transform this site into a national Tomb of the Unknown Soldier in the late 1920s.[52] Built in 1817–1818 as a military guard station and symbol of Prussian victory over Napoleon, the Neue Wache became under Tessenow's hand an austere monument graced only by an oak wreath made of silver and gold, a tomb in the shape of an altar, a stone engraved with the years of the war, and a circular ceiling opening. Tessenow had wanted to create a pure gold wreath, but cost considerations prevented his plan. The oak wreath did not in any event serve only to memorialize the war dead because it was still associated with the idea of military victory, and it recalled Schinkel's design for an oak wreath atop the quadriga on the Brandenburg Gate, also an important symbol of Prussian martial prowess. Architectural critics were ambivalent about the redesigned Neue

Wache, in any case, and the public never embraced it as a centerpiece of the Republic's memory culture.

Despite Tessenow's austere design, the sheer size of the structure created an appropriate monumental space for Nazi commemoration. The National Socialists would later transform it into a site of memory for their own heroes, adding the Christian symbol of an oak cross to the inside rear wall of the memorial. Buoyed by various groups' insistence that "true Christianity and heroic nationality [*Volkstum*] belong together," the Prussian finance minister Johannes von Popitz agitated to have the cross added. The Nazis accommodated the wish in part to further their campaign to mobilize church support. Even so, the Neue Wache again failed to have the cathartic effect on the public its designers had envisioned. After World War II the East German government, also exploiting the oversized proportions of the Neue Wache, would turn it into a monument against war and fascism, replacing the cross with the emblem of the hammer, compass, and oak wreath. In 1993 it would be reinaugurated as a controversial memorial to all German victims of the two world wars commissioned by the newly unified Federal Republic. Each regime imposed its own layer of memory as well as its own chapter to a story of contention over the possibility of a national German war memorial. It would be possible to say that the Neue Wache became a true palimpsest of German culture were it not for the fact that each regime eradicated the previous state's symbolic creations. What united each period's handling of the monument was the diffidence with which both expert opinion and the general public reacted to official efforts to make the Neue Wache a constitutive element of German national memory.

Mosse has written of the way the Myth of the War Experience was affected by the postwar brutalization of politics. In all countries, the war contributed to a sense that life was cheap, a feeling that made it easier for the majority of people to contemplate if not accept even greater bloodshed in the Bolshevik revolution, the slaughter of Armenians in Turkey, the Holocaust, and World War II. In Germany, the brutalization of politics derived from the inherited instability of the German state and party system, a lost war, revolutionary violence, and economic crisis. From the concatenation of these factors emerged an increasingly nationalistic memory of the war in the late 1920s. Before 1928, themes of Christian sacrifice and mourning could be found on war monuments, but after this date nationalist defiance gained the upper hand. The growing power of radical nationalist veterans' groups such as the Steel Helmet (*Stahlhelm*) and the popularity of von Hindenburg himself played a

Figure 18. Neue Wache, Berlin, 1930s. Bildarchiv Preussischer Kulturbesitz.

role. Another factor was the desire to discharge the emotional content of guilt feelings many Germans had about surviving the war when so many of their loved ones had died. In effect, many Germans said, "We have felt guilty too long."

But more intense nationalism was also a product of the fragmented nature of German collective identity. A structural characteristic of the German past made the conjunctural factors mentioned above all the more palpable. The evolution of the Neue Wache reminds us that German national memory remained multicentered after World War I. This is demonstrated by a brief comparison. The abstract Cenotaph, a tomb for the unknown soldier, became *the* British war memorial in both public processions and popular imagination. An elegant structure created by the geometrician Sir Edwin Lutyens and unveiled in 1919 in Whitehall, in the heart of London, the Cenotaph was based on simple yet ancient Greek forms that riveted public attention through brilliant minimalism. It has been rightly compared to the similarly minimalist and popular Vietnam Veterans' Memorial of 1982 by Maya Lin. The Cenotaph served a public interest in mourning the loss of loved ones without

Figure 19. The Cenotaph, London, 1932. Deutsches Historisches Museum.

necessarily celebrating Allied victory in the war. So popular was the Cenotaph's draw on the public imagination that British elites, alarmed by the potential that war commemoration would escape official control, tried to make the Grave of the Unknown Warrior in Westminster Abbey equally central to popular memory. Although the Grave was a success, it never rivaled the Cenotaph's ability to focus public devotion in the interwar period.[53]

In contrast to the more centralized English memory culture, in Germany the Neue Wache competed with other monuments and sites to shape World War I commemoration. Its lack of public effect, much criticized by contemporaries, was due primarily to the larger commemorative context, not its reduced and minimal aesthetics or its difficult siting on the busy Unter den Linden. The national monuments of the imperial period continued to work as centerpieces for war-related memorial activities, and many local veterans' monuments were more effective foci for war remembrance than the Neue Wache or the Tannenberg-Denkmal could be. Whereas the multiplicity of activities and memories surrounding such monuments produced much energy, their impact was dispersed. Geertz has argued that the symbolics of power require both a "center" (which is not to be interpreted only or even primarily in geographical terms) and a "cultural frame" that defines, advances, or subverts authority.[54] German political memory, and hence German political authority, had no real center at this time, and its cultural frame was contested. A more radical form of nationalism and more nationalistic memory of the war were responses to this sense of dispersal and decenteredness.

Who would focus these responses? Who would cut away the multiplicity of perspectives contained in the memory landscape to give it a more crystallized orientation to the past and a more concerted purchase on national identity itself? Who, in short, could master the unruly and decentralized German past in a new framing strategy?

"A RACE HAS ROOTS"

Emphasizing dynamism and militancy, the Nazi movement's political style and emotional content drew directly on memories of World War I. Hitler himself recalled on many occasions that the wartime trenches had been his Heimat, his true home. Despite Nazism's violent manipulations of the German past, one cannot ignore that the Führer's political vision rested on this deeply felt association between personal experience and collective mission. Already during Weimar the National Socialist movement glorified martyrdom and death in service to the Fatherland. The sixteen party members who died in the abortive Beer Hall Putsch of November 1923 quickly became an integral part of National Socialist political liturgy. Terrorists such as Albert Leo Schlageter and street fighters such as Horst Wessel were lauded as true sons of the Fatherland whose sacrifice was put on a par with that of the fallen of World War I. An entire calendar of celebrations and memorial services was built around death and martyrdom. Death and resurrection were of obvious importance to the Christian religion. Despite Nazism's criticism of organized religion, or its later, contorted efforts to describe a "positive Christianity" distinct from that of the churches, its cult of death was thoroughly within Christian tradition and iconography—all the more so in the 1920s when "barefoot prophets," amateur messiahs preaching a new form of political religiosity, predicted the imminent coming of Judgment Day to an anxious German population searching for a new spiritual identity as it mourned the fallen of World War I.[55]

Still, before the seizure of power, the Nazis' influence over the memory landscape, whether this was oriented to the war dead or some other aspect of German history, was more rhetorical than real. A Schlageter memorial was dedicated in 1931, though the Nazis were not included in the ceremonies, which were controlled by the conservative Right. The Nazis were thwarted by the Munich and Bavarian authorities in their efforts to have a common grave for the martyrs of the Beer Hall Putsch, and only in 1935 were they able to erect a monument at the Feldherrnhalle, the site of the debacle. The cemetery graves of Horst Wessel and Herbert Norkus, a Berlin Hitler Youth member killed by Communists in 1932, became sites of pilgrimage for the Nazi faithful, but before Hitler gained power no major monument was built to honor them. Like all movements on the doorsteps of power, the Nazi party still had to maneuver between the monuments of preexisting regimes and epochs instead of creating their own "poetic spaces."

This did not prevent them from turning others' monuments to their own purposes. Using preexisting buildings and monuments to support National Socialist ideology was of course crudely opportunistic, as much Nazi propaganda was, but it was also much more than this. For National Socialist ideologues, national monuments were inverted symbols of Germany's moral decay—ruins that had been given over to a process of dissolution, the origins of which lay with the inherent tendency of the larger society. "To feel that culture lies in ruins can sometimes be a way of saying its motive force or conviction wanes or is lost," Harbison tells us.[56] No less than modernist architects or avant-garde painters, no less than nationalists who embraced the war dead in patriotic rhetoric, the Nazis believed the motive force of German culture after World War I had been lost.

In 1928 the Nazi Gauleiter of Berlin and later propaganda minister, Joseph Goebbels, wrote a scathing critique of the urban environment that had grown up around the Kaiser Wilhelm Memorial Church, which today stands as one of the Federal Republic's few urban ruins from World War II.[57] Built from 1891 to 1895 in the neo-Romanesque style favored by Wilhelm II, the Gedächtniskirche was a fitting example of a national monument from the imperial period. Its monumentality was evident in its 113-meter-high central steeple. It contained a memorial hall with mosaics and marble reliefs depicting scenes from the life of Wilhelm I and the history of the Hohenzollern dynasty. The stained glass windows included scenes from the life of Christ and representations of biblical virtues that integrated Christianity with dynastic and national history. But the church lay on Auguste-Viktoria-Platz in Charlottenburg, a district increasingly filled with busy traffic, cabarets, theaters, coffee houses, business offices, and restaurants.

For Goebbels, this juxtaposition of national monument and modern commercial life was obscene. He railed against the neon advertisements of the new cinemas announcing *The Girl from Tauentzien Avenue* and *Just One Night*. He decried the "so-called men [who] stroll to and fro, monocles glinting" and the "harlots" with their "artful pastels of fashionable women's faces." These individuals ignored the deep symbolism of the church, wrote Goebbels; they "perhaps have never gazed up at its towers." Their business was not the business of national memory but of "the eternal repetition of corruption and decay, of failing ingenuity and genuine creative power, of inner emptiness and despair." Berlin West was the "abscess on this gigantic city of diligence and industry. What they earn in the North they squander in the West." And who was it that was bilking the workers from Berlin's northern suburbs and "stealing day and night from the dear Lord"? Goebbels answered without hesitation: "The Israelites."

The national monuments of the empire were now foreign objects on their home soil. The Memorial Church was "alien in this noisy life" of Berlin West. "The German people is alien and superfluous here," wrote Goebbels. "To speak in the national language is to be nearly conspicuous." The Gedächtniskirche was now a prisoner in this "stone desert." "Like an anachronism left behind, it mourns between the cafes and cabarets, condescends to the automobiles humming around its stony body, and calmly announces the hour to the sin of corruption." The images of swindlers, dealers, and hawkers of pornographic magazines could remind the reader of Spengler's notion of the *fellaheen,* decadent remnants of past greatness who sheltered in the ruins of the decaying

Figure 20. Kaiser Wilhelm Memorial Church, Berlin, 1932. Bildarchiv Preussischer Kulturbesitz.

world cities "like men of the Stone Age . . . in caves and pile-dwellings."[58] Still, Goebbels predicted that the monument would have its revenge on these people. The "true Berlin" was beginning "to recognize the Judas who is selling our people for thirty pieces of silver." When Judgment Day came, the true Berlin would "demolish the abodes of corruption all around the Gedächtniskirche; it will transform them and give them over to a risen people." The threat of violence, a militancy stemming from the moral outrage of a "risen people," could not have been clearer.

This combination of opportunism, moralistic commentary, and racism could be found in other parts of Nazi propaganda dealing with architecture and monuments. For example, the Nazis helped organize conservative Heimat architects against modernists once the political potential of such action was recognized. Conservative architects had reacted vociferously to modernist critiques of tradition as well as to modernist successes such as the Weissenhof exhibit. They railed against aspects of modernist style that were seen as "un-German," such as the flat roof, which was not only maladapted to the snow and ice of northern climates but also reminiscent of Mediterranean or Middle Eastern cultures. They argued that modernist creations violated one of the central standards of architecture, namely the need for all new buildings to fit their historical context. They were by no means uniformly opposed to the use of new materials or the unadorned qualities of the new architecture, but they insisted that architecture be adapted to cultural tradition and national memory. As racist ideologies became more prominent in the interwar period, the cultural critique of modernist architecture took on a more racist character. Nazi ideologues such as Alfred Rosenberg and Walther Darré strengthened this tendency by endorsing and elaborating Nordic mythology, antiurbanism, anti-Semitism, and ruralist imagery of "Blood and Soil." Conservative architects would later find that the Nazi regime neither gave full endorsement to Heimat architecture nor opposed all aspects of the modernist architectural vocabulary. But the Nazi party's support of conservatives' attack on the Bauhaus and functionalism in the Weimar Republic nonetheless established a relationship through which cultural criticism of the new architecture and racist politics joined forces.

Spengler had made the point succinctly: "A race has roots. Race and landscape belong together. Where a plant takes roots, there it dies also."[59] The Nazis used this idea to place themselves in a centuries-old continuity of German history. Because the destiny of the race was inextricably interwoven with the centuries-old formation of both nature and characteristic styles of the built environment, to be removed from those surroundings was a form of collective death of such world-historical significance that the fate of individuals or even of other competing races was necessarily regarded with indifference. To avoid this relationship was to invite certain decline. In this sense Nazis portrayed themselves not as proactive or even as revolutionaries, but as simple, loyal stewards of racial destiny. If the surroundings of the Gedächtniskirche or modernist architecture alienated the German race from its relationship with the environment, and therefore alienated it from true destiny, then not only the perpetrators of this crime, but also the products of their subversive labor had to be eliminated. Like the adherents of Kyffhäuser symbolism, Nazis were devoted to eradicating internal enemies. Like the adherents of the Hermann Monument, they were also devoted to defending Germany against foreign forces. Victimization of the nation by enemies within and without would be met with violent resistance.

Consistent with such goals, Nazism transformed the memory landscape into a biologized terrain of meaning. This was not entirely suited to Spengler's ideas because the philosopher had avoided the biologistic connotations of racial categories. Nationalist leaders had used the term "race" since the nineteenth century, but they often treated it as a cultural attribute and an aspect of the ethnie. For Hitler, in contrast, race was neither a philosophical concept nor a cultural marker but an immutable and irreducible biological reality, something "below" and more authentic than the ethnie itself. "Every animal mates only with a member of the same species," wrote Hitler, who used this homely observation to argue that human race-mixing constituted a "blood sin," a perverse act against the laws of nature.[60] Like Spengler, Hitler thought in terms of racial destiny. A part of this destiny was the already mentioned obligation to eradicate the nation's enemies—or to perish. But there was also a "positive" element that obliged the regime to improve the race, nurture its best qualities and traditions, and steel it for the inevitable world-historical battles to come. On the basis of this obligation, the eugenics movement, which brought together practitioners of so-called racial hygiene, made great strides in Germany and other countries in this period. To the considerable degree that the effort to use the memory landscape as a symbol of racial destiny took heart from this positive element, it too had a strong eugenic quality. Monuments and historical places had been assimilated into the goals of racial hygiene.

CULT OF DEATH

Once in power the Nazis institutionalized such impulses. Aware that the "seizure of power" might be seen by some Nazi party members, especially in the disgruntled Sturmabteilung (SA), as a time to realize the social revolutionary potential of National Socialism, Hitler reoriented the movement toward an apocalyptic future. The cult of death became a national ritual that drew on the past, radicalizing it to strengthen the nation not for immediate political victory but for future world-historical battles. In response to the decentralized culture of war memory in the Weimar Republic, the Nazi regime saw to it that as of 1934 there would henceforth be a single day of mourning, a "Heroes' Commemoration Day" recognizing not only the World War I dead but (after 1940) the fallen of the new war of racial conquest as well.[61] Individual death in the struggle for the Nazi party became a necessary sacrifice to the higher good of a race that would be engaged in a decisive, final battle for supremacy. The terrain of memory became a network of sites of martyrdom for those who died in the racial struggle and who would inspire others to die in the future. Nazi ideologues now captured the Schlageter memorial, brought the Neue Wache into the culture of Nazi martyrdom, and erected a monument to the fallen comrades of the Beer Hall Putsch in Munich. Consisting of a bronze plaque and swastika encircled by an oak wreath, a traditional Germanic symbol, the Feldherrnhalle monument bore the inscription "On 9 November 1923 at the Feldherrnhalle and at the War Ministry the following men died believing firmly in the resurrection of their Fatherland." Commemoration of the putschists of 9 November became the central ceremony in the Nazi party calendar as each year party faithful performed a dramatic torchlight procession from the Bürgerbräukeller, where the insurrection began, to the spot near the Feldherrnhalle where police fired at the demonstrators. Accompanied by funereal music, the celebrants carried the so-called "blood flag," which, it was said, had been stained with the blood of its martyred holder, Andreas Bauriedl. Nazi leaders reinforced the idea of the Feldherrnhalle as a sacred space by requiring passersby to give the Hitler salute. Many people regarded this as an absurd regulation and avoided the Feldherrnhalle by taking a detour on a nearby street.[62]

The Nazi cult of death was of course anything but a German invention, and Hitler took his cue from Mussolini on this finer point of political symbolism. The Italian dictator had begun to fashion a cult of martyrs soon after gaining power in 1922. Here too the idea of death and

Figure 21. Nazi cult of death at Neue Wache. Deutsches Historisches Museum.

resurrection was captured in a revolutionary calendar arranged around observations of martyrdom and worshipful ceremonies at monuments designed to symbolize "the nation in the black shirt."[63] Themes of struggle, bloody sacrifice, and ultimate triumph played a central role here just as they did in the cultic practices of Nazi Germany. Similarities between the fascist martyrs' calendar and Catholic tradition should not be overlooked. This is obvious in the case of Italy, where Mediterranean Catholic culture lent itself well to the idea of an annual cycle of remembrance organized around saints. But even in Germany, where the Nazi party had deep roots in Catholic Bavaria, and where more than once Hitler insisted he was a devout Catholic, the essentially "southern" and Catholic contributions to the new memory culture were easy to see.

In Germany many sites associated with the cult of death were referred to as "admonitory memorials," or *Mahnmäler*. An SA guide to Berlin referred to the "commemorative sites," or *Gedenkstätten*, of the Nazi struggle for the Reich capital. The *Mahnmal* or *Gedenkstätte* did not only remind observers of an event or the victim of an event but rather exhorted them to remember and be vigilant to prevent the recurrence of

Figure 22. Passersby give mandatory Hitler salute at Feldherrnhalle memorial, Munich, 1937. Bildarchiv Preussischer Kulturbesitz.

the tragedy. Many such admonitory memorials were erected after World War II, illustrating an important continuity in the memory landscape. Whereas in the imperial period the themes of victimization, admonition, and future vigilance could be found most explicitly on the great national monuments such as the Kyffhäuser or Hermannsdenkmal, they were now more ubiquitous in the Weimar Republic and Nazi periods as motifs on soldiers' monuments and sites of memory for Nazi martyrs. In the years after 1945, they would appear most often on memorials to victims of the Resistance and the Holocaust. But it is important to note their presence during the Third Reich because some have argued that memorials of admonition did not exist in Germany before the end of World War II.[64] This is inaccurate unless we define *Mahnmäler* only as antiwar or antifascist monuments.

Whether they built war monuments or memorials to Nazi martyrs, National Socialist designers were stylistically quite conservative. They added few new symbols to nationalist iconography, and the swastika was often integrated into other traditional forms, as in the Feldherrnhalle monument, where a swastika was placed in an oak wreath. The spectrum of motifs and forms used for war monuments narrowed greatly in the Third Reich when compared to earlier times. Realism lurched to the foreground, as Nazi architects and sculptors abandoned the allegorical language of earlier periods. The point was to create monuments that were not too hard to decipher by the masses. Symbols such as the eagle, present on national and war monuments in the nineteenth century, now commanded greater attention. A symbol of manly courage and aggression, the eagle's genealogy could be traced back to Roman iconography. The Christian cross remained an important symbol, but its possible meaning was limited to that of victory and sacrifice to the nation. Soldier figures were still used on war monuments, but they now usually struck active poses rather than remaining on guard, as they so often did in Weimar-era monuments. Even though the Nazi party permeated the memory landscape with nationalist and party symbols, then, they did so in a way that reduced and simplified the iconographic possibilities.[65] It might be added that such artistic reduction was thoroughly in line with the increasingly popular modernist aesthetic, which in architecture, advertising, and other areas of the design world eliminated ornamentation.

The integration of the swastika within earlier design contexts highlights the concept of "associationism," an idea applied to eighteenth-century landscape gardens and later transferred to nineteenth-century historicist architecture. The concept refers to the ideological, historical, and emotional associations one brings to a work of art. Designed by Hitler himself, the swastika was the most important symbolic representation of the Nazi party, and Goebbels's propaganda machine worked tirelessly to promote it in all areas of public and private life. In the ancient Middle East, Japan, Tibet, Greece, India, and among some American Indians, it had been a religious symbol as well as an "evil eye," and in some civilizations the swastika recalled the rotating sun, a symbol of the continuous reaffirmation of life. By linking the swastika with other well-known symbols, viewers learned to associate Nazism with a sense of ancient or even prehistoric heritage. By incorporating Imperial Germany's colors—a black swastika on a white circle against a red background—the relationship between Nazism and nationalist traditions became stronger. (Hitler in addition argued that red in the Nazi flag stood for the party's social idea while white stood for nationalism.) As with the cult of death, Italian fascism supplied ample models for National Socialism on this score. Italian architects and sculptors used the ancient Roman fasces, a bundle of rods attached to an ax carried by Roman magistrates as a sign of authority and justice, to associate Mussolini's rule with Roman tradition. One of the most evocative and successful architectural uses of the fasces at the time could be found in the Monument of Victory, a war memorial erected in Bolzano from plans by Marcello Piacentini. Designed to embrace the memory of World War I soldiers and fascist martyrs in a single gesture, this monument substituted powerful fasces for columns in a triumphal arch reminiscent of classical designs. It was said that the idea for Piacentini's design came from Mussolini himself.[66]

Simultaneously, a cult of Teutonic prehistory based on earlier influences, especially from the 1920s, established itself within a part of the Nazi party. It was pushed with particular energy by the leader of the SS, or Elite Guard, Heinrich Himmler and the chief Nazi philosopher Alfred Rosenberg. Hitler thought such ideas were nonsensical, and no official Teutonic cult grew up within the Nazi movement as a whole. As always, Hitler had his eye on popular opinion, and he feared that visions of Teutonic warriors clad in bearskins as they slaughtered their enemies and worshipped at cultic sites in the German forests were too far-fetched even for some of his most feverish supporters. So attached had the German media become to such ideas that the propaganda ministry demanded a retreat. "The National Socialist movement is too close to reality and life to deem it necessary to drag forth outmoded and dead concepts from the dark past, concepts which in no way are able to support the difficult political battle of today," read one ministry warning from 1935.[67]

Still, ideologues within and without the party promoted such ideas. Himmler venerated old Teutonic tribesmen, who were models for his plans to build up the SS as the purest representatives of German blood. The sites, artifacts, and symbols of prehistoric Teutonic tribes were explored and analyzed. Popular researchers as well as professional scholars sifted through ruins, pottery, ancient wall paintings, early medieval inscriptions, and other sources for the history of the swastika, which was said to represent the eternal return of the Aryan soul in world history. New SS architecture such as the Ordensburgen, drawing on a combination of Gothic and Germanic motifs, created centers where the modern SS tribes would meditate and renew their commitment to the racial cause. Himmler hoped that such places could be modeled on the old Teutonic Order. The Hitler Youth and other Nazi subsidiaries built shrines to their martyrs duplicating the form of ancient Germanic halls. The *Thing*, or "folk gathering," movement created outdoor fora based on ancient models and designed to stage plays and festivals that would transport audiences to prehistoric times.

An even more bizarre aspect of such associationism was a tendency to see the fabled lost continent of Atlantis as an Aryan ruin, and thus as a kind of mythic precursor to the Third Reich. A string of Atlantis novels by Edmund Kiß and others appeared in the 1930s paralleling the destruction of an Arctic Teutonic kingdom of Atlantis with the "time of troubles" in the Weimar Republic or with a more nebulous image of a decline of Western civilization. The existence of the ruins of Atlantis would spur contemporaries to fight to the death for the survival of a new Teutonic kingdom in the making. In one of Kiß's novels, the noble caste of warriors made homeless by the destruction of Atlantis retreat to South America, where they enslave members of a "lower race." Under a blue banner with a silver swastika, they return to the northern provinces of their primeval homeland, only to find it cold and inhospitable. But they adapt, and they unite with the peasant Nordic race inhabiting their homeland to form a single Volk under a powerful leader. Eventually, they tire of the north, turning southward to establish the Hellenic civilization of the first millennium B.C. The premise of the novel was that the Nordic race had undergone a continuous cycle of decline and renewal, an "eternal return" that strengthened racial characteristics and steeled the Volk for even greater challenges in the future.[68]

Beside creating their own network of palpable and imaginary sites of memory, the Nazi party transformed, remade, or destroyed the monuments of previous periods. No political regime in Germany had ever dealt more ruthlessly or comprehensively with the memory landscape than the Nazi government did. Although they rarely added lists of World War I fallen to war monuments built after 1871, they did occasionally alter monuments from the imperial period to suit National Socialist aims. In one instance, the regime removed the figure of a dying soldier in the arms of his comrade placed before a monument to Wilhelm I in Coesfeld. The image was too explicit in its reference to death in war, and the Nazis wanted to use memory not only to honor those who had fallen for the Fatherland but to prepare Germans for another war. In the case of the busy Gothic Wilhelm I monument in Hohensyburg, the regime transformed a monarchical monument into a Reich monument by adding the Führer and the military to the inscription, placing statues of Bismarck and Moltke in a more central spot, replacing the kaiser's birthday with the date of the founding of the Kaiserreich, and reducing the number of figurines and details to present a simplified message. The resultant monument did less to honor the monarchy than to stress the military's role in the wars of unification and to place the Third Reich in a direct line with the tradition of German military prowess.[69]

These were rather mild treatments of the past when compared to Nazi policies toward the memory of the regime's enemies. The Nazis saved their greatest hatred for the traces of the Weimar Republic. Arguing that monuments should recognize "racial sentiment," the Nazi ideologue Fritz Wilkendorf claimed that the monuments of the Republic were symbols of "the political chaos of a sunken liberal epoch" in which "so-called artists inspired by Bolshevism" created forms that emphasized "caricature and the pathological." Wilkendorf criticized modernist motifs as well as the "dishonorable tendency to scorn war" one found on monuments of the Weimar "system."[70] Begun in the last stages of the Republic, this attack intensified once Hitler came to power and took an even more drastic turn after 1937.

The result of this critique was a Nazi war on monuments that forecast the coming assault on internal "enemies" and other European peoples. In some cases, the Nazi seizure of power enabled local groups to complete a campaign against particular monuments that had begun in Weimar. In Düsseldorf the sculptor Jupp Rübsam was commissioned to create a memorial for the fallen of the 39th Fusiliers' Regiment. Dedicated in 1928 and placed before the Rheinhalle, the monument sparked immediate opposition from nationalist groups, who thought that the portrayal of a soldier desperately helping his wounded comrade was unheroic. General Erich Ludendorff, who along with Hindenburg had established a virtual military dictatorship in Germany during World War I, made a public show of demanding that his name be removed from the monument. The edifice's Cubist style also offended, as did the rather Egyptian motifs. Opponents tried to dynamite the granite monument, succeeding only in blowing off the chin of one of the soldier figures. But after Hitler became chancellor, the monument was quickly demolished on 28 March 1933. It was replaced at another site by a more stylistically traditional monument that portrayed a heroic group of marching soldiers. Later in the post–World War II era, what remained of Rübsam's unlucky creation was reassembled and displayed as a "monument of a monument."[71]

In addition to such actions, the Nazis renamed streets to obliterate memory of the "November criminals" of the Weimar Republic and commemorate military heroes and Nazi party figures. In Munich, the regime tore down or moved monuments commemorating the assassination of

Kurt Eisner, leader of the Bavarian Revolution of 1918–1919, and created new monuments to celebrate the right-wing reaction that brought down the revolution. The most dramatic of these was a twenty-four-foot-high monument depicting a naked male strangling the snake of "degeneration and decline." Completed in 1942, this monument praised the actions of the paramilitary Freikorps, bloody suppressers of the Munich revolution. In many cities, streets with the names of trade union leaders were renamed to recall the sites of World War I battles. An entire urban district, the predominantly working-class Friedrichshain in Berlin, was to be renamed "Horst Wessel City." So great was municipal administrations' desire to have streets and squares named after Adolf Hitler that the regime had to issue a decree limiting such practices.[72] Meanwhile, socialist monuments in Berlin were torn down, including Mies's 1926 monument to Liebknecht and Luxemburg, quickly demolished in 1933.

The traces of some damaged monuments were left as ruins to symbolize Nazi victory, as in the case of the Reichstag. The work of a single deranged Dutch man with ties to the Communist party, the Reichstag fire occurred on 28 February 1933. It damaged the large plenary meeting room, but other rooms remained functional. During the Republic, the Nazi party viciously attacked the Reichstag and parliamentary politics, and thus it was unsurprising that Hitler chose not to rebuild the damaged sections of the monument. But the Nazis did use the trial (held partly in the Reichstag itself) of the unfortunate arsonist as a pretext for a violent campaign of repression against the Communist party and other political enemies. And they allowed the damaged Reichstag to stand as a reminder of the political chaos that allegedly characterized the Weimar Republic. Speer wanted to demolish the building as part of his urban renewal plan for Berlin, but Hitler admired the Reichstag's neo-Renaissance architecture and allowed the ruin to stand, telling his disappointed chief architect the plenary room could be used as a grand library for parliamentarians.[73]

There was some support to have the structure rebuilt but even this reflected negative assessments about the building and its history. The architectural critic Joseph Tiedemann wrote in the summer of 1933 that the Reichstag should be reconstructed in order to take account of the "popular uprising and renewal" sweeping Germany. The Reichstag was a product of a time of "internal disorientation," argued Tiedemann, and reconstruction should eliminate the problematic features of the building. Architects could remedy the "overcrowding and pathos" of the cornice

Figure 23. Berliners view the smoldering Reichstag, 28 February 1933. Bildarchiv Preussischer Kulturbesitz.

by eliminating many of the figures and statues, and they could remove the ugly cupola. A "correction" of "false pathos" rather than a renewal, according to Tiedemann, these modifications were in fact carried out after much debate over the postwar fate of the badly bombed building in the 1950s.[74] It was not the first time that plans derived from aesthetic ideas prevalent in the Nazi years were realized in the 1950s. In the meantime, the massive edifice remained a public curiosity, suspended between a conflicted past and an uncertain future. The Grieben tour guide to Berlin of 1936 noted rather disingenuously that parliament would meet in the nearby Kroll Opera until the restoration of the Reichstag finally occurred.[75]

The monuments of Jewish culture were also reduced to ruins in the Nazi dictatorship. Nazi persecution of the Jews became increasingly radical and violent during the course of the regime, culminating in mass extermination in World War II. At first, the regime's policy was "purification" of Germany. There were attempts to remove Jewish names from German war memorials, although because of complications associated with such efforts, Hitler decreed in 1939 that Jewish names would remain but that new war memorials would not mention Jewish soldiers. Purification also meant renaming streets that commemorated Jewish personages or neighborhoods. This process caused Nazi officials much anxiety. In Munich, the city administration found that despite having renamed many streets after 1933, eleven still bore Jewish names in 1937. These streets were immediately renamed, but the city somewhat nervously directed the municipal archive to continue research on the subject to see if more local streets could be identified as "Jewish."[76] It was as if the Jewish past kept bubbling up through the memory landscape from some subterranean level the source of which Nazi officials could only partially identify. "Paradoxically," writes historian Omer Bartov, "just as the Reich was declared progressively *judenrein* (Jew-free) the specter of Jewish presence seemed to haunt people's imagination even more."[77]

The Nazi onslaught against Jewish sites in the memory landscape reached a new level of violence in 1938. In the summer of that year Nazi party squads vandalized and torched synagogues in Munich and Nuremberg. Then, in the so-called Reich Night of Broken Glass, a violent anti-Semitic pogrom engineered by Goebbels on the night of 9 November 1938, 267 synagogues throughout Germany were plundered and burned, 7,500 businesses damaged, and several hundred Jews killed. Many damaged synagogues were left standing as ruins, as in the case of the massive Oranienburger Straße synagogue of Berlin, which could still be used for Passover in 1939, only to be extensively damaged in a late 1943 bombing. The Levetzowstraße synagogue in Berlin was damaged in the pogrom, then used as a deportation center for Jews sent to extermination camps.[78] Such examples reflect the fact that although the Nazis aimed to eradicate Jewish culture from Germany and Europe, they had a "museal" attachment to some of the remains of this culture. Himmler had indeed drawn up plans for SS-run museums that would display the artifacts of an all but extinct Jewish life in Europe. Similar plans were announced for Freemasons. This amounted to a perverse and murderous inversion of the Musée des Monuments Français of the French Revolution of 1789, the first museum to formulate an explicit strategy for preserving the artifacts of a defeated regime.[79] On the ruins and artifacts of these "inferior" histories, the Nazis would build their violent empire.

In all these examples, one finds a more comprehensive, a more totalistic, approach to the memory landscape than any previous German regime had. In this sense Nazi memory work anticipated later developments. For instance, in a move that later in the twentieth century became

Figure 24. Fasanenstrasse synagogue after Nazi pogrom, November 1938, Berlin. Bildarchiv Preussischer Kulturbesitz.

typical of urbanistic thinking, cities were redefined as whole topographies rather than as networks of discrete elements. A good example comes from an extremely detailed 275-page "guide through the sites of commemoration of the struggle over the Reich capital" published in 1937 by the SA.[80] Although the larger purpose of the guide was to celebrate the Berlin Nazi party's victory over Communism, the methodology and focus were social-historical because they catalogued the everyday sites of SA history during a time when Germany "came precariously close to the brink of Bolshevist chaos."[81] The party faithful were led to dozens of sites where SA men had been killed, restaurants and pubs that had served as SA headquarters (*Sturmlokale*), and mainly working-class neighborhoods where bloody battles between Communists and Nazis occurred. The guidebook devoted much attention to what might be called "negative monuments," giving, for example, almost a full page to the so-called Wanzenburg in the Moltenmarkt, which in the nineteenth century had been a prison, but was then transformed into an apartment building by a "rich Jew" who "squeezed the last pennies" out of mostly Communist proletarian families who rented there.[82] It was torn down in

1935–1936 as part of the urban renewal scheme for the city. Here the history of ordinary folk "from below," the struggle of what were portrayed as simple German workers against rapacious Jewish property owners, was put to the service of Nazi racism.

Famous Berlin landmarks were not entirely absent in the SA publication. Just as other guidebooks did, the SA handbook led its readers to some of the city's most memorable historical sites, giving practical advice on when monuments or museums were open for viewing. But whereas the popular Grieben guidebook to Berlin would get fourteen lines on the architectural and political history of the Brandenburg Gate from its erection in 1788 to the return of the famous "Viktoria" from its Parisian exile in 1814, the SA guide devoted only two lines to this history. In its place were eight separate references throughout the guide to the gate's significance to the history of the Nazi party, including a paragraph on the triumphant torchlight procession through the gate the night Hitler received the chancellorship. Only one sentence referred to the Reichstag's complex architectural history, and, noting that Hitler never spoke there before 1933, the guidebook stated that the building had been torched by "Communists" on the night of 27 February 1933.[83]

Another goal of the SA guide was to record contemporary history before it was eradicated. The guide mentioned that many places in Berlin where the SA had held meetings or where fierce battles between the SA and Communists took place had changed ownership since the Weimar Republic. Many sites had been destroyed or were about to fall victim to Nazi urban renewal schemes. The guide would record the events and personalities of the movement to ensure that this important part of the National Socialist memory landscape would not be obliterated. The compilers of the guide explained that they relied on interviews and oral histories to carry out their job. The urgency with which this task was undertaken derived in part from the drastic decline in the SA's political power following the bloody purge of its leadership by Hitler in 1934. But the tour guide was more than a response to a specific political crisis. Its use of oral history, its sense of recovery of an "alternative" history about ready to fade, and its transformation of the Berlin cityscape into a topography of Nazi memory traces gave it a strikingly anticipatory quality. Like the martyrs' monuments and fabricated historical cores of Nazified cities (see below), the SA guidebook pointed to forms of memory work that would become widespread in the Western world in the 1970s.

POLITICAL LIFE-FORMS

If comprehensiveness defined such approaches to urban physiognomies, then Nazi architecture and planning were among the key influences to encourage this trend. The regime called for coherent nationalist initiatives in new construction and the planning of German cities. Stylistically, this resulted not in a specific form of National Socialist architecture but in a rather eclectic mix. Neo-classicism characterized the work of Albert Speer, Hitler's chief architect. But functionalist styles appeared in industrial buildings and the bridges of the new Autobahn. Heimat style persisted in new residential building and in plans for the occupied areas of Poland and Russia. Hitler admired Renaissance and baroque architecture. Himmler and the SS promoted what they regarded as ancient Germanic motifs. Many National Socialist buildings done up in neo-classicist style shared architectural modernism's love of austerity and lack of adornment, and indeed after the war, Speer would see European modernism's antecedent in Prussian neo-classicism of the nineteenth century. Modernism made less headway in Nazi architecture than it did in Italian Fascist architecture. In Italy the totalitarian and quasi-religious elements of modernism were used to full advantage by a regime trying to represent Fascism as the inheritor of the grandeur and power of the Roman Empire. Architectural modernism grew and matured alongside the Fascist movement in Italy.[84] In contrast, in Germany, modernism appeared before the Nazi party had gained its decisive electoral victories, and Nazism gained political leverage by opposing modern architecture because of its alleged bolshevik or decadent qualities. Nonetheless, one could not argue that modernist influences were absent in the Nazi architectural pantheon.

If no single style characterized Nazi architecture, the rule of political functionality did. All Nazi buildings were to be judged according to the principle of *Volkstümlichkeit,* which may be translated as the quality of "nationalness" or even "racialness." Speer said it well: "People talk of a 'built National Socialism,' and by that they mean that with contemporary German architecture it is not a matter of technical questions or aesthetic values but of a political life-form speaking from the buildings."[85] National Socialist architecture would be measured according to the standard of political efficacy. If buildings, monuments, and entire cities maximized popular mobilization in service to the racial community, then they conformed to Nazi standards. An austere classicism characterized the transformation of Munich's Königsplatz, renamed the Adolf-Hitler Platz, where the party built a grand commemorative temple to the martyrs of 9 November. But the real significance of the square was that it served as a forum for rallies, demonstrations, and exhibits. It fulfilled its function of giving architectonic voice to a "political life-form."

Such architecture had also to fulfill the new demands of Nazism's historical perspective. Speer had been put in charge of creating the grand complex of buildings and spaces that would serve the Nazi party's annual rallies in Nuremberg, the *Reichsparteitagsgelände,* or Party Congress Grounds. In order to construct the building on the Zeppelin Field, the Nuremberg streetcar depot had to be torn down. Its rusted iron reinforcements protruding from broken concrete reminded the young architect of how badly modern buildings withstood the pressures of time. Using what he later admitted was the impossibly pretentious title of "a theory of ruin value," Speer pondered ways of making buildings that would provide a more lasting "bridge of tradition," to use Hitler's term, to future generations than modern constructions did. "By using special materials and by applying certain principles of statics," Speer recalled, "we should be able to build structures which even in a state of decay, after hundreds or (such were our reckonings) thousands of years would more or less resemble Roman models."[86] Speer's idea thus projected Nazi remains into a distant future, envisioning how later generations would regard the Third Reich in memory and history.

To illustrate his law of ruins, the architect prepared a drawing of what the reviewing stand on the Zeppelin Field would look like after generations of decay. It was depicted overgrown with ivy, its columns and walls crumbling and cracked. That Nazi architecture could be portrayed in a state of such decomposition was of course very controversial, and members of Hitler's entourage regarded the sketches as blasphemous. Hitler was not shocked. He considered such ideas as logical and useful and ordered that all regime buildings should be constructed according to his young architect's theory of ruin value. The planned Great Hall in Berlin, which would have contained the Capitol of Washington D.C. many times over had it been built, was to be constructed according to this theory, as were many other Nazi monuments. (It was a fitting monument to Hitler's failed plans that after the war the only remaining trace of the great domed hall aside from sketches and models was the ruin of a partial structure built near Berlin to test the strength of the enormous concrete foundation that would bear the weight of the projected colossus.) In all such cases, grandiose monumentality was to impress and intimidate not only contemporaries but many future generations. As late as 1943, when the Third Reich was on its way to becoming a total ruin, architectural theorists such as Friedrich Tamms continued to endorse such ideas. "Without mass . . . without extravagance in the use of materials, no monumental effect can be achieved," he wrote.[87]

If new monuments with "ruin value" occupied the imagination of the Nazi leadership, this reflected not a specifically German conceit but once again a larger fascist attraction to such objects. Ruins figured prominently in the iconography of Mussolini's regime. Italians had of course learned to live with actual ruins, and even to occupy them comfortably or to raid them for use in new buildings, as in the popes' notorious rummagings through Roman artifacts. Although ruins had long lost their centrality to urban planning, they retained an inestimable value in the Fascist government's drive to create a "new Italy." Italian national identity would be strengthened by reviving Italian power in the image of the Roman Empire. In Rome, this led to a massive renewal project in which the extensive ruins of the Roman fora were uncovered and a monumental street, the Via dell'Impero, was laid out right through the exposed archaeological zones of ancient Rome. Connecting the center of Italian government, the Piazza Venezia, with the ruin of the Colosseum, the nine-hundred-meter-long avenue was thirty meters wide including a ten-meter-wide sidewalk where tourists could stroll along viewing the archaeological riches and gardens displayed on either side of the street and where massed throngs could cheer the regime's parades and marches. Related to plans first developed in 1911, the project got underway after Mussolini's order of 1924, and the complex was finally dedicated in a ceremony on 28 October 1932, the tenth anniversary of the regime, in which *il Duce* and his entourage rode on horseback down the monumental street accompanied by blackshirted guards. A popular tour guide to central Italy celebrated the "magnificent artery" created by the genius dictator.[88]

If the Via dell'Impero excavated and displayed the ruins of ancient Roman glory, it also created many new ruins through a process of planned demolitions called *sventramenti.* In order to implement the project, hundreds of buildings were torn down, including several artistically important baroque palaces and churches like the SS. Annunziata de' Pantani and the S. Lorenzo de Ascesa. Many neighborhoods that had grown up on and around the archaeological remains since the Middle Ages were leveled. Supporters of the project made a point of insisting that many such neighborhoods had hardly been picturesque. For his

Figure 25. Roman Colosseum (upper right) and Mussolini's troops, 1938. Deutsches Historisches Museum.

part, Mussolini linked this process of destruction with his own social agenda. "Everything that has been handed down to us that is great, beautiful, and honorable, that we shall maintain . . . and not just that, we will enhance its value," he said. But the goal was also to disencumber the city, "to free Rome from its overcrowding, destroy all unsanitary housing, disperse the residential sections, and give the people sun, light, and air."[89] Neither Mussolini nor his German supporters noted that, from a Spenglerian point of view, the excavated fora were symbols of a long-lost empire that was already facing inevitable decay in the grander scheme of world history, and that the new Via dell'Impero was thus nothing more than a nostalgic gesture by a culture whose moment of glory had passed centuries before.[90]

Like Mussolini, Hitler also wanted to give the people "light and air" through restorations that were historically authentic. Like urban planning in Rome, Brescia, and many other cities, National Socialist policies aimed to "thin out" and modernize historical urban cores. To achieve this goal, Hitler ordered a massive urban renewal program that would remake Berlin as the new capital of his world empire and simultaneously renew major German cities such as Hamburg, Nuremberg, Kassel, Braunschweig, and Cologne. In Cologne urban renewal entailed the destruction and restoration of many districts as buildings from one site were torn down and reconstructed on another. Preservationists admitted that such radical plans created urban districts that were "historical" only in the vaguest sense of the term. Such districts were not only important examples of the regime's social resolve but also major successes for tourism.[91]

This too was more of an international tendency than a Nazi invention. The United States was in the forefront of a trend toward manipulating the urban past and reconstructing and restoring historical edifices at a level never dreamed possible before World War I. Henry Ford organized Greenfield Village in Dearborn, Michigan, in the 1920s, reassembling ninety old buildings to represent U.S. development through invention, agriculture, and technology. In the 1930s Colonial Williamsburg was re-created with Rockefeller monies as a patriotic gesture. Both were immensely successful tourist meccas. There were many significant differences in such projects. But all of them—from the Via dell'Impero to Williamsburg, from Hitler's renewed cities to Greenfield Village—relied on aggressive fabrication and restoration. They looked ahead to the reconstructions of the post–World War II age, which aimed for a more complete sense of historical ambiance rather than historical accuracy of the kind nineteenth-century restorationists had wanted. It also should not go unnoticed that the Williamsburg restoration entailed the demolition or relocation of many of the homes and community institutions of blacks who were living in the community. White tourists looking for eighteenth-century ambiance were uncomfortable seeing African-Americans as anything but servants.[92] Nazi urban renewal took a more activist approach to the culture of "inferior" peoples in its historical productions. Instead of being a byproduct of restoration, the removal of "defective" folk comrades was a preordained feature of urban renewal schemes as property changed hands and landlords in some of the affected districts were obligated to rent only to morally unobjectionable "Aryans."[93]

Many Nazi ideologues considered the historical core of German cities to be a new, internal "living space," or *Lebensraum,* which a healthy race would in effect recolonize for the good of the nation. The Lebensraum motif was most fully used with reference to areas outside the borders of the German state. Poland and Russia were the ultimate objects in the search for living space, but one cannot overlook the close connection between the drive to the East and the recapturing of Western territories lost to Germany as a result of World War I. As in the East, these terrains of memory had to have their foreign influences expunged, though not as ruthlessly as in Poland and the Baltic, just as historical urban cores had to have defective and "asocial" comrades removed.

One example comes from the industry-rich Saarland, lost to Germany in the postwar settlement and placed under international administration. A plebiscite was to be held in 1935 to determine if the region would be reunited with the Reich. Nazi propaganda for the Saar plebiscite reflected the degree to which representations of the historical landscape were used to denigrate or minimize French influences and emphasize German heritage. In illustrated books and brochures produced by the Germans, streets and buildings in French areas appeared dirty and run-down, while historical monuments were badly maintained and in urgent need of repair. The ruinous quality of the built environment reflected the alleged moral decay and superficial cultural impact of the people. In contrast, in German-speaking areas, picturesque half-timber houses and tidy village streets along with scrubbed, well-maintained German churches and public buildings were the rule. The Saarland consisted not only of industrial settings, but also, on the left bank of the Saar river, beautiful nature and sleepy, ancient villages. These places were said to evoke the long historical existence of the German race, whose culture shown brightly everywhere in the memory landscape. The primeval character of the village of Wadgassen was evident in its name, which "came up from the deep" of historical legend. Once called Wuadegozzingen or, in Latin, Wadegotia, the village was claimed by local antiquarians to have been a Celtic or Germanic site of cult sacrifices, the first part of its name referring to the Germanic god Wotan.[94] Such arguments contributed to a belief that the German race had roots in the Saarland that could not be expunged by political settlements and treaties. The Saar would eventually vote overwhelmingly to return to German control.

Where World War II enabled Germany to recover lost territories, the ruins of foreign culture and military presence were duly noted and displayed. Approved and encouraged by official circles, a 1942 Baedeker travel handbook to Alsace-Lorraine (taken back from the French in 1940 in a swift German military victory) exemplified this perspective.[95] The guide was introduced with surveys by noted German academics, including the geographer Friedrich Metz, who wrote that "all the political measures of the French have not succeeded in changing the German character of the landscape or above all of the people." Metaphors of center and periphery were important to Metz's geopolitical interpretation of German history. He proclaimed that "the entire tragedy of Alsace has been determined by its place as a borderland which in truth represented a German nucleus and heartland." (Metz conveniently overlooked the fact that French nationalists made precisely the same argument about the "lost provinces" after 1871.) Tourists to the new German heartland were advised to follow the traces of the Maginot line, the complex system of bunkers and other defenses erected by the French military after World War I. By train or car, tourists could reach the province's ancient castle ruins, products of French military victories in the seventeenth century, of the Franco-Prussian War, or of the "Greater German War of Liberation" of 1940. The guidebook pointed out that visitors could view original medieval reliefs from the famous Strasbourg cathedral in a museum on the Schloßplatz. These reliefs included symbols of the Christian church and Jewish synagogue, which was depicted as a blindfolded woman in a highly stylized and elongated form. The index of the guide contained no reference to Jewish culture other than that of the *Judenhutplan,* which was a shelter for hikers near the small city of Gebweiler. In all such instances, the message was that Germany's recapturing of the region was predetermined in its deeply planted historical and racial roots.

One of the most fully worked-out and murderous narratives of racial destiny and long German presence on what was then non-German soil was developed in relation to Poland and the East. Here the Nazis drew on well-established symbols and memories. They did so, however, in response to political conditions that were historically specific. Poland, the Baltic, and other Eastern regions had been victims of German military aggression in World War I, and many Germans interpreted wartime imperialism as a return to territories that had been a legitimate and substantial part of Prussian and German history since the Middle Ages. The boundaries of the reduced political core of the German ethnie as it existed before 1938 were now to be expanded to encompass the full radius of German racial influence. Ludendorff argued in 1915, "It is up to Germany to continue the comprehensive settlement policies of the Teutonic Order and to bring to completion, after centuries of interruption, the work that it began." In the 1920s, this theme became even stronger, partly because World War I had raised the curtain on a possible new future of German aggrandizement there. But the idea of "completion" of a German mission in the East became popular also as a response to perceived victimization of Germans at the hands of the Allied powers after 1918. A long, symbolic tradition was nurtured by political expediency and feelings of vengeance integral to national memory. After Nazi Germany attacked Poland in 1939 and began a bloody campaign to Germanize the country, the press was instructed by Goebbels not to use the word "colonization" but rather terms such as "recovery," "restoration," "reclamation," and "retrieval." The SS, increasingly successful in the competition between rival groups within the Nazi state, was the most murderous enforcer of policies of Germanization. One of its handbooks stated explicitly: "For centuries the German East has been the German people's destiny. And in centuries to come it will remain so."[96]

If Germanization was to be a completion of ethnic history, then the memory landscape would be a key resource in identifying and renewing the symbols of long-established racial presence, and architectural iconography of the East would be framed as a product of German racial destiny. The Germans had indeed built cathedrals, roads, factories, farms, and cities throughout the East. These were symbols of a constant German-Polish interaction as much as they were of a continuous and "pure" German presence. Yet Nazi planners and propagandists saw every part of the built environment between the Oder and Vistula rivers as products of German labor alone. Moreover, German influence testified to the superiority of the culture that exercised it. Ewald Liedecke, chief planner of the province Danzig-West Prussia, argued that the humble ruins of a German cottage represented a more substantial cultural achievement than a contemporary Polish government palace.[97]

East Prussia in particular emerged in propaganda as a "land of castles" shaped by the systematic conquest of the Teutonic Order in the Middle Ages. Marienburg was the jewel in the crown of this impressive web of medieval fortresses. For many centuries under Polish rule, the Marienburg returned to control of Prussia in the eighteenth century. It became a symbol of Prussian cultural politics and Wilhelmine national identity in the nineteenth century. After the peace settlement of World War I created the free city and enclave of Danzig, the town of Marienburg, Danzig's nearest German neighbor, was cut off from its largely German hinterland and oriented exclusively toward East Prussia. Once the center of the Teutonic Order's empire, the Marienburg became a castle on the border between East Prussia and the Polish corridor. "In the brilliance of the rising sun, the shadow of this imposing capital of the Order no longer has a place on politically German ground," read one highly ideological tourist publication. But the ground on which the Marienburg cast its morning shadow was indubitably German ground, according to this publication: "Rich prehistorical excavations directly before the gates of the city [of Marienburg] prove scientifically that Germanic peoples have settled here for centuries."[98] Midsummer open-air plays that took place at the foot of the Marienburg in the 1920s and 1930s featured famous German actors in productions with as many as five hundred performers and audiences of ten thousand visitors. These spectacles testified to the "frontier spirit" that enlivened the Marienburg and its politically fraught milieu.

Armed with such perspectives, economic and urban planners in the Eastern territories developed the goal of re-Germanizing Europe on the ruins of decadent or inferior peoples. The East would be resettled with ethnic Germans, new towns would be built, and new Germanic architecture would radically change the Polish landscape. Germans wrote disparagingly of "Polish innkeeping," an epithet for Polish state policy since 1919 that had allegedly transformed the East's roads, towns, and villages into ruins. German propagandists recalled the words of the nineteenth-century writer Gustav Freytag. Writing of the Prussian monarch Frederick the Great's rebuilding of West Prussia after having annexed that land in the eighteenth century, Freytag gushed: "The very rottenness of the country became an attraction for him . . . Everywhere there was digging, hammering, and building. Cities were peopled anew, street after street rose out of the heaps of ruins."[99] The great monarch's Faustian reconstruction of the East would be reenacted by the Nazis.

As one might expect, the role of the Jews, who numbered more than three million in Poland, was a purely negative one in such rhetoric. Propaganda transformed Jews into a symbol of racial decline, and as a source of filth, disease, and decay. Anti-Semitism was hardly a German import to Poland in 1939. In 1935 and 1936 more than 150 Polish cities had seen violent pogroms against Jews.[100] Partly an attempt by the regime to adapt to the growing power of German racialism, Polish anti-Semitism was also homegrown and popular. It is a chilling fact that some, and not always those who thought badly of Jews, foresaw the elimination of Jewish culture from Polish life well before World War II. The journalist Ludwik Stasiaski, stopping over in Oświęcim in 1920, wrote of the "narrow streets and charming alleys" of that city's Jewish ghetto. Although half of the town's ten thousand inhabitants were Jews, Stasiaski saw a bleak future for the picturesque urban quarter. "All of this will disappear from the surface of the earth," he wrote. "Every civilized person wishes to have such a Jewish corner painted, but none wants to live in such a corner. And so these courtyards, so very picturesque, will be swept away by modern utilitarianism and hygiene."[101]

Under Nazi rule Oświęcim became Auschwitz, the site of the notorious extermination center. This city's fate would indeed be the result of a form of hygiene, but it would be a Nazi racial hygiene based on modernist planning techniques through which human and material resources would be "maximized." In Nazi planning strategies, this also meant the eradication of "inferior" peoples. Oświęcim had for centuries been at the crossroads of cultural and economic interactions between the inhabitants of Silesia, Bohemia, Galicia, Poland, and other regions. More than most places, it was truly a palimpsest of Central European memory. But National Socialism demanded a radical simplification of this history: layers of memory would be torn away, and the East was to be seen as purely German. On one level this goal coincided with the Kaiserreich's attempt to control the past and unburden Germany from the complexities of history by establishing a new, "cleaner" memory. But where the Kaiserreich settled for compromise, the Nazi state demanded total resolution; where the Kaiserreich sought identity tempered by the "normal" workings of politics and war, the Nazis sought total clarification ensured by utter annihilation. A "final solution to the Jewish question"—which also meant a final, uncompromising solution to Germany's tangled orientation to Central Europe—had to be found. One of its most murderous centers would be located in this picturesque town, an ethnic switching yard in the Central European memory landscape.

Auschwitz was mentioned briefly in a 1943 Baedeker guide to the General Government in Poland, an area of nearly forty thousand square miles occupied by the Nazis adjacent to the annexed Polish territory in which Auschwitz lay.[102] This travel guide was inspired and sponsored by Hans Frank, the ruthless administrator of the General Government. Its introductory material made several references to the allegedly nefarious influence Jews had on the Polish economy and culture. But for tourists or soldiers going by train to Cracow, Auschwitz was only "an industrial town of twelve thousand inhabitants." In fact, the Auschwitz site had been up and running since April 1940, when the Germans reinforced and electrified the fences surrounding the former Polish army barracks there, erected guard towers, and converted the complex into a concentration camp. For the killing center, the Nazis razed the Polish village of Brzezinka three kilometers away from Auschwitz-I and set up barracks, gas chambers, crematoria, and burning pits. Its foundations a bed of ruins, Birkenau became the place where the Nazis would kill 1.6 million people, 90 percent of them Jews. Visitors to Łódź, renamed Litzmannstadt (also in annexed Poland), where a deathly Jewish ghetto had been formed as of February 1940, would read in the same guidebook that this city "like many American cities, still showed the signs of hasty and inorganic development." "Since 1940," the guide continued, "a generous urban renewal program based on the most modern urbanistic and social-hygienic principles has been set in motion." One of the few instances in which preexisting Jewish culture was mentioned in the guidebook's itineraries was in the description of the city of Lublin, the population of which had been nearly 60 percent Jewish. Now, however, the city was "Jew-free," or *judenfrei,* and the Altstadt, badly damaged in 1939 and once populated "for the most part by Jews," was slated for an ambitious reconstruction.

Some forty-five years later, Karl Schlögel, a West German journalist traveling to the Lithuanian city Wilna, once the "Jerusalem of the East," would note with horror that no plaques or memorials commemorated the more than sixty thousand Jews who once lived in that town's picturesque Altstadt. One could walk through the city's narrow lanes and never realize how pervasively Jewish life and customs once shaped this community. One could gaze at the city's landmarks and shops and have no idea that just sixty individuals survived the seven streets that made up the ghetto. The city's historical buildings were implicated in the silence. "The steeples of churches and cloisters lost their innocence as art-historical objects—the Dominican cloister, the All Saints' Cloister, the Lutheran Church in German Street: they saw everything."[103] Wilna was hardly unique; many states and communities throughout Europe, some much more than others, chose not to remember who had lived in their midst and what their fate had been. Yet it is clear that forgetting had begun in World War II, and that Nazism had set the precedent. "Judenfrei" cities were also "judenfrei" memory landscapes. The post-1945 world had accepted much of the Nazis' radical plans to "unburden" Europeans of a very complex past.

MEMORY LOOKS TO THE FUTURE

That the Holocaust was being forgotten as it happened indicated that the postwar world began in World War II, indeed that memory anticipated the future. Germans' reaction to the bombing of their cities reaffirms this statement. Based on ideas developed well before 1939, the aerial bombing of cities was undertaken to damage enemy morale, gain retribution, and debilitate industry. The German air force had undertaken vicious bombing campaigns against Polish cities in 1939, and the ruins of this campaign were identified throughout the 1943 Baedeker guide to the General Government. The first major bombardment of a German city took place 28–29 March 1942, when the British air force attacked Lübeck in northern Germany. Supposedly intended as revenge for the German raid on Coventry, this attack damaged Lübeck's medieval core and 30 percent of the central area of the city. British and U.S. raids on German cities, transportation networks, and industrial centers would develop in conjunction with the Allied war effort, and by the period from August 1944 to April 1945, more than two hundred air raids were carried out, more than ninety on Berlin alone. The most devastating came on 13–14 February 1945 in Dresden, where masses of civilians and priceless architectural treasures were annihilated. As many as six hundred thousand German civilians died in the Allied air raids, and on average Germany's major cities lost about 50 percent of their built-up areas.[104]

In one respect it is useless to ask what the piles of rubble left behind by such devastation "meant" to the German population. Physical hardship, demoralization, and psychological disorientation characterized the lives of those individuals who survived the bombings and continued to live amidst the ruins. Survival could be the only goal. Nazi officials demonstrated extreme anxiety about the ruins, and especially at the beginning of the air war, they forbade journalists to photograph the rubble or to write reports of the damage.[105] Even so, Nazi propagandists did try to use the ruins for their political purposes. Hitler hoped they would be a spur to radical struggle against the Allies, saying that "even the dumbest person now grasps the fact that his house will never be rebuilt unless we win the war."[106] The Führer declared that defenseless cities should be classified as fortresses, leaving them at the mercy of the armies closing in on them from air and land on both fronts. This move corresponded to the Führer's insistence that Germans, in true Spenglerian fashion, fight to the finish or perish. Notwithstanding Hitler's growing insanity, the idea of ruthless battle against outside forces had been a continuous element of German nationalist thought. The ruins of Berlin, Hamburg, Cologne, and Dresden somehow connected with Hermann's raised sword. Hitler's seemingly senseless declarations were consistent within the context of German national memory work. The idea of resistance to assaults from beyond the nation's borders would also be carried into the postwar era, though only after bombs and tanks were transformed into automobiles and refrigerators.

The ruins could also symbolize a desire to complete the National Socialist revolution. Hitler joked with Speer that the latter would have had to tear down more than eighty thousand buildings in Berlin alone to realize the Führer's scheme to transform the capital. "Unfortunately the English have not carried out the plan according to your guidelines," he told his architect, "but at least a start has been made!" Hitler remained undaunted, telling Speer "We will build our cities in a fashion even more beautiful than they were before." Goebbels' position was even more ruthless. Deriding German culture for its attachment to "tradition and reverence," the propaganda chief cheered the destruction of German cities. "Under the ruins of our destroyed cities are finally buried the so-called accomplishments of the bourgeois nineteenth century. Along with the cultural monuments, the last obstacles to the fulfillment of our revolutionary goals now also fall."[107] Here, too, old ideas worked to create an image of the decline and fall of the German nation, the ruins of which could now be used to predict even greater national glory. In the postwar era, the notion of national resurgence would be reinforced not with visions of new National Socialist cities but with capitalist and antifascist ones.

British writer Stephen Spender was so impressed with the debris of Berlin in the fall of 1945 that he wrote: "One goes to the ruins with the same sense of wonder, the same straining of the imagination, as one goes to the Colosseum at Rome."[108] The ruins of German cities worked as the national monuments of the last years of the Nazi dictatorship. Clemen's nightmare vision of the German city as a sea of ruins was realized and exploited by a political system whose goal may have been death and radical renewal but whose real accomplishment was, simply and tragically, death. It did not take a commitment to Nazi ideology to derive yet another meaning from the ruins. Many Germans rightly saw themselves as victims—of a murderous regime, of ruthless Allied bombing, of incompetent and fanatical local Nazi leaders who wanted to fight to the finish, and of immoral schemers willing to exploit material and psychological hardship for personal gain. For more religious Germans, victimization was just retribution for the sins of the nation. But even then, victimization could also mean sacrifice and renewal, in the Christian sense of these terms. Guilt for the crimes of the regime was less easily felt in this context. And in any case, the enormous weight of certain cultural traditions and etched-in ways of seeing worked against a thorough, self-critical assessment of what had been done in the name of Germany. In this instance as well, postwar forms of memory had begun to operate in World War II.

CHAPTER THREE

Reconstructions

Tourist guidebooks introduce strangers to new countries and cities. In the bombed-out cities of occupied Germany, the strangers were the inhabitants themselves. The first new guidebook of the post–World War II era to appear on German soil was for the city of Leipzig, a major urban center that could trace its history to the eleventh century. More than one quarter of Leipzig's buildings were destroyed in the war and more than five thousand people died. As many as 40 percent of all buildings in the city had some damage, and more than one thousand bomb craters made streets and squares all but impassable. Leipzig had been known internationally for its publishing industry, but the publishing district had been almost leveled, wiping out an integral part of the city's economic base and identity. After German capitulation, the city's population was fewer than six hundred thousand, a 17 percent drop from 1939. In the first years after the war, people gradually returned, many of them natives of Leipzig. But there were also those who were driven from more badly damaged cities in Germany or from Poland, Czechoslovakia, and other East European countries, whose governments expelled ethnic German inhabitants from areas they had lived in for centuries. The mayor's honorary preface to the guidebook pointed out the double function of the publication. Tourism could hardly be considered for the badly wounded city, the mayor argued, but natives could use the handbook to appreciate their "now very diminished cultural heritage," while newcomers would use it as an aid "to grow with [Leipzig] so that it becomes not only a place of residence but a new hometown."[1]

How would the now-strange city be made both more precious and more familiar to old and new inhabitants? The mayor maintained that "every trace of our past puts us in touch with all parts of Germany and with all periods of its history." The goal was to maintain what had been saved, to reconstruct important buildings and monuments that had been damaged, and where exact reproductions were undesirable or impossible, to re-create the historical forms and silhouettes if not the precise contents. The Baedeker thus led its readers to the damaged central train depot, one of the largest in Europe, and a monument of the imperial era, noting, "It is planned to give all parts of the train station their old appearance." The guide pointed out that three damaged but still intact medieval churches of the city would be maintained, while the ruins of a fourth, the fifteenth-century Matthäikirche, would not be reconstructed but replaced with a new theater adapted to the proportions of the surrounding ensemble. Readers were informed that despite the destruction, the layout and general character of what native citizens traditionally called The City, a square-kilometer grid whose origins went back to the twelfth-century layout of the town, would remain the fundamental core of the community.[2] The guidebook was thus a reminder of what had been there and what would be in the future—a reconstructed city whose old and new monuments would link Leipzig inhabitants with a long historical continuity palpably symbolized in the urban landscape.

The guidebook's vision was colored by the political reality of the moment: after being captured by U.S. forces in April 1945, Leipzig was occupied by the Soviet army, and in order to publish the guidebook, a license from the Soviet zonal authorities was necessary. The guidebook is full of references to the social revolution then underway in the Saxon city's institutions. In contrast to past ages, the guidebook pointed out, "talented and motivated working-class students were now particularly encouraged" at the democratically reorganized university. Street names also reflected the new situation. By August 1947, 113 streets and squares in Leipzig had been stripped of their Nazi or Wilhelmine names and replaced with those of Marx, Engels, Rosa Luxemburg, and antifascist resisters.[3] Many outsiders would argue that the Soviets and their German Communist allies were obliterating the old society in an effort to break with the past. Their historical analogy was the Bolshevik revolution three decades before. Destruction occurred, of course, but the

Figure 26. Damaged central train depot, Leipzig, 1948. Bildarchiv Preussischer Kulturbesitz.

critics failed to see that even revolution required reconstruction—of institutions and social networks as well as monuments. Leipzig was somewhat atypical. Other cities in both East and West experienced heavier damage, and in comparison to Dresden, Berlin, Hamburg, and Cologne, Leipzig's problems were moderate. Still, all these cities were like Leipzig insofar that rebuilding, regardless of its form, regardless of whether it emphasized modernization and revolution or the preservation of tradition, could never be divorced from the German past.

"Reconstruction describes the re-creation of vanished buildings on their original site," explains the architecture scholar James Marston Fitch. "The reconstructed building acts as the tangible, three-dimensional surrogate of the original structure, its physical form being established by archaeological, archival, and literary evidence. This is one of the most radical levels of intervention. It is also one of the most hazardous culturally: all attempts to reconstruct the past . . . necessarily involve subjective hypotheses."[4] Reconstructions involve hypotheses, but they are not inventions or simply products of the imagination. Subjectivity does not entail being out of touch with reality. Fitch referred to individual buildings, but the experience of the Germans and the Poles after World War II, or of the French and Belgians after World War I, tells us that reconstruction could also mean reestablishing entire urban morphologies even when individual buildings were not exact copies. Reconstruction always meant something had been broken or lost and would now be reestablished and reconnected. The idea of forgetting the past was never a serious option, even when the builders of monuments or the stewards of historical places searched for new meanings. What *was* optional was to ask which past would be remembered, and with which past one was to reconnect. Reconstruction was, in short, a framing device over which various groups competed as they remade cities, buildings, places of resistance to Nazism, and former concentration camp sites. Monuments and ruins had once dominated ways of thinking and speaking about the German memory landscape, but reconstructions in all their varied forms now commanded attention from 1945 to 1970, as Germany emerged from the most murderous military and racial struggle in human history.

GERMANY AS CHARLIE CHAPLIN

Germany in 1945. These words connote unexampled ruin and devastation for people throughout the world. Millions of tons of rubble and fifty million deaths were the result of Hitler's empire. In German cities alone, as many as six hundred thousand civilians died in the air raids and perhaps another eight hundred thousand were injured. Ernst Jünger, who once praised the armored warrior-worker as the symbol of the age, now likened Germans to a stumbling, disoriented Charlie Chaplin after he had received a blow to the head.[5] Scenes of devastation in German cities not only reminded people of interwar observers' fearful images of ruins after World War I but eerily recalled even older memories of devastation. German cities had been burned and ransacked, their inhabitants killed and raped, in the Thirty Years' War of 1618 to 1648, to which the poet Andreas Gryphius reacted with the following words:

> The towers stand in flames, the church is overturned,
> The town hall lies in ruins, the stalwart are hacked to bits,
> The maidens are deflowered, and everywhere we look
> Fire, plague and death oppress the heart and soul.[6]

It was neither uncommon nor historically illegitimate for Germans to recall the devastation unleashed on German cities three centuries before.

Yet what made the aftermath of World War II very different than that of the Thirty Years' War was the rapidity with which life was reorganized. Having toured the former German capital, the poet Gottfried Benn wrote of a "Mongolian border town still provisionally called Berlin."[7] But the diary of the German resister and journalist Ruth Andreas-Friedrich reflected the impressive beginnings of social reconstruction in Berlin in the first three weeks after German surrender.[8] Although the Nazis had been defeated, Berliners still had to avoid the Russians, who harassed and intimidated men and raped women at will. Work details forced people to clear rubble from the streets while their families waited for food at home. Radios, telephones, and typewriters were confiscated by Soviet authorities, then returned in a matter of days. Looters and sightseers sifted through the ruins of Berlin's devastated buildings. Hitler's chancellery was now a burned-out hulk guarded by a Russian soldier lounging on a green, silk-covered armchair. Near Tiergarten Park, Andreas-Friedrich discovered a small mound on which had been planted a primitive wooden cross. On this homely monument was an inscription in blue ink: "here lie one captain, one lieutenant, two sergeants, and six privates." On the Charlottenburger Chaussee the smell of decaying horse carcasses permeated everything; Berliners had cut the meat off the bones and left the rest to rot in the streets. Yet soon ration cards were distributed, and the city council began issuing

Figure 27. Temporary graves in a Berlin courtyard, near Kurfürstendamm, 1945. Deutsches Historisches Museum.

directives. *Antifa,* or antifascist, groups sprouted everywhere, and the rumor was that Stars of David went for five hundred marks. Those who could prove they were Jews, it was said, or even those who could prove they had helped Jews, would be treated leniently by the occupiers. Former members of the Nazi party who could not produce character references were subject to forced labor, which meant breaking stones, digging up bodies, and cleaning the clogged sewers. Just three weeks after the last shot was fired in Berlin, one of Andreas-Friedrich's musician friends announced he would conduct a concert of classical music on 26 May.

The rebuilding of the physical environment was based on these small but often heroic human beginnings, but its rate and form were determined by larger political forces. In the political arena the theme of reconstruction was clear for all to see even if first appearances suggested otherwise. Germany ceased to exist as a sovereign state, its power being transferred to the four occupying powers. With growing tensions between the Allies as a result of the Cold War, two German states were formed in 1949. In the West, the Federal Republic of Germany was founded on democratic and federalist principles. A desire to avoid Nazi centralization placed the new republic in the national state tradition of the imperial period, which had also given much authority to the federal states. This federalism in turn offered a vehicle whereby an older sense of the nation could be reaffirmed. National identity had been based on the principle of unity between the princes and the Volk. The princes were now gone, or they had become citizens like everyone else, and it can be argued that this was a consequence of Nazism's modernizing impulse.[9] National Socialism had after all claimed that all Germans were equal as long as they were racially correct. But the federalist vision still resonated with cultural attributes associated with the older meaning of the nation. It was unsurprising to find that in opinion polls most Germans over the age of sixty regarded the Kaiserreich as the best period of their life. Even for generations too young to remember pre–World War I Germany, the Kaiserreich could be seen not only as an age of relative tranquillity before thirty years of upheaval, but as a time when provincial government, the power of place, and a multicentered culture of regions and towns balanced the forces of state centralization.

Federalist meanings and persistent cultural attributes also lent themselves well to the idea of a society based on mass consumption guaranteed by market principles and state welfare. The social market economy, associated above all with the Federal Republic's finance minister and later chancellor, Ludwig Erhard, reasserted a sense of economic progress and state involvement that appeared first in the emerging territorial states of the eighteenth century and was then reaffirmed in the Second Empire and the Weimar Republic. But it did so by extending the idea of economic citizenship to the masses in theory and practice. Bonn was not Weimar, argued politicians and pundits, who meant that the Federal Republic would not make the same political mistakes the ill-fated Weimar Republic did. Yet this could also be interpreted in terms of material progress and consumption: the promise of mass consumption would no longer be just a promise, as it most certainly was in the interwar decades, but a reality. Celebrating its "economic miracle," the Federal Republic picked up on a tradition of identifying the nation with prosperity, reinvesting it in the future, and transforming it into the dominant motif of the age.[10] The new republic was aided in this effort by the fact that it had inherited Germany's most industrialized and wealthiest regions; that an inconsistent policy of denazification had left many elites in their former positions or reinstated them, thus minimizing economic disruptions; that "corporatist" arrangements between industry, trade unions, and the state held labor conflict in check; and that Marshall Plan monies from the United States supplemented West German efforts.

Soviet occupation in combination with structural features created a very different starting point in the East. Here, with several exceptions, one found the least industrialized regions of occupied Germany, having a quarter of the German population but only a tenth of its wealth. The Soviet occupiers were ruthless in extracting reparations, especially after their efforts to get payments from the other zones were thwarted. They dismantled factories and rail lines, leaving the badly damaged occupation zone without valuable resources in manufacturing and transportation. More successfully than in the West, denazification in the Soviet zone eliminated many people from skilled positions in the economy and administration, but it also disrupted reconstruction until new individuals were trained. Many German Communists and Soviet occupiers wanted revolution, but this did not mean they wanted a complete break with the past. The new state would reformulate the working-class movement's traditional vision of the future as it had developed in the imperial and Weimar eras. This past taught that history was moving toward a bright new era of egalitarianism and socialism, an epiphany in which social conflicts would be resolved on a higher level of civilization. Here was the functional equivalent to the social market economy's utopian embrace of federalism, mass consumption, and democracy. The Communist party of the German Democratic Republic, the Socialist Unity Party, or SED, would reaffirm this tradition and incorporate it into antifascist ideology.

In both the Federal Republic and the Democratic Republic, the past was very much alive, if for no other reason than to give Germans a sense of orientation. Much of this was quite spontaneous as films, novels, newspapers, urban festivals, and other media picked up on historical themes. Yet the politics of memory could not be overlooked. In the West, politicians used the centenary of the 1848 revolution to pledge they would make good on the promise of liberal democracy voiced one hundred years before. A debt would be repaid. In the East, 1848 served as a symbol of the "other"—democratic, socially minded, egalitarian—Germany that had been repressed by the forces of capitalism, imperialism, authoritarianism, and fascism. Eighteen forty-eight was celebrated as the beginning of "scientific Communism" and the opening of a long narrative of working-class struggle starting with Marx and Engels and extending right through to anti-Nazi working-class resistance and the founding of the GDR.[11] It is important to remember that Marxism was as much a part of German national identity as völkish and right-wing nationalism was. The East German version of Marxism reaffirmed and adopted many elements of the German national tradition—the idea of the West (read: capitalism) as irretrievably tainted; the idea of humankind alienated from its true nature; the notion that individual identity was possible only when subsumed in a larger collectivity; the utopian desire for fundamental and total resolution of societal contradictions; and an emphasis on intellectuals' primary responsibility of bringing about the hoped-for revolution.[12] It may go too far to aver that the "*Sonderweg*, the definition of the German nation as the opposite of the West, survived the destruction of Nazi Germany and lived on in different discourses in East Berlin."[13] Yet East German Marxism did recombine and reorient such etched-in national traditions, including a particular form of anti-Semitism based on Communist notions of irreligiosity and rationality.

History also nurtured hopes of reunification. The division of the two Germanys was increasingly evident soon after the war to political leaders as well as ordinary citizens. Already in September 1948, thirteen years before the Berlin Wall was erected, Ruth Andreas-Friedrich envisioned a "Chinese wall with battlements and watchtowers" between the occupation sectors of the city.[14] Even so, Germans did not give up on the idea and hope of national unity. The promise of unity was kept alive through the manipulations of postwar politicians, to be sure. West Germans institutionalized memory of the workers' revolt against the GDR on 17 June 1953 by making the "Day of German Unity" a national holiday. Torchlight processions along the German-German border as well as ceremonies at traditional sites of German national identity such as the

Hermannsdenkmal provided the backdrop for (West) German politicians' predictions of coming unity.[15] The German chancellor Konrad Adenauer and the Christian Democrats pandered to revanchist desires among expellees from the East just as Stalin (until his death in 1953) and the German Communists dangled the possibility of a neutral, unified German state before a hopeful world. Pundits on both sides of the border performed complex rhetorical calisthenics to address "the German question." Did "Germany" consist of two states in one nation? Or two separate nations and states? Despite the propaganda and despite the acceptance of material well-being and stability as compensation for lack of political unity, many continued to think of the German nation as one, as a single ethnie, and to hope for a peaceful solution to Cold War division. It should be recalled that in the aforementioned Leipzig guidebook, each local building, each local artifact was said to put Germans in touch with all parts of their history and nation. This was more than a publisher's conceit.

From the end of the war to the start of the Cold War—Herf refers to these years as the "Nuremberg interregnum"[16]—the Nuremberg war crimes trials, denazification, the indictment of Nazi criminals, and the actions of German politicians in all the occupation zones contributed to the memory of the war and the Holocaust. Individual Germans discussed questions of guilt and responsibility with one another and with foreign visitors; clergymen, political party leaders, journalists, novelists, and artists debated how German society should work through what had happened.[17] A significant minority of Germans made efforts to create a critical and comprehensive public memory of Hitler's racial policies beyond the immediate postwar years. The philosopher Karl Jaspers heroically referred to the Germans as a "pariah people"—a stunning and provocative term once reserved solely for Jews. Jaspers and his students tried to face up to the catastrophe Germany had just unleashed by giving reconstruction a new (more liberal and Western) ethos and by placing Auschwitz at the center of political discussion.[18] But these efforts were often dispersed and sporadic. A vigorous and sustainable public interest in *this* dimension of the German past did not exist in the decade after the war. In the Federal Republic in particular, the need to establish a democratic consensus worked against a full and critical assessment of the immediate past. West German policies on restitution to the victims of Nazism, on the reintegration of former members of the Nazi party into German society, on policies toward war criminals, and on rearmament—all reflected the need to play down the stark historical fact that only a few years previously, a large part of the German population supported a regime that undertook a murderous war of aggression.[19]

It is difficult to maintain that this was a uniquely German inability to face up to the crimes of the Nazi regime. In France, Italy, Yugoslavia, and many other countries, the conflicts and sins of the past were covered up or at the very most left only partially exposed to the light of public debate. The Italian realist novelist Romano Bilenchi, who repudiated his earlier ties to fascist culture, summed things up well in November 1945 when he wrote "the war has recently ended, and at times none of us can remember what his life was like before. None of us recognizes his own past."[20] In all such cases, the political and cultural need to rediscover a point of commonality for populations torn apart by the war was most compelling. This was a European endeavor, not solely a German one.[21] Thus it may be argued that the revival of German memory in the first years after the war was necessary to the survival of the country as both a national and European entity. If a critical memory of Nazism and the Holocaust were to develop, as it would in the last quarter of the twentieth century, it could do so only with the reestablishment of a broader German sense of belonging. The revival of a German orientation to the past was not a failed attempt to "master" history but a necessary and understandable development on which later generations would build. If a nation were to remember, if a nation were to take responsibility for its deeds, it had to be reconstructed as a nation first, in the heart of Europe. As the Cold War developed, this effort necessarily took place on two tracks, but it did not lose its urgency. It is possible to argue that Germans traded a national identity for a European one (or for two European identities, one democratic and one Communist) in this period. Jost Hermand has argued that in the Federal Republic the Europeanization of memory was a "trick" that allowed West Germans to extricate themselves from the national guilt.[22] My analysis suggests that a sense of German identity was retained—even if the problem of guilt was left unresolved—in a broader European reassertion of national traditions.

AN ALLERGY TO RUINS

In light of the need for historical orientation in all occupation zones, it is unsurprising to find that much agreement existed among Germans about clearing rubble and reconstructing individual landmarks. Some Germans called for the maintenance of ruins as a grim reminder of German history, but this was the position of a small and, in the eyes of many, a peevish minority. Whether the city was Berlin or Cologne, where irreverent locals gave the name "Hitler mountain" to the pile of rubble, ruins were obstacles to the smooth functioning of the community. Too, since the nineteenth century, urban planners had rejected the ruin as anything more than a secondary motif. Between the world wars, ruins were the metaphorical and literal clothing of an age of war and revolution, but nobody advocated allowing extensive ruins to remain. In East Germany, planners and preservationists would develop theories for using ruins in urban ensembles, but this was out of necessity rather than a desire to revive the earlier Romantic embrace of the ruin. GDR political leaders would transform some ruined landmarks into antifascist memorials, such as the Frauenkirche in Dresden. Photographers, film makers, poets, and novelists would use the ruins of Berlin and other cities as evocative motifs. Some would actually mourn the passing of the ruins in the early 1950s because the piles of rubble had given forth such rich bouquets of wildflowers in the middle of urban grayness.[23] Still, no one really expected or wanted the ruins to remain, and out of this conviction grew an impressive public commitment to rebuilding historical places. Even where rebuilding had not taken place, ruins were transformed into virtual buildings, such as Munich's once scenic Odeonsplatz in the early 1950s. A travel guidebook to this square read: "This is one sight of Munich which you may still appreciate as before the war; for while many of the buildings are empty shells, the facades still remain, and the general effect has not been lost."[24]

The collective allergy to ruins was not a flight from memory of the war but rather an attempt to resurrect a certain version of history. Widespread public support existed for the repair of the Cologne cathedral and the reconstruction of Cologne's many Romanesque churches, for example. The cathedral had been spared serious destruction, although one of its buttresses had a massive hole in it and the area surrounding it was leveled. The Romanesque churches, most built between the tenth and thirteenth centuries, had been heavily damaged. The debris from these venerable buildings left the British novelist Stephen Spender no other choice than to characterize the Rhenish city as "a vast sandy waste of blowing dust, derelict walls and maimed monuments."[25] The question on the minds of Cologne citizens was not whether the maimed churches would be reconstructed but how the process would be carried out. Beyond their meaning to Rhenish and local identities, the churches symbolized Christianity's importance to German national thinking. Christian themes of sacrifice and renewal also played a role, as they had after World War I. Too, some churches had opposed the Nazi regime. This gave them a moral authority and a degree of political power with the occupation authorities in the West, who conveniently forgot that the churches had supported Nazism's attack on the Left and on the alleged decadence of Weimar culture. All in all, support for the reconstruction of churches was a powerful indicator of how traditional attitudes continued to influence the postwar world of the Western occupation zones and the Federal Republic.[26]

Reconstruction projects involving secular buildings were much more controversial in the West. Frankfurt am Main was one of the most severely damaged cities on German territory, having experienced eight major air attacks in 1943 and 1944. The city's *Altstadt,* or historical center, traced its origins to the fourteenth century and retained its general outlines in virtually complete form until World War II, when more than five centuries of urban tradition were quickly destroyed. "I can still imagine Munich," wrote the Swiss architect Max Frisch, "but no longer Frankfurt."[27] Despite this abrupt break in the historical continuity of the city, Frankfurt's leaders decided not to rebuild the Hessian metropolis in more traditional styles, concentrating instead on modernization and a more historically accurate reconstruction of a few key landmarks. A local civic group agitated for a less modernizing approach, but except in a few important instances, they failed to push through their agenda.

The most important Frankfurt landmark from the point of view of German political history was the Paulskirche, which had been the site of the first freely elected parliament on German soil in 1848. That the revolution of that year had failed gave the building all the more poignancy, especially because the centenary of the event was to be celebrated just three years after the end of World War II. Moreover, German political and business leaders anticipated that the city on the Main River would become Germany's capital in the postwar era. The symbol of a thwarted liberal revolution of the nineteenth century would become the symbol of a successful liberal republic in the twentieth.

The two-story building was a classicist structure built in 1789 on the former site of a Gothic church. It had an elliptical central building with Romanesque windows, and a tall steeple with a tambour (circular wall) and cupola. Inside it had a dramatic gallery supported by ionic columns. A March 1944 air attack gutted the interior, leaving the red sandstone ruins of the circular building and steeple. When Frankfurt decided to rebuild the Paulskirche in time for the May 1948 centenary, those supporting a more historicist reconstruction of the city wanted to see the landmark re-created as an exact copy. But supporters of a modified historicist reconstruction, led by the architect and planner Rudolf Schwarz, carried the day. The architects in charge of the project wanted a building in which "no untrue word should be possible."[28] This meant that the Paulskirche would be rebuilt as an assembly hall with a flat roof rather than the previous mansard roof; that the gallery and much interior decoration would be eliminated; and that the building as a whole would be more austere and lighter in appearance. The architects resorted to an old architectural trick, lowering the entrance to the building and thereby enhancing the impact of one's entry into the reconstructed central meeting room, which evoked simplicity, transparency, and democracy. Frankfurt would not be the new German capital, and the Paulskirche did not become the parliament of the new republic, but it did serve as the site of the West German book industry's coveted Freedom Prize in literature, and it was a fitting symbol of the democratic aspirations of Frankfurt city fathers and German political leaders.

German liberal traditions were evoked by another Frankfurt landmark, the birthplace of the poet and philosopher Goethe at Großer Hirschgraben 23.[29] Built 1755–1756, this house was set up as a monument to the great literary figure in 1863 and then restored to its original eighteenth-century appearance in 1884. It was an impressive three-story, half-timbered building with a commanding gable and elaborately decorated iron window covers on the ground floor. Not only did the Goethe House symbolize the proud civic and domestic traditions of the well-to-do eighteenth-century Bürgertum, it also evoked the orderliness and clarity of an urban architecture that went back as far as the Gothic period in the Frankfurt Altstadt. World War II had left the Goethe House a complete ruin.

As with the Paulskirche, a vocal group of Frankfurter wanted to see the Goethe House rebuilt as an exact copy of what had been at the site before the war. For them, the Goethe House symbolized German cosmopolitanism and liberality. Opponents argued that to reconstruct the Goethe House was an act of historical amnesia. A reconstruction, regardless of whether it reproduced the previous building or abstracted from it as the Paulskirche did, would erase memories of wartime destruction. Even more seriously, it would obscure the intimate connection between the heritage of Goethe's thought and the rise of Nazism. Regardless of the great poet's intentions, argued the opponents, he had helped to create a German tradition of idealism that led many German Bürger to avoid their political and civic responsibilities in favor of "inwardness" and individualism. In addition, the poet's "Faustian" striving had given German culture an air of unreality and Romantic flight that was murderously realized in Nazism's quest for world domination by a master race. Goethe was hardly a symbol of liberality in this view, but instead part of the fatal logic of fascism.

The proponents of an exact historical copy won the battle. They benefited from the fact that reconstruction had an international constituency that went well beyond the Germanophone world. Financial contributions came from all over North America and Europe, including the Soviet zone. Goethe was as much a symbol of the liberal West as he was of German tradition. Given the unanimity with which the West was committed to the reconstruction of Germany in the evolving Cold War, it is not surprising to see the little house on the Großer Hirschgraben assume such importance. Symbols in place, a reconstructed and liberal West Germany was a political bulwark against the East as well as a key stimulant of economic growth. Was not the coming "economic miracle" as Faustian as the actions of Goethe's character had been? Still, the ceremony celebrating the new Goethe House in 1951 left many left-leaning German opponents embittered, and at least one newspaper commentator expressed his concerns about the "ghosts" of Germany's past hovering over the dedication ceremonies in the city on the Main River.[30]

Neither the fact nor the form of reconstruction were inevitable. Leaving aside for a moment those buildings closely linked to the history of Nazism, the GDR's rebuilding of parts of Berlin meant that some artifacts of the past would be removed because of their reactionary political associations as these were broadly defined. The famous equestrian statue of Frederick the Great, a forty-four-foot-high monument designed by Rauch and towering over the east end of Unter den Linden since 1851, disappeared in 1950, only to return three decades later after the great Prussian monarch was rehabilitated in public memory.

More spectacularly, the East German regime's dynamiting of the imperial palace of Berlin was an example of how the effort to reframe German history could lead to outright destruction. Referred to most often as the Berlin castle, or *Schloß*, this massive landmark enclosed two large courtyards in a rectangle that was 192 meters long and 116 meters wide. Its monumentality was a fitting symbol of the Hohenzollern monarchy's centrality to Berlin's history. Although its origins could be dated back to a small fifteenth-century fortress built by the elector Friedrich II, the palace gained its architectural fame through the gifted architect Andreas Schlüter, who worked on it from 1698 to 1706 at the behest of the first

Figure 28. Frederick the Great statue removed from Unter den Linden by GDR, East Berlin, 1950. Deutsches Historisches Museum.

Prussian monarch, Friedrich I. The baroque monument commanded the cityscape of central Berlin as it faced the Lustgarten on one side and the Schloßplatz on the other. Through its massive portals and courtyards, visitors streamed to the castle's museums and exhibits. At the end of war its hulking facades stood as mute witnesses to the fighting that had gone

Figure 29. Ruins of the imperial palace, East Berlin, 1950. Bildarchiv Preussischer Kulturbesitz.

on all around it. Despite the damage, several architectural exhibits were held in the castle in the first years after the war, and the GDR magistrate had made at least one proposal to restore another part of the building as an art gallery.

Some regime officials maintained that in addition to bomb damage, heat from the fire caused by the conflict over Berlin in the last days of the war had reduced the strength of the ruin's walls by more than 20 percent, making it technically impossible to rebuild. Building officials were confident nonetheless that the massive monument would be restored. "As many as possible so-called historic buildings are supposed to be maintained as long as they did not originate in the Nazi period," said the building office of Berlin-Mitte in whose jurisdiction the ruin lay in early July 1949. "Also the old castle should be maintained as a cultural and historical landmark."[31] In subsequent months, inspired by Soviet planning models, the SED and other agencies voiced their commitment to a reconstruction plan that "would begin to free Berlin after eight hundred years' existence from [its] dishonorable burden of the past" and create a new era for a "unified, democratic Germany."[32] This burden had been left behind by Berlin's association with the Hohenzollern monarchy, Prussianism, militarism, capitalism, and finally Nazism. Although such rhetoric appeared to endanger symbols of Prussian history, regime officials continued to argue that the castle and other landmarks would be maintained. But on 23 August 1950, GDR authorities decided to demolish the massive ruin. The area of the Lustgarten and the site of the palace would be used for a tribune and a great open space in which as many as eight hundred thousand people could be assembled for regime demonstrations and other collective actions. It would be named the Marx-Engels-Platz. The Schloß did not fit the image of a city that was to be remade as a socialist capital in which workers and peasants were to be the dominant force.

The decision aroused protest from various groups, and one regime newspaper noted that "a lively debate over the pros and cons" of the decision occurred. Among the most articulate opponents was the well-known art historian Richard Hamann, who regarded the palace as an unusually important example of north German baroque architecture. Hamann's memorandum of September 1950 to Otto Grotewohl, minister president of the GDR, compared Schlüter's masterpiece to Michelangelo's St. Peter's in Rome and the Louvre in Paris. Restoring the palace would not arouse popular memories of the monarchy or loyalty to Prussia, argued Hamann, for "in several years, to say nothing of generations, nobody will think any more about the Hohenzollerns; the building will speak for itself alone, and for its creator, Andreas Schlüter."[33] This argument proceeded from the premise that, by allowing the edifice to stand, Germans would depoliticize its history and focus only on its architectural importance.

Hamann's argument met strong criticism from the East Berlin mayor Friedrich Ebert and several SED agencies. Significantly, regime supporters also stressed the historical importance of the palace, though from an explicitly political direction. From one of its balconies, the Prussian monarch was forced to review the grisly parade of dead bodies carried by demonstrators who wanted the king to see the consequences of his troops' battles against the revolutionaries of 1848. From one of its windows, revolutionaries proclaimed the republic during the November struggles of 1918. Within its walls, "freedom fighters" from the paramilitary People's Marine Division defended the new republic against counterrevolution. Arguing that this political history provided "insight into the necessity" of tearing down the palace, a government publication argued that even the working class would have to eliminate some monu-

Figure 30. Demolition of the imperial palace, East Berlin, 1951. Bildarchiv Preussischer Kulturbesitz.

ments of its past in order to make way for a newer, brighter history of socialism. A product of both Prussian militarism and working-class struggle, the palace also became a symbol of German victimization in a much more explicit way than landmarks in the West did at that moment. One regime newspaper wrote of the "barbaric lust for destruction of the bombers, for whom this uncontrolled act of destruction was merely a matter of sport, a business deal from which they returned home with satchels stuffed with dollars."[34] Allied attacks on Germany—leaving Hitler aside!—had created a problem that the GDR leadership would have to solve on its own.

The destruction was completed in February 1951 after 150 days of work. Crowds gathered to watch the giant structure disappear stone by stone. Although regime supporters insisted that the cost of restoring even part of the palace made preservation prohibitive, later estimates indicated that some form of restoration was financially feasible. The SED had promised that at least valuable parts of the structure would be preserved. What this amounted to, however, was an alarmingly small number of artifacts: from the Lustgarten facade, portal IV, where the revolutionary Liebknecht proclaimed the socialist republic in 1918, was inserted in the facade of another government building on the Karl-Marx-Platz in 1963; sculptures and statues by Schlüter and his studio were scattered in displays in three Berlin museums; the bronze statuary "St. George with the Dragon," initially placed in one of the palace's great courtyards, found its way into the Volkspark Friedrichshain. Significantly, even in its absence the palace was still celebrated as a major historical landmark. The GDR's most authoritative guidebook to German historical architecture continued to devote one-and-a-half pages to the wonders of the old Schloß, whereas the building that replaced it in 1973, the modernist "Palace of the Republic," received just three lines.[35] Even in the former East Germany, the old castle led the life of a virtual monument.

The tone of the Schloß controversy also calls attention to a theme that would become more important in the GDR as the postwar period developed. Blame for the ruined landmark was not placed mainly at Hitler's feet, as it should have been, but at the feet of the Allied bombers. In East German cities such as Dresden, rich with architectural and art treasures, the theme of victimization at the hands of bloodthirsty U.S. and English bombers was fully elaborated. Here the terror attacks on the night of 13 February 1945 on a city congested with refugees from the Eastern front were described as "modern barbarism." Dresden's destruction was indeed an act of senseless slaughter. Dresden had little strategic value, and the German air force was powerless to defend it. More than thirty-five thousand people died in the bombing, and many more were injured. The incendiary bombs created a horrifying five-day-long firestorm that engulfed many of the city's renowned architectural landmarks, including the eighteenth-century Frauenkirche, the dominant element of the cityscape and one of the most important Protestant churches in Germany. Max Seydewitz, a postwar Communist and Red Cross official in Dresden, wrote that the Nazis contributed to the Frauenkirche's demise by storing highly flammable Luftwaffe film of German air attacks on European cities in the basement of the church. Nonetheless, Seydewitz's account of the destruction of the city placed most emphasis on the "unspeakable torment and terror" caused by the Allies. Seydewitz's disturbing descriptions of human beings transformed into burning torches in the "hell" of Dresden placed the air attacks on the same moral plane as Nazi atrocities. But Nazi crimes were never explicitly spelled out, and Seydewitz argued that American imperialists now carried forward the German capitalists' destructive goals of war

Figure 31. "Attention! You are now leaving West Berlin." Brandenburg Gate, 1964. Bildarchiv Preussischer Kulturbesitz.

and world conquest. Consistent with this view, and despite a postwar inventory of its stones as a prelude to reconstruction, the Frauenkirche would remain a ruin, only to become an antifascist memorial against war in the 1960s. Dresden as a whole would remain a subject of GDR memory, as with the photographer Ulrich Lindner, whose photo collection, *Death in the City,* published in 1984, featured haunting, romanticized images of ruins taken by Lindner since the 1950s. Near the end of the East German state, Dresden became a symbol of victimization not only in relation to the West but also in relation to the GDR regime itself, as East German human rights activists chanted, "Don't destroy human rights as Dresden was once destroyed" in 1988.[36] I return to the victimization theme below when considering monuments to the victims and resisters of Nazism.

There were some landmarks that had the potential to symbolize the common heritage of the two Germanys, most notably the Brandenburg Gate.[37] This eighteenth-century Prussian structure became a national monument in the imperial period, and Hitler had used it as a backdrop for his own military parades. Allied bombing left the gate severely damaged, but East German architects embraced the structure and debated the future of the quadriga, the casts of which had been made by the

Nazis and deposited in what became West Berlin. In the 1950s, at the height of the Cold War, the two Germanys decided to cooperate to restore the monument, with the East taking responsibility for the gate itself and the West reconstructing the quadriga. The finished quadriga was placed at the sectoral boundary in 1958, but the East Germans did not return it to the top of the gate until they removed what they regarded as two key symbols of German militarism, the Prussian eagle on the goddess's staff and the Iron Cross inside the wreath. West Germans attacked the East for its vandalism, while the East derided the West for its acceptance of the artifacts of Prussian aggression. Once a symbol of national unity, the gate now earned its grandeur as a reminder of what divided the two Germanys. As such, it was also a grand touristic success, and visitors from all over the world delighted in the vicarious thrills of the Cold War as they had themselves photographed in front of the foreboding sign placed at the gate on the Western sectoral border: "Attention! You are now leaving West Berlin." For their part, East German tourist guidebooks failed to mention that the restored monument was a product of German-German cooperation.

URBAN VARIATIONS

Decisions to rebuild or destroy individual landmarks were embedded in a larger context of choices about how to reconstruct entire cities. Given the massive destruction of the German urban fabric, it was necessary for municipal governments to find quick solutions to the overwhelming number of problems they faced. They had to remove rubble, build temporary housing, and engage planners and architects. For their part, the planners, many of whom had reached professional maturity under Nazism, had their own aims and wishes. Based on precepts shared by all the major Western powers since before the war, urban planners in both East and West Germany agreed that cities should be organized as flowing, organic entities consisting of cell-like units. Population densities in inner-city residential areas were to be reduced, suburbs guaranteeing green space and a neighborhood atmosphere were to be promoted, and urban centers were to be linked via modern transportation networks with other cities. German planners approached the postwar period as an opportunity to realize such long-standing goals. They took a structural approach to the city, looking for ways to make urban centers healthier and more efficient. Aesthetic matters and issues of identity would take care of themselves if historic landmarks and monuments were maintained in a larger effort to restructure and reconstruct a rational city. The advocates of historical ambiance and historical architecture would have to assume their assigned place in the hierarchy of planning needs. This applied to the West as well as the East, although the ideologies that were mapped onto planning initiatives served as mirror images in the two states.

But what to do about the undeniable psychological wounds of the war, the "spiritual rubble" that the exiled modernist architect from Berlin, Martin Wagner, argued had to be cleared away before the physical rubble was removed?[38] Wagner's comment reflected that urban reconstruction was not only a matter of practicality. Aside from the moral depredation left behind by the bombing and its aftermath, the German city, its layout and skyline, was itself a symbol of German local and regional identity. Despite the Nazi regime's attempt to eviscerate the complexities of the German past with a racist ideology, German national memory remained the result of accommodation and compromise between Prussians, Hessians, Rhineländers, Bavarians, and Saxons. Despite planners' structural approaches to the city, urban communities were still embedded in a long tradition of memory and sense of place evocatively captured in the notion of Heimat. Here again the pre–World War I era remained the central historical horizon of the politically divided ethnie. To reconstruct the German city as a complete entity, whether modernized or preserved, was also to reconstruct this thread of morality, tradition, and memory. The inventive or imaginary qualities of reconstruction could not be denied, and the practical demands of the moment could hardly be avoided; but neither could the weight of the past nor the substantial cultural limits on the process of reconstructing Germany.

An attachment to the power of the historic place was a European rather than German phenomenon. For citizens from Avignon to Worms, from Stockholm to Dubrovnik, the European urban core in particular "remained the symbol of survival."[39] Consider the example of Warsaw, 85 percent destroyed during Nazi occupation.[40] Like their counterparts in other badly damaged European cities, Polish planners and architects were initially uncertain about whether Warsaw would be rebuilt on its former site or moved to the still intact Praga district across the Vistula River. But the tradition of "place memory" ("the coalescence of social identities around particular sites of events and their subsequent commemorations")[41] was strong in postwar Poland, and eventually the choice was made to rebuild the historical city center in its original location. State funds as well as a vigorous campaign to collect private donations financed

Figure 32. Rebuilt Warsaw, from the Vistula River Bridge, 1950. Deutsches Historisches Museum.

the extensive reconstruction. Not only were hospitals, roads, and factories rebuilt, but most of the city's 987 memorials and monuments (782 of which had been destroyed or damaged) were restored over time. Such evidence demonstrates that Poles gave much more attention to monuments of cultural and national history than did Germans in the first postwar decades. Poles' emotional investment in the project was clear for all to see. When the restoration of the thirteenth-century Royal Castle was finally completed in 1974, its tower clock chimed at precisely 11:15 A.M., the moment that it had been silenced by German bombs in 1939. Moved by joy and sadness, thousands of Varsovians wept on the castle square and surrounding streets as they heard the chilling peal of the bells.[42]

The conditions for such reconstruction were of course favorable, not from the point of view of material and money, which were in exceedingly short supply, but from a symbolic and emotional perspective. Warsaw's status as a victim of Nazi aggression was unambiguous, and the Polish national tradition of resistance to outside forces was stronger than ever after 1945. This tradition was reinforced by the fact that Warsaw's destruction had not come as a result of war damage but as part of a thoroughly designed plan of demolition by the Nazis, who wanted to liquidate the Polish metropolis and replace it with an entirely new German city. More than that of other European cities, Warsaw's reconstruction was a direct repudiation of everything for which Nazism stood. The self-assurance of its historical position was captured in the city's motto for the rebuilding effort: "A Whole Nation Builds Its Capital." But this was also more than a national project. East European capitals such as Warsaw and Bucharest had identified strongly with the West since the nineteenth century, partly because their membership in advanced European culture was rendered unclear by geographical distance and socioeconomic marginality. The reconstruction of Warsaw, despite taking place under a Communist regime and the boot of Soviet authority, was also a reaffirmation of the European character of the Polish ethnie. Not to be underestimated, moreover, is that one of the key avenues to Western currency would be the steady stream of tourists from capitalist countries who delighted in the historical ambiance of the rebuilt Central European metropolis.

Germany's status as perpetrator complicated the symbolic effect of urban reconstruction and made unambiguous gestures like the rebuilding of Warsaw more difficult. Too, the multicentered quality of German urban tradition made uniform responses to destruction unlikely if not impossible. German planners and the historicists were by no means diametrically opposed to one another, but they did have different goals. In the process of working out those goals, the German city, taken as a whole, emerged as a negotiated reconstruction, a compromise between various interpretations of the past and present. One can speak of three vectors of reconstruction.[43] In places such as Münster, Nuremberg, and Freiburg, the historical qualities of old city centers were retained, though often in heavily modified forms. In contrast, in Berlin, Kassel, Frankfurt, and other metropolitan centers, more aggressive modernization diminished the presence of historical buildings and monuments in the cityscape. Communities such as Lübeck, Munich, and Cologne maneuvered between these poles. The varied patterns and forms of the reconstruction of German cities reflected differing urbanistic framing strategies with reference to the past.

In the long run the advocates of functionality and modernization won the day on both sides of the German-German border. In the West, architecture and planning adopted functionalist perspectives not only as technical solutions but as symbols of economic growth and adaptation to Western values. Of the modernists, Gavriel Rosenfeld has written: "Their structures, built of glass, steel, and concrete, and arranged in asymmetrical compositions, were touted as a light and transparent style of architecture that symbolized the openness and humanity of democracy." Architecture that did not fit this style—and specifically anything remotely resembling the neo-classical, monumental motifs that characterized German architecture under Hitler—was regarded by the modernists as reactionary and "fascist."[44] Although many people associated functionalism with a flight from the past, it was in fact a reinvestment of a particular tradition of modernism. Drawing on the design vocabularies of early pre–World War I abstracted historicism and the interwar Bauhaus, postwar planners and architects reduced the variability of early modernism. They emphasized buildings as space-enclosing volumes rather than as masses. They derived the appearance of a building from the repetition of its horizontal and vertical elements. They insisted buildings should have an industrial or even mass-produced look to reflect the realities of a machine age. And they stressed technical achievement and fineness of proportion to reflect engineering qualities and aesthetic effect gained in the absence of decoration.[45] The Federal Republic's cities emerged as reconstructions, then, not strictly speaking as products of a negotiated settlement between past and future but between alternative versions of the past. The functionalist version, deriving its view from a reduced perspective of the tradition of modernist design, was triumphant, at least until the 1970s, when postmodernism challenged some of the most strictly observed modernist taboos.

In the East, a similar kind of victory was won, though its characteristic forms at first seemed to differ from those in the West. GDR planners dismissed modernist architecture and the Bauhaus as products of a capitalism that had been imposed on the German people from outside. A recurrent theme of German national identity, resistance to alien influences, was thus carried forward in design theory. East German architecture and planning would adopt forms that fit the sensibilities of the Volk and promoted revolutionary goals. Classicism was seen as the last truly innovative architectural style on German soil and a fitting expression of revolutionary impulses. GDR architects' interpretation of the classicist tradition could be seen in the massive offices, apartments, and monuments lining the Stalinallee (formerly Frankfurter Allee, later the Karl-Marx-Allee) in Berlin, a planned seven-kilometer-long project built largely with material from World War II ruins. Never completed, the Stalinallee was described by critics as a combination of "speculative baroque" and "barrack classicism" that was related to Berlin planning of the late 1920s and Speer's ideas for remaking the city as the capital of a Nazi world empire. While in prison Speer noted the affinity between

Figure 33. Construction on the Stalinallee, near Strausberger Platz, East Berlin, 1952. Bildarchiv Preussischer Kulturbesitz.

Berlin and Prussian classicism and the modern movement. Both stressed austerity, balance, and moderate or no ornamentation. Later in the postwar era, the GDR would adopt a "socialist" architecture that, with its prefabricated slab construction and extreme lack of decoration, mirrored the "no-frills modernism" of the West.[46] Here too the functionalist tradition became an integral part of official design culture.

BUNKERS, TEMPLES, AND EMPTY SPACES

All such efforts reconstructed and reframed German histories, but what to do about those buildings that unavoidably reminded Germans of the Nazi regime? The built environment was of course full of artifacts from the National Socialist period, from Autobahns and regime buildings to more prosaic structures embedded in everyday life. The period of National Socialism saw extraordinary building activity, much of it based on regime initiatives, but much of it also due to the building programs of churches and other nonregime groups. One approach to this heritage was simply to eliminate the reminders of the Third Reich, a solution widely turned to in the first decade or so after the war. Berlin had been the center of Hitler's empire, and postwar officials there were confronted with especially difficult questions of how to deal with Nazi architecture. One famous example was what remained of the grand Reich chancellery, which Speer had built for Hitler in the city's main government quarter, centered by the Wilhelmstraße and located after 1961 next to the Berlin Wall. Underneath the chancellery was a series of bunkers, including the so-called *Führerbunker,* which Hitler had used in the last months of his life before killing himself there. The bunker in particular fascinated foreigners more than Germans after the war, and until 1948, many soldiers from the West and the Soviet Union and not a few visiting dignitaries, including Winston Churchill, visited it. Stephen Spender noted that as late as fall 1945 there were still shelves of books on architecture above Hitler's bed in the bunker.[47] In 1948, the Soviets leveled the chancellery and closed the bunker (the East Germans would completely destroy it in secret in the 1980s). The stones of the chancellery were used in a nearby train depot and in two imposing Soviet war memorials in Treptow and the Tiergarten.[48] No more radical reconstruction could be imagined. Another sort of reconstruction would await the area covered by the buildings that housed the SS and secret police (Gestapo) headquarters on the Prinz-Albrecht-Straße in the government quarter. Although these ruins were leveled in the decade after the war, they would reappear as the Topography of Terror in the 1980s.

Munich was another big city in which National Socialism left many architectural traces. As the "Capital of the Movement," the Bavarian metropole had played a central role in the Nazi party's symbolic universe. After the war, local newspapers featured vigorous debates between planners and preservationists, who discussed whether to save buildings such as the Temple of Honor on the Königsplatz, where Hitler had the remains of the Beer Hall Putsch martyrs reburied. The decision on the Temple of Honor was negative. "Three bursts of a siren, a detonation, a cloud of dust. Of the two stiffly classical 'temples of honor' only piles of rubble remain for the excavators to clear away," wrote the correspondent from *Heute,* a German-language illustrated magazine published by the U.S. occupation authorities, on 1 February 1947. Despite the drama of the event and the contentiousness of the intellectuals, most people from Munich were unconcerned with the fate of these buildings: "They have to struggle with other, more immediate cares," noted *Heute.* The temples' foundations would be used for purposes more appropriate to the "tradition of the city of art," namely for badly needed exhibition halls the supply of which had been all but depleted in Allied bombing raids.[49]

Even older buildings that the Nazis transformed were victims of postwar destruction in Munich. Outside its Altstadt, Munich had been a city of renaissance, baroque, and Gothic palaces and ensembles. One of the most architecturally famous examples was the Wittelsbacher palace, commissioned by Ludwig I and built from 1843 to 1848 in a restrained Gothic style for the crown prince Maximilian. In the Third Reich, the Gestapo occupied this building. After the war, the surrounding gardens, which had once had an elegant stand of chestnut trees, were replaced by a huge bank building, and the palace itself was torn down even though it was not badly damaged. Nothing physical remained of the Nazi secret police activities in the Bavarian capital. A tourists' guidebook to Munich published in 1951 failed to mention the site as a former Gestapo headquarters, noting only that the famous palace, "the first important work of Romanticism in Munich," had to be torn down because of "severe damage."[50] It was easier to contemplate the palace's now abandoned place in German art history than its place in recent political history.

In many cases, the method followed was not to destroy Nazi buildings, but to remove traces of the regime. In a society hard-pressed to find functioning office buildings, schools, and other facilities, officials often chose to obliterate the evidence of the former rulers rather than do away with the buildings altogether. This was a reasonable approach, though fraught with consequences for collective memory. The Reichsbank in Berlin was the Nazi regime's first major office building in that city, a fitting symbol of the economic might that stood behind the dictatorship. GDR authorities removed the Nazi eagles and other reminders of the regime, choosing to use it first as the finance ministry, then as Communist party headquarters.[51] Throughout East and West Germany this scene was repeated again and again in less spectacular fashion—a swastika removed from an army barracks or a war monument, an inscription from Hitler sanded off the stone portal of a youth hostel, a Nazi painting removed from a school assembly hall. In such cases it was as if Germans assumed that superficial ornaments of the Thousand Year Reich could simply be removed in order to reintegrate buildings in the postwar flow of life. To a degree, they were correct: Nazi culture was in part a process of agglutination through which swastikas or other figures were added to the preexisting symbolic landscape of eagles, iron crosses, and the like. Remove the swastika, and the older symbols—assuming they too had not fallen into disrepute, as so many did in the GDR—could seemingly return to their prior meanings or at least be absorbed into the indistinct world of cultural "heritage."

Another way of dealing with the Nazi past was simply to ignore it. In the rubble-strewn, overgrown fields left behind in Berlin at the site of the former chancellery and the government quarter of the Wilhelmstraße, the history of National Socialism lay buried. Not far away, few realized that the empty fields north of the Reichstag and west of the Potsdamer Platz in Berlin were the product not only of Allied bombing but of Speer's demolition work as he prepared the city for a major north-south axis of monumental proportions. At the southern edge of the former government quarter were the remains of the SS and Gestapo headquarters on the Prinz-Albrecht-Strasse, which lay on the border between the Western and Soviet zones of occupation. Although planners envisioned new uses for these spaces, all such ideas were made irrelevant by the building of the Berlin Wall in 1961, which ran along Prinz-Albrecht-Strasse and made the area unusable. These sites remained desolate fields, or they were used as a dumping site for construction refuse and an automobile race track. Urban planners have recently begun to speak of a "geography of emptiness" as they discover the varied cultural meanings of empty spaces in modern cities.[52] But few such theories have dealt properly with the vast array of meanings and memories associated with the empty spaces of National Socialist Germany. For most Germans, these spaces required little comment—and very little was given until the 1970s.

In many instances, it was not empty spaces but extant artifacts that were the objects of public silence. In the Third Reich, Munich architects demolished four Florentine-style buildings from the nineteenth century on the Ludwigstraße and replaced them with the Central Ministry building, a colossus designed to reflect Nazi power. This was one of the first Munich buildings to experience severe damage in World War II bombing. Although it suffered much more damage than other notable buildings in the Ludwigstraße, the Central Ministry was reconstructed after the war, later becoming the Agricultural Ministry. Not the finely proportioned Florentine palaces but the example of Nazi monumentality reappeared. In 1937 the architect Leo von Klenze's beautifully proportioned Herzog-Max-Palais, built in 1827 in the style of the Florentine Renaissance for a cousin of King Ludwig, was leveled to make way for a more "monumental" building designed to house the new Reichsbank. Only the first story of the new building was completed before the end of the war, but when reconstruction took place, architects completed the edifice more or less as it was planned in the Third Reich. The building, designed to house a bank, thus assumed the style Nazi planners had envisioned for it. The landmarks register's official description of the bank stated innocently that it was a "neo-classical monumental building adapted to the image of the street."[53] Without mentioning the full history of the site, the city thereby completed what essentially had been a National Socialist project.

To ignore the traces of Nazi architecture in Nuremberg was even more challenging. Here the burden of the Nazi past was as great as in Berlin. Rightly celebrated as a city where medieval architecture could still be seen in great quantities, the Bavarian metropolis became the site of the annual Nazi party rallies and the place where the racial laws instrumental to the Holocaust were passed. After the war, the trials of the leading Nazi war criminals added another layer of infamy to the city's memory. To accommodate the Nazi party's annual rallies, the city had created the Party Congress Grounds, or *Reichsparteitagsgelände,* a huge complex of buildings and spaces situated outside the boundaries of the old town and designed for mass effect. More than fifteen times the size of the Altstadt, the development comprised a number of notable structures including the main tribune of the Zeppelin Field and the horseshoe-shaped Exhibition Hall, designed to accommodate thousands of Nazi party members but never completed.[54] The severely damaged Bavarian city decided to celebrate its nine hundredth anniversary in 1950 in the hall without mentioning the history associated with the monumental edifice. Thereafter various parts of the parade ground were used for concerts, assemblies, and sports events. For more than two decades after the war, officials remained silent about the complex's relationship to the Nazi period or the city. Few noted that in addition to the NSDAP rallies having taken place there, the grounds housed a POW camp in which many Soviet soldiers had lost their lives and a train depot from which Jewish citizens of the city had been deported to concentration camps. Tourists complained that signs directing visitors to the grounds were all but impossible to find. Even English-language tourist literature, which one might have expected to be more direct than German sources were, demonstrated unusual cowardice. A 1956 guidebook was maddeningly vague, noting only that "in the south-eastern part of Nuremberg, on the exhibition site near the Dutzendteich, formerly the scene of political meetings, is the unfinished horseshoe-shaped Exhibition Hall." A decade later, Speer's massive but incomplete towers on the military parade grounds, the *Märzfeldtürme,* were dynamited.

Figure 34. Dynamiting Märzfeld towers, former Nazi Party Congress Grounds, Nuremberg, 1966. Archiv für Kunst und Geschichte, Berlin.

As the Nuremberg case suggests, the Nazi past was muted or suppressed also when, intentionally or unintentionally, buildings took on new functions. Built 1935–1936, the Air Ministry in Berlin was a symbol of Hitler's military might and the center from which terror bombings of European cities were planned. Because of its size and good condition after the war, the building became the GDR's "House of Ministries" and the site where the new republic was proclaimed. No mention was made of the building's previous history. In the West, the Olympic stadium and complex had been planned before Hitler came to power. But they were impressed in public memory because of their use in the Nazis' propaganda show at the 1936 Olympics. After the war, the Olympic complex's fraught political history was lost in sporting and other events, and the stadium itself became West Berlin's main soccer stadium. The entrance of the massive, curved Tempelhof airport was to have been aligned with the eastern approach to Hitler's triumphal arch in Berlin. In 1948–1949, the U.S. military used the airport to circumvent the East Germans' blockade of the Western occupation zones, providing West Berliners with food and supplies in a heroic effort that was commemorated two years later in a dramatic monument at the entrance to the airport.[55] The Tempelhof example alerts us to the fact that the line between intentionality and chance was very thin. Those who thought of Tempelhof as a symbol of postwar German-American friendship may have wanted to forget the Nazi past. Yet the force of circumstances and the unquestionable drama of events also compelled them to remember the airport for its postwar historical significance.

ANTIFASCIST RESISTANCE

On balance, it was easy to see how German buildings and urban layouts could mute or suppress the memory of Nazism. In the context of widespread destruction, buildings were needed for everyday functions, not mourning. But there were some sites Germans and other Europeans wanted to remember as scenes of massive violence. Nazism had been a European phenomenon, and throughout Europe vestiges of Nazi crimes were numerous. Understandably, the theme of antifascist resistance became a central motif in the memory landscape.

Although this theme emphasized heroism and struggle, it was in fact rooted in a sense of deep sacrifice and bittersweet victory. So great had been their humiliation by the Nazis, so shocking the loss of human life, that Europeans, even those who won the war, shared a memory of exhaustion, loss, and desperate determination to recover. A narrative of resistance thus grew in the soil of "defeatist" memory, in the East even more than in the West.[56] Germany, the chief loser, shared in the general European sense of immense tragedy. But just as the rise and fall of Nazism's plans for European domination unfolded as part of a national project, the sense of defeat and the resistance theme developed in sync with the rhythm of political contention in each country. Martyrdom became "nationalized," in the words of historian Pieter Lagrou, as Europeans searched, often not without conflict, for "the kind of patriotic epic that only the Resistance could deliver." For the French, Belgians, Italians, Yugoslavs, Dutch, and Poles, there were dark corners in the memory of the Resistance that had to be avoided or suppressed. And there were numerous points of ambivalence, as with workers who had been deported to Germany during the war for forced labor, but were often suspected of collaboration. In Belgium forced laborers managed to have their story seen as both a form of national martyrdom and resistance, while in France they were vocal but less successful in this regard, and in the Netherlands they were ostracized from the community of national memory.[57] To reconstruct the past on the basis of stories of recovery and resistance was to inspire as well as potentially to embarrass the national society such stories were designed to serve. It was not only the German past that had to be "mastered."

In no country were martyrdom, deportation, and resistance conflated and nationalized with more political energy than in France. Seeking to expand a rather shaky coalition of supporters, General Charles De Gaulle used his wartime heroism to build a "generous and collective vision of the French combat to liberate France."[58] The key result was "resistentialism," which Tony Judt has referred to as "a strange, self-induced amnesia" that turned military defeat and occupation by the Nazis into a heroic national struggle against fascism. Instead of admitting the limits to popular opposition against Vichy and Nazism, both the Right and the Left, with little discussion or dissent, welcomed last-minute resisters, labor conscripts, former collaborators, and many other questionable types into the postwar "community of resistance."[59] Right-wing Gaullists believed in the French nation as an eternal cycle of decline and resurgence in which resisters threw off the Vichy state in order to reassert Republican France. Without acknowledging its heritage, this perspective incorporated many elements of nationalist thought as they had been elaborated under Pétain's rule. The Communist party relied on a linear model of history in which the struggle against fascism was the latest chapter in a story of class conflict between socialism and reaction. Yet such narratives were told and retold with a degree of embarrassment. The Right used resistance narratives to reconstruct national dignity after the humiliation of military defeat and the passivity of the majority of the French under Nazi occupation. The Left avoided evidence reminding the nation of tensions between left-leaning resisters and local populations, whose innocent members were often the chief victims of Nazi reprisals.

A good example of such complexities comes from the site of a Nazi atrocity at the village of Oradour-sur-Glane in the Limousin in west-central France.[60] Ordered to suppress Resistance activity at the time of the Allied landing in Normandy, an SS division moved into this small town on the afternoon of 10 June 1944, killed 642 men, women, and children, and set the town on fire. Only five people survived, and the village itself was a complete ruin. After the war, the French parliament quickly made the forty acres of ruined houses, shops, and farms into a national monument, and the incident became the paradigmatic story of French victimization. Oradour was with equal speed transformed into a symbol of French Resistance even though the villagers themselves had been innocent of resistance activity. The government, local citizens, and resistance groups claimed the "village martyr" of Oradour as a central example of Nazi repression and barbarism.

Other such villages, including what the Dutch press called the "Dutch Oradour" of Putten,[61] but most notably the industrial and mining town Lidice in Czechoslovakia, were also transformed into commemorative sites. In Lidice the Nazis killed 173 men, sent 203 women and their children to concentration camps and gas chambers, and razed all the houses. The Nazis claimed that townspeople had sheltered the assassins who killed the SS official and Reich protector of occupied Czech territories, Reinhard Heydrich, in 1942. Towns in the United States, Cuba, Brazil, and other countries named themselves after Lidice to express solidarity with the victims, and English, Scottish, and Welsh miners took up collections to support the survivors. The Soviet army erected a provisional monument at the site soon after the war, and the Czechoslovak government rebuilt an entirely new town near the old one. By the 1960s, the remains of the cellar where the murdered men were initially herded, the excavated base of the wall where they were shot, a marker showing the site of the destroyed church and the house of the village priest, a stark cross wreathed in barbed wire placed over the mass grave of the murdered men, a statue symbolizing Lidice women grieving for their loved ones, a huge memorial garden with some twenty-nine thousand rose bushes (donated from all over the world), a beautiful stand of trees (including walnuts and oaks from Oradour), a semicircular monument-wall engraved with the town seals of other communities wiped out during World War II, and a museum were among the physical reminders of the massacre.[62]

Oradour, however, was the only such martyred village to be preserved *in toto*. The new town overlooking the old also served as a powerful symbol of the French nation's postwar revival. As the commemoration of Oradour unfolded in the postwar decades, organizers and local citizens de-emphasized matters of political context and the Resistance in favor of memories of Christian sacrifice and individual and national suffering. The original plan for the old site was to stop history: to represent the town as it had been on the day after the massacre. This framing device was widespread in Europe because the sites of atrocity still referred to events recent in time and palpably remembered by the victims and survivors. Ruined buildings, bullet holes in the walls of the church where village women were burned to death or sprayed with German gunfire, the remains of the church bell—all would be preserved in their original spot or placed in a memorial exhibit inside the ruins. At the cemetery, the only part of the town to survive the attack, bones and ashes of the victims were deposited, and plaques bore the names and ages of all 642 victims. Relatives of the victims placed individual funerary plaques at the ossuary or on individual graves. Survivors and tour guides told stories of individual suffering. Approximately three hundred thousand people visited the site annually, almost 90 percent French. Their experience was more like that of Christian pilgrims attending a shrine than of students of history inspired by tales of the glorious Resistance. One could hardly imagine a starker contrast to the documentary impulse that would characterize many German sites of commemoration. Little was done to enlighten these visitors about the messier details of Oradour's history: that many Frenchmen had not only passively accepted Nazism and Vichy but also collaborated; that mass resistance was belated and often self-interested; and that Resistance fighters themselves often unintentionally signed the death sentence for innocent bystanders like the villagers of Oradour, who paid with their lives for the Resisters' sometimes empty or incompetent acts of heroism.

In Italy, Nazi atrocities also resulted in martyred villages. Here as elsewhere, political tensions compelled Italians to commemorate some parts of the memory landscape while ignoring or de-emphasizing others. On 29 June 1944 an SS division of the German army, retaliating for a spontaneous partisans' attack on four German soldiers who had lost contact with their unit, killed around 250 men in the Tuscan villages of Civitella, Cornia, and San Pancrazio. These quiet medieval hill towns had done little to deserve their fate. Devoutly Catholic and conservative, Civitella had celebrated the fall of Mussolini in July 1943, but it had never been a center of Resistance activity. Even so, after the war the Italian Left commemorated the massacre and heroized the people of Civitella in an attempt to keep alive the antifascist coalition. But some Civitelli resented the partisans' recklessness, and the Christian Democratic party attacked the Resistance for its immaturity. Civitella's equivocal relationship to the Resistance led Italian Communists to give more attention to towns such as Marzabotto, another site of Nazi reprisal, the inhabitants of which were strongly Communist. It was finally the simple human memory of the murdered men—and of the women who were left behind to bury them and raise the children of Civitella—that most powerfully shaped the legacy of the town.[63]

In Eastern Europe and the Balkans, the theme of resistance also served national political aims, all the more so given the fact that Nazi occupation had been so much more brutal there than in the West. France lost less than 2 percent of its prewar population in World War II, but Poland lost almost 18 percent and Yugoslavia more than 10 percent. Although Soviet occupation and the emergence of authoritarian political systems muffled open debate in the East, there were also complex crosscurrents and antagonisms in the formation of a public memory of resistance to Nazism. One can see how compelling memory of resistance was in Poland by considering the history of the famous Warsaw Ghetto Monument. Erected in 1948 at a time when Warsaw remained a landscape of desolate rubble, the ghetto monument commemorated the Jewish uprising against the Nazis in 1943.[64] It was established at the site of the actual ghetto, a move that again reflected the direct connections between commemoration and historic place in the immediate postwar era. Established in October 1940, the Warsaw ghetto at one time included more than five hundred thousand Jews, most of whom would be sent to extermination camps. By the early months of 1943, only sixty thousand Jews remained. In pitched battles starting on 19 April and continuing for six weeks, the ghetto survivors fought the Nazis until they were killed in the struggle, executed, or sent to extermination centers. A handful escaped to join the underground Resistance. The Polish sculptor Nathan Rapoport received the commission to memorialize the resistance of these heroic fighters. Having spent part of the war in the Soviet Union, Rapoport created a monument that combined elements of Stalinist heroism and myth with traditional Jewish images of a people in exile.

Situated in a cultural and political environment in which the Jewish community had been radically decimated (though by no means extinguished), the Warsaw monument did not become primarily a symbol of Jewish resistance but one of Polish resistance to foreign aggression. I have noted the persistence of Polish self-identity as the "Christ of Nations" whose sacrifice would contribute to national resurgence. This tradition was extended and even strengthened in the new postwar context, as Poles continued to see themselves as members of a "disenfranchised ethnic population" trapped by more powerful European neighbors and lorded over by a Communist state.[65] During and after the war, many Poles thought of the ghetto revolt not as an event in Jewish history but as an inspiration to sacrifice themselves in the heroic struggle against Hitler. More than two hundred commemorative tablets marking the sites of Nazi executions of Poles were distributed throughout reconstructed Warsaw.[66] But soon Poles resented the ghetto monument because it became a symbol of the *absence* of commemoration of the 1944

Polish uprising. In this uprising, the Polish Home Army struggled valiantly as the Germans liquidated the city block by block. Meanwhile, the Russian army, camped across the Vistula river, watched passively as 180,000 Poles lost their lives. The Polish regime's strong support for Rapoport's monument was seen by some as suppression of the memory of the Polish uprising. Such resentment led some Poles to dub the Brotherhood in Arms Memorial to Soviet soldiers who liberated Warsaw as the "Monument to the Sleeping Soldiers." As time wore on, the ghetto memorial would become the site of dissidents' memories and demands, including those of the Solidarity movement in the 1980s, which most vocally supported a monument to the events of 1944. A central symbol of Jewish memory of the Holocaust in Israel and the United States, Rapoport's creation on Polish soil became much more closely tied to Polish national history and to the triumphs and embarrassments, the moments of light and darkness that that history embraced.

The preceding examples remind us that it is impossible to make a simple distinction between a relatively homogeneous and self-confident public memory of resistance in non-German countries and a more constricted tradition of commemorating resistance in Germany. Even those who had triumphed over Nazism shared a defeatist memory. Yet the German remembrance of resistance was complicated in a way other national memories were not. Many elements of the Nazi experience had no precedent in German history. Even after the slaughter and military defeat of 1914–1918, Germans could console themselves that their young men had fought valiantly for a good cause, and their war monuments could symbolize noble heroism. After Hitler's war, no such consolation was available, at least not for the majority of the population. That majority had identified with Hitler on some level even if less than half of the voting population had ever voted for him. Now the crimes he perpetrated were clear for all to see. Perhaps only Croatians could look back (had they chosen to do so) on a roughly comparable history of organized brutality in their wartime campaign to liquidate Orthodox Serbs, Jews, and Sinti and Roma, although here too the comparisons take us only so far. Most Germans were not yet ready to face fully the fact they had seen themselves in Hitler. Nor could they bring themselves fully to pinpoint who had run the system of mass extermination. Not until after 1970 would more than a tiny minority of Germans in the Federal Republic gain a more critical perspective on these aspects of the history of Nazism. Until then, German identity was expressed in reconstructions and monuments symbolizing either the plight of those who were persecuted and in some way victimized by the Nazi regime, or of that small minority who resisted it. In public memory it was often difficult to separate these categories, just as it was difficult to separate them in real life. It is worth doing so, however, for analytical purposes.

In West Germany, the most important heroes of the Resistance were those military officers and civilians who tried to assassinate Hitler on 20 July 1944. Goebbels referred to this group of perhaps two hundred Resisters as putschists and traitors, and for many Germans, especially the elderly and those who had fought at the front, there was much ambivalence about these mostly elite individuals who turned against Hitler at a time when Germany was assaulted from all sides. After the war, veterans' groups as well as the neo-Nazi Right continued to maintain that the resisters of 20 July betrayed Germany. For the advocates of democracy, moreover, the plotters left behind an ambivalent heritage. The conservative aristocrats, officers, and officials of the July plot had after all supported or gone along with Hitler until the last stages of the war, and they had more in common with the nationalist opponents of the Weimar Republic than with the proponents of democracy. Still, it was politically useful for the West German leadership to promote the memory of the conspirators because the theme of resistance to Hitler aided attempts to reintegrate the Federal Republic in the West.[67] The European and transatlantic dimensions of the resistance story were thus as important to West German identity as the strictly national dimensions were.

The assassination plot had been organized from the former headquarters of the military high command in the Bendlerstraße in Berlin's Tiergarten district. It was here that the five officers who led the conspiracy were executed according to their military rank the night of the assassination attempt. Their bodies were at first buried in a cemetery in nearby Schöneberg, but the SS later exhumed the corpses, cremated them, and scattered the ashes. The reconstruction of this site reflected a long commemorative tradition in Germany. Like German cemeteries and monuments of the past, austerity and simplicity were the key features. A lone statue marked the bare inner courtyard of the building where the executions had taken place. Constructed in 1953 by Richard Scheibe, who earned a national reputation as a sculptor in both the Weimar Republic and Nazi period, this statue depicted a naked youth in the tradition of war monuments after World War I. Its form combined naturalistic and classical motifs, suggesting an unhistorical humanistic tradition rather than the specific political history of Nazism and World War II.[68]

Figure 35. Sculpture by Richard Scheibe, Bendlerblock Memorial, West Berlin, 1953. Bildarchiv Preussischer Kulturbesitz.

In 1955 the Bendlerstraße was renamed after Colonel Claus Schenk Graf von Stauffenberg, who had placed the bomb at Hitler's feet. This act reflected the tendency in the first years after the war to personalize the memory of the Resistance either with reference to single individuals or to specific groups. Sponsored by the Berlin Senate, a memorial plaque placed in the courtyard bore the names of the main conspirators, noting only that the five had died "for Germany." This part of the memorial drew attention to the conspirators as defenders of the ethnie in a moment of grave crisis rather than as historical subjects in a political context fraught with great ambivalence. This message would become more complex and inclusive by the mid-1960s, after which time a series of exhibits over the next two decades turned the memorial into a documentation and learning center. For the time being, however, the memorial in the Stauffenbergstraße would serve the purpose of reminding Germans that a relatively small group of their countrymen had sacrificed their lives in an attempt to end Hitler's brutal rule and thereby preserve the national community.

Most of the July 20 conspirators were executed at another site of terror, the Plötzensee prison in Berlin-Charlottenburg. This was one of the main sites for the torture and execution of political prisoners in Nazi Germany, and it was estimated that more than three thousand prisoners were guillotined or hanged here. More than 200 were executed here for their part in the July plot. It thus lent itself more readily to a broader sense of who had resisted Nazism than the Stauffenbergstraße memorial did. In 1952, before it commemorated the Bendlerblock, the Berlin Senate established a "Memorial to the Victims of the Hitler Dictatorship." This included a wall of honor inside which was buried a document stating "Berlin hereby honors the millions of victims of the Third Reich, who, because of political conviction, religion, or racial heritage, were vilified, abused, robbed of their freedom, or murdered." Near the wall was a simple urn containing earth from all Nazi concentration camps, placed at the site in 1957, and near the urn was a large wooden cross. The site included a small documentation center and, most chillingly, the execution room, where in the first year after the war a guillotine stood, and where visitors could still see five of the original eight meathooks from which victims hung. Even the wash basins where the executioners cleaned up were preserved. The site was also noted for the fact that Hitler had the executions of July 20 conspirators filmed here, only to have the grisly propaganda film stopped once one of the camera crews refused to continue.

At first glance, the prison memorial seemed to balance symbolic gesture, emotion, and criticism based on historical fact.[69] Its startling authenticity needed little embellishment to remind visitors of the methods with which the regime dealt with its enemies. That the group of enemies was large and varied, including many different nationalities and political opponents, including Communists, was evident from the text of the buried document and the wall inscription. The memorial was situated on the Hüttigpfad, named after Richard Hüttig, the first Communist to be executed at the site on 14 June 1934. But the inclusive approach also blurred the distinctions that authenticity and documentation (there

Figure 36. Plötzensee Memorial, Berlin-Charlottenburg, 1965. Bildarchiv Preussischer Kulturbesitz.

would later be a documentary center at the site) supposedly established. By mentioning all the victims of the regime, both Jews as well as former supporters of the regime who ran aground of the system would find their way into the circle of heroes. By including those persecuted for religious, racial, and political reasons, the victims' status would be obscured. Communists lost their lives under Hitler's ruthless rule, but they had made a political choice. Jews killed in the concentration camps had no choice about changing their supposedly immutable racial characteristics. The large urn with earth from the German concentration camps also recalled an earlier theme of German national identity, namely the close relationship between the landscape and the national community. Meanwhile, the large wooden cross symbolized Christian themes of sacrifice and renewal in the manner of so many other German monuments.

Even the themes of authenticity and documentation picked up on commemorative traditions that, paradoxically, the Nazis themselves had used. Although based on emotional appeals to the racial community, Nazi sites of memory had an important critical and documentary perspective. Warped by racial and radical nationalist ideals, Nazi propagandists nonetheless worked diligently to pinpoint the alleged crimes of other nations and domestic opponents. They used realistic motifs on monuments, in film and newsreels and other media to develop such critical memory. They used photography and film to document their own actions, even those which later in the post–World War II period would provide damning evidence of the barbarity of the regime. They did so perhaps partly because they were attracted by the site of murdered victims, a kind of *Schaulust,* an irresistible desire to look, similar to that felt by individuals attracted by grisly scenes of human suffering at automobile crashes. Yet there was also a sense of disbelief that *they* were doing *this*. The need to document such gross crimes thus counterbalanced the desire to cover up, to destroy evidence, to obliterate the remains of former death camps, and later to be silent.[70]

German monuments of the post–World War II period would strengthen a documentary and critical element. So immense were the crimes of the Nazi regime, so harrowing the loss of life and the destruction of World War II, that memory demanded precise analysis of past crimes. But even more important was the fact that emotional identification with those who had been victimized—if this were at all possible—necessitated a cognitive bridge between the victims and the national community remembering them. A documentary path was required to lead the nation across the great divide that in the Nazi years had separated the "community of the Volk" from its many "enemies." The documentary path did not substitute for but was rather a first step toward "thinking the unthinkable." It was a prerequisite of mourning, a form of memory based not on melancholy or anxious immobility, but on acceptance of loss, clearsighted recognition of past mistakes, and acute willingness to safeguard the future against recurrences.[71]

To the degree that the German Left now played a central role in public memory, the documentary impulse assumed a new importance as it drew on radical democratic and socialist traditions of critical memory. For some on the Left, dispassionate analysis and authenticity did not continue the realism of the Third Reich but was a countermeasure against Nazi-inspired "fanaticism," a key word of the National Socialist vocabulary. This was the approach of the philosopher Theodor Adorno, whose views on German memory were expressed in a public lecture broadcast on German radio in 1959 and circulated in journals and books in the following decade. Adorno was convinced that cognition and analysis would lead Germans to see a fundamental point: that their allegiance to Hitler stemmed from capitalism's tendency to divide society into "the dominating few and the dominated masses." Adorno called for "mobile educational task forces" that would educate the German people about what had happened at Auschwitz.[72] With its emphasis on rational analysis and dispassionate criticism, Adorno's proposal was reminiscent of the architect Bruno Taut's Weimar-era idea to build reading rooms throughout Germany to create a critical memory of World War I. Adorno's treatment of the subject influenced many younger West Germans in particular; it was adopted in only piecemeal fashion by political and economic elites, who realized that the pedagogical scheme riveted critical attention on capitalism. But the Adornoesque approach had an impressive half-life, particularly because it called on socialist and democratic thinkers to represent "the real" through a critical analysis of the past that did not fall prey to the conservative notion of stable and homogeneous national history. This approach to memory continued to inform the work of the painter Anselm Kiefer, the novelists Peter Handke and (in East Germany) Christa Wolf, and the artist and philosopher Alexander Kluge in the 1970s, 1980s, and beyond.[73]

The first major memorials to commemorate resistance to Nazism in the West, the two reconstructed sites at the Bendlerblock and Plötzensee retained their significance in the 1970s and 1980s, as we will see. Given their origins in the first postwar years and their continued recognition, they became paradigms for the memory of the Resistance. Both drew on existing commemorative traditions, including national and Christian themes. Both tried to balance critical memory and documentary effect with an emotional appeal to the memory of Resisters as representatives of a national identity. But in the form they assumed early in the Federal Republic, the two monuments parted ways in the manner they envisioned the Resistance itself. For the Bendlerblock memorial, the Resistance consisted of a small group of individuals committed to the overthrow of Hitler. In this view the victims of the regime could be arranged in a hierarchy of commemoration with the aristocratic-conservative-military resistance at its peak. This view of the Resistance thereby reaffirmed an older sense of the German ethnie as a unity of the princes and Volk, using the Kaiserreich as its referent. The early Stauffenbergstraße memorial was thus of a piece with the reconstruction of German churches and Altstädte. Subsequent controversy over the site stemmed from attempts to widen this representation.

In contrast, the Plötzensee always contained the possibility of a very broad and undifferentiated view of the Resistance. All those who suffered under Nazism, regardless of specific actions or intentions, might enter the pantheon of victims, who in turn symbolized the nation. This way of viewing the past looked to the future, when, after the late 1960s in particular, the memory landscape would be conceived in terms of broad topographies rather than specific monuments and reconstructions. In the first fifteen years after the war, however, the Plötzensee's inclusiveness was limited by political events, as the Communist party and the Communist-influenced Association of Persecutees of the Nazi Regime (or VVN, for *Verein der Verfolgten des Naziregimes*) were banned by the Federal Republic. Such political repression ensured that the history of Communist resistance was all but purged from public memory.

German cities were dotted with memorials and reminders of the Resistance in the first two decades after the war. These memorials fell along a spectrum defined by the paradigms sketched above. No central monument honoring Resisters existed, but then none had to. German national identity remained the product of a multicentered sense of community with strong federal, urban, and regional traditions. Dispersed commemoration of Resistance fighters throughout the Federal Republic was appropriate to this vision of the German past. The Federal Republic had just two secular national holidays, 1 May, the traditional labor day, and 17 June, which commemorated a spontaneous workers' uprising against the East German regime in 1953. The absence of 20 July in the commemorative calendar leads some scholars to argue that memory of the Resistance was a matter of official embarrassment. While there is certainly something to this argument, if one considers the continuities of German memory in the Federal Republic, the absence of a centrally directed holiday for the Resistance is not so unusual. Instead of a national campaign to establish an official memory of the Resistance, it is to be expected that the Federal Republic would have chosen a decentralized and relatively unfocused approach to the subject dependent largely on local initiatives. The mere fact of decentralization was a symbol of the Federal Republic's commitment to mastering a difficult past using the etched-in syntax of tradition. The content and iconography of memorials mattered less in this instance than the continued existence of particular local commemorative practices. This continuity had a tactical function as well, as regime officials, cognizant of many Germans' bitter memory of Nazi centralization, wanted to avoid the appearance of directing cultural life from Bonn.

If we turn our attention to the GDR, we see both parallels and stark differences. In East Germany commemoration of the Resistance had much in common with the more hierarchically arranged memory symbolized in the memorial to the July conspirators in Berlin. This was true all the more so because the regime, unlike its counterpart in the Federal Republic, directed the commemoration of resistance from above, ensuring that plaques and monuments would be distributed throughout the state. If in the West the history of Communist resistance to Nazism was an object of "cultivated oblivion," as Eve Rosenhaft has written, then in the East it was the focus of the regime's "pious celebration."[74] The regime's first goal was to honor the Soviet army and German working-class resistance to fascism. All other resisters, whether members of the intellectual class or non-Communists, or other victims, whether Jews or Sinti and Roma, occupied a secondary position in the pyramid of official memory. It was as if the West German hierarchy symbolized by the axis of the Bendlerblock and Plötzensee had been turned upside down. The inverted hierarchical arrangement was also directed toward members of the Communist resistance themselves. The postwar GDR leadership consisted of individuals who had been in exile in Moscow during the war. Their memory of resistance was quite different from that of German Communists who had spent the war in underground activity or in the camps. The leadership criticized the "sectarianism" and ineffectualness of Communist underground activity and established an official memory that often marginalized the old rank and file.

The hierarchy of memory could also be seen in the way it embraced three basic forms of memorials in the GDR. The first and most important consisted of three "National Sites of Admonition and Memory," or *Nationale Mahn- und Gedenkstätten,* the former concentration camp sites of Buchenwald, Sachsenhausen, and Ravensbrück. In the second level of priority were other former concentration camps and sites of resistance comparable in many respects to those in the West. Finally, there was a third level of "antifascist heritage" comprising monuments, streets, and buildings in various communities. Because I treat former concentration camp sites in both East and West separately below, I discuss several illustrative examples of the second and third tiers of memory in the GDR in the following paragraphs.

The regulating force of the GDR's approach to the past was the ideology of antifascism.[75] Rooted in the experiences of German Communist leaders in the Weimar Republic and in exile during the war, antifascism was an ethical category resting on two premises. First, it was based on the acceptance of the Soviet Union's historical role as the victor over imperialism, capitalism, and fascism and as the model of a new society inspired by the goal of universal freedom. Second, it depended on the building and maintenance of an antifascist political coalition derived from the struggle against Nazism but guaranteed in the daily policies of the GDR. Antifascism transformed the GDR into a country based entirely on history. It was not only appropriate but necessary that the GDR, perhaps more than any other postwar European state, "set about defining a historical tradition and creating the iconography and symbolic landscape for a newly invented state with no previously accepted physical, cultural, or linguistic boundaries."[76] Antifascism derived its legitimacy from the argument that fascism was the outcome of a historically documented logic of capitalist aggression and imperialism, and that antifascism would in turn eradicate the economic and social roots of such perfidy, pointing the way to a socialist future. Once the system based on this historical argument and its accompanying symbolism fell, as it did in 1989, the state on which it rested also disappeared. It was significant that none of the GDR's socialist neighbors disappeared as national communities once Communism was gone.

One of the not-to-be-overlooked advantages of this historical argument for the East German state was that it necessitated rooting out the remaining traces of fascism. Anti-Hitler resistance was carried over into the postwar era as a fundament of the new state's political culture. This led to an aggressive program of denazification in which, unlike the Federal Republic, the GDR eliminated Nazi influences in government, schools and universities, and cultural life. More than a half-million former members of the Nazi party were removed from their professions. Important though this was, East German denazification did not entirely eliminate former Nazis from positions of influence. Such individuals gained prominence in the press, various sectors of the economy, the arts, the schools and universities, and even in the SED bureaucracy. Nonetheless, the substantive and propagandistic successes of denazification legitimized the GDR leadership's claim to have broken with the past. Not surprisingly, this claim also made it impossible to discuss the new state's responsibility to the victims of the Third Reich. The regime operated according to the formula "Our Goethe, your Mengele."[77] In this simple juxtaposition, the GDR appropriated the progressive traditions of German culture as represented by Goethe, and left the memory of Auschwitz and the gruesome medical experiments carried out on camp inmates by Josef Mengele to a still culpable West German political culture.

Antifascism also made it impossible to look beyond economic logic as the fundamental basis of fascism. Thus when the victims of fascism were to be honored, those groups that had been persecuted and killed not because of their economic significance but because of "racial" heritage or religious affiliation represented a challenge to official antifascist memory. Racial war, the core of Auschwitz, found no place in antifascist historical perspectives other than as an epiphenomenon of the violent logic of capitalism. Because the historical experiences and social situation of ethnic minorities in general, and Jews in particular, had always been of secondary importance in prewar antifascist discourse, the East German inability to see the Holocaust as something more than a product of the most nefarious tendencies of capitalism was consistent with German Communist tradition. For only a brief moment in the immediate postwar years, after German Communist exiles in Mexico such as Paul Merker and former concentration camp prisoners had made their way back to East Berlin, did the "Jewish question" and the problem of anti-Semitism gain more than a marginal significance in antifascist discourse.[78]

GDR memory drew heavily on prior commemorative practices even as it proclaimed revolution. This strategy was also consistent with the ethics of antifascism, which gained moral legitimacy through the historically specific struggle against National Socialism, and which therefore posited socialism as an historical outcome rather than a first premise. Prior traditions and practices could therefore be combined in antifascist memory as long as they could be defined around the core of state ideology. In this context GDR iconography was no less associationist, in the sense the term was used in the previous chapter, than Italian Fascism or German National Socialism. National traditions and even Christian motifs could be deployed just as easily as traditions derived from the Soviet Union. When later in the postwar period the GDR would distinguish between heritage (*Erbe*) and tradition (*Tradition*), it would do so partly because antifascist perspectives on the past allowed for a certain eclecticism. Heritage was the sum total of the culture and history of the ethnie, which in the German case included the seeds of radical nationalism, unfettered materialism, and finally fascism. But tradition could be maintained through a healthy nurturing of positive elements inherited from the past such as socialism, working-class history, and even progressive bourgeois thought and culture. Antifascist ideology defined the positive elements of German history and deployed them in the official memory of the regime.

Soviet war memorials were among the most visible and monumental symbols of the antifascist resistance in postwar East Berlin. Completed in 1949, the Treptower Park memorial symbolized the Soviet army's struggle against fascism and contained the graves of five thousand Soviet

Figure 37. Visitors at Treptow Memorial, East Berlin, 1949. Bildarchiv Preussischer Kulturbesitz.

soldiers and officers who died in the battle of Berlin. It was a reconstruction insofar that it used the ruins of Hitler's Reich chancellery for building materials. The massive memorial included the statue of a woman mourning her slain sons, a symbol of the grieving motherland. Dominating the memorial was the sculptor E. V. Vuchetich's "Soldier-Liberator," a massive bronze statue of a Soviet soldier carrying a German girl and holding a sword over a shattered swastika. The scene was said to re-enact an event that happened during the last bloody days of the battle for Berlin. Yet like many of the war memorials of the past this monument had little to do with the reality of battle. The use of the sword was interesting because it gave the struggle against fascism a premodern quality even though it had of course been a highly mechanized war. In this sense, the memorial drew on "medievalist" forms of war commemoration prevalent after World War I.

The sheer size of the monument indicated how heavily it drew on a Soviet tradition whereby Communist history was transformed into overpowering myth. The Soldier-Liberator in particular was the central image of the cult of the Great Patriotic War in the Soviet Union for the entire postwar period. The forty-fifth anniversary of the Soviet victory over Nazism in May 1990 included a float with a live tableau of the

Figure 38. The Soldier-Liberator, Treptow Memorial, East Berlin. Deutsches Historisches Museum.

monument, complete with a tall uniformed man holding a small girl in a white dress.[79] Yet monumentality was no alien element in the history of German commemoration either. The Soviet war memorials could thus also stand in the tradition of the Second Empire's colossal national monuments, as the heroic Soviet warrior of East Berlin answered the monumental figures of Hermann or Barbarossa. Whereas the Western parts of Germany had now forsaken this tradition of monument building, the GDR embraced it. The Treptower Park memorial was reminiscent of the German national monuments in another important respect, namely its treatment of Nazism as a foreign occupying power. The monument portrayed the Soviet army and its German Communist allies as heroic defenders who threw off an alien force in much the way Teutons bested Roman invaders in the first century A.D. and Prussian and Russian forces drove out the French in 1813. The heroic Soviet soldier followed in the tradition of the Hermann Monument and the Leipzig monument by symbolizing the nation in arms vigorously defeating foreign threats.

If the Treptower Park monument sounded the theme of Soviet heroism and antifascist resistance, another major memorial, the Neue Wache, alerted viewers to the need for political vigilance.[80] Having lived previous lives as a symbol of anti-Napoleonic military victory by the Prussians and as a national site of mourning under the Weimar Republic and the Third Reich, the neo-classical temple assumed yet another identity as the "Memorial to the Victims of Fascism and Militarism" after restoration in the 1950s and dedication by the GDR leadership in 1960. At first many wanted to leave the Neue Wache as a ruin, including the architect who had designed it as a war memorial in the Weimar Republic, Heinrich Tessenow. Its entrance was partially collapsed, the roof had a large hole in it, and graffiti (some of it pro-Nazi) marred its outer walls. The granite slab in the interior of the memorial was heavily scarred, and the gilded wreath of oak leaves had been stolen by vandals. Some wanted to use the building as a Schinkel museum, others as a university bookstore (it was near the Humboldt University) or a monument to Goethe. Still others suggested that a Kollwitz sculpture should be placed in the ruin, anticipating the transformation of the memorial in the 1990s. Among the suggestions could also be heard the idea that the forlorn ruin should simply be bulldozed. It was finally the insistence of the Soviet authorities that saved the structure: they saw it as a symbol of German-Russian friendship because of its association with the anti-Napoleonic coalition of 1813.

At first, it was decided to restore the building with traces of wartime damage left in place in much the same manner that the architect Hans Döllgast had reconstructed the Alter Pinakothek, a famous Munich museum. But in the 1950s the GDR leadership chose a more ambitious plan to transform the building into a memorial to the victims of war and fascism. The architect and planner Hermann Henselmann retained much of Tessenow's original design, including the granite monolith, although the crucifix placed on the rear interior wall by the Nazis was removed, as was the floor plaque reading "1914–1918." Originally, the great poet Bertold Brecht's line, "Mothers, let your children live," was to be placed on the rear wall, but for reasons still unclear the inscription "To the victims of fascism and militarism" was chosen instead. For the twentieth anniversary of the GDR the Neue Wache received another major facelift, including the addition of the East German state symbol (a hammer and compass embraced by a Germanic oak wreath); an eternal flame housed in an imposing glass cube; and urns for the Unknown Soldier and the Unknown Resistance Fighter as well as for earth from nine concentration camps and nine World War II battlefields.

Partly a reflection of the East German regime's new sense of its own authority, the 1969 facelift was also a concession to international taste. The memorial had become an important stop in the touristic pilgrimage to various Berlin sites, and since 1962 (the year in which the GDR got universal military conscription) visitors would organize their itinerary in order to be present when goosestepping East German soldiers changed guard before the Neue Wache. Throughout such displays the message was clear: only diligent antifascist awareness of the threat posed by militarism and fascism would preserve the hard-won peace made possible by German Communists and their Soviet brothers. Yet beyond that, the message reflected a general tendency toward blurring distinctions between various victim groups. If antifascist ideology organized a pyramid of victims with Soviet and German Communists at the top, who could guarantee that visitors to the memorial would not also mourn for Jews, dissident Christians, aristocratic military officers, ordinary German soldiers, or even former members of the Nazi party—indeed *all* victims equally? More than the Treptower Park memorial, the Neue Wache pointed to a homogenizing tendency of German public memory that would begin to characterize both East and West in later decades.

Still, the importance of antifascist and Soviet ideology in such German national monuments could not be denied in this earlier period. A comparison to Poland illustrates the point more directly.[81] Of the four major monuments erected in Warsaw 1945–1950, only one, the Brotherhood in Arms Memorial, dealt with the USSR. Another commemorated the Warsaw Jewish ghetto's uprising against Nazism while the other two dealt with the Polish astronomer Copernicus and the Polish monarch Sigismund. A collective Polish-Russian design, the Brotherhood in Arms Memorial was put up immediately after the war to commemorate "Soviet liberation" of the city. It was a massive granite pedestal on which stood realistic figures of Soviet soldiers in full battle dress. No other major monument dealing with Polish or international socialism or with the Soviets was erected in the city. Indeed, one observer of Polish public art has estimated that only about 5 percent of Warsaw's historical monuments could be described as "socialistic" even when something like 30 percent of all the city's monuments dealt with the memory of World War II. Overall, monument building in postwar Warsaw addressed cultural and national rather than socialist themes much more strongly than in Soviet-occupied Germany or the GDR. This difference stemmed in part from the Poles' long tradition of using monuments as symbols of national resistance and cultural survival. But it also reflected deep Polish ambiguity toward the Soviet liberators.

Despite the overpowering presence of objects such as the Treptower Park memorial, GDR commemorative practices were quite variable. Less extravagant monuments to the German Communist resistance were also extremely important to the regime, for instance. The history of early Communist agitation linking Rosa Luxemburg to antifascist resisters and finally to the early leadership of the GDR was symbolized in a cemetery and memorial at the Friedrichsfelde near the Treptow war memorial. Inaugurated in 1951, the site of large annual commemorative ceremonies, it featured gravestones for Luxemburg, the Communist party chief Ernst Thälmann, and other Resisters, and Wilhelm Pieck and Otto Grotewohl, the first president and first prime minister of the GDR respectively. The Berlin-Karlshorst memorial site was the building in which the Nazi regime made its unconditional surrender on 8 May 1945. Exhibits there combined memory of the Soviet victory with German antifascist heroes. A heroes' grove with urns containing the remains of executed German Communist resisters was set up in Dresden. The form of this site recalled both the heroes' groves of the post–World War I era and the use of the urn at the Neue Wache and Plötzensee memorials. In the same city, a documentation center and memorial were set up to commemorate more than a thousand political resisters executed in the former district court, the *Landgericht,* which after 1945 was part of the

Figure 39. An East Berlin school group commemorates Arno Phillipsthal, antifascist resister. Deutsches Historisches Museum.

Technical University of Dresden. These were only the most visible and well-known sites. Hardly a town or village in the former GDR was without a small memorial site or cemetery that symbolized Communist antifascist resistance to Hitler. Most such sites were adorned with wreaths or bouquets of flowers placed there by school groups, factory collectives, and individual mourners. By 1970 the memory landscape of Halle, a city of some 230,000 inhabitants, would have more than fifty commemorative plaques, statues, monuments, and cemetery sites, which cumulatively wove together the history of the formation of the Communist party, workers' struggles against the right-wing Kapp Putsch of 1920, antifascist resistance and death in the concentration camps, and the victorious creation and building up of socialist states.[82]

"That can hardly be only the mere expression of party ideology," wrote one observer in the late 1980s of such commemorative activity. "More than in the Federal Republic, the GDR has a stronger sense that remembering the victims of history is a daily obligation."[83] It is useful to note the difference between *legitimate* and *legitimizing* antifascism when considering such practices and sites.[84] Legitimate antifascism was based on the positive memories that the history of resistance to Nazism engendered and the ethical principles it implied. It was rooted in the *idea* of antifascism rather than the self-serving strategy of the regime, which used popular memory of resistance for its own political interests. Although engendered by regime policy, the innumerable monuments and rituals may also have spoken to this more quotidian, pious, and spontaneous form of antifascism.

A telling example of how memory of Communist resistance saturated daily life was in the renaming of streets. Street names were a significant element in the memory landscape in bombed-out cities such as Berlin, Dresden, and Cologne, where street signs were often the only objects standing in the middle of broad gray-brown stretches of rubble. There was much public support for renaming as many as one-fifth of Berlin's nearly two thousand streets, parks, bridges, and squares. Just sixteen days after the end of the war, the new Berlin civil administration met for the first time to discuss urgent problems such as the food supply and housing, but also among the topics was the renaming of streets—an indication of how important the symbolic element was even as the city was digging out from the Nazi carnage. The goal was to remove reminders of aristocratic, militarist, and Nazi traditions but at the same time to honor those heroes who had fought for a better Germany. Officially, renaming streets was under the jurisdiction of each of the separate municipalities within the Berlin conurbation. Although the names of Nazi heroes were removed, ambitious plans to enshrine the memory of resisters or socialist heroes in hundreds of West Berlin's postwar streets never got off the ground. A street was named after Stauffenberg, as we have seen, and in other Western cities such as Cologne, Hannover, Munich, and Hamburg streets or squares were also renamed after this resistance hero. But in the GDR the regime used its influence to turn the streetscape into a web of names recalling Soviet and German Communist heroes and resisters as well as Third World revolutionaries, other European Communists, and figures from the early German socialist and Communist movements, including Marx, Engels, the feminist Communist Clara Zetkin, and Rosa Luxemburg. No street name or square reminded East Berliners of Stauffenberg, and in the entire GDR, only one city, Leipzig, recalled the officer's feat of heroism. Although the East German authorities emphasized that Stauffenberg was less reactionary and anti-Soviet than many of his coconspirators, they could not bring themselves to include him in the canon of antifascist resistance fighters.[85]

Each renaming had its own peculiar history. In a typical example of

Nazi aggression against working-class foes, the Third Reich renamed the Bülowplatz in the Berlin proletarian district of Friedrichshain after the Nazi martyr Horst Wessel. After World War II, Horst Wessel's name was removed, but the old name was not returned. Instead, the square, on which the German Communist party headquarters and the editorial offices of the Communist newspaper *Die Rote Fahne* had stood in the Weimar Republic, received the name of Rosa Luxemburg. This was no idle gesture. Besides Luxemburg, authorities could have chosen the Weimar-era Communist leader Karl Liebknecht or the party head Ernst Thälmann, who had been murdered in the Buchenwald concentration camp in 1944. A 1946 map of the city in fact referred to the square as Liebknechtplatz, while another map from the same year still carried the name Horst-Wessel-Platz. But finally only Luxemburg's name seemed appropriate to the square that had once been a Communist nerve center. German Communist authorities emphasized that they sought a "German road to socialism" as early as 1945, and it was Luxemburg's impressive theoretical writings that seemed to be the most appropriate antecedent of this political goal. Luxemburg's stature as an intellectual also enabled GDR authorities to see her as the German equivalent to Lenin, even though Luxemburg and Lenin disagreed on questions of both theory and practice. Luxemburg's Polish background also made it possible for the GDR to exploit her memory when it promoted fraternal relations between Poland and East Germany, as happened in 1951 when the official newspaper *Neues Deutschland* referred to her as "the great champion of German-Polish friendship." Little was said about the fact that Luxemburg was also Jewish.[86]

THE ICONOGRAPHY OF MASS MURDER

The most important locations of East German antifascist remembrance were former concentration camp sites. In discussing this theme, it is important to point out that on German soil, public memory of the group of victims most systematically targeted by the Nazis, European Jews, would face extraordinary obstacles. Any nation would have tremendous difficulty absorbing the historical fact that its leadership had undertaken a racial war with the goal of total annihilation of "the enemy." Recollections of the Holocaust in these decades would rarely take account of the act of mass killing or of the individuals responsible for the crimes. The enormity of the crimes made such a viewpoint impossible until well after World War II. Until Germans faced up to their role as perpetrators, they would reconstruct identities around distorted images of the victims. Some would resort to quasi-metaphysical reflections on the "darkness" that befell the German "soul" under Hitler, a perspective thoroughly consistent with the language of Romanticism. And still others would argue that the point was not to dwell on the past but to ensure that nothing of a similar nature would occur again. This approach, held by many morally courageous and upright Germans, would place a premium on contemporary political activism or solemn religiosity rather than on systematic historical reflection on the "hows" and "whys" of the Holocaust.[87]

One of the most serious obstacles to memory was that the major extermination centers were outside Germany and that few non-Jewish Germans had experienced life in the major killing centers as opposed to the camps for mainly political prisoners.[88] Life in these camps had been harsh, to be sure, but the conditions were nonetheless very different than in those in Auschwitz or Treblinka. At the end of the war, only about 5 percent of all concentration camp prisoners were Germans, and most of them were there for reasons of political affiliation. Most Germans' experiences with the Holocaust derived not from direct contact with the killing process but with its preliminaries or outcomes: persecutions, deportations, the nationwide pogrom of November 1938, and the deaths in Belsen, Buchenwald, Dachau, and other camps of thousands of Jewish prisoners brutally deported from killing centers on Polish soil in the last, desperate months of the war. This perspective was typified in the West German public in the first decade after the war, when the diary of Anne Frank, published in 1949, became a bestseller. Although this moving account put a human face on a victim of the Holocaust, especially for younger German readers, it dealt with life *before* entrance into the camp system, the terrible workings of which were barely imaginable.[89]

Memory of the Holocaust was a good deal more abstract in this sense than was memory based on direct experience with the Allied bombings of German cities or with the rape and murder of innumerable German women by Soviet soldiers, who were urged on in East Prussia by signs reading "Take revenge on the Hitlerites."[90] Memory always reflects the interests and experiences of those doing the remembering. Even though they were not set up as extermination centers, Dachau, Buchenwald, and Belsen became symbols of the Holocaust in Anglo-American eyes because these camps were liberated by British (in the case of Belsen) or U.S. troops. In Germany, people with no direct experience of the camps often made up the majority of those who commemorated Holocaust victims, and if commemoration was at first oblique, then this reflected the rather oblique nature of many Germans' relationship to the events in question. Too, many of the initial postwar books, articles, and memoirs about the killing centers in the East often came from Allied sources and from Jews—the two were often the same. This only increased the skepticism of older Germans, who bitterly remembered Allied propaganda stories of atrocities by "the Hun" in World War I in Belgium and France, and of younger Germans, who, it must be remembered, had grown up with the anti-Semitic rhetoric of the Nazi state, and who in some cases continued to express anti-Semitic prejudices. But even professional historians outside Germany reproduced this skepticism, writing the first comprehensive scholarly treatises on the genocide that pointedly avoided using survivors' testimonies in the interest of objectivity and analytical distance.[91]

In terms of both iconographical vocabularies and cultural understandings, Germans and Europeans were unprepared to memorialize something as momentous as the Holocaust. Much of the iconography of death after World War I was derived from Christian and national themes. These were not only unconvincing or offensive to the survivors of the Holocaust; they also renewed the cultural legitimacy of the perpetrators themselves. Even more seriously, Christian authors took up traditional anti-Semitic themes, decrying the genocide but calling for a "different anti-Semitism" and insisting that Christians would continue to struggle against "Jewish hegemony."[92] Europeans often responded to the mass deaths of World War I with individual or familial perspectives even if they endorsed the nationalist myths of the war experience. The soldier-hero of Verdun or the Somme was both a patriot and family man, a father, husband, son, or brother. But the Holocaust was defined by anonymous mass murder in which individual life histories and even whole families were extinguished and made unrecoverable to future generations. The political scientist Hannah Arendt wrote of the concentration camps as sites of "organized oblivion" where the goal was "to treat people as if they never existed." In Arendt's (and many others') view, this totalitarian domination of the human soul made individual as well as public memory impossible after the war.[93]

Yet Europeans did remember. Instead of an iconography of individual suffering and death, Europeans would resort initially to collective motifs, including most notably themes of national martyrdom and resistance. Even then, the fact that no internationally valid meaning of the Holocaust was established left the problem of memorialization open to much controversy. The issue had been broached quite early, at least in literary terms, when in 1943 Ernst Sommer, a German-speaking Czech Jew in exile in London, wrote a novel about a Jewish work camp in occupied Poland. Published in 1944 and available to German audiences one year after the war, *Revolte der Heiligen (Revolt of the Saints),* while depicting heroic Jewish resistance against Nazi persecution, anticipated the unprecedented difficulties facing those who would try to represent the camps in literature. The great artist Henry Moore, selected to chair an international competition for the design of a Holocaust memorial at Auschwitz, conceded the difficulty of memory as it pertained to the plastic arts when he asked in 1958: "Is it in fact possible to create a work of art that can express the emotions engendered by Auschwitz?" Some scholars, including most notably Berel Lang, have responded to Moore's question in the negative, arguing that only "literal" representations could adequately address the memory of this, the century's most viciously literal event. Taking a related view on the victims' memory, Lawrence Langer has argued that the oral testimony of the camps' survivors "resists the organizing impulse of moral theory and art."[94]

The sites of former concentration camps were among the most moving reconstructions of the entire postwar period. Europe was covered with more than sixteen hundred concentration camps and their satellites during the Nazi occupation of Europe.[95] Many such camps were destroyed in the last stages of the war, wholly or partially dismantled after liberation, used for firewood and building materials, or reworked by the new authorities to house prisoners of war, refugees, or (as in the case of Stalinist reprisals) political prisoners. If the sites survived as postwar memorials, they did so almost always as reconstructions, that is, as products of new framing strategies. As such, they experienced all the problems reconstructions did in their historical "afterlife." In the ruins around Auschwitz-Birkenau local farmers and their families plowed fields, strolled, rode bicycles, and fished; their activities turned the camp into an everyday "landscape."[96] Nearer major population centers, former camp sites were either covered over with new housing and highways, or, to the extent their remnants could still be seen, integrated with the cityscape and its daily machinery of existence. This integration tangibly and symbolically obfuscated the traces of the surrounding community's involvement with the camp when it was in operation, an involvement that has still not received sufficient scholarly attention.[97] When significant parts of a former camp were still extant, they required an apparatus of explanation—informational plaques and signs, exhibits, photographs, reconstructions—in order to be made meaningful to viewers. The meaningfulness of this apparatus was often entirely dependent on the language in which its message was given. At Auschwitz, the modest and out-of-the-way "Jewish pavilion," opened in 1978, spoke to the issue of the Holocaust, but its displays were in English and French only, and thus inaccessible to many Polish and other visitors.[98] As for memorialization outside Germany, the victims of the camps would be remembered as national heroes. And heroization was in turn based on a more general European blindness. "It seems that the awareness, the *prise de conscience* of the specificity of the Jewish experience," writes historian Pieter Lagrou, "had not permeated contemporary public opinion."[99]

At the most notorious Nazi concentration camp, Auschwitz, in southwestern Poland, only the part of the camp originally established to subjugate Poles was preserved intact, and even this camp was a reduced and distilled version of what had been a much larger complex. A 1947 law established the camp museum to commemorate "the martyrdom of the Polish nation and other nations in Oświęcim [Auschwitz]." The museum contained large glass bins of artifacts including human hair, luggage, eyeglasses, shoes, and clothing of the victims. Pavilions at Auschwitz-I commemorated different nations' citizens at the camp (victims from twenty-three countries had been murdered there) but also downplayed the fact that the majority had been Jews. A gas chamber and its ovens were reconstructed from rubble left behind by the Nazis after they dynamited the camp in November 1944. The site of the mass murder of most Jews lay two miles away, in the vast, 430-acre Birkenau camp, where the four main crematoria were in ruins, and where the inscription of a memorial failed to mention that most of the camp's victims were Jews. Fifty years after the end of the war, visitors could still uncover flints of human bone in the fields and pond near the camp where the ashes of the victims were dumped. An official tour guide to Poland mentioned both Auschwitz and Birkenau but failed to point out they were sites of Judeocide. A guide from the 1980s would note that "Auschwitz was selected as the place where the program of complete extermination of the Jews was to be realized," but it did little to specify the size of the victim groups.[100]

The memory of Jewish victims was not so badly effaced at Treblinka, an equally deadly former Nazi concentration camp in Poland where none of the original camp buildings stood at the end of the war. Here a dramatic and deservedly famous memorial of seventeen thousand granite shards set in concrete around a twenty-six-foot obelisk was dedicated

Figure 40. Auschwitz, February 1945. Archiv für Kunst und Geschichte, Berlin.

in 1964. A menorah graced the top of the obelisk, and the densely packed and unevenly spaced shards reminded many of the ancient Jewish cemeteries of Eastern Europe. The aforementioned Polish tour guide did not fail to mention that Treblinka consisted of both a slave labor camp and an extermination center, and that more than eight-hundred thousand Jews were gassed here.[101] But Auschwitz remained the most well-known symbol of the Holocaust, and the displacement of memory of Jewish victims there was paradigmatic.

That Auschwitz was a site of brutal Nazi mass murders perpetrated against Poles, that the Polish nation was the object of an unprecedented campaign of annihilation, and that many Poles paid for their lives by resisting the Nazis—all this could hardly be denied. But the tendency to avoid narrating the history of the camp in all its complexity was a serious distortion. This reluctance was not only a function of the incomplete or ruined character of the historical site, for in another place of Nazi atrocities, the Polish city of Łódź, no historical markers indicated where the Jewish ghetto had stood even though most of the original buildings survived. Such perspectives befitted a country that traditionally called itself "the Christ of Nations," an identification with suffering and redemption that in the postwar years excluded Jews almost entirely from historical memory. When Jews were included, their suffering was put on a par with that of other non-Jewish Poles. In 1978, the Polish minister of culture Janusz Wieczorek would say that Auschwitz and other sites of the Holocaust were "all stages of extermination, stations of the Cross of Polish Jews and Jews treacherously brought from other countries of Europe. We know their gehenna [Calvary], the misery of Poles." In this view, Jews and Poles not only shared first place in the hierarchy of victims, but political extermination, the fate of Poles, and racial extermination, the fate of Jews, were equated in a generalized memory of "the misery of Poles."[102]

It should not be overlooked that, until the fall of Communism, the official estimate of 4 million victims at Auschwitz-Birkenau (instead of the more accurate 1.1 to 1.5 million) enabled the regime to enhance memory of the misery of Poles and Soviet POWs at the camp at the expense of Jews and many others who died there. Nor should it be overlooked that in using religious metaphors of the Cross and Calvary, the Polish official also rendered Jewish victimization in purely Christian terms. This tradition would be strengthened throughout the postwar years, most notoriously in the 1980s, when a group of Carmelite sisters occupied a building adjacent to the camp where poison gas had been stored by the Nazis. They were responding to the message of Pope John Paul II, who in 1979 had called the site "the Golgotha of the contemporary world," and who eight years earlier, while still Cardinal Karol Wojtyla, had called for the erection of a church there to commemorate a rabidly anti-Semitic priest, Maximilian Kolbe, who was beatified for having voluntarily exchanged himself for another Polish prisoner at Auschwitz. Jewish groups and many others were offended by the Carmelite sisters' actions and by the twenty-four-foot wooden cross whose shadow loomed over the site of Judeocide. The controversy aroused bitter recriminations among Poles, Jews, and the Catholic Church, and was solved only by papal intervention in 1989, when the removal of the nuns and the building of a new convent were assured. It also highlighted a central difference between Christian and Jewish memory, the former demanding redemptive prayer and commemoration of martyrs at the site of so much suffering, the latter demanding only that defiled ground be left untouched and unconsecrated. Similar tensions emerged in the late 1990s, when without official approval, Polish Christians erected small wooden crosses at the site.[103]

The Poles were not the only ones to use such reconstructions (or to ignore extant artifacts) to manipulate history. Yugoslavia suppressed information about a major extermination camp in which perhaps hundreds of thousands of Orthodox Serbs, oppositional Croats, Jews, and Sinti and Roma were killed in World War II.[104] Situated in Jasenovac, a small city in Slavonia on the border with Bosnia, the camp was run by the Ustasha party, the Croatian fascists who from 1941 to 1945 erected the violent Independent State of Croatia, under Nazi Germany's protection. With the support of many members of the Catholic Church, the Ustashe undertook a brutal campaign of forced conversions and executions against Serbs and others. Even Nazi officials were shocked by the viciousness with which the Ustashe liquidated their victims. The camp commander, Vjekoslav Luburić, took special pleasure in informing prisoners of the date and method of their forthcoming torture and liquidation. The Ustashe shut down the camp and removed all traces of the massacre in April 1945, and soon thereafter the Yugoslav army captured the camp and demolished and burned its buildings.

Mass graves at Jasenovac continued to reveal their ghastly secrets in excavations and investigations undertaken by Bosnians and Serbs in the postwar decades. In 1968 officials created a Memorial Park at the site. Partly because of the Yugoslav Communist leader Tito's program of fostering harmony between ethnic communities, the extent of Ustasha brutality was never examined fully. Instead, Jasenovac, like so many former camps throughout the Eastern Bloc, became a site of memory for "victims of fascism." Nor was study of the complicity of certain leaders of the Catholic Church encouraged. Even so, in 1978 Franjo Tudjman, later to be the leader of post-Communist Croatia, told an émigré newspaper that memory of World War II and Jasenovac was being used within Yugoslavia "to exaggerate the collective and permanent guilt of the Croatian people." This, in combination with other statements and interviews, landed him in prison. Tudjman was penalized less for his fanning the flames of memory than for his implying that Croatia's treatment under Communism was different from that of the other member republics.[105] After the fall of Communism, no state in Europe has been less able or less determined than Croatia to come to terms with its fascist past. Croats and Serbs continued to debate the number of victims of Jasenovac, and many Serbs used the memory of Jasenovac as a pretext for violence against the Croats in the Yugoslav Civil War. Jasenovac continues to have the same meaning for Serbs as Auschwitz does for Jews.[106] In 1992 the Croatian Diet exacerbated tensions even more by planning to have all Croatian victims of World War II moved to a central memorial complex at Jasenovac. This tendency toward homogenization of memory of the victims of the war occurred in reunified Germany as well.

Other examples abound. Well into the postwar period, exhibits at the Mauthausen camp near Linz, the harshest of all concentration camps within the boundaries of the Third Reich, depicted Austria as Nazism's "first victim." [107] This perspective, encouraged initially by the Allies during World War II to encourage Austrian resistance to Nazism, later became the official narrative of the postwar Second Republic.[108] Official historiography overlooked the deep strain of Austrian anti-Semitism, which was widespread before Hitler incorporated Austria into the Third Reich in 1938, which gained violent expression in many Austrians' enthusiastic participation in the Final Solution, and which remained important to Austrian identity after 1945. Not until the 1980s was this version of the Austrian past seriously challenged, first in the Waldheim Affair,[109] then in the building of sculptor Alfred Hrdlicka's Monument against War and Fascism on the Albertinaplatz in Vienna. By including references to the Holocaust and to Mauthausen in his monument, Hrdlicka portrayed Austrians not only as victims but as perpetrators as well. But even this gesture had ambiguous effects. One part of the monument depicted a hunched-over, street-washing Jew, a reference to the many Austrians who actively humiliated and beat Jews in the streets of Vienna in the public euphoria following Austria's union with Germany. But tired tourists and shoppers used the crouched figure as a bench, and when Hrdlicka placed a thorn of crowns on top of the street-washing Jew to prevent such uses, Viennese Jews understandably protested this use of Christian iconography to depict Jewish suffering.

The French built a memorial and museum at Natzweiler-Struthof, southwest of Strasbourg, because it was the only concentration camp the Germans put up on French territory. More than forty thousand people entered Struthof and ten to twelve thousand died there. But the French ignored internment and transit camps erected and run by the French at Gurs, Les Milles, and other sites through which Jews and others were deported to Germany and the East. Such reticence emerged directly from a larger public inability, lasting until the 1970s, to come to terms with the fact that the French had been deeply anti-Semitic without the prompting of the Nazis in both the occupied and unoccupied zones in World War II. Even in countries with no direct experience of the Holocaust, distorting or forgetting the history of the event was the rule. In

England and the United States, the reluctance of public officials as well as trade unions to accept more Holocaust refugees and government unwillingness to bomb mass killing centers remained controversial and, until recently, largely unexamined topics for the general public.[110] In this broader international context of distortion or denial, the intensity of German societal involvement with the history of the concentration camps from a relatively early point after the war was impressive even if its results were not always what one would have wished.

On one level, of course, German memory of the concentration camps was necessarily different and more intense than that of the Poles, the French, or the Croats. The Nazis had undertaken a brutal campaign of military conquest, political liquidation, and racial war. Their totalitarian system brooked no resistance and reduced enemies to oblivion. Nazi concentration camps, especially the major extermination centers, raised mass murder to a new level of sophistication that deserves to be called industrial mass killing. One can compare European memories of the camps, then, but it is impossible to overlook the incomparability of what the Nazis did there. This point makes it somewhat easier to explain why in West Germany a more substantial and critical memory of genocide eventually developed—and why from one perspective there were fewer obstacles to this kind of memory in Germany than in other European states. To take the Polish example again, the Poles' record toward the Jews was of a "radically different moral weight," as Irwin-Zarecka correctly pointed out in her study of Jews in 1980s Poland. "But precisely because it is so much more ambiguous than what Germany has to come to terms with," she continued, "precisely because it can so easily be read as a clean record, in short, because it has so much potential to be neutralized, it becomes both extremely difficult and absolutely necessary to examine it with the sharpest of critical eyes."[111] Let us turn a critical eye to German memory as it crystallized around the remains of Nazi concentration camps.

Of all the sites that contributed to antifascist remembrance in East Germany, three concentration camp sites were of central significance. The Curatorium for the Building of National Memorials in Buchenwald, Sachsenhausen, and Ravensbrück was set up in 1955 to ensure not only ideological correctness but also uniformity between the three sites. Functionaries of the SED, the Free German Youth, and former camp inmates served on the curatorium. The sites were to be financed through government funds, donations, and contributions from survivors' organizations.

The sites were to concentrate on three main subjects: fascism and monopoly capitalism, persecution and resistance, and liberation and education through historical knowledge.

Buchenwald became the major jewel in the GDR's commemorative crown—some called it the "Red Olympus"—not only because it was the site of a prisoners' "insurrection" in April 1945 but because it already had a deep national significance.[112] Established in 1937 near the famous city of Weimar, the Buchenwald camp was set up with the legendary "Goethe oak" as its center. This was the spot on a green hill where the great poet and scholar sat with his friends Eckermann or Schiller and contemplated literature and the Thuringian landscape. Nature conservation legislation enabled Germans to build a fence around the great oak and preserve it when the surrounding forest was cleared to make way for the concentration camp.[113] The oak was burned in an air raid in August 1944 and its forlorn stump, now filled with concrete to prevent it from rotting, may still be seen today at the original spot in the camp.

Exploiting popular memory, Himmler tried to invoke the meaning of the place as the cultural center of Germany, a meaning that would be expressed again when the former camp was inaugurated as a GDR memorial. The main camp and satellite camps housed 239,000 inmates, 56,500 of whom lost their lives due to executions, malnutrition, or exhaustion from brutal forced labor. Inmates capable of work did so mostly in the armaments industry for Junkers, Krupp, BMW, and other firms. The entrance to the camp carried the words "To each his own," a chilling phrase meant to be read by inmates from *inside* the camp rather than from the other side. Viewing the gate from the *Appellplatz,* where inmates answered roll calls, prisoners would understand it was their indisputable fate to be worked to death or killed. It was in the courtyard of the Buchenwald crematorium that the Communist party head Ernst Thälmann was murdered in September 1944 (although Thälmann had not in fact spent much time at Buchenwald), making the camp all the more important to regime ideology. The SS ran the camp according to the principle of "annihilation through labor," and as in other camps, grotesque medical experiments also took place there.

The majority of Germans at the camp (probably fewer than 10 percent of the total at liberation) consisted of political prisoners from the Communist and Social Democratic parties, whose members discussed the shape of a future socialist Germany while interned at Buchenwald.

Their actions would later give credence to the view that Buchenwald was the seedbed of the postwar Communist party in Germany and the beginning of the first socialist state on German soil. The GDR would of course ignore or suppress evidence, taken in direct testimony by U.S. military officials soon after the camp's liberation, that Communist inmates pursued their political goals as ruthlessly as the SS did theirs. Highly organized and determined to survive, the hundred or so Communist inmates active in underground politics at Buchenwald were locked in a battle over status and influence with criminal elements among camp prisoners.[114]

Since most Jews were being sent directly to extermination camps in the East, few of them appeared for long in the ranks of Buchenwald's "permanent" inmates, although the ones that did would later identify with the camp in political rather than religious terms. Along with partisans and others from as many as thirty different nationalities, German Communists and Social Democrats established a multinational camp committee that shared information, organized a clandestine memorial ceremony for Thälmann, and even gathered weapons in preparation for an uprising against the SS camp guards. The "uprising" came on the afternoon of 11 April 1945 after the SS's murderous evacuation of prisoners left more than twenty thousand inmates behind, and after the camp commandant formally handed over control to a committee of prisoners. Inmates seized weapons, turned off the electrified fence, and at 3:15 drove the remaining watchtower guards out of the camp. The takeover would later be commemorated by freezing the camp clock at this time. The idea of capturing a moment in history was widespread throughout the European memory landscape in this period, as we have noted for Oradour-sur-Glane and Warsaw. After liberation by U.S. troops late in the afternoon of the eleventh, the surviving prisoners, on 19 April 1945, made the "Oath of Buchenwald." They said: "On this parade-ground that has seen the horrors of fascism, we swear to all humanity that our fight will not be over until the people of the world have called each and every one of these criminals to justice! Our quest is to tear out the Nazi evil by its roots. Our goal is a new world of peace and freedom."[115]

As early as 15 or 16 April, former inmates made two piles of corpses from individuals who had died of disease and malnutrition since the liberation of the camp. Flanked by wreaths and placed in the courtyard of the camp crematorium and an adjacent spot, these "memorials" were reconstructions of a gruesome pile of cadavers left behind by SS operatives

Figure 41. Cadaver memorial, Buchenwald, April 1945. State Historical Society of Wisconsin, Whi(X3)51764.

unable to dispose of the bodies before fleeing from advancing U.S. troops five days earlier. Under the order of General George Patton, commander of the U.S. Third Army, American soldiers forced thousands of Weimar citizens to view the grisly scenes and later exhibited newly reconstructed piles of corpses for visiting U.S. and British political delegations. The U.S. Army Signal Corps photographed these events to document and narrate German war crimes for both the U.S. and the German public. The cadaver memorials reflected what amounted to a deep, albeit temporary, rupture in the memory landscape. Without reference to any preexisting mode of memorialization, the unburied bodies referred only to themselves. They collapsed representation and the represented in a grim, horrific tableau. They suggested "no sign or symbol but the mute identity of the dead with themselves and their death."[116]

Yet even as the cadaver memorials suggested an end to traditional practices of the memory landscape, after liberation of Buchenwald, prior modes of memorialization were continued as they were usurped and transformed. Not far from the main camp stood a Bismarck monument that had been dedicated in 1901. The monument was a popular center of nationalist celebrations as well as a tourist attraction and a site where Buchenwald SS members held their annual summer festival. In early 1945, the SS deposited more than one thousand urns containing the ashes of Buchenwald dead in the vaults of the Bismarck monument, and in March and April of 1945, when fuel shortages curtailed the operation of the crematorium, close to three thousand corpses were deposited in four mass graves to the south of the monument. The U.S. army and the Buchenwald survivors' committee used the Bismarck monument site to bury other individuals who died after liberation. At first, survivors of the camp decorated the burial mounds, situated in front of the monument to the Iron Chancellor, with wreaths and flowers. Later, survivors and local authorities would add more elaborate landscaping, creating commemorative bowl-shaped spaces where the mass graves had been, and planting shrubs and linden, pine, and birch trees in a "grove of honor," or *Ehrenhain* (dedicated in 1949), which recalled the heroes' groves of the interwar memory culture. On the second annual Buchenwald Day, 12–13 April 1947, survivors of the camp held a commemoration, again using the mass graves as foci for speeches and songs that memorialized the still unidentified dead. A wooden red triangle symbolizing the red patch worn by Buchenwald political prisoners hung from the Bismarck monument. Used in a commemoration of camp victims in Weimar a year before, the red triangle signaled the start of a process of "political functionalization" of survivors' memory by East German Communists.[117] The monument itself would be torn down in 1949 and replaced in 1958 by the massive belltower of the GDR national memorial at Buchenwald. What had once been a site of nationalist allegiance to Bismarck, a tourist spot, an SS festival space, and a focus of commemoration of concentration camp victims would become the center of an East German memorial complex celebrating antifascist resistance.[118]

By July 1945 the U.S. soldiers occupying the Buchenwald camp were replaced by Soviets. They in turn used the camp until 1950 to incarcerate more than twenty-eight thousand former Nazi functionaries and opponents of Stalinism, more than seven thousand (some estimates are as high as thirteen thousand) of whom died due to mistreatment and poor living conditions. Left in a ruinous condition, the greater part of the camp was torn down, leaving only the camp gate and its adjoining buildings, two watchtowers, a section of the barbed wire, the crematorium, and two other structures. Outside the camp the well-built former SS barracks and other buildings used by the Russians remained. Soviet use of the camp had made it impossible to consider a German memorial at the original site. But the Russian departure left open the possibility of using both the former camp and the area where the mass graves had been found for memorial purposes. The SED had originally wanted to leave standing only a few buildings from the former camp, planting the remaining empty spaces with trees. Practical considerations prevented the party from destroying more than it did, however. Although the prisoners' barracks disappeared, their layout was marked with stones and the preserved remains of the foundations. The memory of Thälmann's death was particularly important to the East German authorities, who preserved the crematorium and erected a commemorative plaque and a bust of the slain Communist chief.

The initiative for a permanent memorial at the Bismarck monument site came from the Association of Persecutees of the Nazi Regime (the previously mentioned VVN) of the Soviet zone, which lobbied vigorously enough to create tensions with the SED,[119] whose leaders dissolved the association in 1953 because its aims were allegedly now official policy. In its stead, the SED created a Committee of Antifascist Resistance Fighters, which established political resisters as the symbol for all victims of Nazism. Although veteran anti-Nazi Resistance fighters made up no more than 1 percent of the total GDR population, they were seen as the ideological elite and the "founding fathers" of the new state.[120] Yet the regime drastically restricted memory of the scope and meaning of their experience, defining resisters only as those who acknowledged the SED's leadership and continued to support the GDR regime. This was the equivalent to the Federal Republic's 1956 law on compensation to the victims of Nazism, which refused financial reparations to those who opposed the constitutional order after May 1949. In both cases, the regimes retrospectively defined who would enter the pantheon of resisters and victims on the basis of their current political standing.

The Buchenwald Committee of the VVN originally wanted to maintain the Bismarck monument and integrate it into a memorial complex. But the decision was finally taken by the VVN, under considerable pressure from the SED, to destroy the structure. The Soviets supplied the dynamite. Although this occurred in 1949, material and labor shortages as well as technical problems and political infighting delayed further work at the site. It was only in September 1958 that the bell tower and other elements of the new memorial were dedicated.[121] At the inaugural ceremony, GDR president Otto Grotewohl emphasized not only the importance of the memorial to the GDR but to the entire German ethnie.

Figure 42. GDR dedication of Buchenwald Memorial, with Walter and Lotte Ulbricht and Rosa Thälmann (far right), 1958. Deutsches Historisches Museum.

"Buchenwald lies in the middle of Germany," argued Grotewohl, and to remember what transpired there was to undertake "an obligation of the entire German Volk."[122] This reaffirmed the tradition of seeing the forested area around Weimar and Buchenwald as the cultural center of Germany. But now, at the heart of the scenic nation, were the traces of a vicious dictatorship against whose brutality only German Communists fought. Even then, the memorial commemorated the ideas of inevitable victory over fascism and a new socialist existence much more than it drew attention to the everyday and often quite unheroic struggles of those who had lived through the camps. This orientation emerged directly from conflicts between the wartime Communist leadership in exile and the rank and file. As for former Communist inmates of Buchenwald, the most prominent among them were politically emasculated from 1946 to 1952, and one of them, Ernst Busse, would die in a Soviet gulag.[123]

The Buchenwald site became known as the "Kyffhäuser of the GDR,"[124] linking antifascist resistance in the concentration camp to a

Figure 43. Buchenwald Memorial, 1958. Gedenkstätte Buchenwald.

national memorial at the former site of the Bismarck monument, both symbolizing a world-historical struggle for peace and socialism. In contrast to the austere remnants of the camp, the Buchenwald memorial stressed spectacle and monumentality. Not surprisingly, its key referent was the Treptower Park monument of the Red Army. Like national and war monuments of the German past, the Buchenwald memorial was to be seen for miles around and surrounded by a huge space big enough for ten thousand participants. Like most previous monuments, it was to avoid abstract iconography in favor of direct and figurative representations. Like the Treptow monument, the Buchenwald memorial would not primarily be a mournful representation of death but a German victory monument. It is not inaccurate to say that the triumphalism of its various components created "Hegelian moments in stone." [125]

In James Young's words, "The most prominent architects in the country were enlisted to enact a vision of great roads of blood and sacrifice leading to landscaped mountainsides, crowned by victory monuments overlooking the beautiful Ettersberg Valley." [126] An essentially Christian symbolism of pilgrimage and salvation informed the site. Visitors were instructed to begin their tour of the complex along the "blood avenue," the approach to the camp built by prisoners themselves. After touring that, they made their way to the memorial site, where they would de-

Figure 44. School assembly at Fritz Cremer's *Revolt of the Prisoners,* Buchenwald, 1958. Deutsches Historisches Museum.

scend a path into the reconstructed ring graves, dramatic reminders of the "night of fascism." Ascending the "avenue of nations," lined with eighteen pylons that recalled Greek commemorative traditions, they would approach a final ring grave and then make another ascent into the "light of freedom." Here they would encounter Fritz Cremer's 1958 bronze statue *Revolt of the Prisoners,* which depicts eleven heroic concentration camp prisoners, each symbolizing a stage in the growth of antifascist consciousness, looking out over the green Saale River Valley below and imploring all visitors to further action. Looming up over Cremer's creation was the belltower, itself reminiscent of a church steeple and bell. The dialectics of the complex—the concentration camp and the memorial, darkness and light, night and day, the graves and Cremer's heroic statuary, death and resurrection—would finally be sublated inside the tower as visitors would ascend a staircase leading to an opening in the top of the structure. Here distinctions between slavery and freedom disappeared as ascent and light became one.[127] All this amounted to a monument to the future as much as the past, a status reaffirmed constantly in the GDR in commemorations attended by socialist youth groups, school classes, and military inductees. Buchenwald, at the geographical and cultural center of Germany, reflected the assumption that German national identity—indeed the German ethnie—could now be symbolized most effectively in a reconstructed landscape of antifascist monuments, authentic ruins, and nature.

The second largest reconstruction of a concentration camp site in the GDR was Sachsenhausen, near Oranienburg north of Berlin, which had also been used by the SS to torture and work political prisoners to death. Almost one hundred thousand prisoners died at this site. Just as they did at Buchenwald, the Soviets decided to use the camp to intern Germans after the war. They created a facility with as many as sixty thousand prisoners, the largest internment camp in the Soviet occupation zone. As many as thirty thousand lost their lives there.[128] The East German state resolved to turn the camp into a national memorial to the victims of fascism in the 1950s, and in 1961 the site was inaugurated. Besides maintaining several original buildings intact, officials reconstructed two prisoners' barracks with their stark interiors. The goal was authenticity and documentary accuracy. A museum documented the antifascist resistance of prisoners from nineteen nations, most of whom were members of the Communist party. A huge memorial forum and a Monument of Nations would later be erected. The inauguration ceremony on 23 April 1961 reflected the GDR's use of the site in contemporary politics. "We fighters against fascism, military, and war vow at this holy place to engage all our powers for a general and comprehensive world disarmament and for lasting international peace," swore the participants of the ceremony.[129]

The "fighters against fascism, military, and war" recalled a masculine history of victimization, resistance, and triumphal struggle for socialism. At only one former concentration camp site in the GDR did women have the potential of being at the center of a public memory of Nazism. This fact alone suggests a major distortion in the evolving memory of the period. It was after all women, the bearers of the next generation, who were the largest single group murdered in the camps after the men had fled or been evacuated and sent into forced labor. The largest women's concentration camp was at Ravensbrück in the northern German state of Neubrandenburg. The camp was set up in 1938 to provide the regime with female workers for the armaments industry. Men would also be in-

Figure 45. Former prisoners of Ravensbrück, September 1949. Deutsches Historisches Museum.

terned in another part of the complex. By war's end some ninety-two thousand women and children had died at Ravensbrück. It was to their memory that former inmates dedicated a flag consisting of the red triangles worn by camp prisoners in September 1949. Rosa Thälmann, a Communist deputy and widow of the murdered Communist party leader, began agitating for a memorial at the site in the early 1950s. Although she had the support of the government, a large part of what had been the camp was taken over by the Soviet army after the war, and thus the memorial, officially opened in 1959, was a reduction and reconstruction of the original site consisting of the original commandant's headquarters, the camp wall, the crematorium, and the camp prison. While the exhibits and museum at the camp attested to women's resistance to fascism, they also reaffirmed a masculinist bias by portraying women in conventional roles. Instead of hand grenades and radio transmitters, the stuff of masculine resistance, the exhibits showed needlework and dolls fashioned secretly by female inmates. Monuments at the camp depicted women less as active historical agents than as stubborn survivors. "In the historical iconography of GDR sculpture," wrote Claudia Koonz, "heroic males resist and women (if depicted at all) persevere." But this was only a hyperextended version of a broader tendency, in popular representations as well as historical scholarship, to ignore or downplay the actions and plight of women in the Holocaust.[130]

The GDR used concentration camps to formulate a myth of resistance, but the Federal Republic was much less certain about commemorative uses of the camps.[131] The contrast between a centrally organized, ideologically focused memory of Nazism and a more local and discordant public memory in the West is again evident. But this was not a specifically German pattern; Eastern European governments directed Holocaust memorialization on the basis of socialist principles while in the West the memorials were usually left to a memory marketplace shaped by a combination of official agencies, private and local initiatives, tourism, and pilgrimages. I take the Dachau memorial as an illustrative preliminary example for the Federal Republic.[132] Dachau was the first concentration camp of National Socialist Germany and one of the best-known former camp sites due to its accessibility from Munich and its liberation by U.S. troops. More than two hundred thousand prisoners entered its gates during its twelve-year reign of brutality. From 1945 until about 1970, the camp had an uneasy existence in public memory of the Holocaust. The camp was originally for political prisoners; at first there were few Jews in Dachau, and those who were interned there were identified more by their political affiliation than race, as in Buchenwald. Sinti and Roma, oppositional clergy, criminals, and homosexuals were also imprisoned at Dachau. Conditions were relatively survivable compared to concentration camps in the East. But in the last stages of the war, Dachau would turn into a death camp as malnourished and disease-ridden Jews from the extermination centers were evacuated to the West. When the camp was liberated by the U.S. army on 29 April 1945, they found thirty thousand starving inmates and piles of corpses in cattle cars near the camp. These were the images that supplanted the previous years of the Dachau camp, turning the site into a moving and emotional symbol of the Holocaust.

After the war the site underwent continual transformation. First it served the U.S. army's prosecution of SS officers accused of war crimes. From 1948 to 1960 a part of it became a refugee center for Sudetenländer expelled from their homes by the Czech government. In the largest section of the camp, where during the Nazi period the SS maintained barracks and other facilities, the U.S. military set up a huge food-processing center servicing U.S. soldiers in Germany and Austria. Throughout such uses, the physical properties of the site were changed many times. Using the large crematorium, Dachau survivors with the support of the U.S. military created the first exhibit dealing with what had gone on in the camp, including graphic photographs of a prisoner being electrocuted on the outer barbed-wire perimeter of the camp. This exhibit was closed in 1953 when local Dachau officials protested that it damaged the image of the city. Survivors' groups visiting the camp were shocked at the run-down conditions of the camp barracks, the closing of the exhibit, and the city fathers' resistance to memory. The survivors enlisted the help of the U.S. military to open a provisional museum in the crematorium complex.

Commemorative practices in and near the camp complex mirrored the interests and memories of Holocaust victims. A commemorative plaque on a Dachau bank marked the spot where six camp inmates and Dachau citizens were shot by the SS after opposing deadly evacuation marches. The site was dedicated in 1947 by the Association of Persecutees of the Nazi Regime. Dachau would become an important site of Cold War anti-Communism as the concentration camp was seen not only as a symbol of Nazism, a "brown" totalitarianism, but of the "red" totalitarianism of Soviet Russia. Christian themes fit this angle of memory well as the churches could link recollection of their persecution at the hands of the Nazis with their contemporary opposition to the godlessness of Communist states. The first monument to be erected at Dachau honored Catholics, and especially the German and Polish Catholic clergy, who lost their lives at the camp. There were close to three thousand clergy imprisoned at Dachau. Dedicated in 1960, this "monument of atonement" featured a large stone cylinder with an opening in the front leading to a space filled only with a large cross and crown of thorns. In the early 1960s the International Dachau Committee planned a central memorial for the camp, tearing down the housing used by the refugees, reconstructing two model barracks, covering the grounds in white gravel, and establishing a museum and documentation center. From 1964 to 1967 a Jewish memorial temple was erected. It consisted of a simple stone-and-mortar vault, partially submerged, the approach to which was a sloping ramp lined with a stylized barbed wire fence. A committee consisting mainly of survivors and former Dachau inmates held a competition for an international monument at the camp. The competition was won by a Yugoslav, Nandor Glid, the son of Jews killed at Auschwitz, and the monument was dedicated in 1968. This forty-five-foot-long black bronze grid depicts grimacing and emaciated human victims entwined in barbed wire. In a rifle range outside the nearby village of Hebertshausen, a memorial marked the spot where the SS murdered thousands of POWs (most of whom were Soviets, although this was not mentioned) from the Dachau camp; another memorial honored Jewish victims with a Star of David and an inscription reading "Remember the victims 1933–45"; and a third memorial recalled the deaths of Austrian citizens killed at the camp. Since 1970, various groups have worked to modify the site to reflect a more differentiated and historically aware picture not only of the camp but of the ways in which it has been remembered since 1945.

Throughout the period from 1945 to roughly the late 1960s, local people resisted memorializing the Dachau complex.[133] Their arguments mirrored a larger set of narratives West Germans used to remember (or forget) the war and Holocaust. Dachau citizens argued that the camp had been imposed on them by the Nazis, an alien force whose barbarism had destroyed the reputation of a town and a region known for its natural beauty and culture. Hardly an eccentric or politically radical view, this argument found support even in tourist handbooks of the region, as in the popular 1953 Fodor's guide to Germany, published mainly for American audiences. Here one read that the concentration camp had made Dachau notorious, "but before the Nazis provided [the city] with an evil reputation it was a pleasant old town . . . much frequented by landscape painters, for the beauty of its scenery."[134] The Nazis had ruined a perfectly good thing. This was the equivalent to the East German argument that Nazism represented an imposition on the German people engineered by capitalists and fascist ideologues. The Nazis had victimized the German people, the argument went, who after the war were again victims of the Allied occupiers, of survivors' groups clamoring for recognition and financial donations, and of tourists who failed to see the better side of Dachau and Germany. A corollary of this narrative was an argument of ignorance about what had gone on in the camps. Because the people of Dachau knew nothing of the brutalities perpetrated against camp inmates, the argument went, they had no responsibility for commemorating the Holocaust after 1945. Finally, because Germans were victimized for something for which they had no responsibility, they would have to resist all efforts to impose an unjust memory on the nation.

The theme of resistance to unjust alien forces is symbolized in many monuments and commemorative practices throughout German history. The theme had been deployed to legitimize both remembering and forgetting before 1945, and in this regard its use after World War II departed little from previous practices. The Bavarian agricultural minister summarized the argument in 1955 as he advocated tearing down the Dachau crematorium. "At some point we must put an end to the defamation of the Dachau region and its populace because it is impossible that . . . due to an unfortunate past a region can continually be burdened by the concentration camp crime."[135] Resistance to memory of the Holocaust would eventually soften, especially when a younger generation began demanding new forms of public commemoration in the 1970s. But before this period, many Germans, also resisting the "unfortunate past" being forced on them, made arguments analogous to the ones sketched here about the Federal Republic as a whole.

FATED GROUPS

Arguments of victimization and resistance to outside pressures to feel guilty found expression in the memories of other Germans who had in fact suffered under Hitler and Nazism. In France, De Gaulle and his supporters worked to unify all victims of Nazi "deportation," including resisters, forced laborers, and racial persecutees, in a unanimous postwar memory.[136] Within Germany, the German victims of World War II and its aftermath who were not swept up in the genocide took on the collective appellation of "fated groups," or *Schicksalsgruppen.* They encompassed refugees, expellees, victims of bombing, war widows and orphans, the war-injured, and former POWs. One must include the "rubble women," or *Trümmerfrauen,* here as well, who labored to clear German cities of ruins for years after 1945. Elizabeth Heineman has

Figure 46. "Rubble women" at former Nazi Propaganda Ministry, Berlin, 1946. Bildarchiv Preussischer Kulturbesitz.

argued convincingly that not only the experiences of the rubble women but of women in general were "universalized" in West Germany. Women's suffering in the war and occupation lost its gender specificity, and West German politicians and others used women's memory to strengthen a sense of all Germans' bitter experiences. In the process, women gained no concrete advantages for their positive contributions and were criticized for perceived negative behavior such as fraternization with the occupiers.[137] As for the rubble women, in cities such as Berlin they formed a club to retain their "wonderful comradeship" and complain how their contributions to German reconstruction were quickly forgotten.[138] Praised for clearing German streets of the remnants of Hitler's war, the rubble women's specific contribution to reconstruction was suppressed or lost in the broader public attempt to build a memory community of German victims.

Especially widespread in West German public culture in the 1950s were accounts of those who had been expelled from the Eastern territories. Popular memory of these painful treks westward took account of the plight of women, who outnumbered men among expellee groups. Similarly moving were memories of prisoners of war whose odyssey from Soviet internment camps back to Germany made for moving drama in government-sponsored documentation projects, novels, movies, and memoirs. Analyzing the poster of a 1953 traveling exhibit on the experience of German POWs, historian Robert Moeller has demonstrated that important elements of the iconography of Holocaust memory such as shaved heads and barbed wire were transferred to memory of German prisoners of war in Soviet captivity.[139]

Cemeteries and memorials for those who fell in battle furthered the idea of Germans as victims of Nazi aggression. It is true that the "legacy of the dead" was much more difficult to regard positively in Germany after World War II than after World War I because of the taint of Nazism.[140] Nonetheless, veterans' monuments and memorials continued to be built after World War II, perhaps as many as forty thousand in the Federal Republic alone. Stylistically such monuments generally picked up on modernist motifs of the 1920s, eliminating human figures altogether or reducing them to geometrical and cubic forms. The reason for this trend can be explained in part by the cultural authority enjoyed by modernist art after the war. Nazism's use of realistic figures on the war monuments of the Third Reich also did much to discredit more representational approaches. But the sheer number of war deaths and the enormity of human sacrifice also seemed to make abstract motifs more appropriate because of their distancing effect. Still, even when more abstract figures and shapes dominated such monuments, symbols such as crucifixes and the Pietà as well as inscriptions equated the war dead with Christ's suffering. Nationalist motifs or calls to vengeance were of course few and far between. But as noted above, Christianity and Christian iconography had a strong national function in the Federal Republic after the war, and thus it cannot be said that the war monuments of this era dispensed with symbols of national identity and memory. Historian Reinhart Koselleck has argued that to depict death in war on such memorials after 1945 was to offer only questions instead of answers.[141] In the light of postwar West Germany's linking of religious and national motifs, however, Koselleck's argument can be accepted only with substantial qualifications. And who can say definitively that hundreds of thousands of individuals did *not* find both comfort and conclusive meaning in mourning based on Christian beliefs?

Veterans' organizations, church communities, and towns had legitimate reasons to mourn or to make the sad plight of the survivors known to fellow citizens. But one should not overlook that the discourse of suffering had a connection to National Socialist rhetoric as well. Hitler above all, but many other Nazis as well, had argued that Germany was being victimized by the elusive enemy, the Jew, who was both everywhere and nowhere, inextricably tied to the forces of modernity that both enabled and undermined the nation.[142] Too, the idea of Germany as a nation of victims was unintentionally furthered by the occupying powers themselves. In the British zone, 95 percent of the adult population was categorized as "fellow travelers," or *Mitläufer,* in denazification proceedings designed to rid German public life of former Nazis. By categorizing people in this way, and by treating denazification procedures in a quasi-legal manner, the authorities left the impression that most Germans were part of a large mass of rather naive followers of Hitler who could not be held responsible for the regime, and who were in no way comparable to the perpetrators of atrocities. The fellow travelers appeared to have more in common with those who resisted or who were persecuted or murdered in the camps, and their classification gave them what appeared to be an almost juridical acquittal.[143] In the East, the regime's antifascist theorizing in effect excused the German populace for having been hoodwinked by capitalists and their political drones in the Nazi party. Jesus' plea to God from the cross—"Forgive them, for they know not what they do"—had thus become the official if unintended message. Unsurprisingly, Germans' memories of sacrifice and victimization, as well as the uses to which their memory was put by unscrupulous politicians on both sides of the German-German border, too often resulted in silence about Nazi crimes against humanity. Although differing in rhetoric, siting, and styles, war memorials in both West and East Germany led to "the erasure of Germans themselves" as perpetrators and supporters of Nazi atrocities.[144] This silence obtained in public life as well as in dealings with family members and friends.

More difficult to sustain in public life in this period were memories of positive experiences during the Third Reich that had little to do with official political ideology. Germans grew up, went to school, got jobs, made friends, fell in love, and started families from 1933 to 1945. Until relatively late in the war their lives on the home front went on without unusual disruptions, a situation of "normality" purposely promoted by Nazi officials who feared that material shortages or undue alarm would destabilize the regime. Workers of the 1950s recalled that the years right before the war offered employment and economic security of a kind that the Depression had made to seem all but impossible. Even in the darkest days of German military retreat in 1944 and 1945, soldiers had positive experiences of comradeship and friendship. Such memories had little chance of truly public consideration and appreciation when heroic tales of democratic or antifascist reconstruction from the horrors of Nazism and war constituted the official historical narrative. Nonetheless, positive memories did exist, and they reflected how difficult it was to keep memories within categories predefined by the state or powerful social groups.[145] Buildings and monuments most often represented public appropriations of the past, but "between" and "within" the buildings, private memories remained inassimilable to the historiographical politics of the dominant groups.

Reconstructed buildings, cities, sites of resistance, and concentration camps shaped the memory landscape in the two decades after the war. From the perspective of 1990, when a new world of historical inquiry and commemorative activity opened for Germans as well as other Europeans, the immediate postwar decades may have appeared to be a time of forgetting. In the context of economic and political recovery and the Cold War, however, memory was not as constricted as later generations would assume. Distortion or even outright suppression of the past did take place throughout devastated Europe, but groups and individuals strove to remember the dead as well as the circumstances that caused such massive suffering. In the case of the genocide, the problem was not historical amnesia but rather that "the Holocaust as a self-enclosed entity had not yet entered into the general consciousness or memory of the Western world."[146] Germans caused the war and undertook a brutal campaign of racial extermination. It was therefore fitting that they were also among the hesitant leaders in collective memory work in this period. In its broader European context, German history until about 1970 was a story of difficult and ultimately incomplete attempts to remember rather than a saga of unwillingness or inability to "master" the past. That such attempts were undertaken after the war explains in part why, after roughly the late 1960s, the Germanys were also in the forefront of a more intense international trend toward collective memory. How that trend worked itself out in an extraordinary elaboration and pluralization of the memory landscape is the subject of the next chapter.

CHAPTER FOUR

Traces

On 5 May 1985 two Berlin civic groups, the Active Museum of Fascism and Resistance and the Berlin History Workshop, staged a symbolic dig for historical artifacts at the former site of the Gestapo and SS headquarters in Berlin.[1] The fortieth anniversary of the end of World War II, this date was chosen for the dig to demonstrate popular support for transforming this field of weeds and rubble near the Berlin Wall into a memorial and historical exhibit. Although the site was under the control of an official authority appointed by the Berlin Senate to determine the fate of the long-neglected place, the diggers wanted to ensure that their voice would be heard in all such deliberations. Armed with shovels and spades, the two groups unearthed the foundations of Gestapo prison cells on that May day. Their dramatic efforts led to further revealing excavations that would be part of the Topography of Terror, a historical site documenting Nazi crimes.

That the dig combined symbolism and tangible effect surprised no one. The idea of "digging for traces" of history in unconventional places was well established by 1985. In 1973 the philanthropist Kurt Körber and Federal President Gustav Heinemann inaugurated a series of prize competitions for historical writing by groups of high school students that was designed to go beyond evidence derived from traditional schoolbooks. "Go out and find the traces of the Revolution of 1848–1849; search and collect materials and evidence," wrote the organizers of the first competition, which attracted more than seven hundred student

Figure 47. Digging for traces at former Gestapo headquarters, West Berlin, 5 May 1985. Photo by Jürgen Hentschel. Aktives Museum Faschismus und Widerstand Berlin.

groups.[2] The prize competition would become an enormous success, engaging thousands of West German students in subsequent years and producing its own magazine, *Searching for Traces,* or *Spuren suchen.* The most famous and controversial product of the competition was produced by Anja Rosmus, a student who diligently uncovered the role of elites in the Third Reich in her Bavarian home town, Passau, and who published her findings in a book complete with the photographs of all members of the local Nazi party.[3] This event later became the subject of the internationally acclaimed film, *The Nasty Girl,* which portrayed Rosmus's efforts against anxious and ashamed local teachers and officials. Since the late 1970s, local history and civic groups like those sponsoring the Berlin dig have mushroomed in the Federal Republic. Their motto was "Dig where you stand," which signified a program of researching and documenting historical evidence found in one's neighborhood and hometown, the spaces of daily life.

In literary theory the text always bears a "trace," meaning the text loses its "presence" because it refers to something in both the past and future beyond itself.[4] Although the historical diggers of the Federal Republic believed the artifacts and texts they uncovered were more solid and meaningful than the literary trace—there was nothing insubstantial about a former Gestapo cell!—they nonetheless also insisted that their evidence referred to an historical identity with a past and a future. German identity could now be discovered by digging for historical traces, as if the nation consisted of archaeologists searching for something that had been hidden or lost. A previous excess of history had been displaced by the absence of a history that was now to be recovered. The paradigmatic expression of the German memory landscape was now a topography of traces. This transformation had a number of important effects. It resulted in new ways of perceiving historical environments, which were now not simply accretions of monuments, ruins, and reconstructions but broadly defined landscapes whose historical meanings were richer and more differentiated than previously thought. At the same time, it resulted in a new framing strategy that redefined the canon of monuments and historic buildings. A national or war monument from the past, a medieval cathedral, or an Altstadt could take on new and original connotations for groups previously withheld from the court of public memory. Such meanings could be highly personal, or they could be used by groups who felt they had been discriminated against for reasons of ethnicity, gender, political belief, or sexual orientation. The transformation simultaneously furthered and was enabled by a wider (though hardly uncontested) public interest in the history of Nazism and the Holocaust. Sporadic and highly concentrated before 1970, this interest emerged in full force in the following two decades. This in turn would lead to a more subtle and differentiated view of the victims of Nazism and a new willingness to remember the perpetrators of Nazi crimes. The supporters of the Topography of Terror wanted their exhibit to be an "open wound" that reminded visitors they were standing in Germany, the "site of the perpetrators" of the Holocaust. While such changes applied most directly to the Federal Republic, they had analogues in the more constricted context of East Germany.

MEMORY'S STRONGER EMBRACE

To what may we attribute memory's stronger embrace? Eric Hobsbawm has written of the twentieth century as an "age of extremes" in which the bloody era from 1914 to 1945 gave way to a quarter-century of unprecedented political quiescence and economic growth.[5] Throughout Germany and much of Europe, the full arc of the pendulum's swing from one extreme to the other appeared to be complete by the late 1960s or early 1970s, depending on local circumstances. The beginning of the end of the age of postwar recovery and prosperity was at hand. The West German economy's impressive expansion had enabled the well-schooled sons and daughters of the middle and upper classes to attend universities in unprecedented numbers.[6] For these students, like their counterparts in the wealthier countries of Europe and in the United States, the future had promised material and political security to a degree unheard of in the interwar years. But growth and anticipation also produced political ferment as a Christian Democratic coalition government in office since 1949 was followed first by a Grand Coalition of Social Democrats (SPD) and Christian Democrats in 1966 and three years later by a coalition between the SPD and left liberals. Stirred by the Grand Coalition's disturbing prospect of West German politics without substantive opposition, aroused by global political upheaval over the Vietnam War, and encouraged by a growing cultural criticism, the West German Left picked up on a tradition of critical politics that had been slumbering since the first postwar years. When economic growth slowed and Social Democratic reform initiatives appeared to lose steam by the early 1970s, the aura of inevitable progress, so important to the years of stability, was dissipated.

In response to such changes, the West German Left's initial idealism and relative coherence gave way in the 1970s to fragmentation and uncertainty. Activism, terrorism, and escapism jostled side by side for the allegiances of those left behind by the turmoil of the previous years. Many radical students and theorists lost faith in Marxist theory, which, like liberal economic thought, had been predicated on the idea of continued economic growth. The result was a search for new alternatives. In some cases, extreme subjectivity and drug use offered solutions, and for others a compulsion to obliterate the past because of its connections to Nazism seemed the only path worth following. For them, there was a kind of self-induced "lobotomy which afforded the patient his or her wholesale remaking."[7] Environmentalism was also an answer, particularly when it served as a surrogate for thwarted political activism. But environmentalism could also result in nostalgic longings for a notionally simpler society in which nature was unsullied by industry, cities, and wrangling bureaucracies. Not unrelated was a free-floating angst about the direction of an unrepentant materialistic society that promised moral exhaustion at best and environmental or even nuclear holocaust at worst. A ubiquitous theme in plays, novels, and journalistic commentary, angst also hovered over the heads of the historiographical diggers, who feared the future they divined in the traces of the past.[8] The theme of angst was also related to a deeper collective insecurity with historical roots going all the way back to the devastation of the Thirty Years' War in the seventeenth century; in time, this constant sense of insecurity, reinforced again and again in the twentieth century, acquired the patina of national tradition and the unquestioned status of "second nature."[9]

Anxious dissatisfaction with the present also led to an embrace of history. But to what past could West Germany's disgruntled citizens revert? Nazism had misused the past, transforming legitimate cultural memories and identities into a racist ideology. The postwar embrace of progress had devalued tradition and hopelessly commercialized nostalgia. The excess of German memory was buried under totalitarian ideology in one case and capitalist recovery in the other. To reclaim that excess, to mourn and atone for its victims, to emphasize its diversity, and to celebrate its potential for a truly democratic society—these became the goals of the emergent popular historicism. In the search to recover a usable German tradition, many West Germans turned to the history of the working-class movement and resistance or to the history of the victims of Nazism. Youth in particular identified with the victims of the Nazi regime, whose plight was seen—astoundingly, from the perspective of the end of the millennium—as in some way comparable to that of alienated youth in a materialistic society lacking the emotional fulcrum provided by history.

A key result of the new popular interest in history was that the Left embraced an image that no one interested in the German past could quite get around: the idea of Heimat. In one respect of course, Heimat thinking had never left the public arena in Germany. Having been assimilated to the Nazi ideology of blood and soil, Heimat was evoked in the 1950s in various voluntary groups, films, and popular songs as an expression of nostalgic longing for a lost homeland left in ashes by the war or taken over by governments that expelled Germans from the East. Heimat was truly a movable feast. By the mid-1970s, the journal *Kursbuch,* a weathervane of avant-garde political thinking in the Federal Republic, argued that the Left should appropriate and transform the idea of Heimat. Imagery of the homeland and the provinces seemed to offer a useful outlet for environmentalist thinking as well as for more personal longings for attachment and solidarity. Edgar Reitz's wildly popular sixteen-hour film *Heimat* in 1984 was the signature statement of this new evocation. Reitz wanted to portray the many contradictions of the meaning of Heimat; he insisted that Heimat was only memory and longing rather than a real place. Nonetheless, the press and wider public picked up on the more affirmative messages of the long masterpiece and downplayed the critical elements. Critics used loaded terms such as "apologetics" and "rehabilitation" to express their discontent.[10]

The reception to *Heimat* revealed the tensions inherent in the Heimat revival. Leftist popularizers of grassroots consciousness stressed differences between their activity and the Heimat movement of earlier decades. They insisted that Heimat was not rooted in the murky world of "heritage" or race but was the active appropriation of democratic, environmentalist, and antiauthoritarian principles in defense of one's community.[11] They took pains to remind observers that *their* Heimat was not the anti-Communist Heimat of expellee groups from Poland, Czechoslovakia, and Hungary. One cannot gainsay the sincerity with which this attempt to distance the generation of 1968 from the past (or from the toxic present) was undertaken. Adapted to the postwar world and an age of political ferment, Heimat thinking nonetheless retained an older sense of the German nation based on cultural, linguistic, and even ethnic characteristics. As diligently as they tried, and as successfully as they added new meanings to the idea of Heimat, neither Reitz nor the leftist advocates of the new localism could detach the term entirely from prior historical associations. The tradition of the ethnie persisted—at times rather obliquely, at times more clearly—in spite of political conflicts and ideological disclaimers.

The interest in local history and Heimat was often promoted by individuals who were newcomers to their towns or cities.[12] In a highly mobile society, historical knowledge about one's new home was a useful path to social integration and identity. It was unsurprising in this context to find that recently relocated schoolteachers, museum officials, professors, and other educated individuals were in the forefront of the new Heimat movement in the provinces. Again, however, their commitment to transforming Heimat into a democratic ideal expressed a quite old tradition of German culture whereby identity and community were expressed in historical terms, and whereby community rested on a layering of local and national perspectives.

Just as Heimat was to be transformed, so too the nation was to be reinterpreted. Heimat activists stressed a plurality of historical perspectives determined by social interaction rather than a uniform, top-down interpretation of the national past.[13] This was a latitudinal sense of the nation oriented to social exchange, mass consumption, private morality, and "communication" rather than to a longitudinal creation of knowledge reflecting the values and aims of the powers that be. Michael Geyer has described this shift in terms of a transformation of the nation as "vested authority," the prevalent idea of the first half of the twentieth century, into the nation as "civil society."[14] In this view, Heimat and nation could be contradictory terms. But more often Heimat allowed the nation to speak *sotto voce* as the local and everyday dimensions of life were emphasized. Too, popular interest in memory was now more personal, as family and individual histories enriched and often displaced a collective sense of the past and future, and as developing mass markets cashed in on the social interest in the past. This personalization of the past picked up on ideas and critiques from the intellectual and social avant-garde before World War I. Although more elaborated in West Germany, the privatization of memory also had an effect in East German society, as East Germans found familial and personal "niches" that both reinforced and limited the power of the state and party. But personal memory could be applied directly to events with broad historical and collective significance. In the sites of memory to the victims of the Nazi regime such as the Old Synagogue in Essen, where the names of more than three thousand townspeople murdered by the Nazis were listed, the goal was to enable visitors to "undertake a search for the traces of the fate of individual victims."[15] How many individual narratives and painful personal memories were generated on the other side of the German-German border at state-induced ceremonies at former concentration camp sites, memorial centers, and antifascist monuments?[16]

The Left's "radical plurality" was deeply disturbing to conservatives. Their response was to adapt older ideas of the nation to new circumstances, to try to recover a vested authority while also adapting to the formation of a now powerful and fully developed civil society. In all Western European political systems, a "change in tendency," or *Tendenzwende,* occurred in which conservative parties and ideas were revived as social reformist policies became enervated. The timing and content of this shift depended on specific historical and political factors. The German variation on this theme placed the Christian Democratic party at the center of things. After the late 1970s, and especially after Helmut Kohl became the chancellor of the Federal Republic in 1982, the Christian Democrats emphasized the need for a revived sense of national loyalty. This was expressed among other things in a broadly affirmative stance toward German history.

The politicized world of German architectural criticism provided some of the ammunition for the change in tendency.[17] Starting in the last half of the 1970s, architects and critics began to debate the impact of the Third Reich on West German architecture and design. Ostensibly revolving around the question of postmodernism, this debate also confronted the legacy of Nazi architectural practice in the German memory landscape. The debate opened in 1977, when the British architect James Stirling won an international competition for an addition to the Neue Staatsgalerie museum in Stuttgart. Stirling's striking postmodernist design was labeled "fascist" by modernist architects and writers, who viewed its neoclassical references (such as Doric columns) and geometrical forms as a rehabilitation of the brutal architecture of the Third Reich. The debate escalated as supporters of postmodernist design returned fire, arguing that modernist architects had flirted with Nazism in the first years of Hitler's rule and that modernism was institutionalized in Western Germany after 1945 by architects who had come to power during the Nazi years. They also argued that modernist postwar reconstruction in West German cities had brutally marginalized traditional forms of architecture. Postmodernists further rankled the modernists by reviving public interest in the Heimat devotee Paul Schultze-Naumburg and the Nazi architect Albert Speer, whose neo-classicism was praised in a provocative 1985 book by the Luxembourg architect and former Stirling associate Leon Krier. Many of the arguments made by defenders of postmodernist design—that architectural tradition should not be rejected only because of its use by Nazism, that Nazism was not a singularly German phenomenon but a product of modern tendencies inherent in all Western societies, that architectural design could be appreciated independently of the crimes committed to produce it—were analogous to positions taken by conservative intellectuals and politicians in other fields in the 1980s. Such arguments often (though not inevitably) translated into a sense of national identity that marginalized or downplayed the worst traumas and crimes of German history.

The museum industry expanded tremendously throughout the Euro-American world in this period, as states and private groups assembled historical traces in "destinations" for ever more enthusiastic crowds of tourists and pilgrims.[18] It is unsurprising in this context that another area of the memory landscape in which the desire for a more affirmative national history was expressed in the 1980s in West Germany was in two major museum projects, the new museum of the history of the Federal Republic in Bonn and the German Historical Museum in Berlin. The latter was to encapsulate all of German history in a single building. "[The museum] should stimulate a critical coming to terms with the past," read a 1987 statement, "but also make [historical] understanding possible, and allow possibilities for identification."[19] The line of continuity running throughout the museum projects in particular and Christian Democratic cultural politics in general was the effort to recentralize identities and memories around a national state that, rhetoric notwithstanding, accepted the division of Germany. This did not mean that authoritarian traditions were to be revived. For Kohl and his key supporters, such as the historian Michael Stürmer, the goal was to reduce German memory to an identification with Western values as expressed by the Atlantic community, NATO, and the substantial accomplishments of the Federal Republic's liberal constitutionalism. For some, this was simply political sleight-of-hand: "He wants to put Germany on the winning side," said one Berlin historian of Kohl after unification.[20] But for those who felt threatened by the political radicalism of the age, for those who saw the plurality of perspectives of the new Heimat movement as an impossible fragmentation of the national image, the "Atlanticist" argument made sense—from a geopolitical as well as a cultural standpoint. Better than any other postwar option, it controlled and channeled a typically German excess of memory through the newly valued lens of Enlightenment and liberality. It was a winning framing device.

Yet, as before, a unified national memory also expressed the multicentered qualities of the German past. Even as he continued to associate the Federal Republic with a historic German orientation to the West, Kohl courted the nostalgia of German-speaking groups expelled from Eastern Europe after the war. More than a political ploy, this appeal to the expellees kept alive notions of German ethnic identities independent of state boundaries. It also facilitated the idea of a central European German identity standing astride the historical abyss dividing East and West Europe. Stürmer in particular evoked Germany as the "land of the middle," a reference to the country's unique geopolitical situation in the heart of Europe. Multicenteredness was also a characteristic of the Federal Republic's museum politics. As noted above, German officials were proposing two major museums, one reflecting the history of a successful German Republic in Bonn, the other the entirety of German history in Berlin, the divided German capital that many thought might one day be the restored political metropole of a single German national state. A key element of the Federal Republic's historiographical politics, the Bonn-Berlin cultural axis both unified and dispersed national memory in a striking reaffirmation of the idea that German national tradition united the one and the many.

Throughout the rise of the new Heimat movement and conservative reaffirmation of the nation, private and public memory became increasingly focused on Nazism and the Holocaust. Parents and grandparents had said little about their historical experiences in the war to the younger generation. Their reticence was widespread not just in Germany but throughout Europe and even among Holocaust survivors. Younger Israelis commented that until the 1960s they gained little knowledge about the Holocaust from relatives, parents, and grandparents who survived the concentration camps. This meshed with public accounts and monuments of the Shoah in Israel, where, although the history of the extermination of the Jews was part of public consciousness soon after the founding of the state, it was not until the decade of the '60s when this history was fully elaborated and extended to all phases of Israeli life.[21]

Not just the general critical climate of the age but specific events stirred younger Germans to ask questions about the Third Reich. In 1959 the desecration of Jewish cemeteries in Cologne touched off interest in the memory of the Holocaust.[22] In 1961 in Israel Adolf Eichmann, the chief administrator of the Final Solution in the East, was tried, executed, and cremated, and his ashes were spread in the Mediterranean. The trial was a lightening rod for increased historical interest in both Israel and Germany, as was the 1964 trial of Auschwitz SS officials in Frankfurt. An array of German novels, plays, and avant-garde films explored themes related to Nazism, the war, and the camps. Shown in Germany in 1979, the U.S. television film *Holocaust* undoubtedly touched a nerve within families all over West Germany. But the favorable public reaction to the soap opera by no means initiated the popular movement to investigate the past; it had been growing for some fifteen years, and indeed *Holocaust* may be seen as the "culmination" of one period of memory work, as Peter Steinbach remarks, and the beginning of another.[23] The consumption of the Holocaust as a media and public phenomenon had in any case reached a new and unprecedented level internationally at the end of the 1970s. Critics argued that "Shoah business" had gotten out of hand and others, most eloquently the Israeli historian Saul Friedländer, charged that the history of Nazism and the Holocaust was undergoing a dangerous tendency of aestheticization. Representations of death, argued Friedländer, now crossed the line into "kitsch."

Friedländer's remarks were not only accurate but prescient, for after his book appeared even more questionable cultural artifacts relating to the history of Nazism appeared worldwide, including Holocaust video games and a Nazi theme park, Wolf's Lair, in Poland.[24]

The German public's willingness to decipher the past revealed important limits and contradictions about how the perpetrators of wartime crimes were to be remembered. Moreover, as more affirmative responses to German history became increasingly acceptable under Christian Democratic rule, public preoccupation with the darker events of the recent German past generated a backlash, or rather a sense of exasperation that there was too much knowledge—and too much resultant guilt—about the history of Nazism. I examine these developments below. For the time being it is important to emphasize the depth and breadth of the new interest in German history. Journalists and scholars constantly stressed a German "inability to mourn" and to "come to terms" with the past.[25] But in an international perspective, West Germans' approach to the history of the war and Nazism was responsible and impressive. Although the two decades after the war had seen only sporadic attempts to deal with themes such as the Holocaust, the activity of the period after 1970 had hardly started from ground zero.

It is instructive to compare public images of the past in the Federal Republic and France in the same period. French fascism and the wartime Vichy regime were absent from the radar screen of collective memory as the image of De Gaulle's Free France and the Resistance dominated public recollections in the first quarter-century after the war. It was two North American historians, Michael Marrus and Robert Paxton, who, in a book published in 1983, brought to light Vichy's initiative in developing and implementing anti-Jewish policies.[26] By this time, the French were experiencing what could only be described as a national trauma after long-repressed versions of the French past reappeared. Shot in 1969 but not shown in theaters until 1971, banned from television until 1981, the film *The Sorrow and the Pity* belatedly caused much public soul-searching. It portrayed the French during the occupation not as heroic resisters but as passive individuals or collaborators even as it downplayed the Jewish identity of many victims of the Vichy and Nazi regimes. Jewish memory reawakened to uncover seams of anti-Semitism in French culture that could not be explained away only as products of opportunistic collaboration with the Nazis. Previously discussed mainly by former inmates and foreigners, French concentration camps during the war were revealed as part and parcel of a regime's attempt to remake society along the lines of Pétain's national revolution. Through such "discoveries," some French began to see Vichy and fascism not as departures from national history but as integral outgrowths of it. This view was as extreme as the suppression of memory it was designed to combat.[27] By comparison, German engagement with the past in this period was less sudden and more mature and balanced.

THE NEW HISTORY MOVEMENT

Environmentalism put emphasis on preserving scarce resources in the natural world for future generations. This perception now shifted to the memory landscape. What had been seen as expendable and historically uninteresting to past generations was now regarded as an important piece of historical evidence. What was seen as largely a matter of elites was now available for the popular embrace of history and tradition. The conservative daily *Frankfurter Allgemeine Zeitung* called the mid-1970s interest in the preservation of historical architecture a "people's movement," or *Volksbewegung.* It approved of the new dispensation but also reminded liberal critics who criticized the movement for its antiurbanism and nostalgia that the interest in monuments had stemmed from the Left.[28] The West German newsweekly *Der Spiegel* wrote of the emergence of the "new history movement" as an epochal event.[29] Pundits noted that the appearance of many grassroots citizens' initiatives, or *Bürgerinitiativen,* supported the popularization of monuments and historical subjects. A product of the politicization of West German society in the 1960s, the citizens' initiatives embraced a multitude of themes in largely local contexts.

Older types of organizations added to the momentum of the movement. The SPD and unions experienced a revival in historical interest in the late 1970s and 1980s. The workers' movement had always stressed the importance of historical knowledge and legitimized its mission by referring to immutable laws of history that would lead to a socialist society. But in the era of economic reconstruction, the SPD's interest in history faded, reflecting the general trend of the age. After 1970 this began to change. For some, the return to history was an attempt to discover lost opportunities of the German past. What would have happened had Social Democrats and Communists united against Hitler in the Weimar Republic for instance? In the middle years of the 1980s some 365 regional and local histories of the Social Democratic Party were published. Workers' initiatives paralleled the work of the citizens' initiatives, as groups of workers, often in alliance with unemployed or underemployed middle-class intellectuals, mounted campaigns to save industrial artifacts, old factories, and even nineteenth-century proletarian housing such as the Eisenheim complex near Oberhausen in the Ruhr.[30]

The History Workshop (*Geschichtswerkstatt*) movement grew out of the array of citizens' initiatives. Observers maintained that history workshops constituted the fastest growing type of cultural organization in West Germany in the decade after 1980. Internationally the roots of the movement go back ten years earlier to the United Kingdom and Sweden, where by the early 1980s some sixteen hundred "dig where you stand" groups organized numerous local historical projects. In Germany the movement stemmed in part from the "Project Group: Regional Social History" at the University of Konstanz, which in 1979 was looking for alternatives to academic publications as a way of influencing public opinion on local economic growth. Its solution was to organize the Working Group on Regional History, an assemblage of some one hundred professional and amateur historians, teachers, and others who printed up brochures, held exhibits, and conducted sociohistorical city tours. A group with the similar intent of creating historical knowledge outside traditional structures appeared with the Berlin History Workshop in fall 1980. It emerged from the large alternative movement of the city and worked with various Heimat museums in Berlin districts. Soon other groups in Hamburg, Hannover, Göttingen, and much smaller cities pursued similar aims, as the number of communities with history workshops grew to about fifty.[31]

Many such groups were highly specialized, focusing only on the history of a particular local industry or neighborhood, and many undertook their own version of historical preservation by renovating an old warehouse or factory as their headquarters. They often attracted high school and university students as well as younger professional (or unemployed) historians and individuals in cultural agencies. In contrast to these groups, in the mid-1980s adult education schools, municipal cultural offices, and similar institutions established history workshops that attracted older individuals. A typical example was the Volkshochschule Recklinghausen, in which a group of former miners researched their history. In 1982 and 1983 what had been a grassroots movement became a national organization when the History Workshop was officially founded. History Festivals were organized to share information, plan for the future, and create social contacts. More than one thousand people attended the first one in Berlin in 1984. The group also published a successful journal. The movement was highly heterogeneous and by no means without internal conflict. One significant division was that between professional historians with one foot in the history workshops and the other in universities on one side, and amateur enthusiasts who were less theoretical and less engaged with critical political thinking than the intellectuals were on the other.[32]

Citizens' initiatives, labor unions and the SPD, and history workshops "produced" new monuments, or rather they transformed the meaning of the memory landscape to include a whole new array of objects. Because many groups wanted to explore what was close to home or what could be understood "from below" rather than from the point of view of the powerful, a new array of buildings, streets, and spaces came into view as the successful framing strategy took hold. Because the history of states and nations did little to illuminate the feelings of ordinary people, a new world of material culture, of the workshop, factory, home, and neighborhood, would be needed. The memory landscape was no longer defined by a cluster of cathedrals, castles, and city halls, but was a wider and more complex assemblage of historical traces scattered throughout a city, village, or natural setting. These groups also stressed new methods of apprehending and understanding such objects. Oral history became popular as researchers sought out individuals who had experienced historic events firsthand. The point was not so much to explain what had happened on the basis of overarching theoretical models based on Marxism or modernization theory but to empathize with individuals as historical subjects. This applied most frequently to the alternative groups and history workshops, less so to the trade union or Social Democratic initiatives, whose members still often held to ideas of Marxism and class struggle.

Stressing empathy highlighted the hybridized approach to historical knowledge developed by such groups. In 1980 an alternative history group conducted a bicycle tour through parts of Bavaria to rediscover physical traces of the Peasants' War of the sixteenth century.[33] Following the path of peasant masses that held demonstrations, sacked palaces, and burned down estates, participants tried to get a sense of how peasants experienced the landscape. Participants rejected the primacy of professional historical standards of precision and exhaustive research in archives and libraries. Although they did not dispense entirely with such methods and standards, they opted for a mixed methodology of research, discussion, and recreation. History was not studied for its own sake but for its significance to personal identity and contemporary political needs.

Participants also supported a protest against Daimler-Benz's building of a new test track in the area, thus combining historical and environmental concerns. The project on peasant war sites emerged from the imaginatively titled *Traum-A-Land* initiative. This name captured the organizer's dualistic sense of the Franconian province's identity, which was shaped not only by the "dream," or *Traum,* of the beautiful landscape but also the historical trauma of bloody war. The dreamlike/traumatized landscape would also be evoked when the initiative discussed the history of Nazism in Franconia. The initiative wanted to recover such contradictory historical experiences in a larger project of creating a new Heimat consciousness.

The forgotten groups of history such as workers and peasants were the key subjects of these initiatives. So too were women, whose history had always been a marginal element with reference to the memory landscape. The new history movement pledged itself to recovering the history of women in everyday life. It was significant that Reitz's *Heimat* took as its central character a woman whose life history was the axis around which the narrative of the locale turned. But this characterization could also be understood in fairly traditional ways, since Heimat imagery had always stressed the "feminine" and nurturing characteristics of the province and the home town. Moreover, the history workshops' commitment to women's history was often more rhetorical than practical, and practitioners of women's history found themselves as isolated within the new history movement as they were in the West German historical profession or in the antiwar movement, where women photocopied leaflets and cared for the children while men made thunderous speeches and planned strategies. Thus, in the 1980s, women's history became the subject of initiatives such as alternative city tours.

City tours had been part of the touristic itinerary in Germany and Europe since the dawn of mass leisure migration. The Nazis constructed an alternative to commercial city tours by publishing a book about SA struggles for control of Berlin. Starting in the late 1970s, alternative tours tried to create new narratives about well-worn touristic paths, but like the larger society, they invariably left out women. In West Berlin in the 1980s a group of women put together a tour explicitly designed to explore the sites of the women's movement from 1848 to the rise of Nazism. They visited schools that had been distinguished in the early stages of the women's education movement. They visited the grave of the famous Berlin feminist Minna Cauer and the site where Rosa Luxemburg was brutally killed by police in 1919. And they toured the sites of

Nazi repression of the women's movement, including the house on Tiergartenstraße where the Nazi programs of euthanasia, compulsory abortions, and sterilization for "unfit" women were formulated. The tour produced a brochure that included numerous historical citations and photographs. The title of the brochure encapsulated the approach: *Experience the History of the Women's Movement.*[34]

Precisely because they favored experience over analysis, empathy rather than explanation, the history workshops came in for often harsh criticism from leading historians such as Jürgen Kocka and Hans-Ulrich Wehler. Leading trade unionists reacted skeptically to a historiography that highlighted the human costs of industrialization and bureaucratized politics; labor bosses were after all fully implicated in a "corporatist" system based on repeated deals between the unions, business, and the state. Leftist intellectuals charged that the workshops and alternative tours threw out theory in favor of melodramatic stories of heroic "little people." The alternative groups often reacted in kind, attacking what one history workshop member called the "enlightened arrogance of science." This same member argued that the workshops should "describe fascists in such a way that we the living will recognize ourselves in them."[35] This comment reflected how the new history movement rejected historiographical distance and placed fascism firmly within West German society. The Nazi past was a palpable and everyday presence that permeated the most intimate corners of family and individual existence. Despite such vigorous exchanges, by the end of the 1980s many of the new history groups, especially the larger and more active history workshops, had become part of an institutionalized cultural politics promoted by states and cities. This did not mean that the history workshops lost their critical edge entirely. But they had established themselves and could no longer argue they were outsiders in constructing an image of the past in the German public. This presented a host of new possibilities but also many new problems. The breakup of the national history workshop movement into two groups in the early 1990s reflected the growing pains and increasing diversity of the movement.

We should not let the controversies over the new history movement obscure the important strands of continuity between the new practices and previous traditions. Popular participation in history groups and Heimat societies had a long genealogy in Germany since the nineteenth century. In their time those groups were also criticized by university professors and major museum directors, who accused the local societies of amateurishness and imprecision. Many nineteenth-century local history and Heimat groups had demonstrated a marked interest in cultural history, broadly defined and developed before World War I, in the work of Karl Lamprecht. This too found little support among university historians, who remained wedded to political and diplomatic history centered on the evolution of national states. In the 1980s the new history groups' methodologies tended to focus on empathy instead of explanation. But the nineteenth-century advocates of cultural history had also argued that political history left human beings out of the picture and that the history of the Volk consisted of a broad palette of cultural forms reaching to the most intimate spaces of everyday life. The 1980s groups stressed new technologies, including video, television, and computers, just as the history groups of the nineteenth century experimented with exhibits, postcards, and other new media made possible by photography and other innovations.

Neither in the nineteenth century nor in the late twentieth century did the new history groups abandon the book as a characteristic medium. Despite an emphasis on cultural history in the earlier period or on everyday life in the later one, the new historians believed in the necessity of historicist reconstruction of "the facts." The continuation of this historiographical tradition could be seen in the popularity of documentary collections of evidence on historical topics. More broadly, the emphasis on history as such reflected the larger legitimacy of historical knowledge in German culture. Here too the ability to innovate and "construct" was shaped by substantive continuities and marked by tangible historical limits.

Despite the popularity of the new history movement's sense of the memory landscape, many Germans still valued the canon of historical architecture for traditional reasons.[36] Preservation and history societies as well as traditional Heimat groups continued to do their work and attract members. But even here a broader definition of monuments prevailed, as such groups sought accommodation with environmentalist organizations and history workshops. In 1975 Germans and other countries celebrated European Cultural Heritage Year, which focused attention on traditional historical monuments as well as issues such as the relationship between urban planning and the renewal of historic city centers. Preservationist and Heimat societies saw a positive potential in postmodern architecture's emphasis on historical forms and regional motifs. Government preservation policy took account more than before of previously marginal topics such as former concentration camp sites and Nazi architecture. Despite such influences, the impact of the new history movement was so strong in these established fields of preservation and Heimat activity that traces of a backlash were apparent in the mid-1970s. Commentators warned of overzealousness and a new "cult of monuments" that threatened to swamp official channels with demands to preserve historic artifacts of no historical or cultural value. For such critics the popular movement to unearth historical traces was a functional equivalent of the tendency to demand everything from the state, from social security to monuments, from economic welfare to a healthy relationship to the past. When conservators and mayors warned of an excess of memory, they put themselves on the side of Helmut Kohl and other Christian Democratic politicians who wanted to reduce public images of the past to more graspable and (it was hoped) politically less challenging dimensions.

RESISTERS AND VICTIMS

The broader interest in memory and monuments was simultaneously shaped and fueled by greater public interest in Nazism. In part this was a continuation of the narrative of resistance to National Socialism that had begun in the first years after World War II but that now widened dramatically. I have noted that two central sites set the parameters of Resistance memory right after the war, the Bendlerblock in the Stauffenbergstraße and the Plötzensee prison. Whereas the former represented a narrower and more hierarchical understanding of the Resistance based on elite and aristocratic attempts to take Hitler's life on 20 July 1944, the latter suggested a broader definition of resisters that included Communists and a diverse group of nationalities. One could see this distinction break down with time as the Bendlerblock's view of resistance began to look more like that of the Plötzensee.

In more than thirty published lectures from the documentation center at the Stauffenbergstraße memorial starting in the early 1970s, presenters drew a broad picture of a resistance consisting not only of the heroes of 20 July but of less renowned military officers and soldiers, exiles, Jews, Communist and Social Democratic workers, Catholics, Protestants, and Quakers.[37] Exhibits reinforced this impression. In the mid-1960s, the Friedrich Ebert Stiftung put on an exhibit at the Stauffenbergstraße memorial that commemorated exiles who resisted the Nazi regime. Still tainted with the suspicion of treasonous activity in the West, the exiles were nonetheless beginning to be accepted as legitimate foes of a murderous regime, a development that had direct political consequences when at the end of the decade, Willy Brandt, who had spent the Nazi years as a journalist in emigration, and who earlier in the decade had been attacked by Christian Democrats for having written articles critical of Germany during the Third Reich, was elected chancellor. In the late 1970s further exhibits drew public attention to resisters from various political parties, the churches, and the military.

In the early 1980s, Richard von Weizsäcker, then mayor of Berlin and later a very effective president of the Federal Republic, sponsored an ambitious exhibit depicting the wider parameters of the German Resistance. This exhibit proved to be controversial because it juxtaposed groups that had previously been kept separate in public commemorations, such as the heroes of 20 July and the German officers in captivity in the Soviet Union who organized anti-Hitler propaganda and clandestine activity in the National Committee for a Free Germany. Based on the idea that the full range of resistance would be represented without making value judgments, the exhibit sparked criticism from many groups. The Catholic church disliked the fact that the exhibit portrayed Catholic resistance not only as a product of the struggle against Hitler but also as a result of internal Church politics. Christian Democrats disliked the fact that working-class resistance seemed to take precedence. During the fiftieth anniversary of Stauffenberg's attack on Hitler, finally, conservatives raised vigorous protests about honoring the 20 July resisters and including portraits of former GDR leaders Ulbricht and Pieck, both Communists in exile in the USSR during the war, in the same exhibit. Peter Steinbach, director of the German Resistance Museum established at the site, defended this widening of memory as both historically accurate and politically enlightening in the context of continuing public divisions after reunification.[38]

Such controversies revealed three sets of anxieties. First, within the now growing array of groups that counted themselves among those who resisted Hitler, there was extreme discomfort about being represented alongside groups with whom one disagreed on political grounds. Had not the Communist resisters later simply replaced one totalitarian regime with another? Second, the hierarchy of action represented by the first commemorations in the Bendlerblock after the war seemed to have broken down. Military and political officials who wanted to keep alive the heroic attempt to kill Hitler were made uneasy by mention of intellectuals and others who had gone into so-called "inner emigration" in the Third Reich. How could the relative passivity of the latter be juxtaposed to the unselfish activism of the former? Third, the exhibit dashed previous images of an ahistorical and idealistic resistance movement, replacing them with a picture of individuals and groups situated in specific historical circumstances. Instead of people of almost mythic proportions, the resister was more often seen as a flesh-and-blood individual making difficult and sometimes erroneous or self-interested choices. The lines defining resistance, previous political traditions inherited from the Imperial and Weimar periods, internal conflicts, and political interest were not so easily drawn in this more nuanced approach to the subject. A more diverse picture of the Resistance now lent itself to a more complicated analysis of the motives and aims of the resisters themselves. In a highly selective memory where only black-and-white contrasts had prevailed, disturbing shades of gray began to bleed in from the borders of the picture.

More than three quarters of all commemorative plaques to the Resistance in West Germany appeared in the 1980s.[39] What Plötzensee had anticipated in the 1950s and what the Bendlerblock began to realize in the 1970s, was now gaining wide public recognition. This commemorative activity was inspired not only by the fortieth anniversary of the end of the war but by other important events as well. In Berlin the planned 750th anniversary celebration of the city in 1987 included a program to distribute some three hundred commemorative plaques throughout the twelve districts of the metropolis marking the birthplaces and sites of activity of historical personalities. This included members of the Resistance, who would be honored with handsome plaques manufactured in the famous state porcelain works. Other cities had similar programs. In 1982 the Hamburg Senate resolved to mark important historical buildings, streets, and squares in a broad campaign entitled "Sites of Persecution and Resistance, 1933–1945." In 1983 the square in front of the main rail station in Bielefeld was renamed to commemorate sixty Resistance fighters. Not just key figures but also ordinary resisters were honored with plaques, as in Kreuzberg, a district in Berlin, where the transport worker and SPD sympathizer Wilhelm Lehmann was remembered for having been executed at Plötzensee in 1942 at the age of seventy-three after writing on a toilet stall "Hitler, you mass murderer, you must be killed, and then the war will be over."[40]

Just as the Stauffenbergstraße memorial highlighted growing conflicts in the memory of the Resistance, the broader rush of commemorative activity revealed deeper social and cultural differences. Social Democrats argued that socialist workers' resistance had been more level-headed and responsible than Communist resistance. Communists in turn argued that it was only heroic Communist workers who were willing to lay their lives on the line *en masse*. Not without considerable ambivalence, West German advocates of the latter position developed arguments comparable to those in the East German regime's program of antifascist memory. Definitions of resistance widened in academic historiography as well, most notably in the work of Martin Broszat and his research team, which undertook a major historical project on resistance, opposition, and nonconformity in Bavaria during the Third Reich.[41] This careful scholarship put the memory of the Resistance in a new light, for it became obvious that those who had actively resisted the regime on political grounds were a tiny minority of the German population. More important had been a dispersed pattern of noncompliance with regime policies that arose from different economic, religious, and professional interests. This in turn suggested that even when opposition to Nazism had occurred, it rested on a deeper substratum of emotional attachment to the regime, a perspective that even more critical observers had trouble dealing with until the 1980s. Only when Germans confronted the history of the perpetrators of Nazi crimes could this more painful memory of emotional identification be addressed. In the meantime, the organizers of alternative city tours of the Resistance would report that schoolchildren and other tour participants had trouble digesting the idea that "resisters" were not always armed or clandestine fighters like those portrayed in Westerns or action-adventure films but rather simple people involved in small and often forgotten subterfuges.[42]

The memory of the Resistance was now more plural, historically differentiated, and internally conflicted than before, and it was the victims of the regime who now also gained greater public attention. As in the immediate postwar era, the two categories remained difficult to separate, and many exhibits and documentations of this period grouped together "Persecution and Resistance." The Cologne publishing house of Paul-Rugenstein typified this trend in its seven-volume historical topography of resistance and persecution, arranged by region and appearing first in 1984. These volumes alerted viewers to hundreds of sites in everyday life where the Nazis had persecuted Jews, organized euthanasia programs, and tortured and killed working-class resisters. The traces of Nazi terror were everywhere, even in remote suburbs such as Allmendfeld in the Hessian town of Gernsheim, which, the guide pointed out, had been a new settlement under Nazi rule designed in the shape of a swastika.[43]

So ubiquitous were exhibits and publications dealing with the themes "persecution" and "resistance" that public memory took on a ritualistic quality that justifiably raised questions about the content and practical effect of commemoration. This was a disturbing development for those who were interested in teaching younger generations about the Holocaust. Would not the incessant and ritualistic commemoration of victims be seen by young people as part and parcel of an adults' worldview that had to be ignored or even resisted? This was a serious question debated openly and somewhat nervously by pedagogues and officials in the 1980s.[44] The linking of the two themes also suggested that persecution was the regime's draconian response to heroic resistance. This point of view suited the left-leaning proclivities of those who made up the majority of scholars and exhibition organizers, but it also hid the fact that Auschwitz was above all about the deportation and extermination of European Jews, the majority of whom did not and could not have resisted in any significant manner. When Essen opened an exhibit in 1980 on resistance and persecution from 1933 to 1945, it placed more emphasis on working-class opposition than on the history of a centuries-old Jewish community that had been exterminated in that city. This imbalance would be corrected, though not entirely, in later years.

The changing image of the victims thus strongly reflected the political interests of left-wing university and high school teachers, members of the Association for the Persecutees of the Nazi Regime, trade unions, church groups, the SPD, and former or current members of the Communist party. It was no coincidence that historical markers and commemorative events clustered geographically around the spaces where these groups had influence—university towns, working-class neighborhoods, and urban quarters in which countercultural groups flourished. These too were the intellectual environments in which memory of the Holocaust became captive to the abstract and synthetic concept of "fascism," which was used by the West German Left not to give a detailed portrait of the victims or even of the processes whereby the Holocaust occurred, but to explain mass killing with reference to an "alliance" between big-business corporations and the Nazi dictatorship. So strong was the association between Leftist political affiliation and commemorative activity in some quarters that it became an obstacle to the public impact of the new history movement. A good example comes from the history of alternative city tours.

Youth groups in Hamburg, alarmed by the rise of neo-Nazi groups, started the first antifascist city tour in the Federal Republic in 1979. The idea had been broached earlier in the decade by the Association of Persecutees of the Nazi Regime and reinforced in a major commemoration of the fortieth anniversary of the Night of Broken Glass in Hamburg in fall 1978. Instead of focusing on traditional landmarks and monuments, organizers of "Nazi Terror and Resistance in Hamburg" explored the city's history from an entirely different angle.[45] Participants could choose from two bus tours, one carrying them to twenty-six sites associated with the history of persecution and anti-Nazi resistance. This included the local trade union house, the Rathaus market square where Nazis killed twenty city parliament deputies, and the site of the former Jewish ghetto and synagogue. In the second tour, organizers concentrated more specifically on the history of the Neuengamme concentration camp. In 1979 eighty-three such tours were conducted with more than four thousand participants. About 90 percent were young people, the vast majority of tours having been initiated by secondary schoolteachers.[46]

The alternative city tours invited former Resistance fighters and concentration camp inmates to convey their impressions and supplement information provided by the tour guides. Most students responded enthusiastically, and some were so overwhelmed that they cried, fainted, or became ill. However, because the eyewitnesses were often associated with the left-leaning Association of Persecutees of the Nazi Regime, or because they were former members of the Communist party, a minority of the high school–age students reacted skeptically to their accounts. This was by no means a function of peculiar circumstances in Hamburg. In Saarbrücken organizers of an alternative city tour reported that some parents refused to allow schoolchildren to visit former Gestapo sites, questioning the historical accuracy of the left-leaning tour guides' information. In Saarbrücken, moreover, a part of one high school class taking the tour refused to listen to the resisters' accounts because they were convinced they were hearing Communist propaganda. Such opposition was not widespread, to be sure, but it was frequent enough to cause concern among tour organizers. For the most part, the tours had more mundane problems, from overpacked programs lasting several hours to a lack of preparation by the schoolchildren and their instructors.[47]

Still, the alternative tours contributed to a general public tendency toward elaboration and differentiation of the history of victims. This trend could also be seen in the changing representations of former concentration camp sites in West Germany. In previous decades concentration camps had had a limited presence in public memory, but with the trial of Eichmann and Auschwitz officials, and a broader popular interest in the history of the war and fascism, the concentration camps gained greater visibility. In one direction, this meant that the history of the minor camps and the satellites to the major camps received more attention, especially from history workshop groups. More recently, in Germany and elsewhere, this trend has resulted in the further elaboration of a picture of the camps in relation to surrounding civilian communities, as in Claude Lanzmann's controversial film *Shoah,* released in 1985, or Horwitz's study of the Austrian town surrounding the Mauthausen camp.[48] But in another direction, this meant that the main camps moved into the public spotlight by getting more elaborate exhibits and receiving more media attention.

From the late 1960s through the period of reunification, Auschwitz became the central symbol of memory of the victims of Nazism in the West. Some would argue it became the key word of West German political culture, the yardstick against which all variations of political identity could be measured. But public interest in Auschwitz rarely focused on the camp itself. Rather, the memory of Auschwitz became integrated into debates over German national identity. Advocates of German unity argued that only a unified national state could responsibly deal with the memory of horrific events that were after all undertaken by a single German state. Opponents such as the novelist Günter Grass maintained that Auschwitz removed forever the right of the Germans to reunify. In either case, Auschwitz was a symbol but not a historical reality. Little concrete information about the camp and its workings reached a broader public, a fact that could not be attributed solely to the Polish government's skewed commemoration of the site as a place where mainly Poles instead of Jews lost their lives. Popular phrases such as "Planet Auschwitz" and, in a more scholarly key, "*l'univers concentrationnaire,*" did not help matters because they strengthened a sense of the concentration camps as a world apart, or a kind of interstellar nonplace, divorced from both spatial and historical settings. But the lack of specificity of the image of Auschwitz also stood for a lack of specificity in the public's memory of concentration camp victims. This statement even applies to the memory of the survivors themselves. For them, the problem was too much memory and information, or a kind of sensory overload that resulted, paradoxically and with much pain, in a certain numbness about the past. The sheer variety of their experiences, their differing ages, nationalities,

Figure 48. A West German group lays wreaths at International Monument to Concentration Camp Victims, Auschwitz-Birkenau, 1986. Archiv für Kunst und Geschichte, Berlin.

and social backgrounds, their varying degree of exposure to persecution before the genocide, their deportation to different camps, and the conditions of their survival made a comprehensive and detailed narrative of the Holocaust difficult if not impossible. And it applies to historical scholarship in the Federal Republic, though for different reasons and with different outcomes. The most authoritative account of the Nazi period by a West German academic came from the political scientist Karl Dietrich Bracher, who published *The German Dictatorship* in 1969 and soon had it translated into a number of languages. In a wonderfully detailed and erudite book that included a nuanced discussion of Nazi racial politics up to 1938, only thirteen of nearly six hundred pages in the German edition were devoted to the extermination centers and the process of mass killing in the war.[49] West Germans would begin to fill in this historical vacuum in the two decades before unification.

Consider for a moment the history of the commemoration of Bergen-Belsen, about sixty kilometers northeast of Hannover, which had been one of the most brutal concentration camps of the Nazi regime. It was used for many groups, including French, Belgian, and Soviet prisoners of war as well as so-called "barter Jews," or *Austauschjuden,* who were thought to be valuable to the Nazi regime as hostages in international trades of prisoners between the Third Reich and its enemies. Bergen-Belsen would become a site of unspeakable horror in the last months of the war, when diseased and maltreated Jewish prisoners from concentration camps in the East were evacuated there. With the takeover of the camp and the ceremonial burning of its buildings for health reasons by British forces, Belsen became part of Western Allied war history and a widely recognized symbol of German evil in British political culture. The specific identities of the victims were downplayed. To stress the ethnic, religious, or national identities of the victims was to affront British liberal principles of treating all minorities equally in the modern nation-state. Even though no other Nazi camp had more Jewish survivors than Belsen at the moment of liberation, Jewish groups had to fight to have their sufferings commemorated. The more than thirty thousand Jews who lost their lives in Bergen-Belsen were honored with a memorial as early as November 1945. In 1947 the British government began work on a more general memorial featuring a twenty-four-meter-high obelisk and a fifty-meter-long wall of inscriptions in fifteen languages commemorating victims from many nations. Yet such memorials remained rather isolated in the vast empty spaces and stark mass graves of the camp, and visitors received little general information about Belsen's history. It was 1966 before a documentation center was established. No inscription commemorated the deaths of Sinti and Roma victims of Bergen-Belsen until 1982, and not until 1990 was there a detailed treatment of the fifty thousand Soviet prisoners of war who died there.[50] Only hesitantly did Bergen-Belsen help focus attention on the victims who perished in Nazism's exterminatory war.

Other camps underwent comparable transformations. The Dachau concentration camp site was reorganized in 1965 to convey more accurately than before what had gone on in the camp and how the Holocaust in its broadest sense originated and developed. Not only the fate of political prisoners and religious dissidents but also the workings of the Final Solution were now treated as equal parts of the site's historical message. From having been a rather marginal survivor of the war, the camp site became a major documentation and educational center, attracting nearly one million visitors annually by the early 1990s. Besides Dachau, Bavaria had also been the site of another major concentration camp, Flossenbürg, near the Czech border. More than thirty thousand people died in this camp, including criminals, "asocials," homosexuals, Jews, and Russian and other POWs. Some were worked to death in a nearby quarry, whereas others, especially the Soviet prisoners of war, were executed. In 1949 the ashes of Jews who died at Flossenbürg were transferred to Israel and buried in Jerusalem on Mount Zion. But little remained to remind Germans of the camp after the war, as officials used some of the buildings to house expellees from the Sudetenland, bulldozed the barracks of the central installation, and destroyed the numerous satellite camps. Although memorials were built at the site immediately after the war, it was not until the early 1980s that a trade-union group organized a fuller exhibit on the history of the victims of the camp.[51]

In Hamburg the Neuengamme work camp had originally been established as a satellite of the Sachsenhausen camp and a source of cheap labor in the urban renewal of Hamburg under Hitler's direction. More than fifty thousand people from all countries of Europe died in the camp, including some seven thousand who perished in May 1945 when British bombers sank the ships *Cap Arcona* and *Thielbek* as the Nazis desperately evacuated Neuengamme inmates off the Baltic coast. It would take twenty years for Neuengamme to become a full-fledged memorial site, and another fifteen before a documentation center was set up. In the 1980s the camp became an archaeological site laid out in a grid pattern and opened to international youth groups, who painstakingly excavated the foundations of camp buildings and uncovered artifacts of the many different groups that worked and died there.[52] This reflected a characteristic feature of the new emphasis on historical traces: Neuengamme was excavated not only because of its historical significance but because the fate of its victims could be linked to more contemporary issues of pedagogy, international exchanges, and human rights issues. The Austrian historian Gerhard Botz noted that former concentration camp sites had become important not only for their historical legacy, but for the fact that they were increasingly "seminar centers" that inspired visitors to think about parallels between historical and contemporary events.[53] This perspective was tangibly reflected in the archaeological approach to the Neuengamme site.

Creating a more differentiated view of the victims and drawing parallels between the past and present brought about another reorientation. The history of persecution of a racial minority drew attention to West German society's often fraught relationship with Turkish, Yugoslav, and other minorities, just as memory of the Holocaust in Britain and the United States since the 1970s has been linked more and more to other forms of genocide and racism as well as to homophobia, social prejudice, and even domestic violence.[54] But in the Federal Republic, the presence of minorities highlighted the absence of a significant Jewish minority. This absence had already been reaffirmed in the memory landscape, where memorials to Holocaust victims erected by German Jews themselves were often modest or virtually hidden from public view. Sites of Jewish memory often marked empty spaces where a synagogue or a school once stood. Where more ambitious memorials were erected, they did little to garner public attention. A memorial put up by Berlin Jews in the form of a simple bronze wall with the names of the death camps, similar to a wailing wall, was placed in the backyard of a Jewish community center in the Fasanenstrasse. Few Berliners knew of its existence.[55] Empty or obscure places of memory reflected the fact that it was not until the 1960s in Europe that a Jewish memory of the war, as something distinct from the memory of antifascist resistance fighters or political persecutees, began to develop.[56]

In East Berlin, the GDR declared the huge Jewish cemetery of Weißensee to be a major cultural monument. This cemetery, measuring more than forty square hectares, was a moving document of the history of Berlin Jews, encompassing the tombstones of famous politicians, financiers, and scholars but also the simple and somewhat isolated markers of poorer Jews who had migrated to Germany from Eastern Europe in the nineteenth century. More than two thousand gravestones at this site reflected the growing number of suicides in the Berlin Jewish community in the late 1930s and early 1940s as the Holocaust gained momentum, and scores more reminded visitors of deportations in 1938, 1941, and 1942. The site was a major attraction in tourist itineraries of the GDR capital.[57] Yet the Weißensee cemetery deteriorated under GDR cultural stewardship, and vandalism, partly a product of anti-Semitism, partly protest against the regime, reflected a widespread feeling that the site was "a kind of no-man's land without owners."[58] A similar description would have applied to many other sites of Jewish memory in postwar Germany.

The concept of victimhood proved to be inadequate to understand the void left by Jews and Jewish culture. Before 1933, the Jews were not primarily victims but integral historical actors in German society, as the Weißensee site vividly demonstrated. The fact that Nazism virtually eradicated all reminders of the Jewish contributions to German culture necessitated a more archaeological approach to the past, a digging for traces, that would enable people imaginatively to reconstruct lost connections and relationships. The alternative history groups played an important role here. For one thing, they addressed the public's difficulty

Figure 49. Jewish cemetery, Berlin-Weißensee, 1980. Bildarchiv Preussischer Kulturbesitz.

remembering Jews as Jews. In an atmosphere of denial or extreme guilt, many people on both sides of the border found it easier to understand the eradication of Jewish life as an eradication of *German* culture by the Nazis.[59] To emphasize the Jewishness of Holocaust victims was seemingly also to resurrect anti-Semitism's intense prejudices and stereotypes. British liberal culture had displayed a similar reticence in its treatment of Bergen-Belsen. West Berlin's program to place plaques of famous historic personalities throughout the city included many Jewish figures, whose names now dotted the buildings and spaces of the districts of Charlottenburg, Wilmersdorf, and Schöneberg, where many prominent Jews once lived. But how to visualize the way in which these personalities related to the broader Jewish culture to which they remained indebted even if they did not identify as Jews?

The history of everyday life was a natural conduit for addressing this question because it dealt with community life, religion, dress, cuisine, music, and many other subjects that resurrected the subjective dimensions of Jewish life. Such perspectives were clearly developed in a 1988 exhibit by the Berlin History Workshop on Jewish life on the Kurfürstendamm, the city's main commercial street. A subsequent brochure based on the exhibit captured the point with its title: *Als wäre es nie gewesen (As If It Had Never Been).* Traces of Jewish life in the former German capital were now to be recovered in an attempt to envision what the Nazis had extricated. One café on the corner of the Kurfürstendamm and Joachimstaler, was described as a place where the " 'flipped-out' of their time," the avant-garde artists and writers of pre–World War I Berlin, often congregated. Many were Jews, but, as the brochure pointed out, it was difficult to determine how many members of this extremely varied cultural avant-garde identified as Jews. It was an anti-Semitic public before 1914 and Nazi persecutions after 1933 that simplified such distinctions, and it was the Nazis' 1939 ruling forcing all Jewish men to take the name "Israel" and all women that of "Sara" that radicalized the process even more. "Is it still possible," asked the brochure, "to imagine the heterogeneous, the religiously, socially, and politically varied, opposed, and also thoroughly contradictory forms of Jewish life, after the Nazis transformed different individuals into 'the' Jews, Sara and Israel?" Was it possible to imagine such variation when "this arbitrary reduction perhaps still has an after-effect in our heads?"[60]

Such questions could be asked by Germans as they were guided along the busy commercial street and directed to look at what remained, or what could be imagined, of a culture that in its time was much more than the product of victims. In many ways, this remains a central problem of German memory work after reunification, as Michael Geyer and Miriam Hansen have pointed out. Opposing the "facile multiculturalism" of the 1990s, Geyer and Hansen write: "The remembrance of the absent Jews requires a concrete knowledge both of their religious and their secular culture and an obligation to the residual Jewish communities; above all, it means recollecting the loss to German life of that once closely identified community."[61] The organizers of the Berlin History Workshop exhibit of 1988 focused precisely on this kind of "concrete knowledge" of Jewish culture *in German history.*

Such approaches to the past were sophisticated and useful, but they were still embedded in a culture where broader definitions of victims and more varied uses of memory also had many negative consequences. Many groups suffered and died under Nazism, for example, but the broader culture increasingly ratified what could only be called a heightened competition over the status of victimhood. Homosexuals, Sinti and Roma, and Jehovah's Witnesses agitated for public recognition as persecuted groups under Nazi rule. Documentation projects and historical scholarship began to firm up the public record of Nazi policies toward these minorities.[62] But much more alarming and influential was the tendency to emphasize Germany as a whole as a nation of victims. The antinuclear movements beginning in the 1970s, as well as massive protests against the stationing of Pershing Missiles in West Germany in the early 1980s, made political gain out of precisely this emphasis by linking memory of World War II with images of an anticipated nuclear holocaust. Anxiety about the potential obliteration of Germany, the future battleground of World War III, engaged public memory of World War II as a war in which Germany was brought to the zero hour of its history. Domansky has pointed out a consequence of this linkage: "Most memories of the 'World War III–World War II' complex depict German society at war as a community of suffering and not as a society that inflicted war and suffering on others."[63]

This tendency gained official sanction in May 1985 in Ronald Reagan's clumsy and inarticulate commemoration of the fortieth anniversary of the end of World War II.[64] Urged by Helmut Kohl to visit a German military cemetery and a former concentration camp site—it was after all the fortieth anniversary of the liberation of the camps as well—Reagan chose to make a brief symbolic visit to the Kolmeshöhe military cemetery in Bitburg, West Germany, near the Luxemburg border and two miles from a U.S. air base where the president would speak. He chose not to visit a former concentration camp because he did not want to arouse unpleasant memories. "They have a guilt feeling that's been imposed upon them," said Reagan of the German people, "and I just think [a visit to a camp is] unnecessary." He later relented on this decision because of massive criticism from all sides, and he did finally visit Bergen-Belsen. But he held to the idea of visiting Bitburg, which happened to contain forty-nine graves of Waffen SS soldiers as well as graves of the Second SS Panzer Division "Das Reich," which massacred the citizens of Oradour-sur-Glane. Undeterred, Reagan told broadcasters and editors visiting the White House in April 1985 that "There's nothing wrong with visiting that cemetery where those young men are victims of Nazism also . . . They were victims, just as surely as the victims in the concentration camps." Reagan's visit to Bitburg went as planned, despite strong protests in the U.S., West Germany, and elsewhere.

Fortunately, German politicians undid some of the damage caused by Reagan's crude and characteristically inarticulate remarks. Two weeks before Reagan's visit, Kohl himself observed the fortieth anniversary of the liberation of Bergen-Belsen, saying he accepted Germany's "historical responsibility for the crimes of the Nazi tyranny . . . a responsibility reflected not least in never-ending shame." Three days after Reagan's visit, the president of the Federal Republic, Richard von Weizsäcker, addressed the Bundestag in one of the most moving speeches in postwar European history. "All of us, whether guilty or not, whether old or young, must accept the past," said von Weizsäcker. "We are all affected by its consequences and liable for it. . . . We must understand that there can be no reconciliation without remembrance." Given previous evidence, such statements might be seen as nothing more than a verification of what so many alternative history groups or grassroots initiatives had been saying for years. Yet that the president of the Republic had made this forthright statement only days after President Reagan had gone to Bitburg was an elegant and effective rejoinder to the now growing narrative of general German tribulation under Nazism.

Charles Maier has used the term "Bitburg history" to describe the tendency to blur and equate victim groups. Bitburg history put oppressors and victims on the same level. It made it difficult to assign collective responsibility or human agency. It also suggested that Nazi crimes were ultimately less original and searing given the twentieth century's mangled record of massacre and violence. Bitburg history along with the fortieth-anniversary commemorations also set the stage for the so-called "Historians' Debate." This public controversy engaged West German historians and other scholars in a heated exchange of views about the status of Nazism and the Holocaust in German and European history. Without featuring new methodological advances or significant new historical interpretations, the debate reflected what might be called a form of historiographical fatigue with issues of Nazism, guilt, and World War II on the part of conservative scholars. The respected historian Andreas Hillgruber published a book in early 1986 that seemed to equate the bitter fate of German soldiers fighting on the Eastern front in the last days of World War II with the extermination of European Jews. Opening with a discussion of two "national catastrophes," the book was titled *Zweierlei Untergang (Two Sorts of Demise)*.[65] More controversially, the Berlin historian Ernst Nolte suggested that Hitler may have acted preemptively against the Soviets and Jews and that all but the Nazis' use of mass gassings had been prefigured in Bolshevik atrocities of the 1920s and 1930s. Nolte's stated goal was to help Germans deal with their past less obsessively, but his books and articles only inspired the noted liberal philosopher Jürgen Habermas to attack him for trying to reduce the uniquely violent character of the Holocaust and trying to unburden German history.[66]

The impact of the new rhetoric of victimization on the memory landscape could be seen most centrally in efforts to create a national memorial for the victims of World War II. The Weimar Republic's attempts to have such a widely recognized and constitutive memorial had failed, but West German officials continued to keep the idea alive, in part because they believed that foreign dignitaries ought to have a place to conduct impressive commemorative ceremonies on important holidays. This underscored the international dimensions of Bitburg history. Varied sites in Bonn, Munich, and elsewhere had proved inadequate for such purposes. In 1983 a commission recommended "a national memorial for the war dead of the German people" for Bonn that would commemorate the two million dead of World War I and the seven million of World War II. Skeptics from the Green party and Jewish groups argued that to honor all German victims of the two wars, soldiers as well as resisters, Jews as well as Catholic priests, in a single memorial did damage to the many differences that separated the fates—and determined the choices—of the people involved. Christian Democratic and other government officials were undeterred, arguing that "all war dead and victims of the hegemony of force have left to us a testament . . . to fight for the triumph of the good and the genuine over the evil and the false."[67]

The defenders of "the good and the genuine" would have their day after German unification in 1993, when the Neue Wache was dedicated as just such a memorial. Although it would be surrounded with controversy, the postunification Neue Wache demonstrated that the long history of the German rhetoric of victimhood was by no means dead. Indeed it would now be used in yet another attempt to recentralize the fragmented and dispersed memories of Germany's two wars in a broad, unhistorical gesture. Informed commentary suggests that to this date, the redesigned Neue Wache has not met with great public enthusiasm. At the end of the millennium, in any case, planning for a giant Holocaust memorial near the Brandenburg Gate sparked more public discussion than the Neue Wache.

GERMAN MIRRORS

If the memory of victims and victimization reconstructed certain key themes in German culture, then so too did a seemingly new and innovative feature of the surge of public memory after the late 1960s. As West Germans dug for traces of the Holocaust, they increasingly discovered themselves. In the first two decades after 1945, this mirroring process

Figure 50. Dedication in 1973 of memorial at Grunewald freight ramp, from which Berlin Jews were deported to Nazi death camps. Deutsches Historisches Museum.

occurred only sporadically because the perpetrators often still held the mirrors. Now a new generation was more willing to view the Holocaust as a complex process organized and implemented by specific people in specific places. Mass extermination was not something that just happened as if it were a thunderstorm. It is significant that naturalistic metaphors, so popular when used with reference to the Holocaust right through the 1950s, found less favor with the West German public now that the perspective had shifted to real people making real decisions. In most previous reconstructions of the Holocaust, not only the victims but the act of mass killing itself assumed an abstract, otherworldly quality that did little to specify concrete historical connections. The historical diggers of the Federal Republic were now ready to make these connections. It was no longer possible merely to see German trains as metaphors of mass death; the places from which Jews were actually carried away, such as the freight ramps of the Grunewald train station in West Berlin, would now be commemorated in all their chilling literality. In their understandable zeal to specify who the perpetrators were, what they did, and where they did it, however, West Germans also reinvested in an old theme: the Sonderweg.

The path to reconstructing a history of the perpetrators was an extremely hard one. Let us first consider the history of the commemoration of the Wewelsburg, a seventeenth-century fortress that had once served as the residence of the prince bishops of Paderborn in Westphalia.[68] Under Heinrich Himmler's direction the monument was transformed first into an ideological school for the SS, then a cultic site for a new order of racially pure SS leaders, and finally what was to be the "center" of the Germanic world after the victories of World War II. These plans necessitated money and labor, the latter being drawn first from the Reich Labor Service but then from camp inmates of Sachsenhausen. Laborers were housed in a small camp that later became the independent work camp Niederhagen. More than 3,000 workers from the Soviet Union, Germany, Austria, and Poland came through this camp, and at least 1,285 died, some from overwork and malnutrition but many others from physical and psychological torture by an especially brutal SS camp staff. In 1942–1943 the site was used by the Gestapo of Westphalia and Lippe for executions, and at least 56 individuals died in this manner until April 1943, when the camp was dissolved and its inmates sent to Bergen-Belsen, Buchenwald, and Auschwitz. Shortly before the U.S. army was to march into the area, an SS commando dynamited the fortress, and a day later the Wewelsburg burned to the ground.

From 1949 to 1979 the Wewelsburg was rebuilt because of its importance as an architectural monument. But its history as the planned headquarters of an SS empire, the nerve center of a phalanx of racial warriors, was more difficult to confront. The U.S. army forced all Wewelsburg citizens aged nine to seventy to participate in a "burial of atonement" in May 1945. Ringed by armed military personnel, townspeople were forced to excavate the decomposing bodies of fifteen Soviet prisoners shot by the SS for plundering the bombed-out city of Paderborn and buried in a mass grave near Oberhagen. This ceremony was to be concluded at the local cemetery, where a priest was to sermonize on Nazi atrocities. The priest refused, speaking instead on the need for a "retreat from hate and triumph of love." The people of Wewelsburg took heart from the clergyman's opposition to U.S. "shock politics," and in the ensuing decades many local people denied the existence of the camp, wrangled over property rights to buildings expropriated by the often unwelcome SS units, and ignored the trials of Wewelsburg SS officers and prisoner foremen, or *Capos*, for atrocities committed against camp inmates.

Only in the 1970s did the wider public become involved in debates over the Wewelburg's history. A modest plaque commemorating the 1,285 victims of the Wewelsburg concentration camp was put up in the fortress's courtyard in 1964, only to be removed in 1973 after local citizens protested that the Wewelsburg itself had nothing to do with the camp. Three years later, after much controversy in the local parliament and the national press, the SPD Bundestag deputy, Thüsing, and several colleagues put up another plaque without official sanction on 9 November 1977, the thirty-ninth anniversary of the Night of Broken Glass. Their action polarized opinions even more, and three days later *that* plaque was spirited away, reappearing in a military cemetery in Böddeken four miles away. The local Christian Democratic leadership of the county finally agreed to erecting an officially approved commemorative plaque to the victims of the Wewelsburg camp in the above-mentioned military cemetery, and exactly one year after the Thüsing affair, the plaque appeared with the rather anodyne inscription "To the memory of the victims of the war and the rule of violence, 1933–1945." Nothing was said about who unleashed the war or ran the system of violence, and the identity of the victims remained foggy.

More significant for the history of Wewelsburg was the decision taken in 1977 by local leaders to establish a permanent exhibit and documentary center, "Wewelsburg 1933–1945—Cultic Center and Site of SS Terror," set up in the former SS guardhouse of the complex. This exhibit opened in 1982. Three rooms used photographs and photocopies of documents to chart Himmler's transformation of the Wewelsburg. Another room was dedicated to the inhumane conditions of the Niederhagen camp, while another explained the history of the SS. Finally, a sixth room documented the ebb and flow of debate since 1945 over how the Wewelsburg was to be remembered. The inclusion of this subject indicated that the process of memory work itself had become an important theme in public commemorations. More specifically, the subject of how the perpetrators should be remembered came into the foreground. This perspectival shift was reinforced by the preservation and renovation of two of the fortress's rooms that had served as SS "shrines." In these rooms visitors could see how the SS had transformed its racist ideology into a form of quasi-religious mysticism.

Another site of terror was the stately building known as the Wannsee Villa in West Berlin. Like Wewelsburg, its history as a site of commemoration was as revealing, perhaps even more so, than its historical significance. At this SS guest house in a quiet, well-to-do suburb, Nazi and state functionaries met on 20 January 1942 to discuss information relating to the Final Solution. Although mass killings had already begun before this date and all the major decisions leading up to the establishment of extermination centers had already been made, journalists and many others would later inaccurately identify the villa as the site where the Holocaust was planned. For most Berliners, however, the villa was almost invisible, functioning as a children's recreation center after the war. The Berlin Senate hoped to keep it this way, declining offers by prominent Berlin intellectuals and the World Jewish Congress to turn it into a memorial and documentation center in the 1960s. It did so partly out of fear of antagonizing conservative voters, whose views were summed up in a polemical headline in a right-wing newspaper: "Nazi Documents More Important than Working-Class Children?" The leader of the initiative to use the site as a documentation center was the historian and Auschwitz survivor Josef Wulf, who continued his attempts until 1974, when, broken by his lack of success, he committed suicide. His work was continued by the city's Jewish community and persecutees' groups. By the late 1980s attitudes had shifted, and work began on a center for Holocaust scholarship and political education. On the fiftieth anniversary of the Wannsee conference in 1992 a Holocaust Memorial Center was finally established with much fanfare. But the new center reflected Wulf's wishes only indirectly, and critics argued that the permanent exhibit did little to clarify who the perpetrators were and even less to pinpoint the experiences and life stories of the victims.[69]

Wewelsburg and Wannsee Villa were viewed as substantially reconstructed or intact artifacts of a larger topography of the traces of Nazi terror. Another site, much more fragmentary and elusive, not only constituted another part of the topography but also embodied the idea of the topography per se. The already mentioned Gestapo terrain was a paradigmatic empty space in the first thirty years after the war, a place of rubble, ruined buildings, and overgrown fields that tangibly expressed a large void in the public memory of Nazism.[70] This began to change in the 1970s when architects and the historian Reinhard Rürup drew attention to the historical significance of the site as they protested the city's plan to build an expressway across the blighted terrain. Further protest arose when the "Prussia" exhibit was held in 1981 in the Martin Gropius Building, only a few meters away from the open space. History workshops, journalists, and others—spurred in part by the general trend toward memory in the period—increased public awareness of the site. The overgrown fields and ruins acquired powerful geographical metaphors such as Gestapo Terrain and Topography of Terror, both fixing the significance of the site in the public mind. In 1980 a member of the Association of Persecuted Social Democrats wrote the Berlin Senate, arguing that "the Social Democratic Resistance fighters and victims of the Nazi regime expect that at the . . . site where the Gestapo had its headquarters and tortured people, a dignified memorial be put up in remembrance of the National Socialist reign of terror."[71]

Numerous groups agitated to create a memorial at the site. Officials responded by reiterating their commitment to using part of the site for a Museum of German History but also conceding the need to put up an appropriate memorial. At the same time, they wanted to create a usable urban space. The Berlin Senate held a planning competition in which 194 proposals outlined possible solutions. But controversy swirled around the competition, and in 1984 the senate handed over responsibility for the site to a commission in charge of Berlin's 750th anniversary, to be held in 1987. It was in this context of widespread debate and uncertainty that the Active Museum of Fascism and Resistance and the Berlin History Workshop held their symbolic dig on 5 May 1985. The uncovering of the foundations of Gestapo prison cells and the placement of wreaths at these sites a year later created informally what the authorities had been unable to create—an authentic memorial space.

In 1987 the Topography of Terror was officially opened as a temporary exhibit. An austere white building straddled the site of the Gestapo cells, providing shelter for visitors who perused photographs and rather wordy descriptions of what had taken place there. Biographies of resisters, maps, and reproductions of official documents rounded out the exhibit. Around the terrain, organizers placed signs that described which buildings had stood at particular sites. Piles of rubble reminded visitors of how the terrain looked after the war. A portion of the Berlin Wall could be seen from the terrain, powerfully symbolizing the geopolitical reality that had emerged from the violence of the Third Reich. In contrast to a museum, which by its nature tends to muffle the emotional impact of historical events with a rationalistic approach to artifacts, the Topography of Terror was an austere site whose very impermanence and proximity to the tangible effects of Hitler's regime gave it the character of an open wound in the urban landscape. The exhibit was extended indefinitely due to favorable public interest. Given the foregoing information in this book about Germans' sincere and ongoing attempts to understand the history of Nazism, there is little reason to puzzle over the fact that the exhibit was "oddly popular," as Jane Kramer does.[72] The Topography of Terror spoke to a deep-seated need to explain and evoke the past. In 1988 the Berlin Senate put together another advisory board to determine the future of the site, and planning and discussion proceeded through the process of national unification.

A consensus was reached only when another group, "Perspective for Berlin," founded in 1988, proposed a giant Holocaust memorial at the site. This group considered it scandalous that Germany did not have a single, central Holocaust monument to honor the victims of Nazism. The director of the initiative was the rather extravagant television talk show hostess Lea Rosh, who led a glitzy and well-financed public campaign to produce a memorial that would be, in Rosh's own words, "big like the crime." Rosh herself had legally changed her name from "Edith" to the Jewish "Lea," and made a public show of the fact that her maternal grandfather had been a Berlin Jew.[73] Though somewhat nonplussed by Rosh's crudeness, the advisors and organizers of the Topography of Terror were not opposed to honoring the victims. But they were convinced that the Gestapo terrain must be used to symbolize the history of the perpetrators, and they asserted their right, indeed their obligation, to determine what part of the history of Nazism was to be represented at the site.

Karen Till has quite rightly pointed out that this insistence also revealed a deeper sense of collective identity insofar that the German nation was identified as a nation of perpetrators.[74] To honor victims at this site, the terrain's supporters reasoned, was to give in to a growing public conviction that most Germans had been victimized by a regime alien to their traditions and values. But it was also to lose sight of who had perpetrated the Holocaust in the first place. Such rigorous defense of the right to specify Germany as a nation that produced mass murderers could not have happened before this time.

As for the massive Holocaust memorial proposed by Rosh and her supporters, the projected site was finally moved to a prime spot in central Berlin, near the Brandenburg Gate and over what had once been Hitler's chauffeur's bunker. The official title of the structure was to be the Monument for the Murdered Jews of Europe, and because it was intended to be the most expensive memorial ever constructed in Berlin, the Berlin Senate quickly became involved in debates over the project. Inconclusive design competitions would eventually produce many bizarre proposals. Rosh initially favored a vast subterranean Star of David, which visitors would enter through gates over which Auschwitz's infamous words *Arbeit macht frei* would be placed. To be fair, there were also some imaginative proposals, including the Kassel artist Horst Hoheisel's plan to tear down the Brandenburg Gate and use *its* stones for the memorial.[75] The fate of the enterprise remained uncertain through the 1990s, and some supporters wanted to use architect Daniel Libeskind's innovative Museum of Jewish history in Berlin as the memorial. With Social Democrat Gerhard Schröder's election to the chancellorship in 1998, a new plan designed by an American architect, Peter Eisenman, was finally approved and ratified by the Bundestag. Even so, details about the precise relation between the memorial and the information center that was to supplement it had to be worked out before construction could begin.

Cultic sites of the SS, the planning of the Final Solution, the headquarters of the SS and Gestapo—all created a new public memory of a murderous regime and the genocidal war it unleashed. But the varied public struggles that had occurred in drawing attention to these sites and securing them for commemorative use reflected that West Germans had resorted to a well-established theme. Violence and terror of the SS were the products of a nation of perpetrators whose values were those of an exterminatory pariah. Germany's unique path through historical time had resulted in a Sonderweg of violence.

There were of course dissenting voices. The historian Detlev Peukert, who bridged university teaching and the history workshop movement, argued that Nazism was not the result of a peculiar German tradition of antidemocratic values and racism, but of the conjuncture of possibilities inherent in all industrial societies.[76] He did not argue specifically about the Topography of Terror, but his perspective could have been applied to it. The Gestapo terrain might have been represented as a site in which the murderous potential of all modern industrial states had been realized under Hitler's direction. Despite the organizers' rather exclusionary emphasis on German peculiarity, some have argued that the Topography gestured to a form of postnational identity. Jürgen Habermas has been among the most vocal proponents of the idea that Germany's future depends on disengaging political and cultural identities. Without giving up the idea of cultural or even ethnic identities, argued Habermas, Germany must opt for a "constitutional patriotism" that embraces universal values of democracy, tolerance, and free speech, and rejects older forms of nationalism. From this perspective, the Topography of Terror could be seen as a site that symbolized the nation's commitment to such universal values in the political realm.[77] Not a self-isolating preoccupation with the history of a single nation's unique and horrific war of extermination, but the universal and civic lessons to be drawn from that history made up the central focus of Habermas's message.

Such nuanced views belonged to a minority, and they were in any case often lost in the heated debates over public memory. Moreover, the organizers of the site opted for what amounted to a neo-historicist approach, stressing documentation and "the facts" about the terrain rather than broader interpretations and the possibility of universalizing themes. For the most part, just as the Topography of Terror had to be secured and defended as a site of German perpetrators, the German nation had to be established as the unexampled instigator and perpetrator of momentous crimes against humanity. It is conceivable that the dissenting views could gain ground over time; no monument is set in stone, least of all a paradigmatic empty space. But the Topography of Terror remained for the time being the symbol of a decidedly *German* collective memory based on notions of national peculiarity. The motto chosen by Rosh's otherwise ungainly campaign for a Holocaust memorial made perfect sense in this context: "We, as Germans, do this."

One could argue in much the same way about the phenomenon of countermonuments, or *Gegendenkmäler.* Appearing most frequently in the 1980s, countermonuments were conceived of as "self-abnegating" entities that questioned the didactic logic and value of the traditional monument. In Hamburg, Jochen Gerz and Esther Shalev-Gerz erected a structure consisting of a twelve-meter-high, one-meter-square pillar out of hollow aluminum covered with a thin layer of soft lead. This pillar was lowered into the ground as visitors filled up its surface with memorial graffiti. At the end of the process, which occurred in stages and was duly celebrated at each ritualized lowering of the monument into the ground, all that would remain was a small burial stone with the inscription "Hamburg's Monument against Fascism." A monument had thus become a historical trace. In the Neukölln district of Berlin, meanwhile, Norbert Rademacher constructed a monument in which passersby at the former site of a satellite camp of Sachsenhausen would trip a light beam that switched on a high-intensity slide projection with written information about the camp and its inmates.[78] In this case, the historical trace was provided by electronic means. Even the highly publicized "wrapping" of the Reichstag by the concept artist Christo, a project debated for years and finally realized in 1995, qualified as a countermonument because it was a temporary display. Moreover, the shimmering silver fabric in which the Reichstag was sheathed gave the building an ethereal quality.[79]

Whether because of their transience and immateriality or their breaking down of barriers between the monument and usually passive spectators, the countermonuments questioned traditional forms of commemoration and used historical time itself to emphasize the temporality of history and memory. Memory changes constantly, the countermonuments pointed out; monuments should do all they can to symbolize this transience and actively involve the viewer in the process of seeking out such fleeting traces.

The Topography of Terror and structures such as the Gerzes' countermonument were radically different in the sense that the former was defended as a permanent site whose meaning was unambivalent whereas the latter celebrated impermanence. The former was meant to serve an explicit and unitary didactic purpose whereas the latter could be taken in a variety of ways—and in fact was by tourists, journalists, politicians, and many others. Yet the historical site and the countermonument had more in common than one might assume. The countermonuments were designed to address aesthetic problems that were international in scope, to be sure. Rademacher for example wanted to create public art that was radically participatory and ever changing, and thus inassimilable to the museum and the marketplace. Such cleverness could only be imagined from the point of view of a privileged artist living in well-to-do Europe. Yet in the Gerzes' cases, the goal was also to create a specific torment for visitors as well as individuals living in proximity to the disappearing monument. Laughing at their clientele, the Gerzes likened the monument to a great black knife in the back of Germany, whose citizens rejoiced in their self-mutilation.[80] Did not this highly cerebral and elitist mischievousness also speak to a supposedly unique quality of tormented "inwardness," a trait not defined solely by memory of Nazism but by a much longer cultural tradition in Germany that brought the supporters of the countermonuments and angst-ridden survivors of the 1960s into line with the German Romantics? The very notion of a disappearing monument, a celebration of absence, had much to do with the special anxiety of how it felt to imagine being German.

EASTERN VISTAS

Only a country that had already attained a high degree of self-consciousness about its relationship to the past could afford and produce countermonuments. Countermonuments made sense only in reference to West Germany's commemorative largesse, just as 1960s hippies made sense only in wealthy and highly materialistic societies. In the German Democratic Republic, there were no countermonuments. Here the cultural politics of the regime marked out a path of commemoration that differed more significantly from that of the West than in the first fifteen years or so after the war. Yet there were still important similarities between the two approaches that revealed the common cultural origins and historical conditions of the two states.

In the first fifteen years of the postwar age, the GDR's leaders concentrated on reconstructing a society traumatized by fascism and war. The goals of relative material stability and political consolidation were achieved, especially after the building of the Berlin Wall in 1961. Antifascist ideology had required historical perspectives, and even more than in the West, the GDR regime looked for historical antecedents for its political and cultural endeavors. The Wall itself was an historical marker or even a memorial in this context: in the 1950s Honecker, who led and administered the building of the "antifascist protective wall," likened the situation in East Berlin to that of the Paris Commune in 1871. The Communards were massacred, argued Honecker, because they failed to seal themselves off physically from the surrounding society.[81] But after the 1960s, historical elements and memories were used to consolidate what was increasingly seen as a mature socialist society. The theme of national reunification continued in the 1960s but was eventually deemphasized in the wake of Brandt's foreign policy of openness toward the East. In the place of reunification came a policy of "demarcation" toward the West in which the GDR would be seen not merely as a socialist alternative to the Federal Republic but a separate national state, permanent and unassailable. Previous historical practices thus took on a different character than before, and new or rather marginalized historical images and objects assumed a new importance.

In the 1960s, but even more so in the next two decades, GDR theorists relied on theoretical and practical distinctions between heritage and tradition to create a new historical context for the regime. If heritage referred to the total German past, then tradition comprised those parts of the past that could be nurtured and developed in the effort to increase popular support for the state. The distinctive characteristic of the period after 1970 was a broader definition of heritage than ever before. The East German state was now not merely a socialist way station on the road to German unity but a fulfilled national entity. This meant its historical roots could be found in the history of the German ethnie as a whole, not only in specific traditions of working-class and socialist history. The regime's primary goal was to strengthen its cultural and emotional legitimacy—which in 1989 proved to be more brittle than even the most hardened skeptics imagined. Still, reliance on a deeper sense of German history also reflected the burden of the past. Despite the regime's insistence on revolution, its future could be secured only with reference to the broad outlines of German tradition and history.

The regime had appropriated German classical heritage early in the postwar era with celebrations of Goethe, Bach, Beethoven, the Prussian generals Gebhard von Blücher and Karl von Clausewitz, the patriotic poet Ernst Moritz Arndt, and even the nationalistic founder of the German gymnastics movement, Friedrich Jahn. In the 1980s, this recognition of historical personalities from the classical era became even more comprehensive. The regime had removed the famous statue of Frederick the Great in Berlin (see Figure 28) in 1950. Frederick returned to his traditional spot in 1980 as his personality was rehabilitated and his visage reappeared on beer bottles and other commercial objects. His return took place in the context of celebrations of Prussia's long history on both sides of the German-German border. But whereas the West celebrated Prussia from a conservative-reactionary point of view, according to GDR ideologues, the East stressed the "other Prussia" of the Wars of Liberation, the Berlin university of Hegel, Fichte, and the Humboldts, and the Berlin working-class movement. With reference to Frederick it was argued that "in contrast to his reactionary goals, many of his policies had in an objective sense positive effects on historical progress."[82]

In 1983 the celebration of the five-hundredth anniversary of Martin Luther's birthday took place. Once derided in East Germany as the "traitor of peasants" because of his opposition to popular uprisings in the sixteenth-century Peasants' War, Luther was now praised as a great humanist whose heritage the GDR took up as its own. The Wartburg fortress in Eisenach, where Luther had translated part of the Bible into German while in hiding, became a center of festivities. Memorials were erected, and restorations of sites that were significant to Luther's life were undertaken in Erfurt, Eisleben, and Eisenach. Luther became a media star on East German television, and regime officials lauded the many German and foreign visitors to the country in 1983 who searched for "the traces of Luther" in the peasants' and workers' state.[83]

As in the Federal Republic, a revived public and regime commitment to the preservation of historic places could be seen in East Germany after 1970. This fact alone indicates that disillusionment with capitalist social relations was not the only motivation for the turn to historic buildings. Indeed the interest in historic places was a worldwide phenomenon, extending from the Anglo-American world to Europe on either side of the Iron Curtain, to Southeast Asia and Japan.[84] In East Germany stronger criticism of the regime's handling of monuments such as the imperial palace could now be heard. Protests against the regime's plans to tear down historical churches in favor of socialist skyscrapers occurred in Wismar, Leipzig, and Rostock. In Leipzig, students and church members attended silent demonstrations, sit-down strikes, and special church services to protest regime decisions to demolish the historic University Church, the foundation of which dated to 1229. Right before the massive landmark was dynamited on 30 May 1968, an artist, surrounded by a group of well-wishers, demonstratively painted a last picture of the church on the Karl-Marx-Platz as Stasi agents looked on. In Rostock, besides protests from local and national Catholic church officials, the mayor received more than fifty petitions against the planned demolition of the neo-Gothic Church of Christ. This building was torn down anyway in 1971 as part of a broader campaign to transform Rostock's downtown into a socialist showplace. The more ambitious urban renewal plan was abandoned for financial reasons, but the Rostock Church of Christ still fell, only to be replaced by a parking lot.[85]

Increasingly, the regime reiterated its commitment to "the good, the true, and the beautiful" in German history, as stated in 1980 by the cultural minister Hans-Joachim Hoffmann.[86] This highlighted a historical perspective that in its aims and objects differed little from West German attention to the classical symbols of German culture. In carrying out this commitment, the state endorsed what became known as "jubilee-preservation" in which anniversary celebrations of cities or historic personalities undertaken for propaganda purposes were used by preservation agencies and groups to promote a preservationist agenda. The Luther celebrations of the 1980s could thus redound to the advantage of preservationists who had their sights set on less ideologically useful half-timbered houses or neglected historic streetscapes. The regime supported and cooperated with the organizers of church restoration projects, which received the lion's share of funding from the West. Technical monuments received more attention, although, as in the case of the Thälmann park discussed below, public desire to protect such sites was by no means always honored by a regime that claimed to cherish the proletarian heritage. The saving of technical artifacts and monuments was in any case as haphazard in the East as it was in the West.[87]

Good intentions abounded. In 1977 the Cultural League of the GDR announced that it was organizing a Society for Historic Preservation that would not only have a much more visible presence in regime decisions but also would engage local groups more than before. Not only the grand monuments of jubilee preservation and regime ideology would have pride of place, but the lesser objects of small town, working-class, and peasant history would as well. Local chronicles of farm villages and working-class districts were typical products of this work. Digging for traces was once again the paradigm. Introducing a Kulturbund chronicle of the peasant village Kössern in Kreis Grimma southeast of Leipzig, a GDR cultural official stated that the author "was researching the traces of how, through their everyday labor, people transformed nature and societal relationships." The goal of his research was to enhance "love for the socialist Fatherland."[88] Such impulses came in the wake of a 1975 preservation law, enacted partially in response to the glitz of European Cultural Heritage Year. The law obliged the owners and users of historic peasant dwellings or half-timbered houses to restore and maintain such structures and even promised financial assistance. But the emphasis remained on those good, true, and beautiful objects that served the ideological goals of the state.[89] Even then, the number of listed monuments in the GDR exceeded fifty thousand in the 1980s,[90] and here too a sense of the memory landscape as a web of traces to be rediscovered and maintained by a broad group of citizens was evident despite the constricted circumstances of state policy.

This information suggests that both legislation and practice allowed an increasing degree of popular initiative and involvement in the formation of the memory landscape in the two decades before the fall of Communism. Yet looking across the border to a country such as Czechoslovakia, it is easy to see how limited GDR policy was in such matters. Czechoslovakia experienced relatively little damage in World War II, and although Prague was modernized in the nineteenth century, its historical center was largely undisturbed. Since its founding in 1948, the Czechoslovak Republic was committed to a broad program of historic preservation. Thus the starting point for maintaining and restoring key monuments was much better than in the GDR. The Czechs and Slovaks listed some 350,000 structures in a registry of historically important buildings, an enormous number for a country so small. Although budget and staffing always limited government and local agencies' conservation efforts, the environment was conducive to a broad program of restoration of both great urban monuments such as the eleventh-century Romanesque St. George cathedral in Prague as well as modest private houses in Telć and Slavonice.[91]

It is nonetheless too easy to idealize the Czechoslovak Republic in comparison with East Germany. Not budget and staffing issues but rather political decisions and prejudice could also determine what would not be preserved in the state, for example. Except for the famous old Jewish cemetery in Prague, which became a successful tourist attraction, the Czechoslovak Republic ignored or destroyed the more than 130 Jewish cemeteries scattered throughout Bohemia, Moravia, and Slovakia. In the eastern Slovak town of Zborov, local inhabitants dug up the gray granite tombstones of the local Jewish cemetery after 1945 and used them in the foundations of new residences. The highly valued black marble gravestones were cut up, used in the entrances of houses, or made into Christian gravestones in the local Orthodox cemetery. Neither the regime, which had as much trouble integrating the Holocaust into socialist ideology as the GDR did, nor the populace had much use for these traces of a now all-but-obliterated Jewish culture.[92]

Nonetheless, more than in the GDR, local initiatives could affect preservation policy in Czechoslovakia, as in the case of the early modern country estate Staré Hrady in the Jiĉín district of north-central Bohemia. Largely neglected until the 1960s, this chateau was the object of a broad popular campaign by preservationists and many volunteers, whose persistent efforts reversed the priorities of preservation agencies in Prague. Officials did not oppose the project, which garnered much media coverage, because the chateau was not a politically sensitive monument. It was rather a site of memory in the cultural and economic life of the local district. By 1986 large parts of Staré Hrady had been restored for art galleries, offices, and other facilities, and more than six thousand tourists visited the complex that year.[93]

In Poland, too, civic initiatives played an important role, as in the case of the imposing broken tombstone memorial to Jewish victims of the Holocaust in the scenic resort town of Kazimierz on the Vistula River. Completed in 1984, the monument came into being because townspeople and members of the Citizens' Committee for the Preservation of Jewish Monuments in Poland dug up Jewish tombstones the Nazis had uprooted and laid as paving stones in a Franciscan monastery turned into a Gestapo headquarters. These tombstones were reassembled in an imposing memorial wall conceived and carried out by the local architect Tadeusz Augustynek. To be sure, the Polish state favored such monuments, and by its own count Poland was at this time the site of more than two thousand Jewish memorials, more than any other country in Europe. As in the case of Auschwitz, such memorials often served the memory of Poles' rather than Jews' victimization. Even when Jews were remembered as Jews, as they increasingly were in 1983, when Poland celebrated the fortieth anniversary of the Warsaw Ghetto Uprising, "the officialdom, the opposition, and the Church went on record as being the rightful keepers of Jewish memory." Poland also effaced many traces of its Jewish past, and in Kazimierz itself an ancient synagogue was transformed into a movie theater after the war. Tourist guidebooks continued to list the site as a historic building and unblinkingly noted its reincarnation as a mecca of secular culture. Nonetheless, the Kazimierz memorial wall, a combination of popular commemorative archaeology and historic preservation, reflected an impressive tradition of public involvement in shaping the memory landscape of a country under Communist rule.[94]

Postwar architecture in Berlin and many other major cities had now also been freed from the Stalinist influences of the 1950s. Socialist realism remained influential in East German culture, but in architecture the earlier emphasis on socialist content embodied in national forms was dropped. In its place there was a theoretical as well as practical acceptance of Western functionalist forms, which were suited to the regime's need to build housing for East German workers as quickly and inexpensively as possible. This meant de-emphasizing ornamentation, accepting and developing procedures for mass production of housing units, and ensuring the efficient movement of people and goods through the city. East German architecture thus took up many of the same goals and forms that architecture in Western capitalist states had.

This also entailed a rehabilitation of the Bauhaus tradition, which in the early 1950s had come under attack from East German ideologues. They had argued that the Bauhaus was a product of capitalist social relations and a malformed result of the domination of American cosmopolitan culture in the Western world. This critical memory now changed, as preservationists got the regime to list the badly deteriorated former Bauhaus school in Dessau as a historic building in 1966, and as architectural theorists emphasized the humanistic and democratic features of the Bauhaus tradition a decade later. What is more, functionalist architecture itself was seen as an originally socialist idea aimed at solving the housing problem of the working masses. The social aspirations of Walter Gropius and the Bauhaus were to be realized not within a capitalist state but in "real existing socialism." "The heritage of the Bauhaus is in good hands in the German Democratic Republic," said the GDR building minister Wolfgang Junker in 1976 at the dedication of the carefully restored Bauhaus building on the fiftieth anniversary of the school's founding.[95] Still, the assurance with which such ideas were propounded revealed yet another insecurity, as in the 1980s postmodern architecture was criticized by GDR theoreticians as a product of the crisis of late capitalism. This criticism could not hide the fact that even in the East, architects and planners, often without broad ideological backing, were turning to more expressive historical forms that in Western culture went under the very name of postmodernism.[96] Such forms revealed a deep dissatisfaction with the machine aesthetic of functionalism. The rehabilitation of the Bauhaus tradition was achieved by the late 1970s, therefore, only to be undercut by history.

Developments in historical and new architecture were also connected to trends in East German city planning. Although the GDR had always placed emphasis on new housing, urban planners increasingly turned their attention to historical buildings and ensembles. For East Germany, as for the West, this was partly a pragmatic consideration: East German planners discovered that old buildings, neglected or incompletely reconstructed after the war, were deteriorating at a much faster rate than new buildings could be put up. To stop the bleeding, a more systematic approach to retaining and upgrading older districts would be necessary. In 1973 the regime stated that its housing and planning program was to be seen as "a unity of new building, modernization, and the maintenance of [historical] value."[97] It would take until the 1980s for the principle of "unity" to achieve enough programmatic coherence to be implemented. Nonetheless, the intent was clear. Having first emphasized the construction of brave new socialist cities, the regime now undertook a program of developing socialist architectural traditions out of a broader historical heritage.

In East Berlin, this project led to the modernization of thousands of old Berlin apartment buildings, many of them "rental barracks" from the Imperial era. Given new sanitary facilities and stripped of their crowded back courtyards and alleyways, such buildings had once symbolized the everyday degradation of German workers by capitalism. Their modernization was used by regime officials to demonstrate how a bad heritage had been transformed into a good socialist tradition. The regime also used such histories to emphasize workers' struggles against inhumane living and working conditions. Memory thus served to reinforce an image of the progressive intentions and accomplishments of the regime as well as its historical inevitability. The traces of working-class struggle—from historical photographs of inferior rental barracks to the gleaming new toilets of modernized apartments—could now be pulled together as the resolution of a completed narrative. Superior working-class housing could also symbolize the nation's high standards of popular consumption, a particularly important rejoinder to West Germany's emphasis on economic citizenship.

Even more attention-getting, however, was the reconstruction of the Nikolaikirche, the oldest parish church of the city.[98] It stood in the historical core of old Berlin, and thus served the regime's purpose of symbolizing East Germany's roots in the earliest moments of German history. Situated between the Spree river and the Red Rathaus and envisioned as part of the commemoration of Prussian history, the Nikolaikirche was to be the centerpiece of an ambitious reconstruction of an entire historical ensemble. Only the walls of the Gothic brick church, built in the fourteenth and fifteenth centuries, survived in the war, and since the 1950s the ruin had given archaeologists an unusual opportunity to dig for the traces of the earliest periods of Berlin history. Among their more notable finds were well-preserved eight-hundred-year-old skeletons. But the entire church and its two tall steeples (one of which was a nineteenth-century addition) were now to be revived in another form of "securing traces." Surrounding the church were to be nearly eight hundred new buildings, all designed with historical facades. The church was to serve as a cultural center, the other buildings as the spur to an Altstadt revival oriented to tourism and street life. Visitors would be able to promenade through the new old historical district and simultaneously have views of the East German television tower and the modern cityscape of central East Berlin. Traces of a very distant past would mingle with symbols of socialist prosperity and consumption.

Whereas much of East German city planning had emphasized monumentality and distance, the Nikolaikirche project emphasized many of the same things Altstadt renewal in the West had: smallness of scale, warmth, medieval ambiance, and intimacy. To achieve this effect, the few remaining old buildings in the district were modernized and restored, but most often older buildings and historical fragments from other parts of the city were moved to the Nikolaikirche district—the facade of a thirteenth-century house, an historic inn from the Fischerkietz, and Bürger houses from the seventeenth, eighteenth, and nineteenth centuries. Museums, restaurants, and workshops rounded out the district.

Because the project was virtually hermetically sealed off from other more modern parts of the city, critics in the West rightly referred to it as a "milieu island" in which more history was represented than actual history had left behind. More disparaging Western critics spoke of a historicized "Disneyland," referring to the fact that the GDR had created a historical fiction, not a reconstructed historic district. Western critics also noted that what had been part and parcel of West German urban renewal schemes, namely the historicization of old urban centers, was now becoming an accepted facet of East German urban planning.[99]

Yet just as such critiques could not overlook the popularity of renovated historic districts in the West, the attacks on the Nikolaikirche project could not avoid the power of this particular historic place. The East German regime's emphasis on historical reconstruction was after all in part a concession to public taste. The Nikolaikirche project's chief architect, Günter Stahn, argued that popular interest could not be denied. "Even in cases of total destruction," he wrote, "one should not be resigned to the loss of historic buildings. As long as these buildings still live on as an idealized memory in the people's consciousness, it is culturally and politically legitimate to integrate them sensibly in the reconstruction and further elaboration of the city." In making this claim, Stahn was not arguing for a total reconstruction, but for an integration of old forms with new ones. The area around the Nikolaikirche was a "cultural landscape," a term that had already come into widespread use in the Federal Republic. The district would enable visitors to shop and dine, and it would be reconstructed to make it more accessible to the handicapped.[100]

Such contemporary concerns and facilities could be built into a project that stunningly revealed the resonance of historic settings, even those that lived on only in the imagination. East Germany had now confronted the limits of its history, belatedly to be sure, and tried to exploit and develop them in such new urban and historical projects. The money and time devoted to the Nikolaikirche development vividly demonstrated how powerful the pull of the past had become. The anticipated circulation of goods and people in the district suggested how strong the future's interest in the past would be. The historical resonance of the place was expressed even more vividly—and, for the regime, more dangerously—in the autumn of 1989, when the Nikolaikirche, like many other churches in the GDR, became a popular site of Monday evening peace services, the nuclei of the public demonstrations that eventually brought the state down. The former East German writer Erich Loest would later publish a novel using the Nikolaikirche as the central symbol in a narrative of the demise of the GDR,[101] and in 1995 German television produced a two-part film based on Loest's work.

Other important historic buildings in Berlin enjoyed less favor in the movement to preserve, restore, and consume. Because antifascist ideology pushed Holocaust victims who were killed for racial or religious reasons to the margins, the regime was ambivalent about too visibly commemorating Jews in concentration camp sites. This ambivalence was carried through more broadly in the case of historic buildings. But even here change was evident in the decade before unification. The great Oranienburger Straße synagogue, hailed in the nineteenth century as a masterpiece of contemporary architecture in Berlin and resplendent in the effect its massive golden dome had on the cityscape, was badly damaged in the Night of Broken Glass, used as an army clothing depot, then reduced to ruins in wartime bombing. The building could have been reconstructed, however, though not by the small and impoverished East Berlin Jewish community left in the wake of the Holocaust. The East Berlin government chose not to reconstruct it and dynamited the structure in 1958, leaving only the front part of the building. Plans for a Jewish museum came to nothing, and at one point local planners recommended tearing down the ruin to make room for a new street. In 1966, the centenary of the building's dedication, the regime placed a commemorative plaque on its facade, and for the next two decades it maintained a shadowy existence on a shabby street. The turning point came on the fiftieth anniversary of the Night of Broken Glass, when plans were announced to reconstruct the main part of the building. On 9 November 1988 Erich Honecker attended a showy ceremony at the ruin, dedicating a plaque expressing the solemn wish that the synagogue would be rebuilt. In the same year a foundation was created to finance and organize reconstruction, which was completed in 1991.[102] It is difficult to estimate how far this resolve to reconstruct synagogues and other sites of Jewish history in East Germany would have gone had the regime not left the historical stage. But the resolve was evident by the late 1980s.

The theme of resistance to fascism had suffused public commemorations since the end of the war, but in the 1970s this theme was reinforced by Erich Honecker, himself a Resistance fighter. Antifascism was not only to legitimize the regime historically, but to link history with contemporary social concerns. In the same way the Nikolaikirche project would use history to promote a new commercial development, the resistance theme would accommodate new social needs. In the Prenzlauer

Figure 51. Remains of the Oranienburger Straße synagogue, Berlin, 1990. Bildarchiv Preussischer Kulturbesitz.

Berg district of northeast East Berlin, a new memorial and park were constructed to honor the memory of Ernst Thälmann on the centenary of his birth in 1986. The GDR leadership had struggled with the absence of a major Thälmann monument for some time, and the existing memorials commemorating the slain leader were either marginal to GDR cultural politics or they were aesthetically inferior to the point of bordering on kitsch.

The new housing estate appeared to offer a solution to the problem. The centerpiece of this complex was to be a monument by the Moscow sculptor Lew Kerbel, who designed a thirteen-meter-high bronze likeness of Thälmann, arm and fist raised in the air before an unfurled flag carrying the symbol of the hammer and sickle, on a base of red Ukrainian granite. Surrounding the monumental sculpture would be a housing development with more than nine hundred units in a twenty-six-hectare-square area that would include green spaces, athletic facilities, schools, and even a planetarium. All this was made possible by a two-year-long program of destruction, as postwar Berlin's oldest gasworks, dating from 1872 and including numerous technical artifacts and workshops, was torn down against the wishes of many East Berliners, who wanted to preserve the complex as an industrial monument and integrate it into the Thälmann park development.[103]

At one edge of the Thälmann park stood a small brick building that housed an "antifascist tradition cabinet." Found in most East German cities and in larger urban districts throughout the country, these museum-like institutions were important building blocks of the SED's antifascist ideology. They contained collections of photographs, uniforms, weapons, flags, the personal effects of concentration camp inmates and resistance fighters, and inscriptions commemorating the anti-Nazi opposition. One of six East Berlin cabinets erected in the two decades before unification, the Prenzlauer Berg institution was especially well organized and designed, and like other cabinets, it was set up for guided tours of schoolchildren, youth groups, factory or party collectives, and units of soldiers and policemen. An estimated fifty thousand visitors went through the Prenzlauer Berg exhibit from 1986 to 1989. The goal in all such tours was not engagement with a complex historical period but reinforcement of antifascist ideology and apotheosis of Thälmann himself, who was portrayed as a freedom fighter and martyr. Jewish, Christian, Social Democratic, and military resistance to Hitler were left out completely. Moreover, as one critic later noted, "instead of civil courage, tolerance, empathy, and independent thinking, [the cabinet] promoted obedience, discipline, belief in authority, and enthusiasm for flags and weapons."[104] The continuity with values propagated during the Nazi period could not be missed, all the more so when in other areas of East German life, a sense of discontinuity with the Nazi years could be felt. Nor could it be overlooked that in West Germany a more differentiated historical perspective on the Resistance had already taken hold.

Yet it would be misleading to see the tradition cabinets or many other artifacts of GDR memory as mere official impositions on an unbelieving populace. After 1989 many tradition cabinets were closed, their holdings dispersed and stored. The Prenzlauer Berg cabinet had a unique experience insofar that the site was retained and supplemented with an exhibit that commented on and criticized the antifascist message. A book exploring the "myth of antifascism" as it was elaborated at the Prenzlauer Berg site was published by the Prenzlauer Berg district cultural office and the Active Museum of Fascism and Resistance in 1992. In response to such criticism, former members of the GDR antifascist resistance group protested. "Antifascism was not myth," they wrote. "There were antifascists, who fought in the darkest moment of Germany's history, even though they were a minority, in prisons and concentration camps, in exile, and in liberation movements in countries occupied by Hitler." If many antifascists were treated unfairly in the GDR or their memory was misused, "nothing justifies speaking of an 'antifascism ordered by the state.'" If certain historical facts were massaged or manipulated in the tradition cabinet, if the ideology of antifascism narrowed the range of resisters who should have been commemorated in GDR political culture, the argument went, the phenomenon of Communist resistance to Hitler nonetheless could not and should not be denied.[105]

The distinction between legitimate and legitimizing antifascism is relevant here again.[106] The defenders of the tradition cabinet held to the idea of a legitimate antifascism based on positive memories and irreducible historical experiences that could not be destroyed, either by Communist state policy or by Western leftist postmortems. One could read the sentiment back into the history of the GDR, where, virtually irrespective of regime policy, the positive connotations of the antifascist message were unassailable in everyday culture. While the regime existed, literary intellectuals in particular also held fast to the tradition of antifascism, partly out of a sense of obligation to those who had fought against Hitler. The writer Christa Wolf said it best in 1990: "We felt a strong inhibition to oppose people who had sat in concentration camps during the Nazi period."[107] This attitude created a bridge between the intellectuals and the less exalted people who put together antifascist tradition cabinets. It also created severe limits on the intellectuals' willingness to oppose regime policies. If the dissident movement in the GDR was weaker than in other East European Communist dictatorships, the power of antifascism, particularly among the intellectuals, explains a large part of the story.

The site of former Nazi concentration camps on East German soil underwent a process of elaboration and development in the same manner they did in the West. The antifascist theme remained the dominant motif here as well, but it was now underscored with even more layers of documentary and educational material. At Buchenwald, the first camp museum was erected in 1958. In 1964 this institution was expanded to include material on the establishment and history of the GDR and the relationship between monopoly capitalism and fascism. A year later Buchenwald saw the establishment of a library, and in 1971 the Buchenwald Archive opened. In the same year the research division of the GDR's national curatorium for memorial sites began work, focusing on the themes of fascism and big industrial concerns, the resistance struggle in the camp and its satellites, the uncovering of Nazi crimes, and imperialism and neo-fascism in the present. Ernst Thälmann was commemorated in two parts of the former camp, an altar-like edifice in the lower level of the former camp "disinfection" area, opened in 1971, and a bronze bust in the yard of the crematorium. On the fortieth anniversary of the liberation of the camp, the newly expanded museum was dedicated. It had nearly doubled its exhibit space and systematized its collections. Like the sites of former West German concentration camps, Buchenwald became an important tourist attraction in the GDR, welcoming more than eleven million visitors in the three decades after 1958. The Holocaust was big business in the East just as it was in the West.[108]

But there were still limits to what would be remembered at places such as Buchenwald. The blinkers of antifascist commemoration not only cut off the view of Nazi racial policies; they also purposely shut out the history of certain kinds of political persecution by the Soviets. In 1983 builders uncovered a mass of human bones in a common grave in the forest outside the perimeter of the Nazi camp. Hushed up and closed after the uncomfortable discovery, this grave turned out to be a mass burial site for prisoners of the Soviets, who herded ex-Nazis, counterrevolutionaries, and even Social Democrats who did not want their party taken over by the Communists into camps soon after the Soviet military established itself as the occupation authority. The Soviets had not treated their captives as harshly as the Nazis did, but fully one-third of some thirty thousand people imprisoned in the so-called Speziallager 2 Buchenwald between 1945 and 1950 died, primarily of hunger and disease rather than forced labor.[109] Only after 1989, when more bones were found, were these remains discussed openly, and even then not always rationally. Some conservatives wanted to use the Buchenwald memorial to symbolize the similarity between the Nazi and East German dictatorships.[110] Today one can see the latest phase of commemoration of these victims of Stalinism, whose remains are marked by austere metal poles. As for other persecutees ignored by the former GDR, a reorganized Buchenwald staff, advised by a commission of historical experts and victims' groups representatives headed by the Stuttgart historian Eberhard Jäckel, began to document the plight of Sinti and Roma, homosexuals, and Jews under Nazism soon after reunification.[111]

Among the visitors to the Buchenwald site in the former East Germany were many youths, including more than one hundred thousand students annually. Not just Buchenwald but the other two major former concentration camps in the GDR, Sachsenhausen and Ravensbrück, became integral elements in the regime's policy of capturing youth for a system that was legitimized in historical terms and demarcated from the West. Since 1954, the *Jugendweihe,* or secular state "confirmation" ritual, would often take place at antifascist memorials and former concentration camp sites. Since the early 1960s at all three camps, history and civics teachers could get instruction on the history of the camps and antifascist resistance. Since 1965, new members of the Free German Youth, the Society for Sport and Technique, and other youth groups were initiated at Buchenwald. Since the late 1960s universities held their ceremonies for newly matriculated students at one of the three sites. All such ceremonies combined the antifascist resistance narrative, rites of passage, and the concept of the socialist nation. Buchenwald became the preferred site for the induction of National People's Army personnel, who recited the following: "With the antifascist resistance fighters as our model, we love and protect our socialist Fatherland."[112]

As in West Germany, East German youth were mobilized to dig for historical traces, though in this case those traces led one to ponder resistance and the origins of Germany's first socialist nation rather than victimization.[113] Youth were to understand themselves as "patriots of their Fatherland and internationalists," as stated by one GDR museum scholar in 1985. This relationship between the national and international planes was also emphasized in the pedagogical goals of West German sites such as the Topography of Terror. If in the East such presentations leaned heavily on indoctrination, pedagogues and officials wanted to encourage self-discovery as well. "A pedagogical problem is to heighten the independent initiative of youth at the memorial centers," stated the same GDR museum worker quoted above. But the message was as rigid as it was at the Topography of Terror. Students were given poems by former Ravensbrück prisoners and, as they memorized and recited them, were encouraged to derive the appropriate political and historical meanings. This did not always work out as planned, for officials noted that often students' subjective impressions and emotional responses overpowered rational analysis and historiographical politics. The point for the regime of course was that students should not identify with the camp inmates as persecuted human beings but as the architects of a socialist revolution. Digging for traces of the (socialist) past could have unexpected consequences. It is doubtful that young people's less-than-correct responses were always a function of the rigidity of Communist ideology, moreover, because even in the West the organizers of antifascist city tours commented on the resistance or inattention of some young visitors. But it is true that a more stultified historical culture in the GDR had more extreme effects: some East German school pupils came to identify with the "heroic" side of the Third Reich, while others, who were unable to see many photos of Hitler because such material was discouraged in history teaching, simply wanted to know what the *Führer* looked like.[114]

One cannot avoid the question: how many of the youthful East German visitors to the camps, unmoved or only partially convinced by the regime's antifascist memory work, were among the demonstrators who brought the German Democratic Republic to its knees in the autumn of 1989? The question could of course be extended to the memory landscape as a whole. We have noted that the GDR resisted popular appeals to rebuild the massive Church of our Lady in Dresden, preferring instead to transform the pile of stones left after the February bombing of 1945 into an antifascist memorial. In the last years of the East German state, the memorial became a favorite symbol of the unofficial peace and human rights movement, and then a symbol of opposition to the Communist regime. Many other historic churches, including the rebuilt Nikolaikirche in Berlin, functioned in similar ways. In Leipzig, the capital of the East German revolution of 1989, the Nikolaikirche was the site of the famous Peace Prayers almost every Monday night since 1982. Virtually untouched by World War II bombing, the Nikolaikirche was the oldest parish church in the city, dating to an original structure of the eleventh century. Initially attracting no more than thirty people, the Peace Prayers would later have as many as a thousand participants as they became a political forum for East German dissidents and would-be emigrants, especially in the last year before the fall of the regime.[115] The line between simply ignoring the antifascist message, using it and its monuments for "subversive" purposes, and ultimately opposing the state was indeed fleeting.

The French historian Pierre Nora has argued that France today wants to write its national history in multiple voices. The central goal, he maintains, "is to define France as a reality that is entirely symbolic" and to reject any attempt to reduce it to a phenomenon of some other kind. This opens the door to a new kind of history:

> . . . a history less interested in causes than in effects; less interested in actions remembered or even commemorated than in the traces left by those actions

Figure 52. Frauenkirche and Luther Monument, Dresden, 1946. Bildarchiv Preussischer Kulturbesitz.

> and in the interaction of those commemorations; less interested in events themselves than in the construction of events over time, in the disappearance and reemergence of their significations; less interested in "what actually happened" than in its perpetual reuse and misuse, its influence on successive presents; less interested in traditions than in the way in which traditions are constituted and passed on.[116]

Suggesting that this observation may apply not only to France but other nations as well, Nora argues that people are now less concerned with "reconstructions" of the past than with its "rememoration," which he sees as a kind of "history of the second degree." One could say that rememoration refers to a framing strategy of remembering to remember the past in the present rather than trying to reconstitute past events in all their detail.

This rather abstract idea does seem to apply to both Germanys at first glance. Many of West Germany's historical diggers were less concerned with history as it happened than with the commemorative effects of uncovering traces of the past. The East German regime's antifascism required attention not necessarily to understanding causes but to guarding the practices and objects of commemoration for each new generation. Yet Nora's statement also goes too far if we are to understand it as a comprehensive analysis of how contemporaries gain a purchase on the past. The organizers of the Topography of Terror were as interested in questions of authenticity and historical fact as their nineteenth-century predecessors were. The legacy of Nazi crimes allowed no deviation from the documentary path. East German ideologues insisted that an unassailable historical reality—Communist resistance to fascism and the Soviet army's role in destroying the Hitler dictatorship—was the foundation of the first German socialist nation's existence. This was more than the regime's conceit, for many ordinary GDR citizens felt the same way. Digging for historical traces undoubtedly contributed to a process of defining the German ethnie as a symbolic reality—especially when the ethnie was split into two, apparently long-lived states. But symbolism was still founded on a past consisting of what were seen as indisputable—and unprecedentedly tragic—events. The past was to be mastered or overcome, but regardless of the metaphor used, the past was a profound reality. And, as Michael Geyer notes, "The German politics of memory was always a moral politics."[117] If the consequence of mastering the past was rememoration, the starting point was nonetheless the firm ground of a real place marked with the traces of human suffering and bloodshed for which a significant minority of Germans felt morally responsible.

Conclusion

I have emphasized that the memory landscape symbolized and shaped German perceptions about the past and the nation. The continuity of the memory landscape depended on the emergent evolution of its forms. From one unification to another, monuments, ruins, reconstructions, and traces have been used in contested framing strategies to build an enduring national tradition that has survived and even facilitated profound political and social discontinuity. In one respect this perspective reinforces a well-established theme, for until fairly recently many scholars have emphasized the peculiar continuities of German history. But aside from the fact that they did little to analyze the memory landscape in the entirety of its forms, some scholars used the theme of continuity to portray all of German history as a prelude to the unique irrationalities of Nazism. This book has focused on another kind of continuity. It is a continuity based on recurring forms and symbols of collective memory that were indeed manipulated by the Nazis (as well as by national liberals, radical nationalists, Social Democrats, Catholics, and Communists) but that also contributed to a deeper cultural and political tradition. The elaboration of this continuity in turn highlighted characteristics of the German past that placed it in the mainstream of the history of modern nations. It is now time to turn to some of the implications of this approach for further scholarship and teaching.

"The heretofore is just as important as the hereafter," wrote the novelist Michel Tournier, "especially as it probably holds the key to it."[1]

The history of this recognition on German soil has been the core of my narrative. Of what did this recognition consist? A general response would emphasize the centrality of perceived ethnic and cultural characteristics of German national memory and identity. Germans have assumed that the primary source of their distinctiveness as a people has rested not on a political act, such as the French or the American Revolutions, but on a cultural substratum consisting of shared descent, language, custom, historical experience, association with a specific territory, and myths and symbols of origin and evolution. The persistence of this "sense" right through to the present is noteworthy if for no other reason than that it challenges the notion, prevalent throughout the Western world for some time now, that we have entered an age of "post-nationality." Just as my argument points to the emergent forms of an enduring memory landscape, the foregoing has also stressed not the end of nationality, especially since the late 1960s, but the evolution of the German ethnie, and the elaboration of framing devices designed to promote a particular understanding of national identity. Efforts to de-emphasize or even deny the idea of the nation's ethnic and cultural fundaments—by the Social Democratic leaders of the imperial period, by the GDR (though with equivocation), by advocates of "constitutional patriotism"—only highlighted its pervasiveness.

It is significant that the history of the German ethnie from the founding of the Second Empire to the reunification of 1990 has embraced a variety of political ideologies including monarchical authoritarianism, democracy, fascism, Communism, and liberal constitutionalism. The tradition of ethno-cultural identity and memory could obviously accommodate an array of framing strategies, collective memories, and state forms. In contrast to the "continuity thesis" of an older cultural and intellectual history, which saw Nazism as a virtually inevitable product of deep-seated ideas and traditions, or of a more recent West German social science history, which pinpointed the roots of Nazism in the persistence of authoritarian political and social structures from the nineteenth century into the twentieth, my discussion suggests that the cultural nation was politically "neutral." The memory landscape is a rich source of evidence for documenting this indeterminate relationship between culture and politics. Numerous monuments and buildings have assumed new and often quite opposed meanings as they were manipulated for political purposes by various regimes and contending ideologies.

Even so, the fact that so much energy was put into manipulating the memory landscape for the sake of political expediency suggests that there was also something resistant, something substantive and unmoving, about the monuments and symbols—and about the cultural nation for which they so often stood. It is not quite right therefore that "It is in the intrinsic nature of public art . . . to adapt, to collaborate," as Marina Warner has written, or that of public art (which includes monuments) "It could be said that it has no coat to turn."[2] The discussion returns to this issue below.

In stressing their ethno-cultural roots, Germans have not carved out a unique position among European nations, but rather placed themselves alongside their Central and East European neighbors, who have also stressed the distinctive ethnic and cultural bases of nationhood. In cases such as Poland, the cultural nation has been an even more important source of survival, for in the modern period that country has been partitioned and occupied, its elite repressed or even liquidated, so that cultural tradition as defined by the nobility and the clergy historically served to prevent the national community's oblivion. One could also point to the Hungarian example, or to the Croats and Serbs, whose history of living on fault lines between civilizations is palpable and enduring. The argument of "ethnicism" turns out to be an important component of a transnational European region. It should be noted of course that historically the idea of ethnic identities in its modern form was not an Eastern European invention but an import from German and Western sources, most notably from Herder's thought. Through adaptation to a Western creation, Eastern and Central Europe developed ethnicism as a frame for building memory and national myth.

As this last point suggests, Germany also shares important characteristics with nations commonly identified with a "Western" model of development. This model is defined by processes of economic integration, state centralization, and cultural coordination that worked themselves out most explicitly in France and Great Britain (and to a degree in Spain) between the sixteenth and twentieth centuries. Germany in the nineteenth century acquired many of the economic, political, and social characteristics associated with France and Britain. Nonetheless, Anthony Smith argues that even modern nations defined by this "triple revolution" are to a degree based on premodern ethnic cores and that the survival of nations in the modern era depended on the persistence and elaboration of etched-in memories and myths.[3] In this view, the "nature of blood," to use the title of a recent fine novel on the recurrence and vast destructiveness of ethnic hatreds, emerges as a preoccupation not just of specific times or regions but of modern existence as such.[4] Logically this observation leads one to de-emphasize mutually exclusive distinctions between the West and the East, or between those countries whose nationhood is rooted more in territorial solidification, political and administrative tradition, and a shared sense of citizenship as opposed to those in which history and ethnicism have the upper hand. My discussion of France and Germany in chapter 1 suggests that even those countries that established a coherent territorial identity and authoritative political and civic practices before the era of the modern national state have also relied on the idea of ethnic characteristics to solidify a sense of shared being.

Germany's distinctiveness thus lies in the fact that a sense of nationhood and national memory has been built up through the use of political as well as ethnic categories, territorial as well as cultural associations, notions of political citizenship as well as of shared cultural (or even racial) descent. The idea of Germany as the "land of the middle" has been used to assert, often with highly dubious political motivations, that country's difficult geopolitical placement at the center of a contentious web of national states. For many centuries Germany had been "encircled," it is said, and this predetermined its peculiarly aggressive political and military history. With respect to cultural history, the term makes somewhat more analytical sense because it expresses Germany's movement somewhere along the middle of a spectrum defining "Eastern" and "Western" political cultures. To add a variation on this metaphorical usage, one could also say that the land of the middle implies not centrality but the experience of being a borderland, a permeable entity lodged "between" larger historical forces and territories.

Whether we choose the notion of Germany's middle position or its status as a border, the foregoing suggests another similarity with the nations of Eastern Europe and the Balkans. Here the Poles, Czechs, Hungarians, Croats, Slovaks, and Slovenes were ruled by foreign but culturally related empires while the Bulgarians, Serbs, Macedonians, Montenegrins, and Romanians were dominated by non-European political and administrative principles in the Ottoman Empire. Here only the Poles, Czechs, and Slovenes developed industry on a significant scale before the twentieth century, while the other groups fell behind or failed to industrialize almost completely before the post–World War II era. Here the collective sense of transition and interplay between West and East, Christianity and Islam, development and underdevelopment, liberal and autocratic political culture, ethnicity and religion, and Western-style nation-states and the religiously defined community (*millet*) of the Ottoman Empire, was constitutive for the entire region.[5]

The implication is that comparing or contrasting Germany with its Central and East European counterparts makes as much sense as comparing it with France or Great Britain, the usual referents of Germany's fated history. This point is applicable even if we take into account Germany's more substantial influence in Europe and the world in comparison to countries such as Poland or Serbia. Yet just as we have relatively little truly comparative cultural history,[6] we have almost no systematic comparison between German and Eastern European cultures. The type of comparisons historians make depend on the questions they are asking and the results they anticipate. Given the end of the Cold War; given the fact that for more than two decades a growing chorus of scholars has raised doubts about the notion of the Sonderweg as a compelling causal narrative for German history; and given the contemporary political, economic, and cultural interest Germany now demonstrates in Central and Eastern Europe, it would be surprising if the questions historians ask did *not* ultimately lead them more consistently to study the East. No less important in this regard is the moral imperative felt by many German scholars and officials to study National Socialism's extraordinary brutality against Poland, Russia, and other countries in World War II. Such reorientations will not make Franco-German or Anglo-German comparisons any less useful, to be sure, but they will begin to right an imbalance and provide a more textured historical viewpoint. The important issue of how ethnie work out their specific sense of shared memory and myth, how they do so under very different historical conditions, and how this process includes demarcation from other nations as well as interplay, exchange, and violence, is an all-important subject for further teaching and research in this context.

It is an important subject for domestic politics in Germany as well. After 1990, Germans have once again taken up the issue of "how the German national state should look."[7] They have discussed the differences between civic and ethnic ideas of nationhood. They have reflected on the continued psychosocial effects of remembering Nazi atrocities as a central aspect of German identity.[8] They have taken note of the important fact that the twentieth century featured not only two world wars, fascism, the Holocaust, and Communist dictatorship, but also more than fifty years of Western-style democracy and economic prosperity on German soil.[9] They have asked whether "blood" or democratic politics will determine the shape of the new nation. They have continued to see Auschwitz as a symbol both of a centuries-long German history in the East and a reminder of Germans' forfeiture of the right to develop German culture further in that area.

Knowledge of the historical hybridity of the German nation might be utilized to remind contemporary Germans that traditions of pinpointing an ethnic core can combine with democratic practices and civic definitions of belonging. German citizenship could after all still rest on enduring ideas of shared history, "custom," or language, but politicians could try to create an environment in which those notions of racial identity or conquest that remain would be isolated and suppressed. Patriotism, recent opinion surveys of the German public tell us, is not only compatible with tolerance and cultural diversity but potentially linked with them in a creative and positive relationship.[10] Even when a continuous national tradition has worked to limit choices at specific historical moments, those choices have never been entirely predetermined. Like the emergent evolution of the memory landscape, the evolution of cultural identity has featured persistence as well as slow but palpable innovation, acceptance as well as rejection of certain traditions. This lesson of history—I, for one, think historians ought to be less shy about using this unfashionable term when discussing their findings—might also be applied, with hopefully humane and productive results, to Germans' conflicted relationships with the Turks, Jews, Poles, and Sinti and Roma within and outside the Federal Republic. Recent Social Democratic efforts to liberalize German citizenship law suggests that many Germans have learned quite a lot from their country's conflicted dealings with minorities.

Smith has argued that the process of cultural identification is highly selective.[11] He has pointed to two key patterns by which ethnie—or rather by which intellectuals who engage the masses for the goals of the modern national community—have developed characteristic maps of identity. These are constitutive moments in the process whereby nations frame the past. One pattern consists of using natural and man-made landscapes to create "poetic spaces" in which the historically sanctioned traits and character of the national community are most clearly represented. The other pattern is to use narratives of the origins and evolution of the ethnie. These narratives have often taken the form of a three-part story in which a Golden Age is followed by an age of decline and tribulation, which is then followed by an actual or promised resurgence of the national community. In the preceding pages, I have considered the uses of the memory landscape to create poetic spaces and narratives of national decline and resurgence. Germany's utilization of such patterns places it squarely in the broader cultural history of national identity in the modern world.

It may be true that in one sense the memory landscape has played a more definitive role for Germans over the past 150 years because of the startling discontinuities of that country's political history. A desire for the "real," thought to reside in the steel, concrete, and stone of the built world, has compensated for the unreality of a chain of historical catastrophes. Yet comparisons with a country such as Poland again reduce the distinctiveness of the German pattern. The rebuilding of Warsaw after World War II reflected an almost feverish allegiance to prior architectural and historical forms, as did the persistent construction (and demolition) of unofficial or popular monuments in Poland under Communist rule.[12] Consider also the power of architectural symbols in the history of modern national iconography in the Western world as a whole. The central referent of the struggle for liberty in the French Revolution was the Bastille, a structure far more important for its symbolic radius than for the specific function it had in the French political system of 1789. More than a half-century ago, the French sociologist Maurice Halbwachs, who had studied not only his native country but also Israel and other nations, noted the centrality of monuments and other topographical features in the formation of collective memory in the modern world. As for narratives of the rise and fall of the ethnie, moreover, it is necessary only to recall the example of Serbian allegiance to the Kosovo legend for evidence that makes German adherence to tradition over the course of the last century seem relatively muted. The notion of German distinctiveness in this regard is thus very much a matter of perspective and comparison.

The issue is of course even broader than this because it touches on a defining feature of what we call European civilization. Scholars have recognized that the Greco-Roman heritage was distinguished historically by its emphasis on the individual's relationship with the physical and cultural environment. The human sense of constant transformation and change put a premium on symbols of stability or permanence in the external world, an emphasis that influenced art, architecture, the formation of cities, and many other developments. In addition, the adoption of Christianity in the fourth century A.D. introduced the idea of reality "in which the present is but a single moment in a meaningful progression of directionally interlinked moments existing in both time and space."[13] Rooted in ancient Jewish culture, this orientation positioned humanity in a universe in which every moment is related not only to a past stretching back to the dawn of human existence but to a future culminating in the human attainment of everlasting life—and timelessness. These traditions evolved to produce a cultural habitus that gave Europe its distinctive and fundamental approach to reality: a sense of ineradicable time and history; a belief in temporal directionality, progress, and change; an embrace of the physical world as a source of symbolic and spiritual meaning; and a compulsion to intervene actively in the outside world to ensure continued progressive movement. Couched in these broader anthropological terms, the German embrace of the memory landscape appears to be just one particularly interesting variation on a much broader European understanding of man's sense of time and place.

The variations within this cultural range have of course been extreme. Any traveler who has flown from the United States to Europe has received a vivid reminder of the way in which human relationships to the environment, and by extension to the memory landscape, have produced enormous differences by simply looking at the terrain below. The pervasive sameness and rectangularity of the American landscape, a product ultimately of the National Land Survey of 1787 but also of the workings of real estate interests, has led one perceptive observer to argue that the "emblem" of the United States is not the stars and stripes but the grid. "I think [the grid] must be imprinted at the moment of conception on every American child," wrote John Brinckerhoff Jackson with characteristic irony, "to remain throughout his or her life as a way of calculating not only space but movement."[14] Europe is different. Here, especially in places such as central Germany, the rectangular grid is not the emblematic feature of the memory landscape but rather a more irregular and ill-defined web of topographical and cultural environments. In one case, the grid shapes perceptions of time and place, and the pervasive sense is one of a landscape founded and developed in a single, constitutive human action; in the other, the landscape appears to have evolved more organically, and its origins appear to be lost in the mists of time.

In the nineteenth and twentieth centuries, poetic spaces and narratives of national evolution were important to the themes of victimization, resistance, and national rebirth discussed in previous chapters. Observers of recent German history have analyzed the way in which the sites of former concentration camps, perhaps the most radical and sinister "places" of the twentieth century, became symbols not of German crimes against Jews but of German resistance to the Nazis. But this book has offered evidence suggesting that such themes extend back in time and can be "read" from the iconography of edifices such as national monuments. It is difficult to maintain that such uses of monuments reveal a Sonderweg, or qualitatively unique national path through history. In all national cultures, collective memory is after all dependent on the filtering element provided by narratives of victimhood.[15] European societies have been victim societies, especially in Central and Eastern Europe, where the influence of powerful economic and political forces to the West and East have made it necessary to rely on national traditions and ideas of ethnicity as a matter of collective survival. The shadings and content of such narratives have varied from country to country and from time to time. In a country such as Serbia, one could argue, they have been much more salient in public life than in Germany. But they have been persistent elements of each national memory landscape, and the German uses of such framing devices have reflected that country's peculiar placement within European history. This has been less of a Sonderweg than one country's attempt to deal with problems arising from its own Europeanness.

As in many other European nations, the medieval age has been a constitutive element of historical imagery in Germany. But other historical periods have also come into play, and thus a large part of this discussion of the emergent evolution of the memory landscape has been a story of how various historical periods and images, from the Renaissance to the industrial age to socialist working-class tradition, have appeared and reappeared. There is little doubt that the uses of such historical indicators are dependent on circumstances that can be pinpointed and analyzed only in their specific historical context. The richness and depth of historical imagery in Germany derives in large part from the continuous need to elaborate national spaces and narratives in response to unexampled violence and change. But I have argued also that such evocations have been based on a substantial and continuous material presence. For example, from the Kyffhäuser (the mountain as well as the monument) to the Marienburg, from the Wartburg to the Burgfrieden of World War I, from the Cologne cathedral to commercialized Altstädte in both Germanys of the post–World War II age, medieval imagery has endured and recombined with other elements to produce a lasting and evocative web of associations in the memory landscape. The centrality of Christian themes and symbols in German national identity has derived in large part from this medievalism, though for some Germans the medieval age was significant as an age of religious unity under the Catholic Church while for others it was an age to be overcome in the interest of more individualistic and progressive forms of religious and political expression.

The central point is that the persistence, restoration, and building up of such historical places made the diversity of meanings and interpretations possible. Against the perceived continuity of the memory landscape, and against the backdrop of an evolution of the memory landscape's paradigmatic forms, memories and meanings themselves could shift and change—or remain the same. "The very structure of memory (and not just its contents)," writes Andreas Huyssen, "is strongly contingent upon the social formation that produces it."[16] Despite Huyssen's stress on contingency, the statement also suggests that the memory landscape, even when it was rebuilt, torn down, or heavily modified, was less a construction or a product of imagination, as a still fashionable theoretical language would have it, than a *re*construction or a product of social and cultural recycling. It is not that the monument has "no coat to turn," as the aforementioned argument of Marina Warner's claims. Rather, the memory landscape had many coats, many often opposed meanings and political colorations, which were draped around a national tradition that could be made to collaborate with and adapt to historical circumstances precisely because it persisted and endured. Perhaps the exiled East German songwriter and dissident Wolf Biermann said it best when he sang "Only he who changes remains true to himself."[17] Remaining "true" to itself, a sense of national belonging was promoted through the emergent evolution of the multifaceted memory landscape.

A comprehensive history of collective memory in modern Europe has still to be written. If it is at all possible, it will have to take account of the commanding presence of the modern national state. If the modern memory landscape is best described as a palimpsest, then to a large degree its layers have been the products of national states' incessant need for the past and for the cultural legitimacy the past has offered. One could make the same observation about the succession of political ideologies that have stamped both European and German history. Even so, Charlotte Tacke has recently warned against writing the history of the "nationalization" of European societies as a story of state initiatives, top-down policies, and dominant ideologies.[18] Throughout the preceding pages I have emphasized the importance of individual and societal initiative in the building up and manipulation of the memory landscape.

To a somewhat more limited degree, I have stressed the centrality of commercialism and the elaboration of complex modern societies based in part on the production and consumption of national identities.

Recent scholarship in the U.S. and Europe has drawn attention to the way in which consumption was not only an important tool of social change but an agent in the creation of individual and collective identities.[19] There is still relatively little scholarship on the history of commercial culture in modern Europe or on the relationship between commercial culture and national identity. These are significant gaps given the degree to which, especially, though not exclusively, since World War II, national states have come to depend on the marketing of their national cultures (through film, museums, monuments, historic urban commercial districts, cuisine, and clothing) in a global economy. For much of the past century, Germany has benefited from such marketing strategies in no small degree. Tourism is one particularly promising theme in this context. In the preceding chapters, tourism, or at least that part of the touristic experience reflected in my sample of guidebooks, entailed not only passive consumption but also the active appropriation of the memory landscape. The act of appropriation emphasized some memories and downplayed others; it supported regime initiatives (including those of racial war and mass extermination) but also suspected or doubted them; it simplified the past but also, often unintentionally, gestured to the complexities of time and memory; it framed history no less consequentially than political ideologues and state officials did. This too is a subject unto itself, and one for which historians and teachers of late modern Europe have very little specialized research to go on. Michael Geyer has recently pointed to the dramatic (and still largely unanalyzed) interaction between the rise of a consumer culture and genocide in Nazi Germany;[20] one can only reiterate the importance of such themes in writing the history of modern Germany.

I have stressed those factors that render Germany more like other European nations. Yet the problem remains that Germany, in twelve short years, achieved a notoriety that is unparalleled in the history of the twentieth century. While it is not my goal in this book to explain fully why and how that became the case, it is necessary to point out that national continuity could also entail moments of enormous change and discontinuity, especially in the political sphere. In World War II, specific political and military events created a situation in which unexampled killing could take place. "An extreme threshold or outer limit of transgression was crossed," as LaCapra writes.[21] All arguments of Germany's normality in the cultural history of national memory must therefore take account of Nazism and the Holocaust. All arguments about the origins and development of the Holocaust must in turn take account of the normal workings of German society and culture during Hitler's rule.[22] The relationship between consumer culture and genocide is worth mentioning again in this context.

If Germany developed poetic spaces and national stories that mirrored its European heritage, it also produced a murderous political regime whose violence toward other Europeans was unprecedented. This fact alone suggests that the workings of German memory after 1945 have had an agonizing quality lacking in other traditions of national memory because those traditions have not had to deal with such an extraordinary level of inhumanity. Perhaps the only exception in terms of historical experience is Croatia, which in its World War II–era fascist version did not in any case have the material resources or popular backing to organize mass extermination on a scale comparable to that of the Nazis. In the Germans' sense of their country as a site of perpetrators, this important qualification, this sense of a German Sonderweg of history and memory, has come through clearly. It appears also in the extraordinary public reception in Germany accorded to Daniel Goldhagen's book on the Holocaust, which essentially (and very misleadingly) transformed all Germans of the wartime generation into "Hitler's willing executioners."[23] Goldhagen's book has been a major media phenomenon not only because of aggressive marketing and certainly not because of the quality of the scholarship, which is flawed. The book has gained an audience largely because its argument suits a generation willing to see its parents and grandparents as unredeemable and uniquely violent perpetrators whose hold on a contemporary and more democratic Germany has now been broken.

But even this sense of historical peculiarity, which in any case has been held only by a substantial minority of the German population, may already be an historical artifact. It is not true that "guilt" has become superannuated, as a 1998 cover of the German newsweekly *Der Spiegel* provocatively suggested.[24] In a recent study of the politics of reunified Germany, two perspicacious scholars predicted that the Berlin Republic will not differ all that greatly from its Bonn predecessor. Democratic institutions are so firmly embedded, they asserted, that it would be difficult to envision a significant German departure from the path laid out in more than forty years of the Federal Republic. Where matters could change, however, is in the exercise of power. "Germany vacillates between an overbearing projection of power (mainly, though not exclusively, in the realm of the economy) and a reticence about admitting that power," they write.[25] This vacillation was inherited from the Bonn Republic, which reacted to Nazi Germany's murderous legacy by stressing democracy and by refraining from the exercise of political might congruent with West Germany's economic clout. The vacillation stemmed from the effect of collective memory, specifically from the effect of Auschwitz, with its extraordinary symbolic radius in postwar German culture, which hampered a full and unrestrained elaboration of power.

If the Berlin Republic will be different in this sense than its Bonn ancestor, argue Markovits and Reich, then it will be so because it will have placed Nazism and the Holocaust in a new historical perspective. A new sense of the Holocaust as a historical event will quite possibly allow Germans to apply their economic and political might in the way "normal" states have in the past. Though Markovits and Reich remain optimistic about the new Germany, they concede that a return to normality on this level creates not a little anxiety. But many scholars have argued convincingly that, by "historicizing" the Holocaust, Germans do not necessarily diminish the horror of the crime.[26] One can continue to emphasize that the Holocaust was unprecedented in its technical ambitions and incomparable in its traumatic effects. One can compare it to other instances of genocide and political atrocity in the past without forgetting its specific historical origins. One can, moreover, continue to emphasize the contemporary significance of the Nazi period while still conceding that it now belongs more in the realm of history than living memory. In short, by situating Auschwitz in a historical time that is now closed to the present, the new Federal Republic will not necessarily deny that some of the historical conditions that produced it can reappear. That *this* form of denial could occur as a result of historicizing the Holocaust is not to say it will, especially if honest citizens and scholars remain alert, and especially if people continue to believe that history informs memory work in the present.

What would the implications of this German future be for the memory landscape? If what the future holds is a new projection of German power, particularly in the economic sphere, then perhaps the regnant element of the new memory landscape will be the citadel, as both economic command post and political-administrative center, as both symbol and guarantor of power and knowledge, as both producer and consumer of the past and future. I have emphasized the continuities of the memory landscape, and certainly the citadel is an ancient form with roots stretching back four thousand years. Its permutations have been varied, as Mumford once pointed out, extending from "the Castel San Angelo to the concrete bunker by the Admiralty Arch in London, from the Kremlin to the Pentagon, and thence to new underground control centers."[27] What Mumford could not have considered in this list because of its recentness was the corporate business center with its offices, shops, theaters, restaurants, nightclubs, malls, and security apparatus—cities within cities whose historical character is increasingly crystallized around bustling and self-policed nodes of information processing and popular consumption. After all, on the brink of urban history, the function of the citadel, or "little city," was not primarily military despite its fortified walls marking it off from the rest of the village. Rather, the king used the citadel as military defense, as a religious shrine, and as a "holding point, where the chieftain's booty, mainly grain and possibly women, would be safe against purely local depredations."[28]

If one looks at developments in modern cities throughout the world, it is clear that new citadels of corporate power have come into being as part of a dual process whereby cities have not only sprawled beyond their former borders but also renewed their central administrative and commercial districts. And despite their significance as symbols of a new global economy and as holding points for goods and services, the citadels also function as symbols of history and national identity. The citadels being built on the Potsdamer Platz in Berlin, once the busiest intersection of the city and now the largest urban construction site in Europe, are as central to the political identity of the new/old German capital as they are to the bottom lines of Daimler-Chrysler and Sony. A substantial part of German identity has been built on a history of technology, economic productivity, and high standards of consumption, and the new corporate citadels emerging in the postunification memory landscape symbolize and further this history of economic nationalism.

"In the center of Berlin," wrote one journalist of the virtual city-within-a-city on the Potsdamer Platz, "building for the future takes place with the myths of the past."[29] In other urban centers, the citadels take in historic city centers as well, making these quarters extensions of their economic reach. In Frankfurt, the hyperdevelopment of the city's West as a corporate and high-rise center takes place outside the historic core. Its roots lay in the redevelopment of the metropole on the Main, and thus remind us that the corporate citadel is by no means an invention of the postunification era. It is difficult to overlook the prescience of the East German regime in this regard as well. Was not the Palace of the

Republic, built from 1973 to 1976 on the spot where the oldest and easternmost part of the imperial castle once stood, also a forerunner of the new corporate citadel? The past decade of public debate over the preservation of the palace reflects that many East Berliners grew fond of the elaborate structure because of its bowling alleys, theaters, and other entertainment opportunities. As a palace symbolizing the power of workers and peasants in a Communist state, the building thus evoked precisely the mix of political identity and consumerist fantasy that the contemporary citadel does. Investment patterns and real-estate capital may further the development of such complexes, especially in East German cities undergoing the transition from socialism to capitalism, since there only large-scale investors with grand schemes have the power to develop neglected urban centers.[30]

The emergent evolution of the new corporate citadel does not mean other artifacts in the memory landscape will disappear. The reconstruction of Berlin as the capital takes place in relation to many edifices that served as national monuments in an earlier period—the Reichstag (wrapped or unwrapped), the statue of Frederick the Great, the Brandenburg Gate.[31] In Dresden the massive Frauenkirche, eighteenth-century jewel in the architectural crown of Germany's "Florence on the Elbe," is being rebuilt. These national monuments remain, even if they can no longer be considered at the forefront of historical consciousness. And the reconstruction of Potsdamer Platz takes place not far from the paradigmatic symbol of the just-concluded era of historical traces, the Topography of Terror, now a permanent installation. Germans will continue to dig for traces of the tragedies and crimes of the national past, in Berlin and elsewhere. They will debate, exhaustively and with great earnestness, how to represent the former concentration camps, some of them sites of both Nazi and Stalinist terror. They will continue initiatives such as the interdisciplinary research project organized by art historian Detlev Hoffmann and historian Jörn Rüsen among others to inventory and interpret what remains of the traces of Nazi concentration camps in Europe.[32] But they will do so as the shadows of looming corporate citadels grow ever longer in the memory landscape. The victimization theme will also not fade away. The recent reconfiguration of the Neue Wache and debates over the forthcoming Holocaust memorial complex in Berlin have reinforced this theme in public life. It remains to be seen whether the Berlin Jewish museum will emphasize the victimization theme to the detriment of a longer history of Jewish involvement in the building of the German nation.

The narrative of victimization as a dominant element belongs more to the eras of the reconstruction and the trace. In those periods, moreover, the theme of national revival also vied for attention and indeed effectively muted the victimization theme at significant moments. The citadel signals an age in which the narrative of national resurgence will radiate much more strongly. But in this as in so many other cases, the history of German memory, like cultural history generally, becomes an innovative recombination of previously existing elements rather than an unambiguous departure from the past, a series of fluid, emergent framing devices rather than a definitive coming to terms with history. The future thus presents a daunting prospect, but it may also represent an opportunity if the half-century of German democracy just concluded remains a continuous and positive element of collective memory.

Notes

INTRODUCTION

1. "Vorwärts und nicht vergessen/ unsere Straße und unser Feld./ Vorwärts und nicht vergessen, / wessen Straße ist die Straße/ Wessen Welt ist die Welt?" The music was composed by Hanns Eisler.

2. Warneken, "Forward, But Forgetting Nothing," 81.

3. Dahn, *Westwärts und nicht vergessen.*

4. Baker, "The Berlin Wall," 709–15, 720–21, 724–25; on representations of the Wall in literature and popular culture, see Schürer, Keune, and Jenkins, eds., *The Berlin Wall.*

5. Kramer, *The Politics of Memory,* xvi.

6. Piero Fassino, "A quei ragazzi hanno negato la memoria," *L'unità,* 7 April 1994, as cited in Ben-Ghiat, "Fascism, Writing, and Memory," 630. The full citation reads: "We must ask ourselves: have we really come to terms with the legacy of fascism in Italian society?"

7. Huyssen, *Twilight Memories.*

8. Kramer, *The Politics of Memory,* xviii.

9. For a recent analysis of German memory from the 1930s through the postwar decades, see Herf, *Divided Memory,* which nonetheless also focuses exclusively on the memory of Nazism and its relationship to certain political continuities in German history. In this context, I also note Michael Geyer's formulation of the problem: "What happens to (the narrative of) German history if we bring into stereoscopic view both halves of the twentieth century, without diminishing the crimes of the first or denying the good life of the second?" See Geyer, "Twentieth Century as History," 666.

10. Maier asks the question for the contemporary period in "A Surfeit of Memory?" He links the late-twentieth-century preoccupation with memory to the exhaustion of transformative politics.

11. Nietzsche, "On the Uses and Disadvantages of History for Life," 60.

12. Confino, "Collective Memory and Cultural History." A major exception to Confino's argument is Mosse, *Fallen Soldiers,* but Confino does not discuss this work.

13. For preliminary remarks on this subject, see Koshar, *Germany's Transient Pasts,* 60–64, 316–17; idem, "'What Ought to Be Seen.'"

14. See for example the recent and controversial argument in Goldhagen, *Hitler's Willing Executioners,* which posits the long continuity of a unique and murderous German anti-Semitism until the post–World War II era.

15. See Haupt and Kocka, eds., *Geschichte und Vergleich,* and François, Siegrist, and Vogel, eds., *Nation und Emotion,* for recent scholarship in comparative history, an underdeveloped field in European historiography.

16. For an opposed view, see Gedi and Elam, "Collective Memory—What Is It?"

17. Assmann, "Collective Memory and Cultural Identity," 130.

18. See Connerton, *How Societies Remember,* esp. chap. 3.

19. Crane, "Writing the Individual Back into Collective Memory."

20. Carr, *Time, Narrative, and History,* 168.

21. I draw on Mayer, "Memory and History," 12–13.

22. Koshar, *Germany's Transient Pasts.*

23. For an engaging and sweeping study of memory and natural environments, see Schama, *Landscape and Memory.*

24. Irwin-Zarecka, *Frames of Remembrance,* 5, for the quotation, and 3–22 for the analytical background.

25. Mumford, *City in History,* 29.

26. See Kammen, *Mystic Chords of Memory.*

27. See Anderson, *Imagined Communities;* Hobsbawm and Ranger, eds., *The Invention of Tradition.*

28. It is significant, however, that a new Germanophone historiography emphasizing the extended evolution of German national identity (and the long-term precedents of late modern nationalism) over centuries is developing, as reflected in Schulze, *States, Nations, and Nationalism,* and Hardtwig, *Nationalismus und Bürgerkultur.*

29. Geyer, "Twentieth Century as History," 665.

30. Smith, "Origins of Nations." For further discussion of the concept as used in my narrative, see below, esp. chap. one. For the quotation, see Smith, *National Identity,* 25.

31. De Certeau, *Practice of Everyday Life,* 200–202.

32. Benjamin, "A Berlin Chronicle," 26.

33. See François, "Von der wiedererlangten Nation zur 'Nation wider Willen.'" Etienne François and Hagen Schulze are undertaking a research program to explore German sites of memory; for the conceptualization of the problem, see François, ed., *Lieux de Mémoire, Erinnerungsorte.* The project by François and Schulze will cover about one hundred sites and, in contrast to the analysis offered here, will emphasize much more strongly the discontinuities of German history. It will also eschew synthesis. For the idea of "realms of memory," see Nora, ed., *Realms of Memory,* the three-volume English translation of

the larger, multipart project by Nora, ed., *Le lieux de mémoire.* For the Netherlands, see den Boer and Frijhoff, eds., *Lieux de mémoire et identités nationales;* for Italy: Isnenghi, ed., *I luogi della memoria,* 3 vols.

34. Judt, "A la Recherche du Temps Perdu"; on the history and politics of heritage, see Hewison, *Heritage Industry;* Lowenthal, *The Past Is a Foreign Country;* idem, *Possessed by the Past;* Samuel, *Theatres of Memory,* 1:205–312.

35. To mention only a sampling of recent book-length studies, dissertations, and collections: Assmann, *Arbeit am nationalen Gedächtnis,* and *Errinerungsräume;* Barnouw, *Germany 1945;* Bartov, *Murder in Our Midst;* Buruma, *The Wages of Guilt;* Confino, *The Nation as a Local Metaphor;* Hardtwig, *Geschichtskultur und Wissenschaft;* Herf, *Divided Memory;* Hoffmann, ed., *Das Gedächtnis der Dinge;* Huyssen, *Twilight Memories;* Kaes, *From Hitler to Heimat;* Koshar, *Germany's Transient Pasts;* Kramer, *The Politics of Memory;* LaCapra, *History and Memory after Auschwitz;* Ladd, *The Ghosts of Berlin;* Maier, *The Unmasterable Past;* Marcuse, *Legacies of Dachau;* Markovits and Reich, *The German Predicament;* Moltmann, et al., *Erinnerung;* Mosse, *Fallen Soldiers;* Reichel, *Politik mit der Erinnerung;* Schmoll, *Verewigte Nation;* Tacke, *Denkmal im sozialen Raum;* Till, "Place and the Politics of Memory"; Young, *The Texture of Memory.*

CHAPTER 1. MONUMENTS

1. Quoted in Schulze, *States, Nations, and Nationalism,* 115.
2. Craig, *The Germans,* 16.
3. Hardtwig, *Nationalismus und Bürgerkultur,* 34–45; Blackbourn, *The Long Nineteenth Century,* 130.
4. Jeismann, *Vaterland der Feinde,* 241–42.
5. Agulhon, *Marianne into Battle,* 173.
6. Mumford, *Culture of Cities,* 435.
7. Riegl, "Der moderne Denkmalskultus."
8. Anderson, *Imagined Communities.*
9. Jeismann, *Vaterland der Feinde,* 242.
10. See Blackbourn, *The Long Nineteenth Century,* 251; on nineteenth-century German historians' contribution to legitimizing the national movement, see S. Berger, *The Search for Normality,* 21–37.
11. Smith, "Origins of Nations."
12. Craig, *The Germans,* 30.
13. Quoted in Tümmers, *Der Rhein,* 209.
14. Smith, "Origins of Nations," 120.
15. Koselleck, "Einleitung," 12.
16. Liman, *Bismarck-Denkwürdigkeiten,* 2: 178.
17. For the following, see Blackbourn, *The Long Nineteenth Century,* 424–29.
18. See Gentile, *Il Culto del Littorio,* 23–28.
19. See Marchand, *Down from Olympus.*
20. Mommsen, "Kaisermacht und Bürgerstolz," 188, 189; Hutter, *Die feinste Barbarei,* 63.

21. Baedeker, *Berlin und Umgebung* [1910], 51. But not everyone reacted favorably to the blocked streets and numerous restrictions on pedestrian traffic that were caused by the emperor's processions; see Fritzsche, *Reading Berlin, 1900,* 167–68.

22. Geertz, "Centers, Kings, and Charisma," 16.

23. Kammen, *Mystic Chords of Memory,* 284–85; Schulze, *States, Nations, and Nationalism,* 169, 173–74.

24. See Rowe and Koetter, *Collage City,* esp. 102–3.

25. Agulhon, *Marianne into Battle,* 186.

26. Hobsbawm, "Mass Producing Traditions: Europe, 1870–1914," 278.

27. Kammen, *Mystic Chords of Memory,* 292.

28. Cohen, "Symbols of Power," 494–95; Ben-Amos, "Monuments and Memory in French Nationalism"; Brown, *Care of Ancient Monuments,* 74–90; Agulhon, *Marianne into Battle,* 70; Tacke, *Denkmal im sozialen Raum;* Winock, "Joan of Arc," 455–67.

29. Smith, *Ethnic Origins of Nations,* 134–38.

30. Hermand, *Old Dreams of a New Reich,* 18.

31. Alings, *Monument und Nation,* 38, 41.

32. Lurz, *Kriegerdenkmäler,* 2: 436; Alings, *Monument und Nation,* 76–78.

33. Lipp, *Natur, Geschichte, Denkmal,* 261–67.

34. Mosse, *Nationalization of the Masses,* 50; Warner, *Monuments & Maidens,* 8; Agulhon, *Marianne into Battle,* 71.

35. Mumford, *Culture of Cities,* 434.

36. Assmann, *Arbeit am nationalen Gedächtnis,* 51.

37. Alings, *Monument und Nation,* 587–90.

38. On the celebration, see Éri and Jobbágyi, "The Millennial Celebrations of 1896"; on the monument, see Gerő, *Heroes' Square,* 5–15.

39. Hoffmann, "Sakraler Monumentalismus um 1900," 270.

40. Alings, *Monument und Nation,* 81.

41. Ibid., 284–301.

42. For much of the following, Tacke, *Denkmal im sozialen Raum;* see also Mosse, *Nationalization of the Masses,* 59–62; and Nipperdey, "Zum Jubiläum der Hermannsdenkmal."

43. On the subscription drive for the Hermannsdenkmal, see Tacke, *Denkmal im sozialen Raum,* chap. 3.

44. Nipperdey, "Zum Jubiläum der Hermannsdenkmal," 15–19. The imagery of Hermann was also connected to the development of Germanic prehistorical studies and archaeology, as discussed in Marchand, *Down from Olympus,* 157–87.

45. Tacke, *Denkmal im sozialen Raum,* is foundational here.

46. Gerő, *Heroes' Square,* 16.

47. Stokes, *Three Eras of Political Change,* 121–22; Judah, *The Serbs,* 29–47.

48. Cited in Körner, *Staat und Geschichte im Königreich Bayern,* 281.

49. Judah, *The Serbs,* 34–37.

50. Alings, *Monument und Nation,* 312; Hutter, "*Die feinste Barbarei,*" 31.

51. Hutter, "*Die feinste Barbarei,*" 69; Alings, *Monument und Nation,* 593.

52. Hoffmann, "Sakraler Monumentalismus um 1900," 250.

53. Ekmečić, "St. Vitus Day as the Principal National Holiday of the Serbs," 339–40; Judah, *The Serbs,* 69–70.

54. Hoffmann, "Sakraler Monumentalismus um 1900," 272; Nipperdey, "Nationalidee und Nationaldenkmal," 575–76; Tacke, *Denkmal im sozialen Raum,* 66–67. For the von Grotthuss quote: Assmann, *Arbeit am nationalen Gedächtnis,* 53.

55. Hutter, "*Die feinste Barbarei,*" 67–68.

56. Cohen, "Symbols of Power," 495.

57. Hutter, "*Die feinste Barbarei,*" 58–79.

58. Ibid., 183–86; Hoffmann, "Sakraler Monumentalismus um 1900," 278.

59. Baedeker, *Deutschland in einem Bande,* 113.

60. Nipperdey, "Nationalidee und Nationaldenkmal," 579–82.

61. Belgum discusses the estimates in "Displaying the Nation," 458.

62. Mosse, *Nationalization of the Masses,* 60.

63. Jackowski, "People's Monuments," 239; Agulhon, *Marianne into Battle,* 167; Belgum, "Displaying the Nation," 460, and *Popularizing the Nation,* esp. 86–98; Alings, *Monument und Nation,* 593.

64. On Hoffman's argument, which appeared in the *Deutsche Bauzeitung,* see Alings, *Monument und Nation,* 16.

65. For the following, see Lerner, "The Nineteenth-Century Monument and the Embodiment of National Time," 176–96.

66. Alings, *Monument und Nation,* 81, 87, 177–86, 564–66; Schmoll, *Verewigte Nation,* 211–12

67. Schmoll, *Verewigte Nation,* 102.

68. Riegl, "Der moderne Denkmalskultus," 149–56.

69. For the following, see Koshar, *Germany's Transient Pasts,* chap. 1.

70. For background, Wright, *On Living in an Old Country,* 48–53.

71. Brush, "The Cultural Historian Karl Lamprecht," 142, 160–61.

72. Nipperdey, *Deutsche Geschichte, 1800–1866,* 403.

73. Gentile, *Il Culto del Littorio,* 26.

74. Harvey, "Monument and Myth," 238–49.

75. See Nipperdey, "Der Kölner Dom als Nationaldenkmal."

76. Cited in Cremer, "Der Kölner Dombaufest," 6.

77. Koshar, *Germany's Transient Pasts,* 68–69.

78. For the following, ibid., 32–34, 57–59.

79. Ladd, *Urban Planning and Civic Order,* 91–92, 126–28.

80. Linse, "Die Entdeckung der technischen Denkmäler," 202–3.

81. Gollwitzer, "Zum Fragenkreis Architekturhistorismus," 7–8; Lewis, *The Politics of the German Gothic Revival,* 9.

82. Schorske, *Fin-de-Siècle Vienna,* 36–37.

83. See Jeffries, *Politics and Culture in Wilhelmine Germany,* 23, 30–31.

84. Cited in Mosse, *Nationalization of the Masses,* 57.

85. Gollwitzer, "Zum Fragenkreis Architekturhistorismus," 9–12.

86. Cited in Ladd, *Ghosts of Berlin,* 86.

87. Mommsen, "Kaisermacht und Bürgerstolz," 192–93; Schmädeke, *Der Deutsche Reichstag,* 32; Jeffries, *Politics and Culture in Wilhelmine Germany,* 27.

88. Lane, *Architecture and Politics,* 13–17.

89. See Pinkney, *Napoleon III and the Rebuilding of Paris.*

90. Quoted in Speitkamp, *Verwaltung der Geschichte,* 56.

91. Sitte, *City Planning,* 85.

92. Schorske, *Fin-de-Siècle Vienna,* 98.

93. Mumford, *The City in History,* 475.

94. See Rollins, *A Greener Vision of Home.*

95. For stimulating if rather disparate commentary on the genealogy of British heritage and ethnic politics, respectively, see Samuel, *Theatres of Memory,* 1:227–41 and 2:60–64.

96. Lebovics, "Creating the Authentic France," 241; Ford, *Creating the Nation,* 17–24.

97. Melman, "Gender, History and Memory," 10.

98. For the following, I rely on Warner, *Monuments & Maidens,* xvii–xx, 18–37.

99. Agulhon, *Marianne into Battle,* 182–85; on Joan of Arc as "anti-Marianne," Winock, "Joan of Arc," 469.

100. Tacke, *Denkmal im sozialen Raum,* 46; Chickering, *We Men Who Feel Most German.*

101. Gall, *Germania,* 6–7, 25–27, 32–37; on the Niederwalddenkmal, Tittel, *Das Niederwalddenkmal.*

102. Alings, *Monument und Nation,* 301.

103. I rely for the following on Tacke, *Denkmal im sozialen Raum,* 105–7, 131–32.

104. Nipperdey, "Sozialdemokratie und Geschichte."

105. For both examples, Hardtwig, *Geschichtskultur und Wissenschaft,* 288–89.

106. Ibid., 295; Lidtke, *Alternative Culture,* 77–85.

107. Frykman and Löfgren, *Culture Builders,* 57–58.

108. Hardtwig, *Geschichtskultur und Wissenschaft,* 272–73.

109. For the following, Domansky, "Der 'Zukunftsstaat am Besenbinderhof.'" See also Projektgruppe Arbeiterkultur Hamburg, ed., *Vorwärts und nicht vergessen,* 320.

110. Baedeker, *Berlin und Umgebung* [1889], 142.

111. Speitkamp, *Verwaltung der Geschichte,* 93; on Jewish culture in the late Kaiserreich, Brenner, *The Renaissance of Jewish Culture in Weimar Germany,* 19–31.

112. Bartov, "Defining Enemies, Making Victims," 773.

113. Kern, *The Culture of Time and Space,* 63, 64, for the quotations.

114. See Hardtwig, *Geschichtskultur und Wissenschaft,* 203–9.

CHAPTER 2. RUINS

1. Clemen, *Die Deutsche Kunst und die Denkmalpflege,* 104.

2. Harbison, *The Built, the Unbuilt, and the Unbuildable,* 99.

3. Simmel, "Die Ruine," 129.
4. Spengler, *Decline of the West,* 5, 248, 252, 375–78.
5. Winter, *Sites of Memory,* 82.
6. Fritzsche, *Germans into Nazis,* 51–66, misses this element by overstating the Burgfrieden's role in breaking with prewar political culture.
7. Eksteins, *Rites of Spring,* 155–59.
8. For numerous examples, see Becker, *La guerre et la foi.*
9. Cited in Applegate, *Nation of Provincials,* 117.
10. For the following, Dumont, *German Ideology,* 57–61, where the author analyzes Mann's polemic.
11. See Koshar, *Germany's Transient Pasts,* chap. 2.
12. Tag für Denkmalpflege, *Dreizehnter Tag für Denkmalpflege,* 63–64.
13. Quoted in Haskell, *History and Its Images,* 236.
14. Clemen, *Die Deutsche Kunst und die Denkmalpflege,* 8, 9.
15. Ibid., 9.
16. My thanks to Valentin Bogorov for this information.
17. Esbenshade, "Remembering to Forget," 74; Miljutenko, "Wir dürfen nicht geschichtslos werden," 23–24; Fülöp-Miller, *Geist und Gesicht des Bolschewismus,* 131, 305–8; Benjamin, "Moscow," 127.
18. Speitkamp, "Denkmalsturz und Symbolkonflikt," 15, 18; on Metz, see Maas, "Zeitenwende in Elsaß-Lothringen," 90, 106n. 43.
19. Lamprecht, *Regiment Reichstag.*
20. Koshar, *Germany's Transient Pasts,* 117–18.
21. Demps, "Die Geschichte der Straßennamen," 18–28, here 24; on Munich, see Rosenfeld, "Monuments and the Politics of Memory," 229–33.
22. Scheffauer, *The New Vision in the German Arts,* 124–30.
23. Quotations from Whyte, *Taut,* 232–34.
24. Pommer and Otto, *Weissenhof 1927,* 1.
25. For the following, Czaplicka, "*Amerikabilder,*" 44–51.
26. See Koshar, *Germany's Transient Pasts,* chap. 3.
27. On the history of war commemoration, see Evans and Lunn, eds., *War and Memory.*
28. Winter, *Sites of Memory,* 78, 93–98, 108–13.
29. Prost, "Monuments to the Dead," 308, 323; Becker, *La guerre et la foi.*
30. It should be noted that war museums were also memorials where the living honored the dead in addition to gaining information about World War I. On this subject, see Brandt, "The Memory Makers," esp. 107–8.
31. Mosse, *Fallen Soldiers,* 106.
32. Ibid., 84–85. Austerity and simplicity were not absent from the culture of war commemoration in England, for the most successful English war monument, the Cenotaph in Whitehall, gained both critical acclaim and popular devotion in part from an impressive starkness, as argued in King, *Memorials of the Great War in Britain,* 145–46.
33. Lurz, *Kriegerdenkmäler,* 3:93.
34. Muirhead, *Belgium and the Western Front,* 40–44; Mosse, *Fallen Soldiers,* 112–13.
35. Winter, *Sites of Memory,* 91.

36. Popovich, "The Battle of Kosovo," 247–53, 304, 307.

37. Mosse, *Fallen Soldiers,* 60–63; the quote derives from Sherman, "Monuments, Mourning, and Masculinity," 103.

38. Dwork and van Pelt, *Auschwitz,* 39.

39. Mosse, *Fallen Soldiers,* 90.

40. Koshar, *Germany's Transient Pasts,* chap. 3.

41. Sherman, "Art, Commerce, and the Production of Memory," 191–95.

42. See Winter, *Sites of Memory,* 86–90.

43. Lloyd, *Battlefield Tourism,* 30.

44. This is the argument in Mosse, *Fallen Soldiers,* chap. 7.

45. Huyssen, *Twilight Memories,* 131.

46. Baedeker, *Rheinlande,* xiii; Lloyd, *Battlefield Tourism,* 119.

47. Michelin & Cie, *Rheims,* 31; on the Michelin battlefield guides' focus on German atrocities, Lloyd, *Battlefield Tourism,* 114–17.

48. Lloyd, *Battlefield Tourism,* 119.

49. See Mayer, "Memory and History," 15, where the author discusses Nietzsche's linking of memory and vengeance.

50. I rely here on Mosse, *Fallen Soldiers,* 92–93, and Becker, *La guerre at la foi,* 111–17.

51. For the following, Tietz, "Ostpreußisches Stonehenge"; Mosse, *Nationalization of the Masses,* 68–71.

52. On the following, see Reichel, *Politik mit der Erinnerung,* 231–46; Tietz, "Schinkels Neue Wache Unter den Linden," 47–64.

53. Winter, *Sites of Memory,* 102–5; Lloyd, *Battlefield Tourism,* chap. 2; King, *Memorials of the Great War in Britain,* 141–55.

54. Geertz, "Centers, Kings, and Charisma," 30–31.

55. Linse, *Barfüßige Propheten;* Behrenbeck, *Der Kult um die toten Helden,* 149–59.

56. Harbison, *The Built, the Unbuilt, and the Unbuildable,* 112.

57. For the following: Joseph Goebbels, "Rund um die Gedächtniskirche," *Der Angriff* (23 January 1928), as reprinted in Kaes, Jay, and Dimendberg, *Weimar Republic Sourcebook,* 560–62.

58. Spengler, *Decline of the West,* 251–52.

59. Ibid., 254.

60. Hitler, *Mein Kampf,* 249, 284.

61. Domansky, "A Lost War," 244–45.

62. Behrenbeck, *Der Kult um die toten Helden,* 197–209; Baird, *To Die for Germany,* 49; Kunz-Ott and Kluge, eds., *150 Jahre Feldherrnhalle,* 66–67.

63. See Gentile, *Il Culto del Littorio,* esp. chap. 2.

64. See Buruma, *The Wages of Guilt,* 203, where the author writes "before World War II there were no admonitory monuments in Germany."

65. Lurz, *Kriegerdenkmäler,* 5:27.

66. Etlin, *Modernism in Italian Architecture,* 404–5.

67. Cited by Emmerich, "Mythos of Germanic Continuity," 43.

68. Hermand, *Old Dreams of a New Reich,* 193–96.

69. Lurz, *Kriegerdenkmäler,* 5:52–53.

70. Ibid., 5:56.

71. Ibid., 5:56–57; Weidenhaupt, *Kleine Geschichte der Stadt Düsseldorf,* 164.

72. Koshar, *Germany's Transient Pasts,* chap. 4; on Munich, Rosenfeld, "Monuments and the Politics of Memory," 232–33.

73. Ladd, *Ghosts of Berlin,* 89; Schmädeke, *Der Deutsche Reichstag,* 113–14.

74. Tiedemann, "Das Reichstagsgebäude," B77–78.

75. Grieben-Verlag, *Berlin und Umgebung,* 81.

76. Friedländer, *Nazi Germany and the Jews,* 229, 292–93.

77. Bartov, "Defining Enemies, Making Victims," 779.

78. Friedländer, *Nazi Germany and the Jews,* 276; Reichel, *Politik mit der Erinnerung,* 202–6.

79. Petropoulos, *Art as Politics,* 171–72; on the Musée des Monuments Français, see Haskell, *History and Its Images,* 236–52.

80. Engelbrechten and Volz, *Wir wandern durch das nationalsozialistische Berlin.*

81. Ibid., 7, where the editors quote Hitler.

82. Ibid., 78.

83. Ibid., 49–51, 55.

84. Ghirardo, "Italian Architects and Fascist Politics," 117.

85. Cited in Lurz, *Kriegerdenkmäler,* 5:139.

86. Speer, *Inside the Third Reich,* 56.

87. Quoted in Hinz, *Art in the Third Reich,* 197.

88. Touring Club Italiano, *Italia Centrale,* 2:272.

89. Ricci, Colini, and Mariani, *Via dell'Impero,* 39.

90. Spengler, *Decline of the West,* 75.

91. Koshar, *Germany's Transient Pasts,* chap. 4.

92. See Hosmer, "Broadening View," 127–28, 129, 132; Kammen, *Mystic Chords of Memory,* 351–74.

93. Schlungbaum-Stehr, "Altstadtsanierung und Denkmalpflege in den 30er Jahren," 86.

94. Kirschweng, "Deutsches Land und Volk links der Saar," 98.

95. For the following, Baedeker, *Das Elsass,* xx, xxi, 5–6, 11, 13, 22, 145.

96. Dwork and van Pelt, *Auschwitz,* 21, 67.

97. Ibid., 26–27.

98. Rades, *Wer kennt Danzig?* 113.

99. Dwork and van Pelt, *Auschwitz,* 36, 47–48.71

100. Friedländer, *Nazi Germany and the Jews,* 218.

101. Cited in Dwork and Van Pelt, *Auschwitz,* 59, 61.

102. For the following, Baedeker, *Das Generalgouvernement,* 10, 15, 129, 131; Young, *Texture of Memory,* 128.

103. Schlögel, "Der Horror einer schönen Stadt," 19.

104. Diefendorf, *In the Wake of War,* 4–13.

105. Bartetzko, *Verbaute Geschichte,* 50–51.

106. Speer, *Spandauer Tagebücher,* 310.

107. Ibid., 309; Schäfer, *Gespaltene Bewußtsein,* 132; Bültemann, *Architektur für das Dritte Reich,* 38.

108. Spender, *European Witness,* 235.

CHAPTER 3. RECONSTRUCTIONS

1. Baedeker, *Leipzig. Ein neuer Führer,* 4. One could quibble with the mayor's observation on tourism since we know that within weeks after the end of the war, urban ruins became a source of fascination for those who could travel, and for foreign travelers in particular; the ruins of landmarks such as the Reichstag in Berlin or Hitler's chancellery spawned a host of tour guides willing to show military, political, and literary personages around. See Spender, *European Witness,* esp. chap. 15.

2. Baedeker, *Leipzig. Ein neuer Führer,* 4, 20–21, 34.

3. On the university, Baedeker, *Leipzig. Ein neuer Führer,* 25. Soviet goals to have more workers and working farmers become university students were difficult to meet in this period, as demonstrated by Naimark, *The Russians in Germany,* 444–45. For Leipzig street names, see Azaryahu, "Renaming the Past," 46–48.

4. Fitch, *Historic Preservation,* 47.

5. Schivelbusch, *In a Cold Crater,* 19.

6. Quoted in Craig, *The Germans,* 20.

7. Quoted in Schivelbusch, *In a Cold Crater,* 14.

8. For the following, Andreas-Friedrich, *Battleground Berlin,* 1–35.

9. See Schoenbaum, *Hitler's Social Revolution.*

10. See James, *A German Identity,* 187–95.

11. Lurz, *Kriegerdenkmäler,* 6:50–53.

12. See Greenfield, *Nationalism,* 386–87.

13. Herf, *Divided Memory,* 159.

14. Andreas-Friedrich, *Battleground Berlin,* 243.

15. Wolfrum, "Der 'Tag der deutschen Einheit,'" 122–24.

16. Herf, *Divided Memory,* esp. chaps. 4 and 7.

17. Spender, *European Witness,* 226–27; Kittel, *Die Legende von der "Zweiten Schuld,"* 49–62; Steinbach, *Nationalsozialistische Gewaltverbrechen;* Benz, "Postwar Society and National Socialism," 2–3.

18. Rabinbach, *In the Shadow of Catastrophe,* chap. 4.

19. See Frei, *Vergangenheitspolitik,* for a comprehensive analysis of government policy in the Federal Republic.

20. Romano Bilenchi, "Letteratura d'occasione," *Società,* 15 November 1945, as cited in Ben-Ghiat, "Fascism, Writing, and Memory," 663.

21. See Bartram, Slawinski, and Steel, eds., *Reconstructing the Past.*

22. Hermand, *Kultur im Wiederaufbau,* 85.

23. See Koshar, *Germany's Transient Pasts,* 227–42, 255–57, 275–77; on East German photography's representation of war destruction, see Kuehn, *Caught,* 13–29.

24. Fodor, *Germany 1953,* 258.

25. Spender, *European Witness,* 60.
26. Koshar, *Germany's Transient Pasts,* 218–22.
27. Cited in Reichel, *Politik mit der Erinnerung,* 72.
28. Ibid., 74.
29. For the following, ibid., 72–73; Koshar, *Germany's Transient Pasts,* 231–32.
30. Koshar, *Germany's Transient Pasts,* 232.
31. Quoted in Zuchold, "Abriß der Ruinen," 179.
32. Ibid.
33. Ibid., 182–83, 191.
34. Ibid., 184, 186.
35. Ibid., 188–89.
36. Seydewitz, *Zerstörung und Wiederaufbau von Dresden,* 81, 101–4, 232; Kuehn, *Caught,* 253–57; Joppke, *East German Dissidents,* 136.
37. See Ladd, *Ghosts of Berlin,* 75–76.
38. Quoted in Diefendorf, *In the Wake of War,* 185.
39. See Heckart, "The Cities of Avignon and Worms," 490.
40. For the following, Gladsky, "Polish Post-War Historical Monuments," 151; Jankowski, "Warsaw," 83–91.
41. Esbenshade, "Remembering to Forget," 80.
42. Szulc, "Rebuilt Warsaw," 109.
43. See Diefendorf, *In the Wake of War,* chap. 4, which adopts this tripartite schema.
44. Rosenfeld, "The Architects' Debate," 192.
45. See Relph, *The Modern Urban Landscape,* 115.
46. Gerd Hatje, Hubert Hoffmann, and Karl Kaspar, *New German Architecture* (New York: Praeger, 1956), as excerpted in McClelland and Scher, *Postwar German Culture,* 408–17, here 409; on "no-frills modernism," Relph, *The Modern Urban Landscape,* 198–201.
47. Spender, *European Witness,* 237.
48. See Ladd, *Ghosts of Berlin,* 127–34.
49. "Eine Kulisse stürzt ein." For the city as a whole, see Rosenfeld, *Munich and Memory.*
50. Baedeker, *München,* 68.
51. Ladd, *Ghosts of Berlin,* 147–48.
52. McDonogh, "Geography of Emptiness," 3–15.
53. Schleich, *Die zweite Zerstörung Münchens,* 20–23; the citation is from Brix, "Monumente der NS- und Trümmer-Zeit," 180.
54. For the following, Dietzfelbinger, "Reichsparteitagsgelände Nürnberg," 69, 73 n. 14; Reichel, *Politik mit der Erinnerung,* 52–59; *Nagel's Germany,* 510.
55. Ladd, *Ghosts of Berlin,* 142–48.
56. See Judt, *Grand Illusion,* 26.
57. Lagrou, "Victims of Genocide and National Memory," 187–88, 197.
58. Ibid., 201.
59. Judt, *Past Imperfect,* 47.
60. I rely for the following on Farmer, "Oradour-sur-Glane." See also Farmer, *Martyred Village.*

61. See de Keizer, "The Skeleton in the Closet," which deals with the ambivalent memory of the village Putten, where in retaliation for the killing of German officers by a Dutch resistance group, the Nazis deported 660 local men to concentration camps and burned down more than 100 buildings. Only 589 of the 660 Putten deportees returned to the Netherlands after the war; over 750 children were left fatherless, and there were some 300 widows.

62. Wheeler, *Lidice,* 8–9, 22–23, 32–37. It may be noted that the monument-wall contained the town seals not only of communities destroyed or damaged by German forces, including Warsaw, Oradour, Putten, Marzabotto (see below), Coventry, and Stalingrad, but also of Dresden.

63. De Grazia and Paggi, "Story of an Ordinary Massacre."

64. For the following, Young, *Texture of Memory,* chap. 6.

65. Kugelmass, "Bloody Memories," 298.

66. Jankowski, "Warsaw," 91.

67. Reichel, *Politik mit der Erinnerung,* 224–25.

68. Ibid., 228.

69. See Czaplicka, "History, Aesthetics, and Contemporary Commemorative Practice in Berlin," 173–80.

70. The point is made effectively in Geyer, "Politics of Memory," 11.

71. See LaCapra, *History and Memory after Auschwitz,* 180–85.

72. I quote here from Lüdtke, "'Coming to Terms with the Past,'" 551.

73. See Huyssen, *Twilight Memories,* chap. 4.

74. Rosenhaft, "The Uses of Remembrance," 369.

75. I base the following on Diner, "On the Ideology of Antifascism," esp. 127–30. On the tradition of German antifascism before 1945, see Herf, *Divided Memory,* 13–39.

76. Farmer, "Symbols That Face Two Ways," 99.

77. Brinks, "Political Anti-Fascism," 210–14.

78. On Merker and others, see Herf, *Divided Memory,* esp. 40–105.

79. Tumarkin, *The Living & The Dead,* 17, as well as caption to illustration between 148 and 149.

80. See Reichel, *Politik mit der Erinnerung,* 237–40; Spies, "Aus einem unabgeschlossenen Kapitel"; Tietz, "Schinkels Neue Wache Unter den Linden," 75–93.

81. For the following, see Gladsky, "Polish Post-War Historical Monuments," 154, 157.

82. Bezirkskommission zur Erforschung der Geschichte der örtlichen Arbeiterbewegung, ed., *Gedenk- und Erinnerungsstätten,* 52–71.

83. Sonnet, "Gedenkstätten für Opfer des Nationalsozialismus in der DDR," 792.

84. Brinks makes the helpful contrast in "Political Anti-Fascism," 208–9, but his analysis also seems to underestimate the degree to which legitimate antifascism continued to play a role in East German everyday life.

85. Berliner Geschichtswerkstatt, *Sackgassen;* Azaryahu, "Renaming the Past," 37, 43; and idem, *Von Wilhelmplatz zu Thälmannplatz,* 66, 196–97.

86. Azaryahu, "Street Names and Political Identity," 584–85; and idem, *Von Wilhelmplatz zu Thälmannplatz,* 74, 174–75.

87. See Herbert, "Der Holocaust in der Geschichtsschreibung," 31–33.

88. For a recent overview of the history and commemoration of concentration camps on German soil, see Schafft and Zeidler, eds., *Die KZ-Mahn- und Gedenkstätten in Deutschland.*

89. Ibid., 34–35. Anne Frank died in Belsen. For a recent statement on the history of the memory of Anne Frank, see Kushner, "'I Want to Go on Living after my Death.'"

90. Cited in Naimark, *The Russians in Germany,* 74.

91. On anti-Semitism in the late 1940s as reflected in U.S. military government surveys, see Herf, *Divided Memory,* 204–5. The first major historical studies of the Holocaust were by Leon Poliakov in France and Gerhard Reitlinger in England; see Kushner, *The Holocaust and the Liberal Imagination,* 3.

92. See Lagrou, "Victims of Genocide and National Memory," 194, where the author quotes Leo Hendricks, an anti-Semitic Dutch writer living in liberated Belgium in the spring of 1945.

93. Arendt, *Origins of Totalitarianism,* 437–59, here 442, 452.

94. Grenville, "The Earliest Reception of the Holocaust"; Moore is quoted by Young, *Texture of Memory,* 135; Lang, *Act and Idea in the Nazi Genocide;* Langer, *Holocaust Testimonies,* 204.

95. The figure of 1,634 is given in Lutz, "Gedenkstätten für die Opfer des NS-Regimes," 191.

96. Young, *Texture of Memory,* 142–43.

97. An exception is Horwitz, *In the Shadow of Death,* which deals with the town around Mauthausen.

98. See Irwin-Zarecka, *Neutralizing Memory,* 153–54.

99. Lagrou, "Victims of Genocide and National Memory," 183.

100. Dwork and van Pelt, *Auschwitz,* 364; *Travel Guide Poland,* 112–13; Smoleń, *Auschwitz, 1940–1945,* 19.

101. Young, *Texture of Memory,* 186–89; *Travel Guide Poland,* 328.

102. For the quotation and argument, Young, *Texture of Memory,* 131–32; see also Irwin-Zarecka, *Neutralizing Memory,* chap. 6.

103. Young, *Texture of Memory,* 144–50.

104. See Boban, "Jasenovac"; Dedijer, *The Yugoslav Auschwitz,* 34, 55, 225–310; Tanner, *Croatia,* 152; Stokes, *Three Eras of Political Change,* 113–14.

105. Quoted in Tanner, *Croatia,* 205.

106. Judah, *The Serbs,* 129, 132–33.

107. On the history of the camp, see Le Chene, *Mauthausen,* and on the Mauthausen town's relationship with the camp, see Horwitz, *In the Shadow of Death.*

108. For the following, Pelinka, "The Great Austrian Taboo," 62–63; Bunzl, "On the Politics and Semantics of Austrian Memory," 10–11, 20–30; Pauley, *From Prejudice to Persecution,* 297, 310. Pauley notes that Simon Wiesenthal, the well-known hunter of Nazi war criminals, made the argument of Austrian complicity in the Holocaust. Pauley also points out that Austrians were heavily involved in deporting Jews and administering the death camps, and that they were statistically overrepresented in the SS.

109. When former United Nations Secretary-General Kurt Waldheim was nominated for the Austrian presidency in 1985, Austrian sources as well as the *New York Times* and the World Jewish Congress revealed that Waldheim, despite his own statements to the contrary, had extensive knowledge of Nazi atrocities during his World War II service in the Balkans.

110. Kushner, *The Holocaust and the Liberal Imagination.*

111. Irwin-Zarecka, *Neutralizing Memory,* 167.

112. For a recent documentation and analysis, Overesch, *Buchenwald und die DDR.*

113. See Buruma, *The Wages of Guilt,* 209.

114. Overesch, *Buchenwald und die DDR,* 41, 44; on the Communist inmates, see also Naimark, *The Russians in Germany,* 260–63.

115. Sonnet, "Gedenkstätten für Opfer des Nationalsozialismus in der DDR," 779.

116. Knigge, "Vom Reden und Schweigen der Steine," 202; on U.S. troops' liberation of Buchenwald, see Abzug, *Inside the Vicious Heart,* 45–59; on U.S. Army Signal Corps photography and the camps, see Barnouw, *Germany, 1945,* passim, esp. 1–87.

117. Knigge, "Die Gedenkstätte Buchenwald," 311.

118. Knigge, "Vom Reden und Schweigen der Steine," 198; Overesch, *Buchenwald und die DDR,* 248–49, 252.

119. The SED worked behind the scenes, allowing the association to appear in public as the main planning instance. Herf, *Divided Memory,* 176, states that planning for the Buchenwald memorial began in 1954, but the SED's role can be traced back to April 1949, as demonstrated in Overesch, *Buchenwald und die DDR,* 261–63. On the history of the persecutees' organization, see Reuter and Hansel, *Das kurze Leben der VVN.*

120. Brinks, "Political Anti-Fascism," 209.

121. Overesch, *Buchenwald und die DDR,* 261–65.

122. Quoted in Sonnet, "Gedenkstätten für Opfer des Nationalsozialismus in der DDR," 780.

123. Knigge, "Die Gedenkstätte Buchenwald," 323, 331 n. 6.

124. Overesch, *Buchenwald und die DDR,* 235. For a comprehensive history of the development of the memorial, see Knigge, Pietsch, and Seidel, *Versteinertes Gedenken.*

125. Knigge, "Die Gedenkstätte Buchenwald," 316–17; on "Hegelian moments," see Herf, *Divided Memory,* 176.

126. Young, *Texture of Memory,* 77.

127. My analysis is based loosely on the discussion in Knigge, "Die Gedenkstätte Buchenwald," 324–26.

128. On the Soviet internment camp and its commemoration in the early 1990s, see Farmer, "Symbols That Face Two Ways," 108–11. For the history of the origin of the Sachsenhausen memorial under the GDR, see Morsch, ed., *Von der Erinnerung zum Monument.*

129. Quoted in Sonnet, "Gedenkstätten für Opfer des Nationalsozialismus in der DDR," 786.

130. Koonz, "Between Memory and Oblivion," 267; on Holocaust scholar-

ship and gender, see Kushner, *The Holocaust and the Liberal Imagination,* 4, 24, 90–115, 280 n. 15.

131. For a very critical account of former concentration camp sites in the Federal Republic, Eichmann, *Versteinert—Verharmlost—Vergessen.*

132. For an overview of the memorial, Young, *Texture of Memory,* 60–72. For Dachau up to 1968, see Marcuse, "Das ehemalige Konzentrationslager Dachau." See also Marcuse, *Legacies of Dachau,* forthcoming, for a comprehensive analysis.

133. I base the following on Marcuse, "Former Concentration Camps" and "Die museale Darstellung des Holocaust."

134. Fodor, *Germany 1953,* 253–54.

135. Quoted in Marcuse, "Former Concentration Camps," 13.

136. Lagrou, "Victims of Genocide and National Memory," 204–5.

137. Heineman, "The Hour of the Woman."

138. Werz, "Erinnerungen an die Ruinen von Berlin."

139. Moeller, "War Stories," 1029.

140. Domansky, "A Lost War," 242–43; for the following information on the number and style of post-1945 war memorials, see Lurz, *Kriegerdenkmäler,* 6:9, 140–42.

141. Koselleck, "Kriegerdenkmale als Identitätsstiftungen des überlebenden," 273.

142. Bartov, "Defining Enemies, Making Victims," 786–87.

143. See Lüdtke, "Coming to Terms with the Past," 549.

144. Lüdtke, "Histories of Mourning," 174.

145. See Niethammer, *"Die Jahre weiß man nicht, wo man die heute hinsetzen soll,"* for numerous examples.

146. Kushner, *The Holocaust and the Liberal Imagination,* 3.

CHAPTER 4. TRACES

1. See above all, Till, "Place and the Politics of Memory," esp. chaps. 4–5.

2. Hagelüken, "Auf den Barrikaden der Geschichte," 43; for one example of the results of the essay competition, see Galinski and Schmidt, eds., *Die Kriegsjahre in Deutschland, 1939–1945.*

3. Rosmus-Wenninger, *Widerstand und Verfolgung: Am Beispiel Passaus, 1933–1939.*

4. Ryan, *Marxism and Deconstruction,* 14–15.

5. Hobsbawm, *The Age of Extremes.*

6. On generational change in the Federal Republic, Preuss-Lausitz, et al., *Kriegskinder, Konsumkinder, Krisenkinder.*

7. Geyer, "The Politics of Memory," 7.

8. Frei, "Geschichte aus den 'Graswurzeln'?" 38–39; see also Geyer, "The Politics of Memory," 6.

9. I extrapolate from Craig, *The Germans,* 22–23, where the author derives the German tradition of obedience to authority from reactions to the angst caused by the Thirty Years' War.

10. Kaes, *From Hitler to Heimat,* 163–71.

11. Paul and Schoßig, "Geschichte und Heimat," 23.
12. For background, see Frei, "Geschichte aus den 'Graswurzeln'?"
13. Lindenberger and Wildt, "Radical Plurality," 82–86.
14. Geyer, "Twentieth Century as History," 682.
15. Lutz, "Gedenkstätten für die Opfer des NS-Regimes," 193.
16. See Lüdtke, "Histories of Mourning," for insights into the complexity of this issue.
17. I base the following on Rosenfeld, "The Architects' Debate," in spite of finding it overly critical of postmodernist architects' historicizing tendencies.
18. See Kirshenblatt-Gimblett, *Destination Culture.*
19. Quoted from Till, "Place and the Politics of Memory," 68.
20. Quoted in Kramer, *The Politics of Memory,* 259.
21. Friedländer and Seligman, "The Israeli Memory of the Shoah," 358–60.
22. Lüdtke, "Coming to Terms with the Past," 551.
23. Steinbach, *Nationalsozialistische Gewaltverbrechen,* 91.
24. Friedländer, *Reflections on Nazism;* Kirshenblatt-Gimblett, *Destination Culture,* 175, 265.
25. The most authoritative statement was by the Mitscherlichs, *Die Unfähigkeit zu trauern.*
26. Rousso, *Vichy Syndrome;* Paxton and Marrus, *Vichy France and the Jews.*
27. Burrin, "Vichy," 201.
28. Korn, "Denkmalschutz als Volksbewegung."
29. Paul and Schoßig, "Geschichte und Heimat," 15.
30. Ibid. For Eisenheim, see Koshar, *Germany's Transient Pasts,* 309–12, 319.
31. Frei, "Geschichte aus den 'Graswurzeln'?" 35–37.
32. Ibid. Schöttler, "Die Geschichtswerkstatt, e.V.," 423–24.
33. For the following, see Herrenknecht, "Geschichte er-fahren."
34. Gélieu, *Geschichte der Frauenbewegung Erfahren.*
35. The criticisms are related in Lüdtke, "Einleitung," 16; the response is quoted in Schöttler, "Die Geschichtswerkstatt, e.V.," 424.
36. For the following, see Koshar, "Memoria ingovernabile?"
37. The first in the series "Beiträge zum Thema Widerstand" was by Andreas Biss, "List als Mittel des Widerstandes," based on a presentation at the memorial on 6 November 1970.
38. Reichel, *Politik mit der Erinnerung,* 228–31; Case, "The Politics of Memorial Representation," 67–76.
39. Reichel, *Politik mit der Erinnerung,* 225.
40. Ibid., 226.
41. See Broszat, Fröhlich, and Wiesemann, *Bayern in der NS-Zeit,* the first of six volumes appearing from 1977 to 1983.
42. Pach, "Alternative Stadtrundfahrten: Das Hamburger Modell," 63–64.
43. See *Heimatgeschichtlicher Wegweiser zu Stätten des Widerstandes und der Verfolgung,* 1:43.
44. See for instance GEW Berlin, *Wider das Vergessen,* published by a prominent Berlin teachers' union.
45. Landesjugendring Hamburg, *Nazi-Terror und Widerstand.*

46. Pach, "Alternative Stadtrundfahrten: Das Hamburger Modell," 61.

47. Ibid., 62–68; and Paul, "Alternative Stadtrundfahrten: Beispiel Saarbrücken," 81–84.

48. Lüdtke, "Coming to Terms with the Past," 555–56; Kushner, *The Holocaust and the Liberal Imagination,* 9; Horwitz, *In the Shadow of Death.*

49. Zimmermann, "Gedenkstätten für die Opfer des Nationalsozialismus," 31–32; Herbert, "Der Holocaust in der Geschichtsschreibung," 37; Kushner, *The Holocaust and the Liberal Imagination,* 8. On survivors' complex memories, see Langer, *Holocaust Testimonies.*

50. Kolb, *Bergen-Belsen;* Puvogel, *Gedenkstätten für die Opfer des Nationalsozialismus,* 391–99; Zimmermann, "Gedenkstätten für die Opfer des Nationalsozialismus," 34; Kushner, "The Memory of Belsen," 23–27; Schafft and Zeidler, eds., *Die KZ-Mahn- und Gedenkstätten in Deutschland,* 33–50; and on liberalism and Holocaust memory, Kushner, *The Holocaust and the Liberal Imagination.*

51. Puvogel, *Gedenkstätten für die Opfer des Nationalsozialismus,* 92–99, 100–107; Marcuse, "Die museale Darstellung des Holocaust an Orten ehemaliger Konzentrationslager"; Friedländer and Seligman, "The Israeli Memory of the Shoah," 358–59.

52. Young, *Texture of Memory,* 59–60; for the most important dates in the evolution of the Neuengamme memorial site, see Schafft and Zeidler, eds., *Die KZ-Mahn- und Gedenkstätten in Deutschland,* 211–13.

53. Fliedl, Freund, Fuchs, and Perz, "Den Toten zur Ehr," 109.

54. Kushner, *The Holocaust and the Liberal Imagination,* 207.

55. Kramer, *The Politics of Memory,* 268; on German Jews' memory, see Bodemann, ed., *Jews, Germans, Memory.*

56. Lagrou, "Victims of Genocide and National Memory," 216.

57. Berlin-Information, *Berlin: Touristen-Tips im Taschenformat,* 124–25.

58. Reichel, *Politik mit der Erinnerung,* 215.

59. Domansky, "A Lost War," 254.

60. Günther-Kaminski and Weiß, " . . . *als wäre es nie gewesen,*" 6, 7.

61. Geyer and Hansen, "German-Jewish Memory and National Consciousness," 190.

62. Plant, *Pink Triangle;* Rose and Weiß, *Sinti and Roma im "Dritten Reich";* Rose, "Der Völkermord an den Sinti und Roma"; Garbe, *Zwischen Widerstand und Martyrium.*

63. Domansky, "A Lost War," 256.

64. For the following chronology and quotations, see Hartman, *Bitburg,* xiii–xvi.

65. Hillgruber, *Zweierlei Untergang,* 9.

66. Maier, *Unmasterable Past,* 9–33; see also Eley, "Nazism, Politics, and the Image of the Past"; Evans, *In Hitler's Shadow.*

67. The quotation comes from a Bundestag intervention by Federal Building Minister Oskar Schneider, 1986, as cited in Reichel, *Politik mit der Erinnerung,* 241.

68. For the following, Hüser, *Wewelsburg,* 107–13; Puvogel, *Gedenkstätten,* 600–603.

69. Ehman, "Gedenkstättenpolitik," 2–3; Ladd, *Ghosts of Berlin,* 153–54; Reichel, *Politik mit der Erinnerung,* 193–96.

70. I base much of the following on Till, "Place and the Politics of Memory," chaps. 4–5.

71. Cited in ibid., 150.

72. Kramer, *The Politics of Memory,* 265.

73. See ibid., 260–62, 283.

74. Ibid., chap. 5.

75. Ibid., 271.

76. See for example, Peukert, *The Weimar Republic.*

77. See the discussion in Till, "Place and the Politics of Memory," 285–88.

78. Young, *Texture of Memory,* 28–37, 40–42.

79. Christo and Jeanne-Claude, *Verhüllter/Wrapped Reichstag.*

80. Young, *Texture of Memory,* 34.

81. Lippmann, *Honecker,* 187.

82. Gerhard Lozek, professor of the Academy of Social Sciences in the Central Committee of the SED, was quoted in Helwig, "'Der Anspruch auf alles Gute, Wahre und Schöne,'" 696.

83. Organisationsbüro des Martin-Luther-Komitees, *Martin-Luther-Ehrung,* 65; Dähn and Heise, *Luther und die DDR.*

84. Relph, *Modern Urban Landscape,* 221.

85. Rosner, *Die Universitätskirche zu Leipzig,* 26–44; Diederich, "Die Sprengung der Rostocker Christuskirche," 567–68.

86. Quoted in Helwig, "'Der Anspruch auf alles Gute, Wahre und Schöne,'" 693.

87. See Koshar, *Germany's Transient Pasts,* 302–6.

88. Berger, *Kössern,* i–ii. The forward was written by Fritz Staude.

89. Helwig, "'Der Anspruch auf alles Gute, Wahre und Schöne,'" 694.

90. Koshar, *Germany's Transient Pasts,* 305.

91. Fitch, *Historic Preservation,* 361–75.

92. Filip, "Geblieben sind nur die Grabsteine aus Sandstein."

93. S. Winters, "Historic Preservation in Czechoslovakia," 270–75, 279–81.

94. Young, *Texture of Memory,* 199–201, 207; for the quotation on rightful keepers of Jewish memory, Irwin-Zarecka, *Neutralizing Memory,* 106; *Travel Guide Poland,* 350; Jackowski, "People's Monuments."

95. Quoted in Hoscislawski, "Die Bauhausrezeption in der DDR," 1593.

96. Ibid., 1593–94.

97. P. Winters, "Wiederaufbau in Ost-Berlin," 1311.

98. For the following, ibid., 1316–17.

99. Ibid., 1317.

100. Stahn, *Das Nikolaiviertel,* 8–9.

101. Loest, *Nikolaikirche.*

102. Reichel, *Politik mit der Erinnerung,* 206–7.

103. P. Winters, "Wiederaufbau in Ost-Berlin," 1318–19.

104. Leo, "Die zweispältige Ausstellung," 10.

105. Quotations in Flierl, "Das antifaschistische Traditionskabinett," 26.

106. Brinks, "Political Anti-Fascism," 208–9.
107. Quoted in Joppke, *East German Dissidents,* 195.
108. Sonnet, "Gedenkstätten für die Opfer des Nationalsozialismus in der DDR," 780–81; Young, *Texture of Memory,* 76–79.
109. For former inmates' personal memories of Speziallager 2, see Müller, ed., *Recht oder Rache?*
110. Buruma, *The Wages of Guilt,* 213–14, 216–17.
111. Hofmann, "Vorwort," 5–8.
112. Cited in Sonnet, "Gedenkstätten für die Opfer des Nationalsozialismus in der DDR," 800.
113. For the following, ibid., 775, 800.
114. See Brinks, "Political Anti-Fascism," 209.
115. Joppke, *East German Dissidents,* 148–54.
116. Nora, "From Lieux de mémoire to Realms of Memory," 1: xxiv.
117. Geyer, "Politics of Memory," 9.

CONCLUSION

1. Tournier, *The Ogre,* 3.
2. Warner, *Monuments & Maidens,* 32.
3. Smith, "The Origins of Nations," 109–17.
4. Phillips, *The Nature of Blood.*
5. See Hupchick, *Culture and History in Eastern Europe,* 121–55.
6. But see the exceptions in the introduction, n. 15.
7. Schulz, "Wie soll der deutsche Nationalstaat aussehen?"
8. Bude, *Bilanz der Nachfolge.*
9. Schildt, *Ankunft im Westen.*
10. Blank, "Wer sind die Deutschen?" 44–46.
11. Smith, "The Origins of Nations," 120–23.
12. Jackowski, "People's Monuments."
13. Hupchick, *Culture and History in Eastern Europe,* 79. I base the argument in this paragraph on the same source, 72–81.
14. Jackson, *A Sense of Place, A Sense of Time,* 153.
15. Markovits and Reich, *The German Predicament,* 16–17.
16. Huyssen, *Twilight Memories,* 252.
17. Quoted in Joppke, *East German Dissidents,* 215.
18. Tacke, *Denkmal im sozialen Raum,* 292–93.
19. Two recent collections may stimulate more research in this area among historians of late modern Europe: see de Grazia and Furlough, eds., *The Sex of Things,* and Strasser, McGovern, and Judt, eds., *Getting and Spending.*
20. Geyer, "Twentieth Century as History," 691–94.
21. LaCapra, *History and Memory after Auschwitz,* 7.
22. See Gerstenberger and Schmidt, *Normalität oder Normalisierung?*
23. Goldhagen, *Hitler's Willing Executioners.*
24. Against the backdrop of the entrance to Auschwitz, the cover read: "Ist die Schuld verjährt? Der neue Umgang mit der Nazi-Vergangenheit (Is Guilt out of date? The new relation to the Nazi past)." *Der Spiegel* 49 (30 November 1998).

25. Markovits and Reich, *The German Predicament,* 203.

26. Still one of the more useful overviews of scholarly positions on the subject: Diner, *Ist der Nationalsozialismus Geschichte?*

27. Mumford, *City in History,* 29.

28. Ibid., 36.

29. Leithäuser, "In Berlins Mitte wird mit den Mythen der Vergangenheit für die Zukunft gebaut."

30. See Häussermann, "From the Socialist to the Capitalist City," 226–28.

31. For a recent statement on Berlin's many layers of historical meaning, see Howe, "Berlin Mitte."

32. See Dittberner and von Meer, eds., *Gedenkstätten im vereinten Deutschland;* Hoffmann, ed., *Das Gedächtnis der Dinge.*

Works Cited

Abzug, Robert H. *Inside the Vicious Heart: Americans and the Liberation of Nazi Concentration Camps.* New York: Oxford University Press, 1985.

Agulhon, Maurice. *Marianne into Battle. Republican Imagery and Symbolism in France, 1789–1880.* Trans. Janet Lloyd. Cambridge, Eng.: Cambridge University Press, 1981.

Alings, Reinhard. *Monument und Nation: Das Bild vom Nationalstaat im Medium Denkmal. Zum Verhältnis von Nation und Staat im deutschen Kaiserreich, 1871–1918.* Berlin: Walter de Gruyter, 1996.

Anderson, Benedict. *Imagined Communities. Reflections on the Origins and Spread of Nationalism.* Revised edition. London: Verso, 1991.

Andreas-Friedrich, Ruth. *Battleground Berlin: Diaries, 1945–1948.* New York: Paragon House, 1990.

Applegate, Celia. *A Nation of Provincials: The German Idea of Heimat.* Berkeley and Los Angeles: University of California Press, 1990.

Arendt, Hannah. *The Origins of Totalitarianism.* New York: Harcourt Brace Jovanovich, 1973.

Assmann, Aleida. *Arbeit am nationalen Gedächtnis: Eine kurze Geschichte der deutschen Bildungsidee.* Frankfurt/Main: Campus Verlag, 1993.

———. *Errinerungsräume. Formen und Wandlungen des kulturellen Gedächtnisses.* Munich: C. H. Beck, 1999.

Assmann, Jan. "Collective Memory and Cultural Identity." *New German Critique* 65 (summer/spring 1995): 125–33.

Azaryahu, Maoz. "Renaming the Past: Changes in 'City Text' in Germany and Austria, 1945–1947." *History & Memory* 2, 2 (winter 1990): 32–53.

———. "Street Names and Political Identity: The Case of East Berlin." *Journal of Contemporary History* 21, 4 (October 1986): 581–604.

———. *Von Wilhelmplatz zu Thälmannplatz: Politische Symbole im öffentlichen Leben der DDR.* Gerlingen: Bleicher Verlag, 1991.

Baedeker, Karl. *Berlin und Umgebung: Handbuch für Reisende.* Sixth edition. Leipzig: Karl Baedeker, 1889.

———. *Berlin und Umgebung: Handbuch für Reisende.* Sixteenth edition. Leipzig: Karl Baedeker, 1910.

———. *Deutschland in einem Bande. Kurzes Reisehandbuch.* Third edition. Leipzig: Karl Baedeker, 1913.

———. *Das Elsass. Strassburg und die Vogesen. Reisehandbuch.* Leipzig: Karl Baedeker, 1942.

———. *Das Generalgouvernement: Reisehandbuch.* Leipzig: Karl Baedeker, 1943.

———. *Leipzig. Ein Neuer Führer.* Leipzig: Karl Baedeker and Bibliographisches Institut, 1948.

———. *München und Umgebung. Tegernsee. Schliersee. Oberammergau. Garmisch-Partenkirchen. Reisehandbuch.* Hamburg: Karl Baedeker/ Munich: Richard Pflaum Verlag, 1951.

———. *Die Rheinlande. Von der elsässischen bis zur holländischen Grenze. Rheinpfalz. Saargebiet. Handbuch für Reisende.* Thirty-third edition. Leipzig: Karl Baedeker, 1925.

Baird, Jay. *To Die for Germany: Heroes in the Nazi Pantheon.* Bloomington: Indiana University Press, 1990.

Baker, Frederick. "The Berlin Wall: Production, Preservation and Consumption of a 20th-Century Monument." *Antiquity* 67 (1993): 709–33.

Barnouw, Dagmar. *Germany, 1945: Views of War and Violence.* Bloomington: Indiana University Press, 1996.

Bartetzko, Dieter. *Verbaute Geschichte. Stadterneuerung vor der Katastrophe.* Frankfurt am Main: Luchterhand, 1986.

Bartov, Omer. "Defining Enemies, Making Victims: Germans, Jews, and the Holocaust." *American Historical Review* 103, 3 (June 1998): 771–816.

———. *Murder in our Midst: The Holocaust, Industrial Killing, and Representation.* New York: Oxford University Press, 1996.

Bartram, Graham, Maurice Slawinski, and David Steel, eds. *Reconstructing the Past: Representations of the Fascist Era in Post-War European Culture.* Keele: Keele University Press, 1996.

Becker, Annette. *La guerre et la foi. De la mort à la mémoire, 1914–1930.* Paris: Armand Colin, 1994.

Behrenbeck, Sabine. *Der Kult um die toten Helden: Nationalsozialistische Mythen, Riten und Symbole.* Vierow bei Greifswald: SH-Verlag, 1996.

Belgum, Kirsten. "Displaying the Nation: A View of Nineteenth-Century Monuments through a Popular Magazine." *Central European History* 26, 4 (1993): 457–74.

———. *Popularizing the Nation: Audience, Representation, and the Production of Identity in Die Gartenlaube, 1853–1900.* Lincoln: University of Nebraska Press, 1998.

Ben-Amos, Avner. "Monuments and Memory in French Nationalism." *History & Memory* 5, 2 (fall/winter 1993): 50–77.

Ben-Ghiat, Ruth. "Fascism, Writing, and Memory: The Realist Aesthetic in Italy, 1930–1950." *Journal of Modern History* 67 (September 1995): 627–65.

Benjamin, Walter. "A Berlin Chronicle." In *Reflections: Essays, Aphorisms, Autobiographical Writings,* edited by Peter Demetz, 3–60. New York: Schocken, 1986.

———. "Moscow." In *Reflections: Essays, Aphorisms, Autobiographical Writings,* edited by Peter Demetz, 97–130. New York: Schocken, 1986.

Benz, Wolfgang. "Postwar Society and National Socialism: Remembrance, Amnesia, Rejection." *Tel Aviver Jahrbuch für deutsche Geschichte* 19 (1990): 1–12.

Berger, Manfred. *Kössern. Geschichte eines Dorfes.* Gesellschaft für Heimatgeschichte. Bezirksvorstand Leipzig. Arbeitsheft Nr. 9. Leipzig: Kulturbund der DDR, 1985.

Berger, Stefan. *The Search for Normality: National Identity and Historical Consciousness in Germany Since 1800.* Providence, R.I.: Berghahn Books, 1997.

Berlin-Information (Autorenkollektiv). *Berlin. Touristentips im Taschenformat.* Berlin: Berlin-Information, 1984.

Berliner Geschichtswerkstatt, ed. *Sackgassen: Keine Wendemöglichkeit für Berliner Straßennamen.* Berlin: Nishen, 1988.

Bezirkskommission zur Erforschung der Geschichte der örtlichen Arbeiterbewegung, Bezirksleitung Halle der SED, ed. *Gedenk- und Erinnerungsstätten der Arbeiterbewegung im Bezirk Halle.* Halle: Bezirkskommission zur Erforschung der Geschichte der örtlichen Arbeiterbewegung, 1971.

Blackbourn, David. *The Long Nineteenth Century. A History of Germany, 1780–1918.* New York: Oxford University Press, 1998.

Blank, Thomas. "Wer sind die Deutschen? Nationalismus, Patriotismus, Identität—Ergebnisse einer empirischen Längsschnittstudie." *Aus Politik und Zeitgeschichte* 47, B13/97 (21 March 1997): 38–46.

Boban, Ljubo. "Jasenovac and the Manipulation of History." *East European Politics and Societies* 4, 3 (fall 1990): 580–92.

Bodemann, Y. Michal, ed. *Jews, Germans, Memory: Reconstructions of Jewish Life in Germany.* Ann Arbor: University of Michigan Press, 1996.

Boer, Pim den, and Willem Frijhoff, eds. *Lieux de mémoire et identités nationales.* Amsterdam: Amsterdam University Press, 1993.

Boockmann, Hartmut. "Das ehemalige Deutschordens-Schloß Marienburg, 1772–1945. Die Geschichte eines politischen Denkmals." In *Geschichtswissenschaft und Vereinswesen im 19. Jahrhundert,* edited by Hartmut Boockmann, et al., 99–161. Göttingen: Vandenhoeck & Ruprecht, 1972.

Brandt, Susanne. "The Memory Makers: Museums and Exhibitions of the First World War." *History & Memory* 6, 1 (spring/summer 1994): 95–122.

Brenner, Michael. *The Renaissance of Jewish Culture in Weimar Germany.* New Haven: Yale University Press, 1996.

Brinks, J. H. "Political Anti-Fascism in the German Democratic Republic." *Journal of Contemporary History* 32, 2 (1997): 207–17.

Brix, Michael. "Monumente der NS- und Trümmer-Zeit. Bewertungsprobleme der Denkmalpflege—Beispiel München." *Kunstchronik* 36, 4 (April 1983): 178–84.

Broszat, Martin, Elke Fröhlich, and Falk Wiesemann, eds. *Bayern in der NS-Zeit.* Vol. 1. Munich: Oldenbourg, 1977.

Brown, G. Baldwin. *The Care of Ancient Monuments.* Cambridge, Eng.: Cambridge University Press, 1905.

Brush, Kathryn. "The Cultural Historian Karl Lamprecht: Practitioner and Progenitor of Art History." *Central European History* 26, 2 (1993): 139–64.

Bude, Heinz. *Bilanz der Nachfolge: Die Bundesrepublik und der Nationalsozialismus.* Frankfurt am Main: Suhrkamp Verlag, 1992.

Bültemann, Manfred. *Architektur für das Dritte Reich. Die Akademie für Deutsche Jugendführung in Braunschweig.* Berlin: Wilhelm Ernst, 1986.

Bunzl, Matti. "On the Politics and Semantics of Austrian Memory: Vienna's Monument against War and Fascism." *History & Memory* 7, 2 (fall/winter 1996): 7–40.

Burrin, Phillipe. "Vichy." In *Realms of Memory: Rethinking the French Past,* edited by Pierre Nora, 1:181–202. New York: Columbia University Press, 1996.

Buruma, Ian. *The Wages of Guilt: Memories of War in Germany and Japan.* New York: Farrar, Strauss, and Giroux, 1994.

Carr, David. *Time, Narrative, and History.* Bloomington: Indiana University Press, 1986.

Case, J. David. "The Politics of Memorial Representation: The Controversy over the German Resistance Museum in 1994." *German Politics and Society* 16, 1 (spring 1998): 58–81.

Chickering, Roger. *We Men Who Feel Most German: A Cultural Study of the Pan-German League, 1886–1914.* Boston: George Allen & Unwin, 1984.

Christo and Jeanne-Claude. *Verhüllter/Wrapped Reichstag, Berlin, 1971–1995.* Cologne: Benedikt Taschen Verlag, 1995.

Clemen, Paul. *Die Deutsche Kunst und die Denkmalpflege: Ein Bekenntnis.* Berlin: Deutscher Kunstverlag, 1933.

Cohen, William. "Symbols of Power: Statues in Nineteenth-Century Provincial France." *Comparative Studies in Society and History* 31, 3 (July 1989): 491–513.

Confino, Alon. "Collective Memory and Cultural History: Problems of Method." *American Historical Review* 102, 5 (December 1997): 1386–1403.

———. *The Nation as a Local Metaphor: Württemberg, Imperial Germany, and National Memory, 1871–1918.* Chapel Hill: University of North Carolina Press, 1997.

Connerton, Paul. *How Societies Remember.* Cambridge, Eng.: Cambridge University Press, 1989.

Craig, Gordon. *The Germans.* New York: G. P. Putnam's Sons, 1982.

Crane, Susan A. "Writing the Individual Back into Collective Memory." *American Historical Review* 102, 5 (December 1997): 1372–85.

Cremer, Wolfgang. "Der Kölner Dombaufest vom 15. und 16. Oktober 1880." *Rheinische Heimatpflege* 17 (1980): 1–11.

Czaplicka, John. "*Amerikabilder* and the German Discourse on Modern Civilization, 1890–1925." In *Envisioning America. Prints, Drawings, and Photographs by George Grosz and His Contemporaries, 1915–1933,* edited by Beeke Sell Tower. Cambridge, Mass.: Busch-Reisinger Museum, Harvard University, 1990.

———. "History, Aesthetics, and Contemporary Commemorative Practice in Berlin." *New German Critique* 65 (spring/summer, 1995): 155–87.

Dähn, Horst, and Joachim Heise. *Luther und die DDR: Der Reformator und das DDR-Fernsehen.* Berlin: Edition Ost, 1996.

Dahn, Daniela. *Westwärts und nicht vergessen. Vom Unbehagen in der Einheit.* Reinbek bei Hamburg: Rowohlt, 1997.

De Certeau, Michel. *The Practice of Everyday Life.* Berkeley and Los Angeles: University of California Press, 1984.

De Grazia, Victoria (with Ellen Furlough), ed. *The Sex of Things: Gender and Consumption in Historical Perspective.* Berkeley and Los Angeles: University of California Press, 1996.

De Grazia, Victoria, and Leonardo Paggi. "Story of an Ordinary Massacre: Civitella della Chiana, 29 June 1944." *Cardozo Studies in Law and Literature* 3, 2 (fall, 1991): 153–69.

Dedijer, Vladimir, ed. *The Yugoslav Auschwitz and the Vatican.* Buffalo and New York: Prometheus Books, 1992.

Demps, Laurenz. "Die Geschichte der Straßennamen in Berlin. Anmerkungen zu einem brisanten Thema." In *Berliner Straßennamen: Ein Nachschlagewerk für die östlichen Bezirke,* edited by Karl-Heinz Gärtner, et al. Berlin: Links Verlag, 1995.

Diederich, Georg. "Die Sprengung der Rostocker Christuskirche vor 25 Jahren: Fakten und Hintergründe." *Deutschland-Archiv* 29, 4 (July/August, 1996): 560–68.

Diefendorf, Jeffry M. *In the Wake of War: The Reconstruction of German Cities after World War II.* New York and Oxford: Oxford University Press, 1993.

Dietzfelbinger, Eckart. "Reichsparteitagsgelände Nürnberg. Restaurieren, Nutzen, Vermitteln." In *Architektur und Städtebau der 30er/40er Jahre,* edited by Werner Durth and Winfried Nerdinger, 64–73. Schriftenreihe des Deutschen Nationalkomitees für Denkmalschutz, vol. 48. Bonn: Deutsches Nationalkomitee für Denkmalschutz, 1994.

Diner, Dan, ed. *Ist der Nationalsozialismus Geschichte? Zu Historisierung und Historikerstreit.* Frankfurt am Main: Fischer Taschenbuch Verlag, 1987.

———."On the Ideology of Antifascism." *New German Critique* 67 (winter 1996): 123–32.

Dittberner, Jürgen, and Antje von Meer, eds. *Gedenkstätten im vereinten Deutschland: 50 Jahre nach der Befreiung der Konzentrationslager.* Oranienburg: Stiftung Brandenburgische Gedenkstätten und Edition Hentrich, 1994.

Domansky, Elisabeth. "A Lost War: World War II in Postwar German Memory." In *Thinking about the Holocaust after Half a Century,* edited by Alvin H. Rosenfeld, 233–72. Bloomington: Indiana University Press, 1997.

———. "Der 'Zukunftsstaat am Besenbinderhof.'" In *Arbeiter in Hamburg: Unterschichten, Arbeiter und Arbeiterbewegung seit dem ausgehenden 18. Jahrhundert,* edited by Arno Herzig, Dieter Langewiesche, and Arnold Sywottek. Hamburg: Verlag Erziehung und Wissenschaft, 1983.

Dumont, Louis. *German Ideology: From France to Germany and Back.* Chicago: University of Chicago Press, 1994.

Dwork, Debórah, and Robert Jan van Pelt. *Auschwitz, 1270 to the Present.* New York: W. W. Norton, 1996.

Ehman, Annegrit. "Gedenkstättenpolitik." Unpublished paper, Berlin, n.d.

Eichmann, Bernd. *Versteinert—Verharmlost—Vergessen: KZ-Gedenkstätten in der Bundesrepublik Deutschland.* Frankfurt am Main: Fischer Taschenbuch, 1985.

Ekmečić, Milorad. "The Emergence of St. Vitus Day as the Principal National Holiday of the Serbs." In *Kosovo: Legacy of a Medieval Battle,* edited by Wayne S. Vucinich and Thomas A. Emmert, 331–42. Minneapolis: Modern Greek Studies, University of Minnesota, 1991.

Eksteins, Modris. *Rites of Spring: The Great War and the Birth of the Modern Age.* New York: Doubleday, 1989.

Eley, Geoff. "Nazism, Politics and the Image of the Past: Thoughts on the West German *Historikerstreit,* 1986–1987." *Past & Present* 121 (November 1988): 171–208.

Emmerich, Wolfgang. "The Mythos of Germanic Continuity." In *The Nazification of an Academic Discipline: Folklore in the Third Reich,* edited by James R. Dow and Hannjost Lixfeld, 34–54. Bloomington: Indiana University Press, 1994.

Engelbrechten, Julius Karl, and Hans Volz, eds. *Wir wandern durch das nationalsozialistische Berlin: Ein Führer durch die Gedenkstätten des Kampfes um die Reichshauptstadt.* Munich: Zentralverlag der NSDAP, Franz Eher Nachf., 1937.

Éri, Gyöngi, and Zsuzsa Jobbágyi. "The Millennial Celebrations of 1896." In *A Golden Age: Art and Society in Hungary, 1896–1914,* edited by Gyöngi Éri and Zsuzsa Jobbágyi, 47–59. London: Corvina/ Barbicon Art Gallery; Miami: Center for the Fine Arts, 1989.

Esbenshade, Richard S. "Remembering to Forget: Memory, History, National Identity in Postwar East-Central Europe." *Representations* 49 (winter 1995): 72–96.

Etlin, Richard. *Modernism in Italian Architecture, 1890–1940.* Cambridge, Mass.: MIT Press, 1991.

Evans, Martin, and Ken Lunn, eds. *War and Memory in the Twentieth Century.* Oxford: Berg Publishers, 1997.

Evans, Richard J. *In Hitler's Shadow: West German Historians and the Attempt to Escape from the Past.* London: I. B. Taurus, 1989.

Farmer, Sarah Bennett. *Martyred Village. Commemorating the 1944 Massacre at Oradour-sur-Glane.* Berkeley and Los Angeles: University of California Press, 1999.

———. "Oradour-sur-Glane: Memory in a Preserved Landscape." *French Historical Studies* 19, 1 (spring 1995): 27–47.

———. "Symbols That Face Two Ways: Commemorating the Victims of Nazism and Stalinism at Buchenwald and Sachsenhausen." *Representations* 49 (winter 1995): 97–119.

Filip, Ota. "Geblieben sind nur die Grabsteine aus Sandstein." *Frankfurter Allgemeine Zeitung* (16 May 1994).

Fitch, James Marston. *Historic Preservation: Curatorial Management of the Built World.* Charlottesville: University Press of Virginia, 1990.

Fliedl, Gottfried, Florian Freund, Eduard Fuchs, and Bertrand Perz. "'Den Toten zur Ehr—den Lebenden zur Lehr'?" *Österreichische Zeitschrift für Geschichtswissenschaft* 2, 4 (1991): 107–10.

Flierl, Thomas. "Das antifaschistische Tradionskabinett als ideologischer Staatsapparat." In *Mythos Antifaschismus. Ein Traditionskabinett wird kommentiert,* edited by Kulturamt Prenzlauer Berg and Aktives Museum Faschismus und Widerstand Berlin, 12–36. Berlin: Ch. Links, 1992.

Fodor, Eugene, ed. *Germany 1953.* Fodor's Modern Guides. New York: David McKay, 1953.

Ford, Caroline. *Creating the Nation in Provincial France: Religion and Political Identity in Brittany.* Princeton, N.J.: Princeton University Press, 1993.

François, Etienne. "Von der wiedererlangten Nation zur 'Nation wider Willen': Kann man eine Geschichte der deutschen 'Erinnerungsorte' schreiben?" In *Nation und Emotion: Deutschland und Frankreich im Vergleich 19. und 20. Jahrhundert,* edited by Etienne François, Hannes Siegrist, and Jakob Vogel, 93–107. Göttingen: Vandenhoeck & Ruprecht, 1995.

———, ed., *Lieux de Mémoire, Erinnerungsorte: d'un modèle français à un project allemand.* Berlin: Centre Marc Bloch, 1996.

———, Hannes Siegrist, and Jakob Vogel, eds. *Nation und Emotion: Deutschland und Frankreich im Vergleich 19. und 20. Jahrhundert.* Göttingen: Vandenhoeck & Ruprecht, 1995.

Frei, Alfred Georg. "Geschichte aus den 'Graswurzeln'?" *Aus Politik und Zeitgeschichte* B2/88 (8 January 1988): 35–46.

Frei, Norbert. *Vergangenheitspolitik. Die Anfänge der Bundesrepublik und die NS-Vergangenheit.* Munich: Beck, 1996.

Friedländer, Saul. *Nazi Germany and the Jews.* Vol. 1, *The Years of Persecution, 1933–1939.* New York: HarperCollins, 1997.

———. *Reflections on Nazism: An Essay on Kitsch and Death.* New York: Harper & Row, 1984.

———, and Adam B. Seligman. "The Israeli Memory of the Shoah: On Symbols, Rituals, and Ideological Polarizations." In *NowHere: Space, Time and Modernity,* edited by Roger Friedland and Deirdre Boden, 356–71. Berkeley and Los Angeles: University of California Press, 1994.

Fritzsche, Peter. *Germans into Nazis.* Cambridge, Mass.: Harvard University Press, 1998.

———. *Reading Berlin, 1900.* Cambridge, Mass.: Harvard University Press, 1996.

Frykman, Jonas, and Orvor Löfgren. *Culture Builders: A Historical Anthropology of Middle-Class Life.* New Brunswick, N.J.: Rutgers University Press, 1987.

Fülöp-Miller, René. *Geist und Gesicht des Bolschewismus: Darstellung und Kritik des Kulturellen Lebens in Sowjet-Russland.* Second edition. Zürich: Amalthea-Verlag, 1926.

Galinski, Deiter, and Wolf Schmidt, eds. *Die Kriegsjahre in Deutschland, 1939–1945: Ergebnisse und Anregungen aus dem Schülerwettbewerb Deutsche Geschichte um den Preis der Bundespräsidenten, 1982/83*. Hamburg: Verlag Erziehung und Wissenschaft, 1985.

Gall, Lother. *Germania. Eine deutsche Marianne? Une Marianne allemande?* Bonn: Bouvier Verlag, 1993.

Garbe, Detlef. *Zwischen Widerstand und Martyrium. Die Zeugen Jehovas im "Dritten Reich."* Munich: Oldenbourg, 1993.

Gedi, Noa, and Yigal Elam, "Collective Memory—What Is It?" *History & Memory* 8 (spring/summer 1996): 30–50.

Geertz, Clifford. "Centers, Kings, and Charisma: Reflections on the Symbolics of Power." In *Rites of Power: Symbolism, Ritual, and Politics Since the Middle Ages,* edited by Sean Willentz, 13–38. Philadelphia: University of Pennsylvania Press, 1985.

Gélieu, Claudia von. *Geschichte der Frauenbewegung Erfahren. Stadtrundfahrt in Berlin (West)*. Berlin: DVK-Verlag, 1988.

Gentile, Emilio. *Il Culto del Littorio. La Sacralizzazione della Politica nell'Italia Fascista*. Rome-Bari: Laterza & Figli, 1993.

Gerő, András. *Heroes' Square, Budapest. Hungary's History in Stone and Bronze*. Budapest: Corvina, 1990.

Gerstenberger, Heide, and Dorothea Schmidt, eds. *Normalität oder Normalisierung? Geschichtswerkstätten und Faschismusanalyse*. Münster: Westfälisches Dampfboot, 1987.

GEW Berlin, ed. *Wider das Vergessen: Antifaschistische Erziehung in der Schule. Erfahrungen, Projekte, Anregungen*. Frankfurt am Main: Fischer Taschenbuch Verlag, 1981.

Geyer, Michael. "Germany, or, The Twentieth Century as History." *The South Atlantic Quarterly*, Special Issue: "German Dis/Continuities," 96, 4 (fall 1997): 663–702.

———. "The Politics of Memory in Contemporary Germany." In *Radical Evil,* edited by Joan Copjec, 169–200. London and New York: Verso, 1996.

———, and Miriam Hansen. "German-Jewish Memory and National Consciousness." In *Holocaust Remembrance: The Shapes of Memory,* edited by Geoffrey H. Hartman, 175–90. Oxford: Blackwell, 1994.

Ghirardo, Diane Yvonne. "Italian Architects and Fascist Politics: An Evaluation of the Rationalist's Role in Regime Building." *Journal of the Society of Architectural Historians* 39, 2 (May 1980): 109–27.

Gladsky, Thomas. "Polish Post-War Historical Monuments: Heroic Art and Cultural Preservation." *The Polish Review* 31, 2–3 (1986): 149–58.

Goldhagen, Daniel Jonah. *Hitler's Willing Executioners: Ordinary Germans and the Holocaust*. New York: Vintage, 1996.

Gollwitzer, Heinz. "Zum Fragenkreis Architekturhistorismus und politische Ideologie." *Zeitschrift für Kunstgeschichte* 42 (1979): 1–14.

Greenfield, Liah. *Nationalism: Five Roads to Modernity*. Cambridge, Mass.: Harvard University Press, 1992.

Grenville, Anthony. "The Earliest Reception of the Holocaust: Ernst Sommer's *Revolte der Heiligen*." *German Life and Letters* 51, 2 (April 1998): 250–65.

Grieben-Verlag. *Berlin und Umgebung. Kleine Ausgabe mit Angaben für Automobilisten.* Grieben Reiseführer, vol. 25. Berlin: Grieben-Verlag, 1936.

Günther-Kaminski, Michael, and Michael Weiß. *"Als wäre es nie gewesen." Juden am Ku'damm.* Berlin: Berliner Geschichtswerkstatt, 1989.

Häussermann, Hartmut. "From the Socialist to the Capitalist City: Experiences from Germany." In *Cities after Socialism: Urban and Regional Change and Conflict in Post-Socialist Societies,* edited by Gregory Andrusz, Michael Harloe, and Ivan Szelenyi, 214–31. Oxford: Blackwell, 1996.

Hagelüken, Alexander. "Auf den Barrikaden der Geschichte." *Spuren Suchen* 7 (1993): 40–43.

Harbison, Robert. *The Built, the Unbuilt and the Unbuildable: The Pursuit of Architectural Meaning.* Cambridge, Mass.: MIT Press, 1991.

Hardtwig, Wolfgang. *Geschichtskultur und Wissenschaft.* Munich: Deutscher Taschenbuch Verlag, 1990.

———. *Nationalismus und Bürgerkultur in Deutschland, 1500–1914: Ausgewählte Aufsätze.* Göttingen: Vandenhoeck & Ruprecht, 1994.

Hartman, Geoffrey, ed. *Bitburg in Moral and Political Perspective.* Bloomington: Indiana University Press, 1986.

Harvey, David. "Monument and Myth: The Building of the Basilica of the Sacred Heart." In *Consciousness and the Urban Experience. Studies in the History and Theory of Capitalist Urbanization,* by David Harvey, 221–49. Baltimore: The Johns Hopkins University Press, 1985.

Haskell, Francis. *History and Its Images: Art and the Interpretation of the Past.* New Haven: Yale University Press, 1993.

Haupt, Heinz-Gerhard, and Jürgen Kocka, eds. *Geschichte und Vergleich: Ansätze und Ergebnisse international vergleichender Geschichtsschreibung.* Frankfurt am Main: Campus Verlag, 1996.

Heckart, Beverly. "The Cities of Avignon and Worms as Expressions of the European Community." *Comparative Studies in Society and History* 31, 3 (July 1989): 462–90.

Heimatgeschichtlicher Wegweiser zu Stätten des Widerstandes und der Verfolgung, 1933–1945. Vol. 1, *Hessen.* Cologne: Paul-Rugenstein, 1984.

Heineman, Elizabeth. "The Hour of the Woman: Memories of Germany's 'Crisis Years' and West German National Identity." *American Historical Review* 101, 2 (April 1996): 354–95.

Helwig, Gisela. "'Der Anspruch auf alles Gute, Wahre und Schöne': Zur Denkmalpflege in der DDR." *Deutschland-Archiv* 14,7 (July 1981): 693–97.

Herbert, Ulrich. "Der Holocaust in der Geschichtsschreibung der Bundesrepublik Deutschland." In *Erinnerung: Zur Gegenwart der Holocaust in Deutschland-West und Deutschland-Ost,* edited by Bernhard Moltmann, et al., 31–45. Frankfurt am Main: Haag + Herchen Verlag, 1993.

Herf, Jeffrey. *Divided Memory: The Nazi Past in the Two Germanys.* Cambridge, Mass.: Harvard University Press, 1997.

Hermand, Jost. *Kultur im Wiederaufbau: Die Bundesrepublik Deutschland, 1945–1965.* Munich: Nymphenburger, 1986.

———. *Old Dreams of a New Reich: Volkish Utopias and National Socialism.* Bloomington: Indiana University Press, 1992.

Herrenknecht, Albert. "Geschichte er-fahren. Mit dem Fahrrad auf den Spuren des Bauernkrieges durch Franken." In *Die andere Geschichte: Geschichte von Unten. Spurensicherung. Ökologische Geschichte. Geschichtswerkstätten,* edited by Gerhard Paul and Bernhard Schoßig, 33–47. Cologne: Bund-Verlag, 1986.

Hewison, Robert. *The Heritage Industry: Britain in a Climate of Decline.* London: Methuen, 1987.

Hillgruber, Andreas. *Zweierlei Untergang: Die Zerschlagung des Deutschen Reiches und das Ende des europäischen Judentums.* Berlin: Siedler, 1986.

Hinz, Berthold. *Art in the Third Reich.* New York: Pantheon, 1979.

Hitler, Adolf. *Mein Kampf.* Boston: Houghton Mifflin, 1943.

Hobsbawm, Eric. *The Age of Extremes. A History of the World, 1914–1991.* New York: Pantheon, 1994.

———. "Mass Producing Traditions: Europe, 1870–1914." In *The Invention of Tradition,* edited by Eric Hobsbawm and Terence Ranger, 263–307. Cambridge, Eng.: Cambridge University Press, 1983.

———, and Terence Ranger, eds. *The Invention of Tradition.* Cambridge, Eng.: Cambridge University Press, 1983.

Hoffmann, Detlef, ed. *Das Gedächtnis der Dinge, KZ-Relikte und KZ-Denkmäler, 1945–1995.* Frankfurt am Main: Campus Verlag, 1998.

Hoffmann, Stefan-Ludwig. "Sakraler Monumentalismus um 1900: Das Leipziger Völkerschlachtdenkmal." In *Der politische Totenkult: Kriegerdenkmäler in der Moderne,* edited by Reinhart Koselleck and Michael Jeismann, 249–80. Munich: Fink Verlag, 1994.

Hoffmann-Curtius, Kathrin. "Das Kreuz als Nationaldenkmal. Deutschland 1814 und 1931." *Zeitschrift für Kunstgeschichte* 48, 1 (1985): 77–100.

Hofmann, Thomas. "Vorwort." *Jahresinformation der Gedenkstätte Buchenwald* (1991): 5–8.

Horwitz, Gordon J. *In the Shadow of Death: Living Outside the Gates of Mauthausen.* New York: The Free Press, 1990.

Hoscislawski, Thomas. "Die Bauhausrezeption in der DDR." *Deutschland-Archiv* 22, 9 (September1990): 1582–94.

Hosmer, Charles B. "The Broadening View of the Historical Preservation Movement." In *Material Culture and the Study of American Life,* edited by Ian M. G. Quimby, 121–39. New York: Norton, 1978.

Howe, Nicholas. "Berlin Mitte." *Dissent* (winter 1998): 71–81.

Hüser, Karl. *Wewelsburg, 1933–1945. Kult- und Terrorstätte der SS. Eine Dokumentation.* Paderborn: Verlag Bonifatius-Druckerei, 1982.

Hupchick, Dennis P. *Culture and History in Eastern Europe.* New York: St. Martin's, 1994.

Hutter, Peter. *"Die feinste Barbarei": Das Völkerschlachtdenkmal bei Leipzig.* Mainz: Philipp von Zabern, 1990.

Huyssen, Andreas. *Twilight Memories: Marking Time in a Culture of Amnesia.* New York: Routledge, 1995.

Irwin-Zarecka, Iwona. *Frames of Remembrance: The Dynamics of Collective Memory.* New Brunswick, N.J.: Transaction Publishers, 1994.

———. *Neutralizing Memory: The Jew in Contemporary Poland.* New Brunswick, N.J.: Transaction Publishers, 1989.

Isnenghi, Mario, ed. *I luoghi della memoria.* 3 vols. Vol. 1, *Simboli e miti dell'Italia unita;* Vol. 2, *Strutture ed eventi dell'Italia unita;* Vol. 3, *Personaggi e date dell'Italia unita.* Rome: Laterza, 1997.

Jackowski, Aleksander. "People's Monuments, 1945–1981." *Polish Art Studies* 8 (1987): 221–42.

Jackson, John Brinckerhoff. *A Sense of Place, A Sense of Time.* New Haven: Yale University Press, 1994.

James, Harold. *A German Identity: 1770–1990.* New York: Routledge, 1989.

Jankowski, Stanislaw. "Warsaw: Destruction, Secret Town Planning, 1939–44, and Postwar Reconstruction." In *Rebuilding Europe's Bombed Cities,* edited by Jeffry M. Diefendorf, 77–93. Hampshire: Macmillan, 1990.

Jeffries, Matthew. *Politics and Culture in Wilhelmine Germany: The Case of Industrial Architecture.* Oxford: Berg Publishers, 1995.

Jeismann, Michael. *Das Vaterland der Feinde. Studien zum nationalen Feindbegriff und Selbstverständnis in Deutschland und Frankreich, 1792–1918.* Stuttgart: Klett-Cotta, 1992.

Joppke, Christian. *East German Dissidents and the Revolution of 1989: Social Movement in a Leninist Regime.* New York: New York University Press, 1995.

Judah, Tim. *The Serbs: History, Myth & the Destruction of Yugoslavia.* New Haven and London: Yale University Press, 1997.

Judt, Tony. *A Grand Illusion? An Essay on Europe.* New York: Hill and Wang, 1996.

———. "A la Recherche du Temps Perdu." *New York Review of Books* 45, 19 (3 December 1998): 51–58.

———. *Past Imperfect: French Intellectuals, 1944–1956.* Berkeley and Los Angeles: University of California Press, 1992.

Kaes, Anton. *From Hitler to Heimat: The Return of History as Film.* Cambridge, Mass.: Harvard University Press, 1989.

———, Martin Jay, and Edward Dimendberg, eds. *The Weimar Republic Sourcebook.* Berkeley and Los Angeles: University of California Press, 1994.

Kammen, Michael. *Mystic Chords of Memory: The Transformation of Tradition in American Culture.* New York: Vintage, 1991.

Keizer, Madelon de. "The Skeleton in the Closet: The Memory of Putten, 1–2 October 1944." *History & Memory* 7, 2 (fall/winter 1996): 70–99.

Kern, Stephen. *The Culture of Time and Space, 1880–1918.* Cambridge, Mass.: Harvard University Press, 1983.

King, Alex. *Memorials of the Great War in Britain: The Symbolism and Politics of Remembrance.* Oxford: Berg, 1998.

Kirschweng, Johannes. "Deutsches Land und Volk links der Saar." In *Kampf um die Saar,* edited by Josef Bürckel. Stuttgart: Verlag Friedrich Bohnenberger, 1934.

Kirshenblatt-Gimblett, Barbara. *Destination Culture: Tourism, Museums, and Heritage.* Berkeley and Los Angeles: University of California Press, 1998.

Kittel, Manfred. *Die Legende von der "Zweiten Schuld": Vergangenheitsbewältigung in der Ära Adenauer.* Frankfurt/Main: Ullstein, 1993.

Knigge, Volkhard. "Die Gedenkstätte Buchenwald: Vom provisorischen Grabdenkmal zum Nationaldenkmal." In *Die Nacht hat zwölf Stunden, dann kommt schon der Tag. Antifaschismus: Geschichte und Neubewertung,* edited by Claudia Keller and literaturWERKstatt Berlin, 309–31. Berlin: Aufbau Taschenbuch Verlag, 1996.

———. "Vom Reden und Schweigen der Steine: Zu Denkmalen auf dem Gelände ehemaliger nationalsozialistischer Konzentrations- und Vernichtungslager." In *Fünfzig Jahre danach: Zur Nachgeschichte des Nationalsozialismus,* edited by Sigrid Weigel and Birgit Erdle, 193–234. Zürich: vdf Hochschulverlag AG an der ETH Zürich, 1996.

———, Jürgen Maria Pietsch, and Thomas A. Seidel. *Versteinertes Gedenken: Das Buchenwalder Mahnmal von 1958.* 2 vols. Spröda: Edition Schwarz Weiss, 1997.

Körner, Hans-Michael. *Staat und Geschichte im Königreich Bayern, 1806–1918.* Munich: C. H. Beck'sche Verlagsbuchhandlung, 1992.

Kolb, Eberhard. *Bergen-Belsen: Vom "Aufenthaltslager" zum Konzentrationslager, 1943–1945.* Fifth edition. Göttingen: Vandenhoeck & Ruprecht, 1996.

Koonz, Claudia. "Between Memory and Oblivion: Concentration Camps in German Memory." In *Commemorations: The Politics of National Identity,* edited by John Gillis, 258–80. Princeton, NJ: Princeton University Press, 1994.

Korn, Karl. "Denkmalschutz als Volksbewegung." *Frankfurter Allgemeine Zeitung* (21 January 1975).

Koselleck, Reinhart. "Einleitung." In *Der politische Totenkult: Kriegerdenkmäler in der Moderne,* edited by Reinhart Koselleck and Michael Jeismann, 9–20. Munich: Wilhelm Fink Verlag, 1994.

———. "Kriegerdenkmale als Identitätsstiftungen des überlebenden." In *Identität,* edited by Odo Marquard and Karlheinz Stierle, 255–76. Munich: Fink Verlag, 1979.

Koshar, Rudy. *Germany's Transient Pasts: Preservation and National Memory in the Twentieth Century.* Chapel Hill: University of North Carolina Press, 1998.

———. "Memoria ingovernabile? Il culto del passato nella Germania degli anni Settanta." In *La Memoria del Nazismo nell'Europa di Oggi,* edited by Leonardo Paggi, 305–28. Florence: La Nuova Italia Editrice Scandicci, 1997.

———. " 'What Ought to Be Seen': Tourists' Guidebooks and National Identities in Modern Germany and Europe." *Journal of Contemporary History* 33, 3 (July 1998): 323–40.

Kramer, Jane. *The Politics of Memory: Looking for Germany in the New Germany.* New York: Random House, 1996.

Kuehn, Karl Gernot. *Caught: The Art of Photography in the German Democratic Republic.* Berkeley and Los Angeles: University of California Press, 1997.

Kugelmass, Jack. "Bloody Memories: Encountering the Past in Contemporary Poland." *Cultural Anthropology* 10, 3 (1995): 279–301.

"Eine Kulisse stürzt ein." *Heute* (1 February 1947).

Kunz-Ott, Hannelore, and Andrea Kluge, eds. *150 Jahre Feldherrnhalle: Lebensraum einer Großstadt. Materialien zu einem Baudenkmal.* Munich: Buchendorfer Verlag, 1994.

Kushner, Tony. *The Holocaust and the Liberal Imagination: A Social and Cultural History.* Oxford: Blackwell, 1994.

———. " 'I Want to Go on Living after My Death': The Memory of Anne Frank." In *War and Memory in the Twentieth Century,* edited by Martin Evans and Ken Lunn, 3–25. Oxford: Berg Publishers, 1997.

———. "The Memory of Belsen." *New Formations* 30 (winter 1996): 18–32.

LaCapra, Dominick. *History and Memory after Auschwitz.* Ithaca: Cornell University Press, 1998.

Ladd, Brian. *The Ghosts of Berlin.* Chicago: University of Chicago Press, 1997.

———. *Urban Planning and Civic Order in Germany, 1860–1914.* Cambridge, Mass., and London: Harvard University Press, 1990.

Lagrou, Pieter. "Victims of Genocide and National Memory: Belgium, France, and the Netherlands, 1945–1965." *Past & Present* 154 (February 1997): 181–222.

Lamprecht, Kurt. *Regiment Reichstag: The Fight for Berlin, January 1919.* London: Constable, 1932.

Landesjugendring Hamburg, ed. *Nazi-Terror und Widerstand in Hamburg: Alternative Stadtrundfahrt.* Fifth edition. Hamburg: Landesjugendring Hamburg, e.V., 1989.

Lane, Barbara Miller. *Architecture and Politics in Germany, 1918–1945.* Cambridge, Mass.: Harvard University Press, 1985.

Lang, Berel. *Act and Idea in the Nazi Genocide.* Chicago and London: University of Chicago Press, 1990.

Langer, Lawrence L. *Holocaust Testimonies: The Ruins of Memory.* New Haven and London: Yale University Press, 1991.

Le Chene, Evelyn. *Mauthausen: The History of a Death Camp.* London: Methuen, 1971.

Lebovics, Hermann. "Creating the Authentic France: Struggles over French Identity in the First Half of the Twentieth Century." In *Commemorations: The Politics of National Identity,* edited by John R. Gillis, 239–57. Princeton, N.J.: Princeton University Press, 1994.

Leithäuser, Johannes. "In Berlins Mitte wird mit den Mythen der Vergangenheit für die Zukunft gebaut." *Frankfurter Allgemeine Zeitung* (7 September 1995).

Leo, Annette. "Die zwiespältige Ausstellung." In *Mythos Antifaschismus. Ein Traditionskabinett wird kommentiert,* edited by Kulturamt Prenzlauer Berg and Aktives Museum Faschismus und Widerstand Berlin, 7–11. Berlin: Ch. Links, 1992.

Lerner, Adam J. "The Nineteenth-Century Monument and the Embodiment of National Time." In *Reimagining the Nation,* edited by Marjorie Ringrose and Adam J. Lerner, 176–96. Buckingham: Open University Press, 1994.

Lewis, Michael J. *The Politics of the German Gothic Revival: August Reichensperger (1808–1895).* New York: The Architectural History Foundation, 1993.

Lidtke, Vernon. *The Alternative Culture: Socialist Labor in Imperial Germany.* New York: Oxford University Press, 1985.

Liman, Paul, ed. *Bismarck-Denkwürdigkeiten aus seinen Briefen, Reden und letzten Kundgebungen sowie nach persönlicher Erinnerungen.* Vol. 2. Berlin: Verlag von A. de Grousilliers, 1899.

Lindenberger, Thomas, and Michael Wildt. "Radical Plurality: History Workshops as a Practical Critique of Knowledge." *History Workshop Journal* 33 (spring 1992): 73–99.

Linse, Ulrich. *Barfüßige Propheten: Erlöser der zwanziger Jahren.* Berlin: Siedler Verlag, 1983.

———. "Die Entdeckung der technischen Denkmäler: Über die Anfänge der 'Industriearchäologie' in Deutschland." *Technikgeschichte* 53, 3 (1986): 201–22.

Lipp, Wilfried. *Natur, Geschichte, Denkmal: Zur Entstehung des Denkmalbewußtseins der bürgerlichen Gesellschaft.* Frankfurt: Campus Verlag, 1987.

Lippmann, Heinz. *Honecker and the New Politics of Europe.* New York: The Macmillan Company, 1972.

Lloyd, David W. *Battlefield Tourism: Pilgrimage and the Commemoration of the Great War in Britain, Australia and Canada, 1919–1939.* Oxford: Berg, 1998.

Loest, Erich. *Nikolaikirche.* Leipzig: Linden-Verlag, 1995.

Lowenthal, David. *The Past Is a Foreign Country.* Cambridge, Eng.: Cambridge University Press, 1985.

———. *Possessed by the Past: The Heritage Crusade and the Spoils of History.* New York: Free Press, 1996.

Lüdtke, Alf. "'Coming to Terms with the Past': Illusions of Remembering, Ways of Forgetting Nazism in West Germany." *Journal of Modern History* 65 (September 1993): 542–72.

———. "Einleitung: Was ist and wer treibt Alltagsgeschichte?" In *Alltagsgeschichte: Zur Rekonstruktion historischer Erfahrungen und Lebensweisen,* edited by Alf Lüdtke, 9–47. Frankfurt am Main: Campus Verlag, 1989.

———. "Histories of Mourning: Flowers and Stones for the War Dead, Confusion for the Living—Vignettes from East and West Germany." In *Between History and Histories: The Making of Silences and Commemorations,* edited by Gerald Sider and Gavin Smith, 149–79. Toronto: University of Toronto Press, 1997.

Lurz, Meinhold. *Kriegerdenkmäler in Deutschland.* 6 vols. Heidelberg: Esprint-Verlag, 1987.

Lutz, Thomas. "Gedenkstätten für die Opfer des NS-Regimes: Landmarken gegen die Wendegeschichtsschreibung." In *Normalität oder Normalisierung? Geschichtswerkstätten und Faschismusanalyse,* edited by Heide Gerstenberger and Dorethea Schmidt. Münster: Westfälisches Dampfboot, 1987.

Maas, Annette. "Zeitenwende in Elsaß-Lothringen: Denkmalstürze und Umdeutung der nationalen Erinnerungslandschaft in Metz (November 1918–1922)." In *Denkmalsturz: Zur Konfliktgeschichte politischer Symbolik,* edited by Winfried Speitkamp, 79–108. Göttingen: Vandenhoeck & Ruprecht, 1997.

Maier, Charles. "A Surfeit of Memory? Reflections on History, Melancholy and Denial." *History & Memory* 5, 2 (fall/winter, 1993): 136–51.

———. *The Unmasterable Past: History, Holocaust, and German National Identity.* Cambridge, Mass.: Harvard University Press, 1988.

Marchand, Suzanne L. *Down from Olympus: Archaeology and Philhellenism in Germany, 1750–1970.* Princeton, N.J.: Princeton University Press, 1996.

Marcuse, Harold. "Die ehemalige Konzentrationslager Dachau: Der mühevolle Weg zur Gedenkstätte, 1945–1968." *Dachauer Hefte* 6 (1990): 182–205.

———. "Former Concentration Camps and the Politics of Identity in West Germany, 1945–1995." Unpublished Paper, Second Annual Upper Great Lakes Consortium for European Studies Conference, Minneapolis, Minn., 20–22 February 1997.

———. "Die museale Darstellung des Holocaust an Orten ehemaliger Konzentrationslager in der Bundesrepublik, 1945–1990." In *Erinnerung: Zur Gegenwart der Holocaust in Deutschland-West und Deutschland-Ost,* edited by Bernhard Moltmann, et al., 79–97. Frankfurt am Main: Haag + Herchen Verlag, 1993.

———. *Legacies of Dachau: The Uses and Abuses of a Concentration Camp, 1933–2003.* Cambridge, Eng.: Cambridge University Press, forthcoming.

Markovits, Andrei S., and Simon Reich. *The German Predicament: Memory & Power in the New Europe.* Ithaca: Cornell University Press, 1997.

Mayer, Arno J. "Memory and History: On the Poverty of Remembering and Forgetting the Judeocide." *Radical History Review* 56 (spring 1993): 5–20.

McClelland, Charles E., and Steven P. Scher, eds. *Postwar German Culture: An Anthology.* New York: E. P. Dutton, 1974.

McDonogh, Gary. "The Geography of Emptiness." In *The Cultural Meaning of Urban Space,* edited by Robert Rotenberg and Gary McDonogh, 3–15. Westport, Conn.: Bergin & Garvey, 1993.

Melman, Billie. "Gender, History and Memory: The Invention of Women's Past in the Nineteenth and Early Twentieth Centuries." *History & Memory* 5, 1 (spring/summer, 1993): 5–41.

Michelin & Cie. *Rheims and the Battles for Its Possessions.* Michelin Illustrated Guides to the Battlefields, Vol. 5. Clermont-Ferrand: Michelin & Cie, 1920.

Miljutenko, Wladimir. "Wir dürfen nicht geschichtslos werden." In *Demontage . . . revolutionärer oder restaurativer Bildersturm?,* edited by Bernd Kramer, 23–30. Berlin: Karin Kramer, 1992.

Mitscherlich, Alexander, and Margarete Mitscherlich. *Die Unfähigkeit zu trauern: Grundlagen kollektiven Verhaltens.* Munich: Piper Verlag, 1967.

Moeller, Robert. "War Stories: The Search for a Usable Past in the Federal Republic of Germany." *American Historical Review* 101, 4 (October 1996): 1008–1048.

Moltmann, Bernhard, et al., eds. *Erinnerung: Zur Gegenwart des Holocaust in Deutschland-West und Deutschland-Ost.* Frankfurt am Main: Haag + Herchen Verlag, 1993.

Mommsen, Wolfgang. "Kaisermacht und Bürgerstolz: Berlin als Hauptstadt des Kaiserreiches." In *Die Hauptstädte der Deutschen: Von der Kaiserpfalz in*

Aachen zum Regierungssitz Berlin, edited by Uwe Schultz, 181–93. Munich: C. H. Beck, 1993.

Morsch, Günter, ed. *Von der Erinnerung zum Monument: Die Entstehungsgeschichte der Nationalen Mahn- und Gedenkstätte Sachsenhausen.* Oranienburg: Stiftung Brandenburgische Gedenkstätten und Edition Hentrich, 1996.

Mosse, George. *Fallen Soldiers: Reshaping the Memory of the World Wars.* New York: Oxford University Press, 1990.

———. *The Nationalization of the Masses: Political Symbolism and Mass Movements in Germany from the Napoleonic Wars through the Third Reich.* New York: New American Library, 1975.

Müller, Hanno, ed. *Recht oder Rache? Buchenwald, 1945–1950. Betroffene erinnern sich.* Frankfurt am Main: Dipa-Verlag, 1991.

Muirhead, Findlay, ed. *Belgium and the Western Front. British and American.* The Blue Guides. London: Macmillan and Co., Ltd., 1920.

Mumford, Lewis. *The City in History. Its Origins, Its Transformations, and Its Prospects.* New York: Harcourt, Brace & World, 1961.

———. *The Culture of Cities.* New York: Harcourt, Brace Jovanovich, 1970.

Nagel's Germany. The Nagel Travel Guide Series. Geneva: Nagel Publishers, 1956.

Naimark, Norman M. *The Russians in Germany: A History of the Soviet Zone of Occupation, 1945–1949.* Cambridge, Mass.: The Belknap Press of Harvard University Press, 1995.

Niethammer, Lutz, ed. *"Die Jahre weiß man nicht, wo man die heute hinsetzen soll": Faschismus-Erfahrungen im Ruhrgebiet. Lebensgeschichte und Sozialkultur im Ruhrgebiet 1930 bis 1960.* 2 vols. Berlin: Dietz, 1983.

Nietzsche, Friedrich. "On the Use and Disadvantages of History for Life [1874]." In *Untimely Meditations,* by Friedrich Nietzsche, 57–123. Translated by R. J. Hollingdale. Cambridge, Eng.: Cambridge University Press, 1983.

Nipperdey, Thomas. *Deutsche Geschichte, 1800–1866. Bürgerwelt und starker Staat.* Munich: Beck, 1984.

———. "Zum Jubiläum der Hermannsdenkmal." In *Ein Jahrhundert Hermannsdenkmal 1875–1975,* edited by Günther Engelbert, 11–31. Detmold: Naturwissenschaftlicher und Historischer Verein für das Land Lippe, 1975.

———. "Der Kölner Dom als Nationaldenkmal." In *Nachdenken über die deutsche Geschichte,* by Thomas Nipperdy, 156–71. Munich: Beck, 1986.

———. "Nationalidee und Nationaldenkmal in Deutchland im 19. Jahrhundert." *Historische Zeitschrift* 206 (1968): 529–85.

———. "Sozialdemokratie und Geschichte." In *Sozialismus in Theorie und Praxis. Festschrift für Richard Löwenthal,* edited by Hannelore Horn, Alexander Schwan, and Thomas Weingartner, 493–517. Berlin: Walter de Gruyter, 1978.

Nora, Pierre. "From Lieux de mémoire to Realms of Memory." In *Realms of Memory: Rethinking the French Past.* Vol. 1, *Conflicts and Divisions,* edited by Pierre Nora, xv–xxiv. New York: Columbia University Press, 1996.

———, ed. *Realms of Memory: Rethinking the French Past,* 3 vols. Vol. 1,

Conflicts and Divisions; Vol. 2, *Traditions;* Vol. 3, *Symbols.* New York: Columbia University Press, 1996–1998.

Organisationsbüro des Martin-Luther-Komitees der DDR, ed. *Martin-Luther-Ehrung, 1983. Bewahrung und Pflege des progressiven Erbes in der Deutschen Demokratischen Republik.* Berlin: Aufbau-Verlag, 1982.

Overesch, Manfred. *Buchenwald und die DDR, oder die Suche nach Selbstlegitimation.* Göttingen: Vandenhoeck & Ruprecht, 1995.

Pach, Sigi. "Alternative Stadtrundfahrten: Das Hamburger Modell." In *Dem Faschismus das Wasser abgraben: Zur Auseinandersetzung mit dem Rechtsradikalismus,* edited by Benno Hafeneger, Gerhard Paul, and Bernhard Schoßig, 56–68. Munich: Juventa Verlag, 1981.

Paul, Gerhard. "Alternative Stadtrundfahrten: Beispiel Saarbrücken." In *Dem Faschismus das Wasser abgraben: Zur Auseinandersetzung mit dem Rechtsradikalismus,* edited by Benno Hafeneger, Gerhard Paul, and Bernhard Schoßig, 69–87. Munich: Juventa Verlag, 1981.

———, and Bernhard Schoßig. "Geschichte und Heimat." In *Die andere Geschichte: Geschichte von Unten. Spurensicherung. Ökologische Geschichte. Geschichtswerkstätten,* edited by Gerhard Paul and Bernhard Schoßig, 15–32. Cologne: Bund-Verlag, 1986.

Pauley, Bruce F. *From Prejudice to Persecution: A History of Austrian Anti-Semitism.* Chapel Hill: University of North Carolina Press, 1992.

Paxton, Robert, and Michael Marrus. *Vichy France and the Jews.* New York: Schocken, 1983.

Pelinka, Anton. "The Great Austrian Taboo: The Repression of the Civil War." In *Coping with the Past: Germany and Austria after 1945,* edited by Kathy Harms, Lutz R. Reuter, and Volker Dürr, 56–65. Madison: The University of Wisconsin Press, 1990.

Petropoulos, Jonathan. *Art as Politics in the Third Reich.* Chapel Hill and London: The University of North Carolina Press, 1996.

Peukert, Detlev J. K. *The Weimar Republic: The Crisis of Classical Modernity.* New York: Hill and Wang, 1989.

Phillips, Caryl. *The Nature of Blood.* New York and Toronto: Knopf, 1997.

Pinkney, David H. *Napoleon III and the Rebuilding of Paris.* Princeton, N.J.: Princeton University Press, 1958.

Plant, Richard. *The Pink Triangle: The Nazi War against Homosexuals.* New York: Henry Holt, 1986.

Pommer, Richard, and Christian F. Otto. *Weissenhof 1927 and the Modern Movement in Architecture.* Chicago and London: University of Chicago Press, 1991.

Popovich, Ljubica D. "The Battle of Kosovo (1389) and Battle Themes in Serbian Art." In *Kosovo: Legacy of a Medieval Battle,* edited by Wayne S. Vucinich and Thomas A. Emmert, 227–307. Minneapolis: Modern Greek Studies, University of Minnesota, 1991.

Preuss-Lausitz, Ulf, et al. *Kriegskinder, Konsumkinder, Krisenkinder: Zur Sozialisationsgeschichte seit dem Zweiten Weltkrieg.* Weinheim: Beltz, 1983.

Projektgruppe Arbeiterkultur Hamburg, ed. *Vorwärts und nicht vergessen:*

Arbeiterkultur in Hamburg um 1930. Berlin (West): Verlag Frölich und Kaufmann, 1982.

Prost, Antoine. "Monuments to the Dead." In *Realms of Memory: Rethinking the French Past.* Vol. 2, *Traditions,* edited by Pierre Nora, 307–30. New York: Columbia University Press, 1997.

Puvogel, Ulrike, ed. *Gedenkstätten für die Opfer des Nationalsozialismus. Eine Dokumentation.* Bonn: Bundeszentrale für politische Bildung, 1987.

Rabinbach, Anson. *In the Shadow of Catastrophe: German Intellectuals between Apocalypse and Enlightenment.* Berkeley and Los Angeles: University of California Press, 1997.

Rades, Werner, ed. *Wer kennt Danzig?* Stettin: F. Hessenland, n.d.

Reichel, Peter. *Politik mit der Errinerung: Gedächtnisorte im Streit um die nationalsozialistische Vergangenheit.* Munich: Carl Hanser, 1995.

Relph, Edward. *The Modern Urban Landscape.* Baltimore: Johns Hopkins University Press, 1987.

Reuter, Elke, and Detlef Hansel, *Das kurze Leben der VVN von 1947 bis 1953.* Berlin: Edition ost, 1997.

Ricci, Corrado, Antonio M. Colini, and Valerio Mariani. *Via dell'Impero.* Rome: La Libreria dello Stato, 1939.

Riegl, Alois. "Der Moderne Denkmalskultus. Sein Wesen und seine Entstehung." In *Gesammelte Aufsätze,* by Alois Riegl, 144–93. Augsburg: Filser, 1928.

Rollins, William H. *A Greener Vision of Home: Cultural Politics and Environmental Reform in the German Heimatschutz Movement, 1904–1918.* Ann Arbor: University of Michigan Press, 1997.

Rose, Romani. "Der Völkermord an den Sinti und Roma und seine gegenwärtige Bedeutung für Deutschland." In *Gedenkstätten im vereinten Deutschland: 50 Jahre nach der Befreiung der Konzentrationslager,* edited by Jürgen Dittberner and Antje von Meer, 68–78. Berlin: Stiftung Brandenburgische Gedenkstätten, 1994.

———, and Walter Weiß. *Sinti und Roma im "Dritten Reich": Das Programm der Vernichtung durch Arbeit.* Göttingen: Zentralrat Deutscher Sinti und Roma, 1991.

Rosenfeld, Gavriel D. "The Architects' Debate: Architectural Discourse and the Memory of Nazism in the Federal Republic of Germany, 1977–1997." *History & Memory* 9, 1–2 (fall 1997): 189–225.

———. "Monuments and the Politics of Memory: Commemorating Kurt Eisner and the Bavarian Revolutions of 1918–1919 in Postwar Munich," *Central European History* 30, 2 (1997): 221–52.

———. *Munich and Memory: Architecture, Monuments, and the Legacy of the Third Reich.* Berkeley: University of California Press, 2000.

Rosenhaft, Eve. "The Uses of Remembrance: The Legacy of the Communist Resistance in the German Democratic Republic." In *Germans against Nazism: Nonconformity, Opposition and Resistance in the Third Reich. Essays in Honour of Peter Hoffmann,* edited by Francis R. Nicosia and Lawrence D. Stokes, 369–88. New York: Berg Publishers, 1990.

Rosmus-Wenninger, Anja. *Widerstand und Verfolgung: Am Beispiel Passaus, 1933–1939*. Passau: Andreas-Haller Verlag, 1983.

Rosner, Christian, ed. *Die Universitätskirche zu Leipzig. Dokumente einer Zerstörung*. Leipzig: Forum Verlag, 1992.

Rousso, Henry. *The Vichy Syndrome: History and Memory in France Since 1944*. Cambridge, Mass.: Harvard University Press, 1991.

Rowe, Colin, and Fred Koetter. *Collage City*. Cambridge, Mass.: MIT Press, 1978.

Ryan, Michael. *Marxism and Deconstruction. A Critical Articulation*. Baltimore: Johns Hopkins University Press, 1982.

Samuel, Raphael. *Theatres of Memory*. 2 vols. Vol. 1, *Past and Present in Contemporary Culture;* Vol. 2, *Island Stories: Unravelling Britain,* edited by Alison Light. London: Verso, 1994–1998.

Schäfer, Hans-Dieter. *Das gespaltene Bewußtsein: Deutsche Kultur und Lebenswirklichkei, 1933–1945*. Munich: Carl Hanser, 1982.

Schafft, G. E., and Gerhard Zeidler. *Die KZ-Mahn- und Gedenkstätten in Deutschland*. Berlin: Dietz, 1996.

Schama, Simon. *Landscape and Memory*. New York: Knopf, 1995.

Scheffauer, Herman George. *The New Vision in the German Arts*. 1924. Reprint. Port Washington, N.Y., and London: Kennikat Press, 1971.

Schildt, Axel. *Ankunft im Westen. Ein Essay zur Erfolgsgeschichte der Bundesrepublik*. Frankfurt am Main: S. Fischer, 1999.

Schivelbusch, Wolfgang. *In a Cold Crater: Cultural and Intellectual Life in Berlin, 1945–1948*. Berkeley and Los Angeles: University of California Press, 1998.

Schleich, Erwin. *Die zweite Zerstörung Münchens: Historische Aufnahmen aus dem Stadtarchiv München und von vielen anderen*. Stuttgart: J. F. Steinkopf, 1978.

Schlögel, Karl. "Der Horror einer schönen Stadt." *Die Zeit* (21 October 1988).

Schlungbaum-Stehr, Regine. "Altstadtsanierung und Denkmalpflege in den 30er Jahren—Fallbeispiel Köln." In *Architektur und Städtebau der 30/40er Jahre: Ergebnisse der Fachtagung in München,* edited by Werner Durth and Winfried Nerdinger, 84–89. Bonn: Deutsches Nationalkomitee für Denkmalschutz, 1994.

Schmädeke, Jürgen. *Der Deutsche Reichstag: Geschichte und Gegenwart eines Bauwerks*. Revised edition. Munich: Piper, 1994.

Schmoll, Friedemann. *Verewigte Nation: Studien zur Erinnerungskultur von Reich und Einzelstaat im württembergischen Denkmalkult*. Tübingen and Stuttgart: Silberburg- Verlag, 1995.

Schoenbaum, David. *Hitler's Social Revolution. Class and Status in Nazi Germany, 1933–1939*. New York: Doubleday, Anchor Books, 1966.

Schöttler, Peter. "Die Geschichtswerkstatt e. V. Zu einem Versuch basisdemokratische Geschichtsinstitutionen und -forschungen zu 'vernetzen.'" *Geschichte und Gesellschaft* 10, 3 (1984): 421–24.

Schorske, Carl. *Fin-de-Siècle Vienna: Culture and Politics*. New York: Random House, 1980.

Schürer, Ernst, Manfred Keune, and Philip Jenkins, eds. *The Berlin Wall: Representations and Perspectives.* New York: Peter Lang, 1996.

Schulz, Eberhard. "Wie soll der deutsche Nationalstaat aussehen?" *Deutschland-Archiv* 28, 4 (April 1995): 337–38.

Schulze, Hagen. *States, Nations, and Nationalism: From the Middle Ages to the Present.* Cambridge, Mass.: Blackwell, 1996.

Seydewitz, Max. *Zerstörung und Wiederaufbau von Dresden.* Berlin: Kongress-Verlag, 1955.

Sherman, Daniel J. "Art, Commerce, and the Production of Memory in France after World War I." In *Commemorations: The Politics of National Identity,* edited by John R. Gillis, 186–211. Princeton, N.J.: Princeton University Press, 1994.

———. "Monuments, Mourning, and Masculinity in France after World War I." *Gender & History* 8, 1 (April 1996): 82–107.

Simmel, Georg. "Die Ruine: Ein ästhetischer Versuch." In *Georg Simmel. Gesamtausgabe,* edited by Otthein Rammstedt. Vol. 8, part 2, *Aufsätze und Abhandlungen, 1901–1908,* edited by Alessandro Cavalli and Volkhard Krech, 124–30. Frankfurt am Main: Suhrkamp, 1993.

Sitte, Camillo. *City Planning According to Artistic Principles.* New York: Random House, 1965.

Smith, Anthony D. *The Ethnic Origins of Nations.* Oxford: Blackwell, 1986.

———. *National Identity.* Reno: University of Nevada Press, 1991.

———. "The Origins of Nations." In *Becoming National. A Reader,* edited by Geoff Eley and Ronald Grigor Suny, 106–30. New York: Oxford University Press, 1996.

Smoleń, Kazimierz. *Auschwitz, 1940–1945: Guide-Book through the Museum.* Katowice: Krajowa Agencja Wydawnicza, 1989.

Sonnet, Peter. "Gedenkstätten für Opfer des Nationalsozialismus in der DDR." In *Gedenkstätten für die Opfer des Nationalsozialismus. Eine Dokumentation,* edited by Ulrike Puvogel, 769–805. Bonn: Bundeszentrale für politische Bildung, 1987.

Spector, Scott. "Beyond the Aesthetic Garden: Politics and Culture on the Margins of *Fin-de-Siècle Vienna.*" *Journal of the History of Ideas* 59 (1998): 691–710.

Speer, Albert. *Inside the Third Reich. Memoirs.* New York: Macmillan, 1970.

———. *Spandauer Tagebücher.* Frankfurt am Main: Ullstein, 1975.

Speitkamp, Winfried. "Denkmalsturz und Symbolkonflikt in der modernen Geschichte: Eine Einleitung." In *Denkmalsturz: Zur Konfliktgeschichte politischer Symbolik,* edited by Winfried Speitkamp, 5–21. Göttingen: Vandenhoeck & Ruprecht, 1997.

———. *Verwaltung der Geschichte. Denkmalpflege und Staat in Deutschland, 1871–1933.* Göttingen: Vandenhoeck & Ruprecht, 1996.

Spender, Stephen. *European Witness.* London: Hamish Hamilton, 1946.

Spengler, Oswald. *The Decline of the West.* Abridged edition. New York: Oxford University Press, 1991.

Spies, Birgit. "Aus einem unabgeschlossenen Kapitel." In *Im Irrgarten deutscher Geschichte. Die Neue Wache, 1818–1993,* edited by Daniela Büchten and Anja Frey, 37–44. Berlin: Aktives Museum Faschismus und Widerstand Berlin, 1993.

Stahn, Günter. *Das Nikolaiviertel am Marx-Engels-Forum. Ursprung, Gründungsort und Stadtkern Berlins.* Berlin: VEB Verlag fur Bauwesen, 1985.

Steinbach, Peter. *Nationalsozialistische Gewaltverbrechen: Die Diskussion in der deutschen Öffentlichkeit.* Berlin: Colloquium Verlag, 1981.

Stokes, Gale. *Three Eras of Political Change in Eastern Europe.* New York: Oxford University Press, 1997.

Strasser, Susan, Charles McGovern, and Matthias Judt, eds. *Getting and Spending: European and American Consumer Societies in the Twentieth Century.* Cambridge, Eng.: Cambridge University Press, 1998.

Szulc, Tad, and Marianne Szulc. "Rebuilt Warsaw Has Put Its Best Centuries Forward." *Smithsonian* 9, 6 (September 1978): 106–17.

Tacke, Charlotte. *Denkmal im sozialen Raum: Nationale Symbole in Deutschland und Frankreich im 19. Jahrhundert.* Göttingen: Vandenhoeck & Ruprecht, 1995.

Tag für Denkmalpflege. *Dreizehnter Tag für Denkmalpflege in Augsburg, 1917.* Berlin: Ernst & Sohn, 1917.

Tanner, Marcus. *Croatia: A Nation Forged in War.* New Haven: Yale University Press, 1997.

Tiedemann, Joseph. "Das Reichstagsgebäude zu Berlin." *Beilage zum "Baumeister."* 31, 6 (June 1933): B77–78.

Tietz, Jürgen. "Ostpreußisches Stonehenge." *Frankfurter Allgemeine Zeitung* (22 September 1997).

———. "Schinkels Neue Wache Unter den Linden: Baugeschichte 1816–1993." In *Die Neue Wache Unter den Linden. Ein Deutsches Denkmal im Wandel der Geschichte,* edited by Christoph Stölzl, 9–93. Berlin: Koehler & Amelang, 1993.

Till, Karen. "Place and the Politics of Memory: A Geo-Ethnography of Museums and Memorials in Berlin." Ph.D. diss., University of Wisconsin-Madison, 1996.

Tittel, Lutz. *Das Niederwalddenkmal, 1871–1883.* Hildesheim: Gerstenberg, 1979.

Touring Club Italiano. *Italia Centrale. Guida Breve.* Vol. 2. Milan: Consociazione Turistica Italiana, 1939.

Tournier, Michel. *The Ogre.* New York: Pantheon, 1972.

Travel Guide Poland. Warszawa: Sport Turystyka, 1970.

Tümmers, Horst Johannes. *Der Rhein: Ein europäischer Fluß und seine Geschichte.* Munich: C. H. Beck, 1994.

Tumarkin, Nina. *The Living & The Dead: The Rise and Fall of the Cult of World War II in Russia.* New York: Basic Books, 1994.

Warneken, Bernd Jürgen. "Forward, But Forgetting Nothing: The Shift in the Use and Meaning of Socialist Symbolism in East Germany Since 1989." *International Review of Social History* 39 (1994): 77–91.

Warner, Marina. *Monuments & Maidens: The Allegory of the Female Form.* New York: Atheneum, 1985.

Weidenhaupt, Hugo. *Kleine Geschichte der Stadt Düsseldorf.* Ninth edition. Düsseldorf: Triltsch Verlag, 1983.

Werz, Günter. "Erinnerungen an die Ruinen von Berlin." *Südwest Presse* (5 April 1980).

Wheeler, Eleanor. *Lidice.* Second edition. Prague: Orbis, 1962.

Whyte, Iain Boyd. *Bruno Taut and the Architecture of Activism.* Cambridge, Eng.: Cambridge University Press, 1982.

Winock, Michel. "Joan of Arc." In *Realms of Memory: Rethinking the French Past.* Vol. 3, *Symbols,* edited by Pierre Nora, 433–80. New York: Columbia University Press, 1998.

Winter, Jay. *Sites of Memory, Sites of Mourning. The Great War in European Cultural History.* Cambridge, Eng.: Cambridge University Press, 1995.

Winters, Peter Jochen. "Wiederaufbau in Ost-Berlin." *Deutschland-Archiv* 18, 12 (1985): 1304–19.

Winters, Stanley B. "Historic Preservation in Czechoslovakia: The Château at Staré Hrady." *Canadian Slavonic Papers* 31, 3–4 (September-December 1989): 267–82.

Wolfrum, Edgar. "Der 'Tag der deutschen Einheit.'" In *Lieux de mémoire, Erinnerungsorte. D'un modèle français à un projet allemand,* edited by Etienne François, 119–26. Berlin: Centre Marc Bloch, 1996.

Wright, Patrick. *On Living in an Old Country. The National Past in Contemporary Britain.* London: Verso, 1985.

Young, James. *The Texture of Memory: Holocaust Memorials and Meaning.* New Haven: Yale University Press, 1993.

Zimmermann, Michael. "Gedenkstätten für die Opfer des Nationalsozialismus in Westdeutschland." *Geschichtswerkstatt* 24 (1991): 31–44.

Zuchold, Gerd-H. "Der Abriß der Ruinen des Stadtschlosses und der Bauakademie in Ost-Berlin." *Deutschland-Archiv* 18, 2 (1985): 178–207.

Index

Numbers in italics refer to figures.

Text: Sabon
Display: Sabon
Composition: G&S Typesetters, Inc.
Printing and binding: Data Reproductions Corp.